FIRST
FOR BRITAIN AND IRELAND

*A Historical account of birds new to Britain & Ireland
1600–1999*

With reference to the Isle of Man and Channel Islands

FIRST FOR BRITAIN AND IRELAND

A Historical account of birds new to Britain & Ireland 1600–1999

With reference to the Isle of Man and Channel Islands

By **Philip Palmer**

ARLEQUIN PRESS

ISBN 1 900159 41 4

First published 2000

Arlequin Press, 26 Broomfield Road, Chelmsford, Essex CM1 1SW

Text: © Philip Palmer
Illustrations and Dust Jacket © Dan Powell

All rights reserved. No part of this book may be reproduced, stored in a retrieval system or transmitted in any form or by any means, electronic, mechanical, photocopying or otherwise, without the permission of the publisher.

A catalogue record for this book is available.

Contents

Acknowledgements vii
Introduction 1
   Categories of Birds on the British List 6
   A history of bird recording in Britain 8
      1100–1600: *An age of myths and poor recording* 8
      1600–1700: *The birth of a science* 11
      1700–1800: *The serious work continues* 14
      1800–1900: *The ornithological revolution* 15
      1900: to the present day: *Systematic recording and increased knowledge* 20
   Specimens, collections and museums 25
      The Hastings rarities and cases of fraud 29
      Further cases of fraud 35
      Meinertzhagen and the British List 36
   Escapes, misidentifications and rejections 38
   Using the systematic list 39
   The Photographs 40
The Systematic List *(acceptable species)* 41
   The Systematic List 41
   Species under consideration 269
   Category 'D' species 276
Near Misses 286
   Rejections 286
and Last 317
   Great Auk 317
References 319
Index 324

Dedication

To Sarah and Max

Acknowledgements

Firstly I would like to thank Keith Naylor who provided my initial list of BBRC accepted 'First' records with an excellent list of reference material; this was the solid base on which I began my work. He also assisted me greatly with certain records and the computer know-how needed to write and compile this work as well as being on the end of a phone when my machine crashed or locked up. I would also like to thank Derick Evans for his help with computer-based problems, contacting other birders via the Internet and for accompanying me to check skin collections. Both he and Keith assisted in finding mistakes made in draft copies.

This project would never have reached the publics gaze without the commitment, hard work and help of Nigel Ede at Arlequin Press. His good judgement brought this project to a positive conclusion and I thank him for believing in me. Nigel Redman, Editor at *British Birds* also provided me with some suggestions, contacts and much encouragement in this work, while John Marchant's comments on an early draft helped me tremendously. Laura Jones edited the final draft and I am indebted to her for the time she spent editing it and providing constructive suggestions. Mike Gaydon and I spent many long hours at Healey's printers going over the typeface and layout and I am grateful for his commitment to make this a beautiful book.

The text would be worthless without the hard work undertaken freely by everyone involved with rare bird record assessment and the publication of reports. From the hard working members of rarities committees to the individuals that undertake research into the vagrancy potential and captive status.

Some of these people made valuable contributions about certain records that had not previously been published, in particular I would like to thank Peter Allard for information about the Norfolk Short-toed Eagle, Roger Long for his contribution regarding Channel Islands reports, Mike Rogers at the BBRC and the county recorders that have helped trace some records, including: J W Donovan, Geof Neal, Deryk Shaw, John Barnes, Chris Booth, Alan Dean and Nick Rossiter. Dr A G Irwin Keeper of Natural History at the Castle Museum, Norwich provided access to, and invaluable information about some Norfolk specimens, while Tim Melling allowed me to quiz him about some BOURC decisions.

Paul Baxter, Stuart Rivers and John Ballantyne helped to track down some details relating to Scottish records and some essential help and comments regarding Irish records were received from Paul Milne and Anthony McGeehan, who also highlighted the concerns of birders in Northern Ireland and the political situation that exists there. I am grateful for their thoughts and input.

My grateful appreciation also goes to the authors alive or dead listed among the reference material whose information I have drawn on to produce this work, especially the journals; *British Birds*, *Ibis*, *Zoologist*, *The Field* and *Birding World*.

I am indebted to the staff at various libraries' including Ian Dawson and staff at the RSPB library, Dr Linda Birch at the Edward Grey Institute Library, Oxford, the Birmingham Central Library and the Denman Library staff at Retford.

The staff at several museums throughout the country provided information about birds in their possession and I am grateful for their assistance and time. Dr Prys-Jones at the Natural History Museum, Tring allowed me to inspect several specimens, as did Steve Woolfall at the Grosvenor Museum, Chester, John Redshaw and Susan Sladen of the Spalding Gentleman's Society at Ayscoughfee Hall, Adrian Norris at the Leeds Museum, Stuart Ogilvie at the Yorkshire Museum, the staff at Mansfield Museum and Art Gallery, and the County Museum at Truro. In Edinburgh, Bob McGowan showed me the specimens held in the National Museums of Scotland, where I was delighted to find that the mounts presented by Eagle Clark are in particularly good condition. At Newcastle, Eric Morton and L Jessop took the time to search for the Red-necked Nightjar. Most kindly allowed reproduction of photographs obtained in their establishments.

Dan Powell's lively sketches complement the text and I am indebted to him for his contribution. Without the aid of several other people it would have been a nightmare to obtain the photographs produced here, and for this I would like to thank John Ballantyne, Killian Mullarney, Tim Loseby, Mike Langman, Dave Cottridge, Mike Parker, Kevin Osborn, Tom Ennis, Roy Dennis, Will Wagstaff, Derrick Evans, Paul Baxter, Anthony McGeehan and Steve Gantlett. The subscribers to UKBirdnet also rallied around admirably to track down certain people. The names of contributing photographers are provided elsewhere and my grateful thanks also go to them.

One person in particular kindled my interest in old records, mounted specimens and the Hastings rarities. His name is John Phillips, the Worksop taxidermist who tragically died while this book was being written. It was his knowledge of the Victorian methods of preserving birds that increased my understanding of the importance of museums and specimen collections. He was a skilled member of the taxidermist's guild and put a different perspective on the records that involved skins and collectors. At the end of the 20th Century, taxidermists have gone from being respected craftsmen supplying the scientist and wealthy collectors to being viewed with suspicion by today's birdwatchers. John's work reflected his broad knowledge of natural history and taught me that the art of preservation should be encouraged rather than looked down upon with ignorance.

I am also indebted to the birdwatchers who found the birds mentioned in this book, provided accurate information. I am also grateful to the future finders of firsts that provided a lift to a site or just a good laugh as part of the many trips I have undertaken to see rare birds.

Finally, I would like to thank Sarah, my wife who has not nagged or moaned while I spent hours at the computer as she did the housework and to Max who was the least demanding baby that an author could ever wish for when trying to concentrate.

Thank you

INTRODUCTION

In a country with such a passionate interest in the natural world, it is unfortunate that news of a rare bird in the British Isles rarely graces the tabloids. To see a bird that has arrived in the British Isles for the first time can be a challenge, and occasionally impossible. Today's birdwatcher is well briefed in the art of identification and needs to make fast decisions to catch up with any rare vagrants that reach these shores, and the pinnacle of such endeavours is achieved with the arrival of a 'first.'

News of a 'first' can elicit a variety of responses: surprise, disbelief, jealousy or blind panic coupled with an irregular heartbeat. Then, birders flailing arms grab car keys, mobile phone, binoculars, coat and a Mars bar with all the skill and grace of an Olympic gymnast. It ends with a swiftly blown goodbye kiss for the suffering partner and an apology for the boss. Or should that be kissing the job goodbye and apologising to the partner.

A whole new set of emotions then comes into play. For some, a supreme wave of elation for others suicidal depths of depression, reserved for those arriving seconds after the bird has flown off. They are known as 'Dippers'. The mother of all negative emotions is reached when all your friends have seen the subject well, as you struggle desperately to connect with it.

Today Britain and Irelands bird populations suffer the effects of intensive farming and habitat loss. Once common birds such as Corn Bunting, Linnet and Tree Sparrow are becoming increasingly harder to find. With fewer migrants or rarities the last year of the millennium was set to be recorded in history books as the worst year that many could remember. That was until the arrival of a 'first.'

In October, the Isles of Scilly (which had so far failed to repeat the excitement generated by the 'big Yank' years of the 1980s) suddenly bounced back. A Siberian Thrush arrived on St Agnes, soon to be joined by a White's Thrush the next day, a good start but totally overshadowed: when a massive Short-toed Eagle flew in to take up residence on the islands for several days- a 'first' for Britain, the making of history.

October is *the* month for rarities in Britain and the last October of the millennium will be indelibly inked in twitcher's notebooks. The Short-toed Eagle was rapidly followed by the first 'twitchable' Blue Rock Thrush, a Veery, Yellow-billed Cuckoo, five Red-flanked Bluetail's, up to 14 Chimney Swifts and five Pallid Swifts; all extremely rare visitors to Britain and Ireland. If modern changes in vagrant numbers and patterns are the result of climatic change then Britain and Ireland can look forward to more unlikely 'firsts'.

It is the ambition of all birdwatchers to find a species new to their local patch or county, but the 'Holy Grail' is to find and correctly identify a species occurring for the first time in the country. The circumstances surrounding these discoveries are often amusing, sometimes astounding but always exciting. This book gives an account of these finds; the icing on a birder's cake, a **FIRST FOR BRITAIN**.

Britain and Ireland have a reputation for producing ornithologists of a high standard and enjoy a high proportion of birders per head of population. Combined with an excellent geographical position, great diversity of habitats and a high human density, the chance of finding rare birds is very high. Compare this to our close European neighbour on the same latitudes just a few miles across the North Sea: the Netherlands. Possessing some expert ornithologists of equal ability, a total area of comparable size, and an excellent political infrastructure, the number of rare birds found there is tiny in comparison.

Prior to 1998 the British Isles had recorded hundreds of American vagrants probably accounting for more than 80% of the grand European total i.e., Green-winged Teal; Britain – *c.*500, compared to just 15 in the Netherlands', 72 Laughing Gulls in Britain where no European country had come close to reaching double figures and for Baird's Sandpiper a massive 210 reports, while the European total is less than 25. This is not just because these isles are closer to the USA, as similar ratios exist between Britain and the Netherlands for Arctic species, Siberian passerines and seabirds; the total number of Iceland Gulls recorded in the Netherlands for example is less than the annual total for Britain! Vagrants from Eastern Europe and Asia also present similar statistics; Arctic Warbler 231 compared to 10, Desert Wheatear 71: 7 and Black-headed Bunting 137: 7. One exception to the rule is large raptors, preferring not to cross large tracts of open water.

Increased protection, expanding populations and release schemes may finally allow old vulture records to be repeated, while the first British Short-toed Eagle was fledging in Spain as the first draft of this book was written.

With an increasing and obsessive British interest in rare birds it was one book above all others that portrayed the excitement of stumbling across a vagrant. In 1982, Dr J T R Sharrock edited a book documenting the occurrence of 83 species found in Britain and Ireland for the first time. His *Birds New to Britain and Ireland* aroused my interest in 'first' records. In the constantly changing arena of birding politics and taxonomy at least one of Sharrock's listed species has been removed from the British List and older records have come to light pre-dating several other accounts.

As Sharrock's book covered the period from 1947 to 1982, this publication aims to update and expand that work. It includes all species and some distinctive subspecies recorded in an apparently wild state in Britain and Ireland for the first time since at least 1800. Prior to this, ornithology as a science was in its infancy. There is practically no detail of new discoveries before 1600 and in the intervening years accounts are unfortunately brief. From 1600 to 1800, common species were recognised and recorded for the first time; they include the likes of Sandwich Tern, Lesser Whitethroat and Reed Warbler.

Conversely, several once-common species now considered rarities, such as White Stork and Great Bustard that were recorded prior to 1800, are also included if sufficient documentation exists. Others listed in early ornithological works with little or no supporting information are only given cursory mention in the preceding chapters.

Unlike Sharrock's work, this book does not include a detailed description of the species involved which can be found in the plethora of field guides or handbook's now available. It is assumed that decisions made by the relevant committees and authorities are correct. For some common species such as Water Pipit, the first report may not necessarily be accurate. Such reports may not have received critical scrutiny at the time lacking any 'official' committee. As a result, the author has made a balanced judgement on the report and also included subsequently better documented records. The age, sex, plumage and race of the individual birds involved are recorded where known.

The inclusion of many species not currently forming part of the 'official' British, Irish, Manx and Channel Islands Lists that involve birds presently regarded as escapes, probables and the objects of possible fraud, are recorded here for interest, accuracy, completeness and amusement in a separate chapter. This may help future generations to locate a report that may help in the re-assessment of a species' status, as new evidence is unearthed. This approach means that this work already includes the first report of birds like Greater Flamingo, Yellow Bittern or perhaps Swallow-tailed Kite, which may eventually officially grace the avifauna of these islands. Who would have believed an 18th Century report of an east coast Red-breasted Nuthatch or an 'at sea' claim of Ancient Murrelet?

On the other hand, documentation of known escapes or the presence of a species in captivity at the time of a suspected vagrant may also rule out future claims of records yet uncovered. The knowledge that Collared Petrel skins were imported from Fiji at the time of a previously accepted record certainly makes today's decision-makers task of record re-assessment easier.

For the potential 'first' hunters there are additions to be made to Britain's avifauna that do not involve trips to the Scillies, Shetland or north Norfolk. Why not pack a shovel and visit Hardwell in Hampshire or Sheppey in Kent? The sediments in these areas have produced the ancient remains of bird species not included in the British Ornithologist's Union's (BOU) current categorisations. Fossils from these two areas and others have included birds probably never seen by homosapien.

The British Ornithologist's Union Records Committee (BOURC) has always included birds occurring in Ireland and the Isle of Man as part of 'British' ornithology. Its British and Irish List covered the whole zoogeographic region. The BOU and British Birds Rarities Committee (BBRC) has shown an interest in birds found on the nearby Channel Islands but the area was regarded as being closer to the continental mainland and not included in any lists. Coverage away from England, Scotland and Wales has always been limited due to fewer observers and changing political divisions. Consequently in January, 1999, at the request of the Irish Rare Birds Committee, the BOURC ceased to produce a joint British and Irish List. Instead they listed birds only recorded in England, Scotland and Wales, excluding Manx, Northern and Southern Irish records. The Channel Islands remained unaffected, having always been separate. While the often heated debate over whether a joint British and Irish List should be maintained, it makes sense to treat England, Scotland and Wales as a single entity for listing purposes. There are also strong arguments that the Isle of Man, Northern Ireland and the Republic of Ireland should be included as they are geographically part of the same archipelago. In fact Ireland lies closer to Britain than either the Shetland Isles or St Kilda and so this presents something of a dilemma for this work.

The decision taken by the Irish Rare Birds Committees (IRBC) to move to independence has led to some calls from within Ireland to reverse the decision. Many birdwatchers in Northern Ireland have since distanced themselves from this decision, refusing to fall under the IRBCs jurisdiction preferring to remain linked closely with the BBRC.

The Northern Ireland Birdwatchers' Association and the Manx Ornithological Society maintain their respective lists and by invitation the BOURC investigate 'first' reports from Northern Ireland and the Isle of Man.

Irish records included here are not on the British List. Anthony McGeehan's article in *British Birds* (92: 212) states the reasons why some of Northern Ireland's birders strongly disagree.

However, this publication covers the species discovered for the first time in all of the above countries as they are inextricably linked geographically, historically and politically. The first record solely attributable to England, Scotland or Wales is mentioned separately.Details of some Irish records have been difficult to track down and may lack some fine detail. There is a lack of published documentation regarding a first report from one country that has already occurred in a neighbour many times. The excitement of such a record is considerably dampened by the fact that by crossing a political boundary the same bird may be regarded as common.

For example, how many birders in England know that the first Reed Warbler to reach Ireland was found in 1908 or that Lesser Whitethroat bred there for the first time in the early 1990s? The first Dartford Warbler to reach Scotland was as recent as 1983, but by presenting such information in a journal solely devoted to Scottish birds or a county report, ornithologists elsewhere may remain oblivious to the importance of such a record.

Of the problems dealt with as part of the record assessment process, the escape likelihood and intention to deceive has always been a thorn in the side of the BOURC. Some reports may be fraudulent and it is impossible to be 100% certain as to their authenticity, particularly the older reports. Two cases in particular received a high profile; these were the 'Hastings rarities' and records submitted by Colonel Meinertzhagen. These are discussed briefly in a chapter of their own, while any potential 'firsts' dismissed following re-assessment are dealt with under the individual accounts.

The first section of the systematic list deals with wild bird species recorded in the areas mentioned above and accepted as a genuine report by the relevant committee (Category A, B and C of the British List).

While it is ridiculous to expect Budgerigars and Penguins to ever grace these lists, Pelicans and ship-assisted birds are worthy of documentation, as are records still pended and waiting further information. The latter species are placed in Category D of the British List by the BOURC and listed in a separate chapter.

A list of some possible, probable and certain escapes not forming part of the British or Irish Lists (Category E species or rejected reports) are included separately, with detailed accounts of the most interesting first reported occurrences.

In this category there is also a mouth-watering array of exotic species that may one-day grace Britain's avifauna if feral populations take hold. The more obvious candidates are included here if their origins are known.

As the BOURC may transfer species to different categories as new evidence comes to light a work such as this is only accurate up to the day it is written.

In Ornithology only one thing is guaranteed and that is:– *nothing is guaranteed!*

CATEGORIES OF BIRDS ON THE BRITISH LIST

Amongst other activities, the British Ornithologist's Union (BOU) investigate the records of all bird species occurring in Britain for the first time. At the request of birdwatchers residing in Northern Ireland, the Channel Islands and the Isle of Man, they also review records from these areas. Additionally, records under consideration include species found at sea within the British Economic Zone, which extends to 200 nautical miles (370 km) from shore. There have been various changes to category definitions since the list's inception, including the creation of Category E and the redefinition of Category D in 1998.

Species in Categories A, B and C make up the present British List, the totals at 20th January, 2000 standing at 553 species (see table below).

The categories currently in use by the British Ornithologist's Union (1998) are:

A Species that have been recorded in an apparently natural state at least once since 1st January, 1950.

B Species that would otherwise be in Category A but have not been recorded since 31st December, 1949.

C Species that although originally introduced by Man, either deliberately or accidentally, have established breeding populations derived from introduced stock that maintain themselves without necessary recourse to further introduction.

C1 *Naturalised introductions*: species that have occurred only as a result of introduction.

C2 *Naturalised establishments*: species with established populations as a result of introduction by Man, but which also occur in an apparently natural state.

C3 *Naturalised re-establishments*: species with populations successfully re-established by Man in areas of former occurrence.

C4 *Naturalised feral species*: domesticated species with populations established in the wild.

C5 *Vagrant naturalised species*: species from established naturalised populations abroad.

D   Species that would otherwise appear in Categories A or B except that there is reasonable doubt that they have ever occurred in a natural state.
   This includes species that certainly arrived with a combination of ship assistance and provision of food and shelter, tideline corpses and birds that would appear in Category C but whose population is not self-sustaining.
E   Species that have been recorded as introductions, transportees or escapees from captivity, and whose breeding populations (if any) are thought not to be self-sustaining.

There are several hundreds in Category E, too numerous to be included in this work, though some of the more interesting ones are listed.

The BOU's codes are used in this work. Notable differences for Irish records occur where the IRBC do not include ship-assisted birds in Category A, instead these are placed in Category D. The IRBC's taxonomic decisions follow the BOURC for Western Palearctic species. Nearctic birds are listed according to the American Ornithologist's Union (AOU).

All species in Category A of the British List and not mentioned in this book regularly occurred in Britain prior to 1800 and are predominantly regarded as common species here.

Category	Britain	Britain, Manx, Northern Ireland and Republic of Ireland
A	531	537
B	13	14
C	9	9
Total	553	560

By 1999, only a few species recorded in one of the other countries had failed to be recognised in Britain. Category A species occurring solely in the Republic of Ireland were: Short-billed Dowitcher *Limnodromus griseus* and Elegant Tern *Sterna elegans,* with Bald Eagle *Haliaeetus leucocephalus* recorded in both Northern Ireland and the Republic of Ireland and Fox Sparrow *Passerella iliaca* solely in Northern Ireland.

Grey Catbird *Dumetella carolinensis* had reached both the Republic of Ireland and the Channel Islands, whose list also included Siberian Blue Robin *Luscinia cyane.* The Isle of Man was the only island to record Mourning Dove *Zenaida macroura.* Of the Category B species Eurasian Griffon Vulture *Gyps fulvus* was recorded in The Republic of Ireland only.

Of the above Short-billed Dowitcher and Mourning Dove had been seen in Britain during 1999 and await official ratification by the BOURC.

References:
Birding World 6: 362; *Brit Birds* 85: 533; 83: 46; 92: 212; BOU 1998: 4-5; Naylor 1996 & 1998; *Ibis* 141: 175-180.

A History of Bird Recording in Britain

1100-1600: *An age of myths and poor recording*

Early reference to British birds can to be found in medieval manuscripts where the artwork recorded recognisable species. There are clear and accurate illustrations of Common Kingfisher, Common Wood Pigeon, Green Woodpecker, Blue Tit and Mew Gull present on the *Tenison Psalter* (pre 1284). Many engravings or ornaments prior to this only allowed birds to be recognised as belonging to a family or group. Several illustrations were confused by combining features from two species; for example drawings of storks often showed additional features only found on cranes and herons.

The *Sherborne Missal* at Alnwick Castle (*c.*1400) shows a grey shrike that has the black mask of a Northern Grey Shrike but the pink chest of a Lesser Grey Shrike.

In the 10th Century Archbishop Aelfric had mentioned the "*ficedula swertling*" which probably refers to the Blackcap; if so, it is the only British warbler mentioned prior to 1500. Prior to this date there had been no reference made to any of the flycatchers, divers or tubenoses.

By 1400, other common species were recorded. In the Holkham Bible Picture Book dating from this time Black-billed Magpie, European Goldfinch, European Robin, Winter Wren and Northern Lapwing are accurately represented, while the Song Thrush even has the correct number of primary feathers illustrated. One document dating from *c.*1340 shows several Long-eared Owls complete with human ears!

The mysteries of birdlife featured prominently in diaries, early journals and literature, with falconry and game birds being particularly noticeable.

The Domesday Book of 1080-85 highlighted the economical importance of raptors as it lists "*hawks aeries*" – almost certainly Northern Goshawk nests, from Sussex to Cheshire.

Poetry and tales of travel mention some of the more obvious birds such as the Common Cuckoo, swans and owls, while the first British record of a Red Crossbill in 1251 was mentioned as an orchard pest in St Albans in the household accounts of a monk – Mathew Paris.

Bird references in 16th Century poems were predominantly the larger species, though Shakespeare mentioned many passerines. Although *King Lear* included a passage that referred to Red-billed Choughs on the cliffs at Dover and listed various raptors, owls and crows, the smaller birds were invariably obvious songsters such as Common Nightingale, Sky Lark and Hedge Accentor.

The earliest significant ornithological records are in manuscripts kept by the medical profession and aristocracy. These were often accounts of birds killed to cure ailments or to provide food. A banquet held at Cawood, Yorkshire in 1466 included 100 Eurasian Curlew on the menu, while in 1512 the Northumberland Household Book at Earl Percy's Yorkshire castles recorded the purchase of Common Redshanks at $1^1/_2d$ each. It also mentioned that Great Bittern's eggs were more to the taste of Fenland inhabitants than Grey Heron's.

Literature

In the 8th Century, 11 species are recorded: Raven, Eagle (White-tailed), Cuckoo, Gannet, Swan (Whooper), Gull, Tern, Curlew (or Whimbrel), Goshawk, Kite and Crane. The first book devoted to natural history was published around 1467 and by 1500 some 80 species had been mentioned. Not all were birds found in Britain and Ireland.

Giraldus Cambrensis included ten chapters of bird descriptions in his *Topography of Ireland* written in 1187 but published in 1587. These were confused first-hand observations of little value and part of a wider natural history interest. The work was unusual in that it added more than a dozen new species to our knowledge.

In 1544 William Turner (1500-1568) from Northumberland published his *Avium Praecipuarum, quarum apud Plinium et Aristotelem mentio est, brevis and succincta historia* (1544) at a time of emerging ornithological interest in Europe. His book principally determined the birds already named by Aristotle and Pliny with additional notes of birds observed personally. Turner separated sightings made in Britain and abroad mentioning species then regarded as common that are now treated as very rare or scarce migrants. His work included accounts of breeding Common Cranes in Britain and scavenging Red Kites inhabiting the towns and villages. Turner also recorded tree-nesting Great Cormorants in Norfolk and breeding Black Terns.

Turner's work raised the number of recorded bird species from 80 to 138 with more than half of the 58 new species discovered by him. However included among them are 33 domestic species or others seen outside Britain. Many passerines were recognised for the first time including three finches, four buntings and three tits. It was the world's first printed book on birds.

Turner possessed a great knowledge of birds and had closely observed several wetland species including White-throated Dipper, Black Tern, Common Sandpiper, Black-headed Gull and Great Cormorant. He noted that the Eurasian Hobby was a summer visitor, describing its habitat and prey items. He separated Hen and Marsh Harriers and listed Common Whitethroat, Meadow Pipit, Brambling and Wood Lark for the first time as British birds.

John Kay, a colleague of Turner, also made new contributions. He kept and studied an Atlantic Puffin in his house for eight months and recorded the food items taken by Eurasian Jackdaw.

Richard Carew included a good number of Cornish bird species in *Account of Cornwall*, part of William Camden's *Britannia* published in 1586. This included a description of a Red Crossbill invasion from at least Gloucestershire to Cornwall that ruined the apple crop: "*cutting an apple in half they would take only the seeds.*"

Carew also recorded the mistaken view that in autumn the Barn Swallows would sing before falling from the sky through reeds into the mud of great lakes to sleep. Fishermen had found them in slimy clods pulled from the lake bed through the holes they had cut in the ice to catch fish. Having taken the swallows home, they were revived by warming them on stoves.

Carew also wrote of Barnacle Geese breeding underwater hanging by their bills onto the sides of ships that had spent long periods at sea.

Carew's survey was thorough. He had a good knowledge of the local natural history and it was probably the first attempt of any substance to write a county avifauna.

It would be inaccurate to put a date to the first recorded occurrence of any species in Britain prior to 1600, so birds regularly encountered prior to this date will not be covered in the systematic list.

References:
British Birds 2: 5-13; 42-50; Yapp 1981; Fisher 1954: 17-21; Birdwatch 90: 6-13.

1600-1700: *The birth of a science*

During this period the cataloguing of Britain's avifauna really began. At the start of the 1600s four very distinctive species were added to the British List. Nicholas Carter's first mention of highly noticeable species such as the Hoopoe, Pied Avocet, Grey Wagtail and Redwing, highlighted the ignorance of scientists at that time.

Christopher Merrett, a Gloucestershire physician, produced the first printed list of British birds in *Pinax Rerum Naturalium Britannicarum* in 1666. This was little other than a list of species previously recorded in Britain taken from the works of Ulysses Aldrovandus which in turn had been compiled from the works of Gesner (published 1599-1603) and Jonstonus's *History of British Birds* (1650). His list included domestic species as well as the occurrence of scarce birds like White Stork, Great Bustard and Smew. It lacked those species difficult to observe, identify or shoot, such as warblers, gulls, terns, pipits.

Merrett's list of English birds:

The Eagle, the Hawk, the Sea Eagle (Osprey)
the Goshawk, the Sparrowhawk, the Stonegall (Common Kestrel)
the Cuckoe (Common Cuckoo)

the forked tail'd Kite, Glede or *Puttock* (Red Kite and Buzzard)
the bald Buzzard or *Kite* (Marsh Harrier)

the white hooping Owl (Barn Owl)
the Raven
a Rook
the Sea Pie (Oystercatcher)

the Shell-apple (Red Crossbill)
the Peacock
the Pheasant

the Hasel Hen, Grous (Hazel Hen not recorded in Britain)
the Bustard
the Partridge
the Snipe
the Wood-cock
the Hoopee (Hoopoe)
a Moor-hen (Black Grouse)
the Kings-fisher

the Lanar (various falcons)

the Foulcon (Peregrine)
Butcher or *murdering Bird* (Red-backed Shrike)
the ring-tail'd Kite (female Hen Harrier)

the Night or *little grey Owl* (Little ? or Short-eared Owl)
the Screech (Tawny Owl)
Carrion Crow
Magpie (Black-billed)
a Bat (this mammal was placed among the list of birds)
the Goat-sucker (European Nightjar)
the Turkey-cock
major Cock of the Wood (Western Capercaillie)

the Guiney Hen (Guineafowl)
a Godwit
the Quail
the Jack Snipe
the Rail or *King of the Rails* (Corncrake?)
a Cock (domestic Hen ?)
a Coot
the common House-Pidgeon and various domestic Pigeon/Dove species

the Turtle Dove
the House-Sparrow
a Gold-finch
the Hawfinch (figured but no English name given)
Brambling
the Yellow-hammer
a Siskin
the tit-Lark
a Bull finch
the Mistletoe Thrush
the Feldefare (Fieldfare)
the Starling
the Green Wood pecker
the Nuthatch
a Wren
the House Swallow (House Martin)
a black Martin (Common Swift)
the less Titmouse (Blue Tit)
the least or long taild Titmouse
the Stone-Chatter (Stonechat)
the Red-start
the Nightingale
the Swan
the Bergander (Common Shelduck)
the Brant Goose
the Duck (domestic duck)
the Wild Duck (Common Pochard)
the Teal
the Widgeon
Razor bill
Arsfoot (grebes)
Tame (Goosander)
Shags
a Shovelard (Spoonbill)
a Ganet (Skua)
the Stork
the Bittourn (Great Bittern)
the Rough, a Reev (Ruff and Reeve)
the Curliewg,
the Lapwing
the Whistling Plover (European Golden Plover)
Trynga (a sandpiper spp)
the Crane
Nun est (Smew) and Gossander

Stock Dove or Wood-Pidgeon
the Reed Sparrow (Reed Bunting)
a Bunting (Corn Bunting)
Chaffinch
the Green-finch
the Linet
the Lark (Sky Lark)
the wood-Lark
the Song-Thrush
the Wind Thrush (Redwing)
the Black-bird
a Clot Bird (Northern Wheatear?)
the Creeper, or Wall-Creeper (Wallcreeper)
the Wryneck
the Hedge Sparrow
the Sand Martin
the Common Titmouse (Great Tit)
the Coalmouse (Coal Tit)
a Water Wagtail (Yellow or Grey Wagtail)
Robin Red-breast
the Wheat ear
the Dotterel
the Goose
Anser ferus (Eider ?)
a Soland Goose (Northern Gannet)
the black Diver (Red-breasted Merganser)
Anas Platyrhincus (Northern Shoveller)
a Gaddel (Gadwall)
the great Ducker (Great Northern Diver)
Worm (Great Crested Grebe)
the Dab Chick (Little Grebe)
the Cormorant
the Pelicane
the Sea Mew (Mew Gull)
the Puphin (Atlantic Puffin)
the Ash coloured Heron (Grey Heron)
Ardea minor (Little Bittern ?)
Red shanks
a Stone Curliew
the Grey Plover
Rallus Itallorum (rail/crake spp)
Sea Lark (Dunlin ?)
a Darker Hen (Corncrake)
Crickaleel (Garganey)

Aided by Sir Thomas Browne in 1668, Merrett added a further *c*.100 bird species (not necessarily recorded in Britain) to his list, but this was not published. Browne is credited with discovering Britain's first Bearded Tit,

Hoopoe, European Roller, Manx Shearwater and Little Auk. Despite sending notes to Merrett, Willughby and Ray some of these accounts were not published until 1835.

Willughby produced the first work devoted solely to birds (1676) and he had worked closely with John Ray. Prior to their publications there had been little scientific study undertaken in ornithology, though Edward Wootton had made an attempt to compile a systematic list. Ray's first work was a poor catalogue of British birds completed in 1674. It was based on species recorded during his travels to various parts of the British Isles. Together with friends he noted "soland-goose" (Northern Gannet) on Bass Rock and in 1662 found Red-billed Choughs near Padstow, Cornwall.

John Ray later arranged Francis Willughby's notes after his death, to form the important *Ornithology of Francis Willughby* (1676).

Ray later added to Willughby's notes and, also using material from Thomas Browne, produced his own work the *Synopsis Methodica Avium*, (published after his death).

Ray was instrumental in finding 30-plus new species, more than half the additions made during the century. This had involved separating Common Redpoll and Twite, Yellow and Grey Wagtails, Coal and 'Marsh' Tits, along with distinguishing Little Tern, four types of warbler and Great Black-backed Gull. In addition, he differentiated between Common Chiffchaff and Wood Warbler.

In 1661, Joshua Childey published a poor natural history book entitled *Britannia Baconi* that was to inspire Robert Plot to write various county natural histories covering, among others, Oxfordshire (1677) and Staffordshire (1686).

Robert Plot's first book had followed work undertaken by Francis Willughby and added no new species. This led to further titles, including Robert Sibald's natural history of Scotland: *Scotia illustrata* (1684) and Charles Leigh's *Natural History of Lancashire, Cheshire and Derbyshire* (1700). Most counties were covered during the following 100 years.

In 1697, Martin Martin visited St Kilda and in his notes give detailed accounts of seabirds. Of these the Fulmar and Storm-petrel had never been documented in Britain but he failed to describe the Leach's Storm-petrel which was to be described from these islands well over a century later.

In 1788, Gilbert White noticed the third British 'wood' warbler: Willow Warbler, though this had been suspected by Derham in 1718.

By the mid-18th Century, regular detailed observations of birds were recorded and, with the invention of taxidermy, specimens-collection started. The bird now had a value greater than just the ingredient of a stew or pie. The study of birds had begun and, though often grossly inaccurate, this period was the birth of ornithology in Britain.

As a result of the work by Willughby, Ray, Browne, Sibbald and Martin the British List stood at 202 at the turn of the century.

1700-1800: *The serious work continues*

Following Ray's death, a lean period in the history of ornithology followed until the arrival on the scene of Thomas Pennant who listed 242 species in *British Zoology* which he began in 1761 and completed in 1776. This was the first important work to include colour plates, 132 in all.

The grandfather of British ornithology Dr John Latham, put the total number of British birds at 268 in *General Synopsis of Birds* (1787) which meant that 104 species had been added to the British List in the 113 years that followed Ray's work.

During the first half of the 18th Century new discoveries had been minimal with only Golden Oriole and Rosy Starling mentioned. However the endeavours of Thomas Pennant and his associates between 1751 and 1796 accounted for a further 16 species; approximately half this century's total! At this time further works on the Birds of Britain were published including those of Thomas Bewick (1797), John Walcott (1789), William Hayes (1775).

The third quarter of the 18th Century showed the first signs that ornithology was becoming a serious scientific subject throughout Europe. At this time it became fashionable to collect or keep birds. Parrots were features of many coffee houses and drawing rooms while waterfowl were released onto the ornamental lakes of the wealthy.

The British Museum was formed in 1753 but failed to appeal to a wide audience, it wasn't until the next century that collecting would reach a grand scale.

An important but crude taxonomic list published by Swedish author Carl Linneaus (1753) was created and the classification of all animals using Latin names was to become recognised throughout the world. This system used only two Latin names while previously some unfortunate creatures had been burdened with many names that virtually described the species and was consequently unworkable. In 1778, the letters, documents and collections belonging to Linneaus were sold by his widow to James Edward Smith for 1,000 guineas. They arrived in Britain with a Swedish warship in pursuit (allegedly) in 1784. By 1788, Smith had founded the Linnean Society of London and become its first president. Britain's leading naturalists were soon attracted and many ornithological records discussed at their meetings. By 1800, the classification system was considered out of date but the basic principal was still universally accepted.

Frenchman Mathurin-Jacques Brisson updated the early ornithological works of Linneaus and John Ray (1676) in 1760. Curator of one of Europe's finest natural history collections, Brisson's work was a catalogue primarily of the specimens held in the Parisian collection of Rene-Antoine Ferchault de Reaumur. His list contained 500 species (three times more than Linneaus) that were grouped according to bill and claw shape. The work lacked information about seasonal plumage change and distribution as no fieldwork had been undertaken to support his claims.

France continued to play an important role in ornithology's infancy and the work of Georges-Louis Leclerc de Buffon ten years later expanded on that of his rival, Brisson. In it, he described all known facts regarding the species listed, including habit and plumage notes.

The studies of the two Frenchmen began a period in Europe's history that launched a series of regional avifauna, including those of: Bonnelli (Italy), Schinz (Switzerland), Nilson (Scandinavia), Naumann and Brehm (Germany) and the laid the foundations on which Thomas Bewick and Colonel Montagu would base their works.

During the 1700s few vagrants were found due to a lack of observers and the poor availability of literature. The small number of ornithologists prepared to devote considerable time to their pursuit began to distinguish several species. Birds separated or added to the British List during this period included Tree Sparrow, Black and Red-throated Divers, Lesser Whitethroat, Dartford Warbler, Tree and Rock Pipits, Greenshank, Grey Phalarope, Lesser Black-backed Gull, Slavonian Grebe, Arctic Skua, Willow Warbler, Sedge Warbler, Wood and Purple Sandpipers, and Rough-legged Buzzard.

By 1799 the British List stood at 241 species.

The works of Gilbert White (1788) and the illustrations of Thomas Bewick (1797) popularised the study of birds, out-selling the more scholarly works and attracting new blood to the hobby.

References:
Gurney 1921: p 229; *British Birds* 2: 109-118, 151-163, 259-266, 290-300; Fisher 1954: 21-23; *Birdwatch* 90: 6-13.

1800-1900: *The ornithological revolution*

A revolution in the printing industry during the 19th Century reduced the cost of producing manuals and journals, coupled with considerable improvements in communication and transport, and the scene was set for ornithological understanding and recording to take a massive leap forward.

The Victorian passion for collecting was instrumental in the search for something unusual and it was an era when anyone taking a little time and effort could name a plant or insect at that time unknown to the scientific world. The microscope became an alternative to the piano or bible to entertain the family or guests after dinner, and the pursuit of some unfortunate creature while 'taking the air' was recommended by doctors.

While the ordinary man studied entomology and botany it was the aristocracy that enjoyed ornithological pursuits. They were the only people with the right to carry a gun and could afford travelling to obtain specimens. Indeed the peak intake of new species in about 1830 is attributed to improvements in gun manufacture. The creation of the Penny Post allowed specimens to be exchanged but many were lost this way.

Lists of eminent naturalist's names were made available to assist beginners. Correspondence between interested parties became easier and various people were soon recognised as authorities in their subject. The goals of these people were partially selfish, based on a desire to classify a new species or increase their own collection.

During the 19th Century the works of Montagu, Macgillivray, Yarrell, Newton and later Saunders and Gurney dominated British ornithological recording. Bird specimens were exhibited at the meetings of respected ornithologists before general acceptance and mention in the literature.

Birds collected before 1800 were poorly preserved and often fell victim to parasite infestations. Consequently few survive to the present day. An improvement in taxidermy techniques led to a boom in shooters, dealers and collectors, indeed most major towns had a resident taxidermist.

In the previous century the sworn oath of a magistrate, clergyman or member of the aristocracy was all that was required for the acceptance of a record. The provision of a specimen was a nicety not a necessity. For the eminent ornithologists of the 1800s it became essential and during this period, rules were made regarding verification of records. This encouraged the growth of fraudulent activity during the period as dealers and shooters were able to command an exorbitant price from the highest bidder for specimens. Importation of specimens began and Leadenhall market in London became the place to find rare birds.

Typical of the era game dealers with market stalls displayed and sold thousands of birds. Mr Durrant of Yarmouth, Norfolk would receive birds from the surrounding area. The common birds would be hung in bunches with the larger ones hung separately, while rarities were placed on conspicuous fruit trays at the front of the stall. His stalls reflected the health of local bird populations at the time, and during a period of hard weather in 1890, he received 1100 Common Snipe alone! Many of these were sent Leadenhall, the most famous bird market. Here many unusual species were found (see Wandering Albatross), with consignments also received from the continent. These included small cargoes of Common Snipe that arrived at the same time as the Norfolk birds which presumably reflected an influx into the Low Countries.

Rare specimens were soon sold in the popular collecting areas like the Norfolk and Kent coasts but the bulk of the commoner species were forwarded to Leadenhall. Occasionally species that were difficult to identify would pass unnoticed through the hands of the dealers and turn up, as is the case with Britain's first American Wigeon.

Several reports from this period are fraught with doubt and suspicion and it was at the end of the 1800s that the infamous Hastings rarities affair began. Various British Lists were published during this period and formal publication of new records appeared in journals such as *Zoologist, Ibis* and *The Field*, now recognised as the accepted forum for discussion and general acceptance.

Until this time, there had been little association with Ireland but, as interest grew, correspondence and specimens were sent to Britain for discussion and display following acceptance in Ireland. Publications and works about 'British' birds started to include Irish records as an integral part of the British Isles and its list. From here on the British and Irish List became the adopted standard.

This was the age of the collector the most notable being Mr E T Booth. While great collectors such as Montagu, Bond, and Gould were content to purchase other people's specimens, Booth would only keep birds he had shot. Many of the Norfolk wildfowlers would send for Booth personally to shoot a rare bird rather than obtain it themselves, as he would refuse to purchase 'second-hand' birds.

Booth's obsession was taken one step further than other collectors; he would obtain an adult pair of birds before making sketches, taking the nest, chicks, eggs, rocks and twigs from the site. Returning to Brighton, the specimens would be mounted and placed alongside the nest and eggs he had taken, all under a painted backdrop depicting the exact site where he had obtained them. Some locations depicted in his specimen cases are recognisable today, over one hundred years later.

The Norfolk marshes became a Mecca for shooters and collectors with several accounts written about the activities of such men. On the Sussex coast a small band of ornithologists dominated the discovery of new British birds as the activities of bird catchers produced exciting migrants among the flocks of Linnets and larks. For example, Little, Rustic, and Black-headed Buntings were all added to the British List courtesy of these people, along with Common Rosefinch and a belated Blyth's Pipit.

The work of Colonel Montagu brought ornithology to a higher level as the study of individual species began. His *Ornithological Dictionary* first published in 1805, followed by his even larger supplement (1813), was constantly corrected and updated by later authors. New discoveries were made regularly and many mistakes noted as the learning process continued; confusion surrounded several 'common' species. Birds with breeding plumages that differed to their winter dress were at first described as separate species. Even into the 19th Century, the Snow Bunting, Common Guillemot and various waders were the subject of some obvious mistakes. With a large variation in plumage, Ruff were recorded as three different species: 'Greenwich', 'Aberdeen' and 'Yellow-legged Sandpipers'. Mistakes were even made regarding the differences between male and female which were named as separate species.

Early 19th Century biological research was clouded with confused issues as the occurrence of hybrids was arousing interest. In December, 1831, the Honourable Twiselton Fiennes exhibited a hybrid Northern Pintail x Mallard from a brood of six. This was possibly the first documented hybridisation of a wild bird in British ornithology. Hybrids among captive wildfowl were the most regularly reported cases and remain a major headache today. In May 1840, the Earl of Derby wrote to the Zoological Society, describing the pairing of a Barnacle and Canada Goose on the Great Lake of his estate. This was unsuccessful but the same Barnacle Goose later paired with a Greater White-fronted Goose and laid eggs. Colour morphs and mutations created additional problems and the Polish Swan (a mutation, where the cygnet of a Mute Swan is pure white instead of grey) was described as a distinct species. This was after a nobleman writing to Joseph Sabine claimed that he had seen a brood of swans that were all white some time before 1836. Subsequent observations collectively convinced Yarrell and others that these birds must be a migratory race of Mute Swan arriving from the Baltic in times of bad weather.

It is also important to record that in 1840 John Gould imported the first Budgerigars, the bird that probably did more for aviculture (and therefore escapes), than any other species.

During the 1800s there developed a difference of opinion between the field naturalists who based their work on observation of birds in their natural habitat, and the studies of the morphologists who indulged in the anatomical studies of dissected specimens (including the chamber or closet naturalists who studied skins and museum specimens). During the early part of the 19th Century there was a period of heated debate between the two camps and much scorn was poured over those daring to make a mistake.

One closet naturalist was unfortunate enough to have named a legless bird of paradise from a specimen sent to him. The matter was only brought to light when a complete bird, with legs still, attached arrived. John Edward

Gray, keeper of zoology at the British Museum in the 1870s attacked the illustrator of a book devoted to the fauna of India. Gray had examined many specimens of a turtle with a hole always present between the 2nd and 3rd digits and so announced the inaccuracies of the artwork, which lacked this feature. Upon hearing of the attack the author, a field naturalist, publicly ridiculed Gray by reporting that the holes were made by fishermen tying up the flippers to prevent escape. A closet man would not be expected to have knowledge of such actions.

The accurate work of Gilbert White written in the previous century remained an inspiration to many field ornithologists.

The early work of Montagu's *Dictionary*, which placed great strength on the study of museum skins, was constantly changed and corrected, and superseded by the works of William Macgillivray and William Yarrell. Both later authors published the first volumes of their books in 1837, which led to an end of the constant arguments regarding the superiority of various systems of nomenclature.

Macgillivray was an accomplished field naturalist, a chamber naturalist and a skilful anatomist, having devised a new scientific classification of birds based on all aspects of ornithology. Unfortunately his work was not as popular as Yarrell's which possessed some skilful illustrations, and a comparison of the digestive systems or shape of the sternum as identification features in addition to plumage details.

Groups of like-minded people formed clubs where unusual records were the subjects of scrutiny. Of these, the Linnean Society, which would eventually spawn the Zoological Society, was at the forefront of record assessment.

In 1859, the British Ornithologist's Union (BOU) was founded by 20 members, all of which but two were active specimen collectors. They were to be widely recognised as the cream of Britain's ornithologists during this period. Many travelled widely.

The original members included Professor Alfred Newton, Oswald Salvin, J H Gurney, Alfred and John Wolley, Canon Tristram, Philip Sclater and Dr Frederick Du Cane Godman, all who were consulted about the identification of additions to Britain's avifauna.

The 20 men had regularly gathered on an annual basis to exhibit specimens to each other and at one such meeting in Cambridge in 1857 it was decided to publish a magazine devoted to ornithology, *Ibis*.

Following Yarrell's death in 1853, his work was updated by Professor Alfred Newton and Howard Saunders who later condensed his work into a single volume entitled *An Illustrated Manual of British Birds* (1899). During BOU meetings Newton examined many specimens and usually had the last word regarding the bird's identity, origin and position on the British List.

The idea of an 'official' British List was agreed upon at the Annual General Meeting of the BOU on 15th May, 1878. P L Sclater and N T Wharton headed the committee given the task of creating the 'List' that considered records prior to 1880. Published in 1883, it listed 376 species but this included some records subsequently removed, several subspecies and some birds not correctly identified until after 1800 despite occurring before. It more correctly stood at 363.

Saunders held the position as editor of *Ibis* and like Newton was often consulted about the validity of a record. His *Manual* was regarded as the published official British List and remained the standard reference until the work of Witherby and Hartert updated it in the next century. At this time, R J Ussher was compiling a list of birds occurring in Ireland culminating in the publication of *Birds of Ireland* in 1900.

This century also saw the invention of the binocular, first patented in 1859, and the introduction of photography as a recording medium; the first photographic contribution to ornithology being in the 1880s. Finally, in 1889, Ludwig Koch made the first recording of bird song at Frankfurt am Main.

References:
Montagu 111; *British Birds* 1. 197-201, 2. 351-361, 389-399; Barber 1980: 17-18; 40-41; Yarrell, 1843: iii, 73, 161, 131-135; Fisher 1954: 24-28.

1900 to the present day: *Systematic recording and increased knowledge*

Saunders maintained late Victorian attitudes as he led ornithology into the 20th Century. Specimen collection, although prolific at first, was replaced by photography, note-taking and ringing activities. At the opposite end of the century, scientists had delved into the biological study of mitochondrial DNA and a long period of taxonomic stability appeared to be drawing to an end.

While *British Birds* magazine (BBRC) and *Ibis* (BOU) had dominated the ornithological press for much of the century, the 1980s saw an upsurge in the number of active birdwatchers. Old arguments between the scientist and field ornithologist were revived. While scientists gauged the distance between species and subspecies, field ornithologists were undertaking studies to decide which side of the line a bird would fall.

Birding World magazine became the voice of the new breed of field ornithologists: the 'twitcher.' Arguments aired publicly in this journal sparked much thought and controversy so that, probably for the first time, the ordinary person in the field was able to actively contribute and influence opinion.

In June, 1907, the journal *British Birds* was launched by Harry Forbes Witherby who was to remain editor until 1943. Indeed, he was to take the crown from Saunders and lead Britain's ornithologists for the first half of the 20th Century. He was responsible for vetting letters from the field naturalists and rejected incorrect submissions of scarce migrants and rare vagrants.

In the first volume of *British Birds,* Saunders updated his list printed in 1899 adding 20 species (including some Hastings rarities) new to the British and Irish List. In the same year, Witherby began his regular updates of rare bird records. One of the original aims of *British Birds* was to keep the work of Yarrell and Saunders up-to-date by drawing together contributions from more than 100 ornithologists across Britain and Ireland. The final judgement pronounced on additions to the British List was left to the BOU, of which Witherby was chairman from 1924-1927.

In 1912, Ernst Hartert, curator of the Walter Rothschild Natural History collection at Tring, together with Jourdain, Ticehurst and Witherby published a *Hand-list of British Birds* giving an up-to-date account of the distribution of each species recorded in the British Isles (an official British List).

Ireland's birds were included in this work despite no distinction in its title, courtesy of Messers Ussher and Warren, with Ussher checking the proofs detailing Irish distribution.

This set the standard for the first half of the 20th Century and was revised periodically by the BOU with the publication of the BOU's own British and Irish Lists; 1915, 1971, 1992 etc. This was in addition to decisions announced in *Ibis.*

At the start of the century the increase in literature and growing number of collectors enabled 23 species to be added to the British List in the first decade. This was the highest number found in any ten-year period since 1799 and was only equalled in 1821-30 when firearms became more accurate. In the decade that followed when World War One took its effect, just three new birds were discovered (between 1921-30). At this time specimen collecting became less fashionable and the noose was tightening around the necks of fraudsters.

After 113 years of publication, *Zoologist* was incorporated into *British Birds* in 1917 following the movement of ornithological readership to the new journal. Between 1938-1941 Witherby published *The Handbook of British Birds* which became the ornithological bible until the completion of *The Birds of the Western Palearctic* in the 1990s.

In 1953, the *Handbook* order of listing was abandoned by *British Birds* and the BOU adopted that of Peters, the order in use at the end of the century, which begins with divers and grebes.

Two ladies dominated bird recording in Scotland during this period: Dr Evelyn Baxter and Miss Leonora Rintoul. They founded the Scottish Ornithologists' Club and co-authored several works – having been steered in the right ornithological direction by Eagle Clarke. Their studies on the Isle of May introduced the concept of drift migration to rare bird hunters and they were to find many scarce migrants, including a first: Pied Wheatear. They are remembered in the image of two lady bird-lovers together on that remote island with Leonora calling: "*Oh Evie, do come quick and bring your gun, there's a dear little Piedy Fly on the Lighthouse wall.*"

In the 1950s a change in thinking led to the acceptance that birds could cross the Atlantic un-aided. On behalf of the BOU, Newton had accepted this phenomenon as early as 1883 but Saunders rejected all records except American ducks, gulls and waders. Bowing to pressure from the large number of Yellow-billed Cuckoo records in Europe, this became the only American landbird allowed onto the British List. The rest were treated as ship-assisted or caged birds.

During the 1950s it became apparent that the numbers of American vagrants arriving warranted serious consideration and by 1960 the Black-and-white Warbler and White-throated Sparrow were officially welcomed to Britain's avifauna. The established vagrancy patterns of other Nearctic passerines became a doorway to acceptance.

It wasn't until 1959 that the British Birds Rarities Committee (BBRC) was formed to judge the growing number of rare bird records. This began with submissions from 1958 and the publication of an annual report. While the BBRC concentrated on identification matters, the task of categorisation and acceptance or rejection from the British List remained the domain of the British Ornithologists' Union Rarities Committee (BOURC). This is still the case today.

Birds in The Republic of Ireland are scrutinised by the Irish Rare Birds Committee (IRBC) and the BOURC have ceased to be involved with any decisions made regarding records there. This separation of The Republic of Ireland became absolute in 1997 when the BOU published its intention to maintain just a British List.

The Republic of Ireland, Northern Ireland, Channel Islands and the Isle of Man maintain their own respective lists but the Isle of Man, Channel Islands and Northern Ireland still permit the BOURC to pass judgement over their records.

At that time the rules governing admission to Category A of the British List changed to include all species recorded since 1st January, 1950. This date had previously been 1958 when the BBRC was formed and the new date brought Britain into line with other European countries.

During the 1990s the work of American taxonomists Charles G Sibley and Burt L Monroe, Jr altered the thinking of Britain's scientists and field ornithologists. The listing of bird species using the results of DNA sequencing as part of the Phylogenetic Species Concept gave birth to a new period of uncertainty. Not only was the old order of birds at risk but several 'new' species were accorded full specific status with others set to follow in the millennium.

Splitting and lumping has always been a contentious issue and to an extent DNA studies backed up what birders in the field had realised for years. Hume's Leaf Warbler and Southern Shrike were made full species in their own right, with others such as Green-winged Teal, Hooded Crow, Black Brant, Whistling Swan, Black Scoter and the 'Herring' Gulls warranting further investigation. Birdwatchers in the new millennium may have to face some dramatic changes to the British List and a new approach to identification. Playback of song to territorial males and taking blood samples seem poised to become as important a tool as museum skins and field observations.

With the launch of many independent magazines, local bird club bulletins and the publication of continental journals in English, information passed freely between field ornithologists and scientists.

As computers became a feature of many households, statistics and records became easier to analyse and the internet presented the opportunity for birds found in Britain to be assessed by birdwatchers living within its normal range far from Britain. However two things remain a thorn in the side of today's birdwatchers: the problem of escapes and the ability of each species to defy all the previously established vagrancy patterns set down by its brethren.

With the relatively recent recognition of high altitude migration on rapidly moving weather systems, and ship-assisted passage, comes the arrival of Britain's first aircraft-assisted bird: a Mourning Dove. How long before a bird is discovered in space?

The listing of British birds has never attracted so much interest. Thorough documentation of new species found in Britain and Ireland is more stringent than ever before, with periodic reviews of older records; while to string or suppress a bird has become the ultimate sin. Each record is subject to the scrutiny of hundreds of observers, recorded by photograph and video, published in a variety of glossy magazines and journals, then subjected to often lengthy debate before a file even reaches the relevant rarities committee.

Fraud, deception, and misidentification are not yet things of the past and never will be; where would we be without rumour and conjecture to spice up the long, birdless winter nights?

Finally a new collector of birds emerged: the twitcher, content to just observe birds as opposed to shooting them. With him has arrived a new language and strange new terminology.

Witherby began to change the 19th Century collector's adage: *"What's hit's history and what's missed's mystery"* which now no longer holds good. The motto of today's twitcher appears to be: *"Anything can turn up in a place and at a time you least expect it – but is it an escape?"*

References:
Mearns 1998: 355-7; *British Birds* 50: 213-223; 37: 162-174; Fisher 1954: 24-28.

SPECIMENS, COLLECTIONS AND MUSEUMS

During the 18th Century collecting became a way to fill increasing amounts of leisure time, with birds slowly growing in popularity. Growth in the taxidermist's skills permitted beautiful birds to be mounted and displayed.

As the first scientists to study birds dealt mainly with corpses, the collection of specimens led to the development of better preservation techniques. Early man had developed the skill of animal skin preparation to provide clothing. From this, experimentation led to mummification and immersion in pickling fluids being practised. Crude and of little use to the scientist at first, taxidermy was the tool that allowed ornithology to move forward out of the Dark Ages.

The first recorded collection concerned a Dutch nobleman who had imported several live tropical birds. They were later stuffed with Indian spices and wire after suffocating when the furnace door of the aviary heating system was left open. The oldest mounted bird specimen in Britain is an African Grey Parrot, which died in 1702. It had belonged to the Duchess of Richmond, a mistress of Charles II. X-rays show that it still contains the complete skeleton, brain and tongue.

It wasn't until the middle of the 1700s that taxidermy reached a workable level but with specimens of the period being poorly mounted few survive today. At that time there was no successful barrier against insect attack.

In Paris, Reaumur devised a technique of drying birds in an oven and he assembled Europe's largest collection of the time. Hans Sloane (who had invented a chocolate recipe that he sold to a Mr Cadbury) provided Britain's contribution to the European collecting scene. His £100,000 collection suffered a serious insect attack after moving to the British Museum and was said to have been better than those already in residence. Unfortunately no records were kept of his "*Knick Knackatory.*"

During the 1800s things improved as many skins were treated with arsenic and placed over a suitable framework, the insides having been removed. Charles Waterton invented an alternative method whereby the whole skin was hollow and lacking any support having been treated in mercurous chloride. His specimens still survive in good condition today.

It was eventually appreciated that sunlight would fade the skins and insects should be kept at bay. Various chemical repellents were created but placing a mounted specimen inside a case became the most effective barrier against infestations. Despite the recognition of preventative measures, several collections suffered attacks and the specimens of several 'firsts' subsequently lost.

The great collector-ornithologists appeared during this century and much knowledge was gleaned from the study of skins. The custodians of the British List held their own collections and all relied on evidence and research based on specimens. Few ornithologists did not collect specimens and those researching new species held their own reference collection to consult. Often the only source of information came from one's own observations or examination of specimens. Research often involved travelling to view others' specimens or European Museums, while popular authors had specimens sent directly to them. The ordinary man had to be content with the less expensive hobby of egg collecting.

Pre-1780 collecting had focused primarily on the luxury trade, being either mounted ornaments or fashion accessories, but between 1780 and 1830 there was a steady shift towards the supply of specimen skins. Collecting expeditions were organised mostly to areas rich in biodiversity, indeed Temminck funded Levaillant's African journey which brought back 2,000 specimens in 1784, while Swainson ventured to Brazil from 1816 to 1819 financed by his military pension and "good connections". It was mainly royalty, governments or the very rich that could fund such trips. Museums often purchased the spoils of these expeditions but generally profit was made from selling to small collectors or the luxury trade.

Diplomatic and military positions allowed the British to bring back foreign skins and many naval journeys included the collection of specimens as part of the voyage to map out and colonise new lands. The French dominated this field in the early 1800s but some British trips were notable, including Franklin's voyage to North America. Additionally the naturalists in each colony, Audubon and Wilson for example, sent information and new specimens. The East India Company possessed so many specimens from its trade with Asia that it opened a London based museum in 1801.

So popular was this activity, that in 1800 Benjamin Leadbeater began a natural history taxidermy agency near the British Museum. With such opportunity for financial gain it is easy to see how fraudulent claims began to trick collectors hungry for new specimens.

Several collections stand out as playing a significant role in the discovery of British 'firsts'. The collections of Montagu, Latham and Yarrell contributed to recognition of many species as did birds obtained much earlier by Sir Ashton Lever.

The Leverian Museum at Blackfriars Bridge Road, London housed a collection of c.28,000 natural curiosities picked up by exploring travellers but lacked any kind of order or classification. Consequently it had little scientific value.

Important as it was, Lever's museum, which possessed Captain Cook's specimens, failed financially and was offered for sale to the Government to join the British Museum. Due to the overcrowding in that establishment it was rejected and sold by lottery. Lever printed 36,000 tickets to be sold at one guinea each while he held 28,000 tickets in the hope of retaining the collection. It was won by a dentist, James Parkinson.

Following an unprofitable period, the museum was divided and sold off in 1806. The 7,879 lots took two months to sell with over 200 purchased by the Imperial Collection in Vienna.

Eminent ornithologists such as Messers Bullock, Swainson and Latham also added Levers specimens to their own. This practice made tracing specimens very difficult as they changed hands frequently or suffered deterioration in poor housing.

The specimens assembled by individual collectors varied considerably in quality and value; William Bullock spent £30,000 creating his museum in London, which became one of the most respected of its day. The skins were well preserved and scientifically arranged. Later they were moved to the Egyptian Hall of the British Museum where 32,000 subjects were displayed.

Marmaduke Tunstall possessed a major collection from which he based his work *Ornithologia Britanica* in 1771, a list of British birds. It was said to have been the best collection in Britain, save for that of Latham. Tunstall's specimens formed the subjects for Thomas Bewick's engravings in his *History of British Birds* (1797-1804).

Like Montagu and Tunstall, Latham based his work on his own collection. He also travelled widely and catalogued much of the British Museum's foreign specimens.

Undoubtedly the most prominent collection remains the British Museum, founded in 1753 by an Act of Parliament. In its infancy it resembled a large aristocratic collection unlike the superior organised museums on the continent, partly because the museum grew out of a collection began by Sir Hans Sloane. The British Museum suffered from frequent insect attack and a lack of space. The bird department was poorly represented and lacking both in quality and quantity.

In 1816, William Leach suggested that the museum purchase Montagu's collection to improve its reputation. This was a bad decision as the skins, costing a total of £1,200, soon suffered the same fate as Sloane's and fell apart. Major purchases included the specimens of Bullock and the East India Company.

Following rehousing, the museum received important specimens from other collectors and today remains the premier ornithological collection in Britain.

At around 1815, all major collections underwent change as museums became places of work rather than places of curiosity. They grew in scale and determined the direction of all classification and identification study. The Zoological Society Collection had been a former rival to the British Museum (it being formed in the 1820s from an offshoot of the Linnean Society). Most notably it had received the specimens donated by Nicholas Aylward Vigors and was more popular than the British Museum in its day.

Mr Gould, curator and taxidermist of the Zoological Society Collection, was part of an elite group of people able to use their position and unlimited access to make new discoveries. Being in receipt of hundreds of specimens, museum curators throughout Europe found and named new species. They included: Bonnelli (Italy), Liechtenstein, Cretzschmar (both Germany), Temminck and Schlegal (both Holland).

The working classes were discouraged from visiting collections as it was thought that they would steal the exhibits but in 1835 John Hancock held open evenings for the public in Newcastle. This was a great success and undoubtedly fuelled an increasing public awareness.

As collectors died, their specimens were sold or donated to museums but a large number of historically important skins were lost, stolen or damaged.

In the 20th Century the passion for collecting diminished especially with the onset of the Great War and the emergence of bird protection laws. The taxidermist's art has changed very little since but collecting specimens is strictly controlled and only allowed under licence. Consequently many of the great collections have suffered from neglect and a lack of interest, though they continue to supply information to authors, artists and scientists.

With an increased interest in identification and the taxonomic changes revealed through DNA study, the work of the curator and taxidermist is again as important as ever.

During the search for museum specimens associated with first records mentioned in this book it became clear that many 'firsts' suffered from ignorance and a lack of museum funding. Consequently many have been lost. How many other important specimens have also slipped away from our grasp?

As new records and species are constantly found in museum trays, it is important that future generations of birdwatcher and conservationist are made aware of the historical contribution and continued importance of good collections.

References:
Stearn 1981; Mearns 1998; Barber 1980.

The Hastings rarities and cases of fraud

The Hastings rarities scandal made British ornithological history as probably the largest case of fraud to be uncovered. The case graced the headlines of the national press and is still discussed a century after the first record was submitted. To this day there are still those who believe many of the records to be genuine and the whole story is the subject of a work on its own. What follows is an introduction to the alleged events, that imported birds were passed off as having been shot in the Hastings area, damaging the British List's credibility.

In 1962, Max Nicholson and Ian Ferguson-Lees revealed the results of an eight-year investigation that rocked the British ornithological world. They published a paper titled *Setting the record straight* in the journal *British Birds*, that removed six species from the British List which have not been recorded subsequently; this was the, so-called Hastings rarities affair.

The six species were Masked Shrike, Black Wheatear, Asian Brown Flycatcher, White-winged Snowfinch, Black Lark and Slender-billed Curlew, although some have been reported but not accepted since and the latter was probably the subject of the BBRC's most important decision.

In the 32 years between 1892 and 1930 almost 600 rare bird records, including *c.*23 species potentially new to the British List, were brought to the attention of the British Ornithologists' Club and the editors of *British Birds*. Norman Ticehurst and Michael Nicoll respected ornithologists of the day had submitted the records. Of these 'firsts,' several now appear regularly in Britain as predictable annual vagrants or scarce migrants, such as Melodious Warbler, Black-winged Pratincole, Semipalmated Sandpiper, Baird's, Terek and Marsh Sandpiper. Another, Cetti's Warbler now breeds regularly in Kent. Others are still rare visitors, such as Grey-tailed Tattler, Belted Kingfisher, Royal Tern, Semipalmated Plover, Rock Bunting, Moustached and Rüppell's Warbler.

The choice of predicted additions to the British List was both accurate and exceptional considering that knowledge regarding vagrancy patterns was poorly understood. In fact, during the 'Hastings' period, records of commonly encountered autumn vagrants such as Pallas's Leaf, Yellow-browed, Greenish and Arctic Warblers in Britain had not even reached double figures.

Included in the suspected list were also the first records of several subspecies or races, such as White-spotted Bluethroat, 'Siberian' Stonechat and Black-headed Wagtail. In addition a handful of washed-up seabirds, such as Britain's first Cory's Shearwater and Madeiran Storm-petrel, were included. In fact nothing too far removed from the reality of the present day British List.

Records of Brown Noddy, Long-tailed Rosefinch and Three-toed Woodpecker were also submitted, but not accepted, though there were already several existing claims from other parts of Britain and Ireland. In fact, escaped Long-tailed Rosefinches are still reported and there are two accepted Western Palearctic records of Brown Noddy from Norway and Germany – so why not Kent?

Many of the specimens had been seen in the flesh as soon as possible after being shot. Others were verbal reports from the original reporters or shooters. However only a few of the birds were actually seen in the field by recognised experts such as Ticehurst and Nicoll.

At the time there was no such thing as the British Birds Rarities Committee and Ticehurst (who co-authored Witherby's *Handbook of British Birds*) was also part of a 12-man team from the British Ornithologists' Club that investigated rare bird reports. Nicoll was also a recognised expert field ornithologist whose reputation was never questioned, even during the 1962 investigation.

The 595 records all came from an area centred around Hastings, stretching from Folkestone in the east to just beyond Eastbourne in the west, including Dungeness, Beachy Head, Romney Marsh and Rye Harbour.

Looking through the amazing list of records it is possible to see why doubts were raised about their origins. There was a large number of birds involved, some of which now appear on a regular basis and are no longer treated as rare, such as Bluethroat, Woodchat Shrike and Barred Warbler. On the other hand 13 Black Larks, three Caspian Plovers and six Slender-billed Curlews would appear to be excessive.

The reports involving skins or specimens all passed through the hands of one man, George Bristow, a taxidermist living in St Leonards-on-Sea, Sussex.

To earn a few shillings, local people would take birds they had killed to him and in turn Bristow would mount the specimens to sell on to the collectors. Here lies the strength of the case against the records being genuine. If Bristow was a criminal it would be relatively easy for this one individual to submit false records.

But the birds were not found or shot by Bristow and each report usually involved a different finder; several of them being interviewed both at the time by Nicoll and Ticehurst or later by the 1962 *British Birds* investigation team. Some locals were asked to swear an oath to back up their reports while Nicoll attempted to see as many as he could to verify the records.

To his credit, Nicoll saw at least 20 live birds including Sociable Lapwing and Pectoral Sandpiper, while he even shot the first claimed British Baird's Sandpiper himself!

The Duchess of Bedford was recorded as finding a Solitary Sandpiper in the Hastings area but her reputation was never questioned when she found Britain's first Blyth's Reed Warbler. If all the records were fraudulent was there a large clique of corrupt people operating in the area?

As a specimen had been obtained in the vast majority of cases, if imported where did they come from?

It was easy to shoot birds abroad, stuff them and send them to England; but it must be remembered that a large number were seen in the flesh by Nicoll before skinning with the blood still wet and appearing quite fresh. So was Nicoll involved?

There has never been any indication or suggestion of this so surely the records where he had observed the bird in the field should stand.

At the time, refrigeration of corpses was not an easy task and ocean journeys often took weeks rather than days. The corpses would have to have been packed in ice, which was expensive and refrigerators were not in use on ships until 1928, two years before the end of the Hastings affair. When questioned about the possibility, Bristow revealed that he once received four albatrosses, a Cape Pigeon and a Hoopoe caught on board a steamer of the Natal Line and frozen for the duration of a journey to Britain.

When the 'Hastings' birds were examined they had shown no signs of being frozen, despite Nicoll and Ticehurst looking for such evidence. In the case of the Bulwer's Petrel (picked up on a beach during a great storm), not only would Bristow have to get the corpse back to England in fresh condition but also time its arrival with prime vagrancy weather conditions.

So far it would appear that Bristow along with a large number of local farmers, shooters, bird trappers, a Duchess and maybe a handful of seamen were involved in the deception, even members of the make-shift rarities committee were possible suspects.

The question must be asked why do it at all? Large sums of money were never proven to have changed hands and Bristow was far from being a rich man. There was obviously the kudos or glory attached to finding a rare bird, but why attempt so many cases of deception when Bristow was never the finder?

Now to the birds themselves: it would seem that the choice of species was exceptionally well thought out. Although c.23 species and several subspecies were new to Britain all but six have turned up since to be reinstated on the British List. The problem would seem to be the number of individuals involved rather than vagrancy potential.

Three Caspian Plovers? Well why not? Of the four British records two different individuals appeared in 1988, while the first British record at Yarmouth also apparently involved two birds together, although only one was shot.

Large numbers of birds or multiple records are not without precedent; in 1888 more than 2,000 Pallas's Sandgrouse were counted in Scotland alone, as part of a massive invasion, and many of them even bred!

So four Slender-billed Curlews? Again, why not? This species often migrates in flocks and multiple records were not uncommon elsewhere in Europe. The species has been recorded 22 times in France, with four records since 1950, despite its decline. This species was probably as common in Europe as the Eskimo Curlew in America; both now facing extinction if not already extinct. Bird populations a century ago were undoubtedly much higher than the present day levels, as habitat loss and pollution or pesticide poisoning have since taken their toll. So the chances are that there was a higher likelihood of vagrancy at the start of the 20th Century.

Climate and weather conditions are constantly changing. In the late 1990s we saw an unprecedented Bohemian Waxwing invasion in winter followed by a record flock of 27 European Beeaters in spring and six Buff-breasted Sandpipers together on Scilly in autumn – so why not a small group of Black Larks in the coldest winter to ever be recorded in its normal range? In fact there are about 15 European Black Lark records. The *British Birds* paper argued that several Black Lark corpses sent from the continent had been on sale at Leadenhall Market, in London.

Most species on the 'Hastings' list concerned several records. For example: three Olivaceous, three Orphean and two Rüppell's Warblers; no less than five Collared Flycatchers, 11 Pine Grosbeaks and five Rock Buntings. Multiple records also existed for Dusky Thrush, of which there were six and White-winged Lark, which recorded 10. This does seem to stretch the imagination a little.

Nelder undertook a statistical analysis. He compared the reports during the period with records from other parts of Britain. His findings illustrated that the concentration of rare bird records in the area was unbelievably high and did not conform to patterns elsewhere in the country; or indeed to earlier and later reports from the same site. He compared the Hastings' birds to those from places high in vagrancy records such as Fair Isle; which had a list of species that consistently appeared on the island at regular intervals throughout the century, rather than multiple arrivals in one or two years only. The species recorded around Hastings differed greatly from the species seen in that area prior to, or following the period.

In 1916 Witherby wrote to Bristow laying down ground rules for future acceptance of his records.

These were that:
1. All birds should be shown in the flesh to Dr N F Ticehurst.
2. When required the bird should be skinned in Dr Ticehurst's attendance.
3. The name and address of the shooter involved be disclosed to Witherby.

A visit was also proposed to the favourite sites involved although Witherby was engaged in active service as a naval officer at the time; it being during the First World War.

Bristow accepted these conditions but never carried them out and so subsequent reports were not accepted by Witherby. These included: Royal Tern, Long-tailed Rosefinch, Belted Kingfisher and Brown Noddy.

1915 was the peak of the 'Hastings' affair with 50 rare bird reports during the year. After 1916 there was an average of 10 reports each year.

As early as 1951, David Bannerman had written several letters to Ticehurst discussing the matter, these letters were found hidden in a book some years ago and make interesting reading:

Ticehurst said both he and Nicoll were constantly on the lookout for fraud as Saunders, Jourdain, Witherby and Eagle Clarke had raised the question at the time. The shooters had been very secretive at first because they killed birds in the closed season and the RSPB were active. Later they were contacted and verified the details.

Ticehurst said it was not unusual for Bristow to receive so many birds as he was the only taxidermist between Dover and Brighton and the dismissal of all the records would be an insult to many good people, including his then deceased friend Nicoll. Bannerman would appear to have agreed with Ticehurst but his campaign to change the opinions of Max Nicholson and Ian Ferguson-Lees would ultimately fail and the Hastings records were all dismissed.

Sir Vauncy Harpur Crewe of Calke Abbey purchased several Hastings specimens. One of the great gentlemen collectors of his day, Crewe was easily tricked into purchasing specimens from other countries. Unscrupulous dealers took advantage of his good nature or lack of knowledge and many important specimens in his collection were subject to some kind of deception or fraud indicating that the activity was far from restricted to the Hastings' area. This collection still remains on public view but the most important skins were sold at auction in 1925 to pay death duties.

A percentage of the Hastings' records probably involved some degree of deception – if one is fraudulent then how reliable are the rest? However if the number of false claims is small, should we accept the majority of records as genuine, allowing a few bad apples to slip through? Maybe an unscrupulous sailor tricked Bristow on the odd occasion and other reports were genuine. From his letters he did not appear to have been even slightly suspicious of their origins. A lot of the records are probably quite genuine, but can we really allow them to be part of our history?

For the purposes of this work any Hastings rarities that occurred in Britain for the first time are mentioned in the systematic list for completeness, but regarded as unacceptable in line with the BBRC and BOURC decisions.

Many specimens relating to the Hastings records still exist today as proof of identification if nothing else. Many specimens bought by J B Nichol's were later sold to A K Maples whose collection remains in good condition and on public display at Ayscoughfee Hall, Spalding, Lincolnshire. It is on loan from the Spalding Gentleman's Society.

Further specimens are also on display to the public at the Booth Museum, Dyke Road, Brighton. Several originate from the sale of Harpur Crewe's birds at Calke Abbey in 1925.

References:
British Birds 55: 281-384; Harrison 1968.

Further cases of fraud

Although the Hastings affair was undoubtedly the most notorious case of ornithological fraud in British History there had already been many attempts to deceive scientists, collectors, museum curators and historians. The motive was usually financial gain or occasionally the kudos that surrounds a notable discovery. Many gamekeepers, sportsmen and taxidermists were involved and at times it is unclear to what extent this activity took place.

During the early 19th Century many of Britain's most respected ornithologists fell victim to fraudsters when the word of a gentleman or member of the clergy was all that was required to allow a species to be added to the British and Irish Lists. Eventually personal opinion and reputation was not good enough to allow acceptance, a specimen was needed. The wise men of the BBRC and BOU made a point of questioning the shooter concerned, however some high ranking ornithologists still remained above suspicion.

Even today, some of the older records are subject to review as new information comes to light. This often leads to the discovery of a hitherto unknown case of fraud. One such case was the 1961 review of Short-billed Dowitcher records. Mr J Baker, a Cambridgeshire taxidermist, had sold a specimen to the British Museum claiming that the bird had been shot in October, 1843. But the condition of its plumage proved it had been killed some time before early September, clearly a case of fraud. His other specimens also seemed highly improbable. Modern knowledge of ageing, moult and feather wear has revealed inconsistencies in written descriptions even those submitted recently. Video and photography is now used as evidence to support a claim but this has its drawbacks. In one instance, photographs of a bird claimed to have been taken in Holland showed a plant species in the background not recorded in Europe, an obvious attempt to deceive the Dutch Rarities Committee.

Investigations continue as new evidence is reported to the BOURC, such as the first Orphean Warbler record published here. The tale of its discovery seems suspicious yet the record has remained acceptable for years. There is a possibility that it had been secured outside these islands and during the course of researching this book I became suspicious about the taxidermist involved with mounting the specimen, Mr Graham of York. He was involved with several records and even at the time some were dismissed. These included a Brünnich's Guillemot, Bald Eagle and an Eastern Screech Owl; the latter an American species that he claimed had been killed in Yorkshire. He was also involved in the first British records of Ross's Gull, Spotted Sandpiper and Houbara Bustard which, at the close of the millennium, remain acceptable.

Hindsight is a wonderful tool and it is clear to me that Britain's first Ross's Gull is unlikely to have turned up well inland, indeed it remains the only such record out of a total of almost 90 records!

The BOURC has been made aware of these suspicions and already these birds are being called "The Tadcaster Rarities". Their position on the British List is under review.

Meinertzhagen and the British List

A case of fraud potentially as important as the Hastings affair has recently come to light; this is the specimen collection of Colonel Richard Meinertzhagen (1878-1967). Over half were allegedly shot by himself but it has been revealed that he also stole skins from existing collections only to re-label them and record them as birds collected by him from a different location. Many of his reports were well conceived and the claimed occurrence of the American races of Merlin, Horned Lark and Common Snipe in western Scotland were not unexpected and aroused no suspicion.

Meinertzhagen was certainly an extraordinary man, his collection of 587,610 ectoparasite specimens alone contained 1,791 type specimens (the first specimen of a species to be collected) the largest amount assembled by one individual. During army service, he collected and sent observations from the Middle East to *Ibis*. But deception was used throughout his career: an intelligence officer he had led the Turks to believe that the British were to attack Giza; by riding behind enemy lines to drop false documents while being chased. He would also drop a rifle covered in fresh horse's blood to indicate that he was wounded. An air of mystery still surrounds the Meinertzhagen story, even his second wife Annie died in somewhat unusual circumstances. She was an accomplished ornithologist and collector before their first meeting and during a shooting practise with Richard, accidentally shot herself in the head.

Meinertzhagen's devious behaviour began at an early stage. When eight-years-old he purchased a drake Garganey from Leadenhall Market to use as an excuse to gain entry to the collection at the Natural History Museum at London. After entering the bird room to identify the bird, he was shown around by Dr Bowdler Sharp. Fifty eight years later in 1954, his own collection of almost 25,000 skins was to join the British Museum of Natural History, by then housed at Tring. The largest acquisition for 75 years.

Many specimens were prepared to a high standard and he held a complete collection of Western Palearctic birds. During Meinertzhagen's lifetime his behaviour was questioned by several ornithologists including Charles Vaurie who wrote to F E Warr saying: "*I can say upon my oath that Meinertzhagen's collection contains skins stolen from the Leningrad Museum, the Paris Museum, and the American Museum of Natural History . . . He also removed labels, and replaced them by others to suit his ideas and theories.*"

Philip Clancey who had accompanied Meinertzhagen during collecting expeditions made further accusations. Clancey described one particular 'Lesser' Redpoll skin in Meinertzhagen's collection that had been shot in Blois, France, in 1954. This particular skin matched that of a bird prepared by Mr R Bowdler Sharpe obtained in southeast England during 1880 and placed in the Natural History Museum, Tring. Clancey stated that Meinertzhagen had never visited Blois, France in 1954.

In 1993, Alan G Knox of the BOURC published a review of the Redpoll specimens and found discrepancies among those obtained by Meinertzhagen. Examination of the preparation techniques revealed that a variety of styles had been used even among a selection of birds apparently killed at the same time in the same locality. One particular style was identified in a considerable number of specimens throughout Meinertzhagen's career – presumably prepared by Meinertzhagen. The other styles belonged to those of collectors he had stolen from. Knox proved that although every Redpoll specimen had been relabelled at least once during Meinertzhagen's lifetime. From 70 skins at least seven had been relabelled incorrectly and formed part of his collection. Knox suspected that this was the tip of the iceberg as they were the most obvious cases within a small group of specimens. It was concluded that he had filled the gaps in his series of Redpoll specimens to establish his claim that *Carduelis flammea britannica* was a valid race.

Meinertzhagen's specimens were investigated, especially those forming part of the British List. Details of these are mentioned later in the individual species accounts. Consequently, all of Meinertzhagen's records have been removed from official records. They included the northern race of Little Auk, and North American races of Horned Lark, Common (Wilson's) Snipe and Merlin.

With easy access to specimens from foreign travellers and stolen museum skins, the unscrupulous dealers had a great opportunity for financial gain. It is easy to see how fraudulent claims were inadvertently encouraged.

There has been a suggestion put forward to remove all rare bird records prior to the formation of the BBRC in 1958 and begin the British List again.

References:
Birding World 10: 441; *Ibis* 135: 320-325, 494-495; Mearns 1998: 35, 192, 310-311, 357-359.

Escapes, Misidentifications and Rejections

Many species recorded in Britain and Ireland have subsequently been found to involve escaped cage birds. The records were submitted in good faith and some have later shown an obvious pattern of vagrancy that has earned them a place on the British and Irish Lists. This includes many American species once thought incapable of crossing the Atlantic.

However many species have no chance of reaching Britain without human assistance; these were originally ignored but are now placed in Category E of the British List. Several first reports of these species are listed for completeness and interest rather than expectation that they may be upgraded. Thorough documentation of escapes is essential to assist the work of future generations and ideally a dated record of all imported birds should be initiated.

Each year since the BBRC was formed, several species have been rejected because the occurrence was poorly documented or the supporting evidence inconclusive. Maybe the bird was misidentified, or salient identification features were not seen, but there is also the possibility of fraud. A list of some rejections that relate to first reports is included as some of these may later be reassessed.

Using The Systematic List

The systematic list includes all species and some interesting subspecies that currently form part of the British List (categories A, B and C) where the first record is known. Also included are species that have occurred only in the Republic of Ireland, Northern Ireland, the Isle of Man or Channel Islands. Decisions which relate to Ireland are those of the Irish Rare Birds Committee which adjudicates over Irish records.

The near misses section includes species/subspecies once acceptable but subsequently dismissed such as Hastings rarities, reports under consideration as of December, 1999 (Slender-billed Curlew, Short-toed and Booted Eagles, etc.), and some sightings accepted by unofficial authorities other than the BBRC, BOURC and IRBC. Also included here are Category D species/subspecies for which the BOURC require further information before acceptance.

Some accounts are included of sightings that fall short of the stringent criteria needed to clinch a first record and some of the more interesting accounts of Category E species (escapes?) are listed.

In the individual accounts, the species/subspecies English name is listed first followed by the Latin name. This follows the BOU's official list of birds of Great Britain (1999). Below this in brackets is its distribution. The next line has the year of the first acceptable record followed by the county and site.

The letter indicates the category in which the species is currently placed by the BOURC, IRBC, MOS or NIBA, while an * indicates that the record is still under consideration. The figure in brackets following this is the total number of individuals that have occurred in Britain, the Isle of Man and Ireland up to the end of 1998. They do not include records from the Channel Islands which are not subject to the British or British and Irish List. These figures adhere to the numbers published by the BBRC concerning officially accepted records.

For example: White-billed Diver: **A (202)** = Category A species, 202 records.

Note [ ] indicates unaccepted reports.

Any discrepancies that may occur involve species now regarded as common, such as Serin (whose true numbers are clouded by large numbers of fledged young) or Woodchat Shrike and Arctic Redpoll (with numbers now into the hundreds).

Where a species was recorded outside Britain first and the category of the British record is different, the species status is indicated twice.

For example for Mourning Dove: Isle of Man **A (1)**   Britain * [1]

For species with the same categorisation only one total is given beside the first account.

Where a British report was under the BOURC or BBRC review in December, 1999 this is mentioned in the text, and occasionally the second record is described in case the first is subsequently removed.

Where a species does not require documented evidence (because it is regarded as common or a scarce migrant and therefore not considered in Britain by the BBRC) the status of this species is indicated by a code (listed below) and replaces the number of individuals placed in brackets. For example, Slavonian Grebe; **A (RB)**. This does not take into account the status of a species in Ireland, the Isle of Man or Channel Islands.

Status Codes: (**RB**)   Resident breeder
              (**SB**)   Summer visitor breeding
              (**WV**)   Winter visitor
              (**P**)   Passage migrant, may rarely breed

These codes, or a statement forming part of the account, gives an indication of that species' status in Britain at the end of the millennium. Some figures may be used to indicate the number of probable breeding pairs in Britain and these are taken from the published *British Birds* Rare Breeding Birds Panel's findings. The status of birds in neighbouring islands at this time was not always available and is omitted.

THE PHOTOGRAPHS

The recording of rare birds relies upon an accurate description of the species involved and credible documentation of the event. Field sketches, artwork, tape recordings, witnesses and specimens have all been used to confirm identification. It has become almost routine for photographs, and more recently video to accompany a submission.

The camera has replaced the gun but photographing a wild bird well can involve weeks of preparation, erection of hides or hours of stealthy pursuit. To get a good photograph the bird needs to be very close and free from distractions. The rarity photographer does not enjoy such privileges and causing a rare bird to move on prematurely is a major consideration when possibly hundreds of birdwatchers are making their way to see it. Though welcomed by rarity committee members, the pictures are rarely competition winners.

The photographs used in this book are of the actual birds mentioned in the text and remain historical evidence of the event. In many cases the image is small or blurred and in normal circumstances would not be saved. With a first record we should be thankful that any photograph exists at all but the images before you remains an important piece of ornithological history. By glancing at a picture when reading the account of its finding the reader will hopefully get a feel for the event.

I have included pictures of museum specimens because previously many have been destroyed or lost, and some may go the same way in the future; the Savi's Warbler is in particularly bad shape. This is not a complete selection as permission was not always granted to photograph them or bureaucracy meant that reproduction fees were too high. Others such as some cabinet skins would be of little use to the reader.

It is important that photographs are published and made available to the public. During my search for them it has not been possible to unearth some material which has been lost following the death of a photographer. Others have gone missing while in the hands of publishers or even rarities committees.

Reproduction in books and journals allows the record to be reassessed in later years, should it be necessary.

This collection includes almost every first that was ever photographed in the wild, good or bad, and so is an important historical record.

THE SYSTEMATIC LIST

Yellow-billed Diver *Gavia adamsii*
(Arctic Russia eastwards to Arctic Canada)
1829 Northumberland, near Embleton.   A (202)

An adult Yellow-billed Diver in winter plumage was shot on a bog near Embleton, Northumberland in December 1829, Mr G Davidson presented it to the Hancock Museum, Newcastle-upon-Tyne. This record was documented by George Bolam whose grandfather had by coincidence shot Britain's second White-billed Diver. It was also killed in Northumberland, the following year (or possibly 1832) and was a fine breeding plumaged adult with "an ivory white bill, the largest specimen he had ever seen". Bolam and his son were being ferried from Old Law to Holy Island by Joseph Shell who recalled the incident in 1902 as he "had never known a *Lyon* with so white a bill". This specimen was lost before Bolam began collecting seriously.

With about half a dozen Yellow-billed Divers recorded annually over 70% of them have occurred in the Northern Isles and NE Scotland, with only two reported inland. An adult at Audenshaw Reservoirs, Greater Manchester 7th-8th December 1987 and an oiled adult at Tattershall, Lincolnshire from 29th February to 2nd March 1996, when it fatally swallowed a fisherman's hook. Almost a third of reports involved dead or dying birds.

References:
Galloway & Meek, 1978: 14; Reviewed in *British Birds* 67: 283-296; Bolam G. 1912: 673-674.

Pied-billed Grebe *Podilymbus podiceps*
(North America)
1963 Avon, Blagdon Lake.   A (28)

The first acceptable individual occurred as recently as 1963, at Blagdon Lake, Somerset. In the afternoon of 22nd December, 1963, H A Thornhill saw a small grebe swimming among duck in a patch of water kept free of ice by the wildfowl. He pointed the bird out to Robin Prytherch who could not put a name to it after three-quarters of an hour of observation.

Two weeks later and no further on with the identification, Prytherch checked field guides covering countries outside Europe. From the *Field Guide to the Birds of the West Indies* he recognised the Pied-billed Grebe and later aged it as a first-winter bird. A short cine film confirmed the identification and the record was accepted by the BBRC.

What was presumably the same bird returned to Blagdon and Chew Valley Lake, Avon, in August, 1965, and made various appearances until July, 1968.

The first report of a Pied-billed Grebe in Britain was an announcement made in *Zool* by Mr J E Harting, referring to a specimen killed at Radipole, near Weymouth, Dorset, in the winter of 1880-81. It still retained traces of the neck stripes visible on young birds. It was purchased from a birdstuffer and exhibited by Mr R B Sharpe at a meeting of the Zoological Society. The record no longer stands.

Pied-billed Grebe has occurred at widely scattered localities and in all months, many remaining for long periods. A bird present in Cornwall from 1992 to 1994 hybridised with a Little Grebe *Tachybaptus ruficollis* in 1994 producing three young.

References:
Zoologist, p 334; Sharrock, 1982:123-126, sketch.

Slavonian Grebe *Podiceps auritus*
(Northern Europe, North America and Northern Asia)
1796 Cornwall, Truro.   A (RB)

Colonel Montagu (1802) first described the "*Sclavonian Grebe*" as a British species from a male specimen killed by a fisherman near Truro, Cornwall, on 4th May, 1796. A friend of Montagu's rescued the specimen as it was about to be plucked and presented it to Montagu for his museum.

This individual was also included in Pennant's list as the first British record.

The Slavonian Grebe winters in small numbers mostly around the coast. A small breeding population of *c.*56 pairs (1997) in Scotland is generally the only birds present during summer.

References:
Yarrell, 1843: iii, 308-312; Penhallurick, 1969: 34; Gurney 1921: 229; Montagu 1813: 133.

Black-necked Grebe *Podiceps nigricollis*
(Western North America, Europe east to Mongolia; isolated populations in China, South America and Africa)
1810 Cornwall.   A (SB & WV)

In the early edition of his *Ornithological Dictionary* Montague had not separated the "Eared" (Black-necked) from the "Sclavonian" Grebe *Podiceps auritus*. However in a supplement updated by Edward Newman and published in 1866 the two were 'split' and a bird moulting into summer plumage described.

Montague's only encounter with the species was a bird shot in Cornwall on 15th March, 1811 by Col. George of Penryn and examined in a fresh condition. The description recorded the difference in bill shape and it places this specimen a full seven years before the widely quoted first record in Norfolk.

The Norfolk bird was caught alive by a spaniel near Great Yarmouth in autumn 1817. Its discovery was published in Shepherd and Whitear's *A Catalogue of Norfolk and Suffolk Birds* 1826. It was remarkably tame and commenced "pluming itself with great composure after it was taken."

It was said to have been rare on Breydon Water or in the Broads and a second specimen was taken in a net soon after, on the River Yare in 1820.

Yarrell mentioned that Pennant had recorded the species breeding in the Lincolnshire fens near Spalding, however Pennant died in 1798 before the two 'eared' grebes were distinguished so the identification cannot be relied upon.

The species was scarce in Ireland during the 19th Century but in 1929 a colony numbering 250 pairs was found at Funshinagh, Co. Roscommon. The area was drained in 1934. Occasional breeding is still suspected but there are only three records from 1959 to 1993.

In 1996, the British population stood at 23-57 breeding pairs.

References:
Paterson 1905: 264-265; Taylor 1999: 104-105; Montague 1866: 130-131; Yarrell 1843 iii: 313-315; British Birds 92: 125; Wingfield Gibbons 1993: 30.

Albatross spp *Diomedea spp*
(Southern oceans)
1836 Lincolnshire/Nottinghamshire, River Trent, Stockwith, near Gainsborough.

A (12)

The first record of an albatross species in the northern hemisphere was an immature bird on the River Trent at Stockwith, near Gainsborough, on the Nottinghamshire/Lincolnshire border. It was shot on 25th November, 1836, where the Chesterfield Canal meets the river. Although the record was accepted, no other information is available. It was most likely a Black-browed Albatross *Diomedea melanophris* and this record pre-dates the first confirmed record of that species. The bird has occasionally been reported as a Yellow-nosed Albatross *Diomedea chlororhynchos* and was apparently identified as such. No specimen has ever been traced.

It was also claimed as a Grey-headed Albatross *Diomedea chrysostoma*, which in immature plumage is very similar to the Black-browed. This confusion arose because the skin of a Grey-headed Albatross allegedly shot at Chesterfield, Derbyshire, on 2nd November, 1870, was claimed to have been the Stockwith bird. The Chesterfield specimen was later found to have been a discarded museum specimen.

In total, 12 unidentified albatross's have been accepted as reaching Britain and Ireland. They were most probably all Black-browed.

Reference:
Ibis 1967: 141-167; Lorand & Atkin 1989: p 211 Apx 1.

Black-browed Albatross *Diomedea melanophris*
(Southern oceans)
1897 Cambridgeshire, Linton. A (27)

Samuel Barker, a farm labourer on the Streetly Hall farm, near Linton, Cambridgeshire caught a large bird thought to be an exhausted gull on 9th July, 1897. He took it to his employer Mr S Owen Webb at the Hall, who then sent it to Mr Travis, taxidermist at Bury St Edmunds. The bird showed no signs of captivity and was in relatively good condition. The Rev G Julian Tuck informed Mr J H Gurney of the record who subsequently examined it as did Saunders, Col E A Butler and Osbert Salvin. Salvin identified it as Britain's first Black-browed Albatross.

An earlier report, in 1894, of an immature bird obtained close to Orkney could not rule out other albatross species.

Some of the recent Black-browed Albatross reports may have concerned just one individual. 'Albert Ross', was a female that first appeared in the gannetry on Bass Rock, Lothian in 1967 and moved to the Saito outcrop, Hermaness, Unst, Shetland in 1972 after failing to attract a mate. She was last seen in 1995.

References:
Ibis 1897: 625; 1967: 146.

Soft-plumaged Petrel *Pterodroma mollis/madeira/feae*
(Central Atlantic)

Recent studies undertaken have resulted in the BOURC splitting the Soft-plumaged Petrel into three separate species with various suggestions for their 'new' names. Fea's, Gon-gon or Cape Verde Soft-plumaged Petrel, *P. feae* which breeds on Bugio and the Cape Verde Islands, Freira, Madeiran or Zino's Petrel *P. madeira* which breeds in small numbers on Madeira and Soft-plumaged Petrel *P. mollis* which occurs in the South Atlantic.

IRELAND
1974 Co. Cork, Cape Clear.   A (26)

Observations from Pointabullaun, Cape Clear between 7.30am and 10am on 5th September, 1974 produced small numbers of Sooty Shearwaters *Puffinus griseus* among typical numbers of Manx Shearwater *Puffinus puffinus* and about 50 European Storm-petrels *Hydrobates pelagicus* passing per hour. When Jim Enticott, Chris Cook and Pete Ewins returned at 3.30pm Storm-petrel numbers had doubled. After about an hour Enticott picked up an unfamiliar seabird at about 1km. He and his companions watched it down to 600m taking note of its unusual plumage and flight manner. Their conclusion was that it was of the *Pterodroma* genus, most probably 'Soft-plumaged Petrel,' but knowledge at this time did not permit the bird to be conclusively identified.

Studies in the identification of this genus allowed this record to be accepted 23 years later.

In 1997, the Irish Rare Birds Committee ruled out the possibility that three 1995 records had involved the South Atlantic Soft-plumaged Petrel. They also admitted that Zino's Petrel was a most unlikely vagrant and the birds were therefore almost certainly Fea's Petrels. The first of these reports to be formally accepted was one or possibly two birds at Cape Clear, Cork, on 27th July, 1995.

All previous Irish records were reviewed resulting in the acceptance of the bird seen passing Cape Clear Island, Co. Cork on 5th September, 1974.

BRITAIN
1989, Cornwall, Porthgwarra.

In 1989, up to five birds were reported from seawatches that involved large numbers of Cory's *Calonectris diomedea* and Great Shearwaters *Puffinus gravis*. The first was a single bird that flew west at Prawle Point, Devon, on 11th August (rejected by the BBRC), followed by sightings from Porthgwarra, Cornwall on 12th, 13th, and 14th, which probably involved the same individual.

The Cornish bird was first seen at about 8.30am on the 12th by around 80 birders. Descriptions were sent to the BBRC by Paul Flint and D Walker with additional notes regarding the following days sightings from seabird expert Peter Harrison and artist Ian Lewington. This was the first British record and since then 'Soft-plumaged Petrels' have been recorded almost annually.

Until August, 1989 there had only been two unconfirmed reports: single birds off Spurn Point, Humberside on 19th November, 1985 and Strumble Head, Dyfed on 2nd September, 1988.

The 'Soft-plumaged Petrel' superspecies was accepted onto Category A of the British List by the BOURC in 1992 when the Cornish sightings were accepted. The birds concerned seemed likely to have been Fea's Petrels, *P. feae*. As a result, all British records are currently accepted as Madeira/Cape Verde Petrels with the Southern Atlantic Soft-plumaged Petrel now excluded.

References:
Birding World 5: 325, 385; 3: 81 & 2: 265-266, painting; Evans 1994: 7; *British Birds* 85: 510; 91: 460; 92: 504-518.

Capped Petrel *Pterodroma hasitata*
(Haiti is the only known breeding site; formerly widespread in West Indies, dispersing to adjacent seas)
1850 Norfolk, Swaffham.   B (2)

Following severe gales in March or April, 1850, a boy on the heath at Southacre, near Swaffham, Norfolk, saw a bird "*flapping for some time from one furze-bush to another*". It became tangled among them allowing it to be captured. Although obviously exhausted it bit the boy's hand so violently that he killed it.

Falconer John Madden saw the boy with his prize and took it to his master, Mr E C Newcombe of Feltwell Hall (or Hockwold Hall, near Brandon in some references) who was hawking nearby. The mounted specimen was later seen by Alfred Newton who initially thought it to be an immature Northern Fulmar *Fulmarus glacialis* but, realising his mistake, later showed it to Messers Yarrell and Gould.

Newton considered that it resembled a skin he had seen of a 'Black-capped Petrel' and this was confirmed by Messers Bartlet and Yarrell. Newcombe recorded the sex as a female.

The bird was presented to the Castle Museum, Norwich on 1st June, 1949 where it remains in good condition and on public display (Accession no. 108.949).

The Capped Petrel, as it is now known was thought to be in danger of extinction and its admission to the British List was thought unlikely. However 100 years later, a juvenile female was washed up on the Yorkshire coast on 16th December, 1984, constituting the second record for the Palearctic. The bird had probably been dead for about three weeks.

Another bird was watched for four hours on 26th February, 1980 some 80km southwest of Rockall and 480km west of Scotland.

References:
Zool, 1852: 3691-8; *Ibis* 1967: 155; Riviere 1930: 176; Mather, 1985: 70, photo plate 57; Evans 1994: 8; Seago, 1977; Y.N.U. 1984: 8; *British Birds* 92: 513-514.

Bulwer's Petrel *Bulweria bulwerii*
(Oceanic islands of North Atlantic and Pacific; nearest population Madeira and Azores)
1837 Durham, River Ure, Tanfield.   A (4)

Europe's first Bulwer's Petrel was found dead on the banks of the River Ure, at Tanfield, Co. Durham, on 8th May, 1837. It was taken to Col. Dalton, of Sleningford, near Ripon, who in turn sent it to Gould. It was described and figured in his *Birds of Europe*.

The skin of this bird was retained by Dalton but later lost casting some doubt on the record. However it was rediscovered 50 years later by James Carter a local naturalist from Masham and Eagle Clarke, curator of the Museum of the *Phil. and Lit. Society* in Leeds.

Capt Dalton had inherited a collection from his father the Colonel and on his death the cases were sold at a local auction. The auctioneer held a list of buyers' names and all had gone to people living near Ripon. Eventually the case was found in the possession of Mr Jacob's, headmaster of the Ripon Choir School but there was no other confirming data with it. Carter visited Capt Dalton's son-in-law, George Clarke, who immediately recognised the case and also produced an accompanying note in an old book recording its location and the preserver, John Stubbs. Prof. Alfred Newton subsequently exhibited it at the Zoological Society on 15th November, 1887. The figures in both Yarrell and Lord Lilford's works on *British Birds* were taken from this specimen. The skin is presumed to be one of two specimens now held at the Yorkshire Museum; the other, the second British record was washed up dead at Scalby Mills, Scarborough in 1908. There has been just one Irish record.

In 1990, a bird seen passing Walney Island, Cumbria allowed Bulwer's Petrel to be upgraded from Category B.

References:
Ibis 1967: 156; Saunders, 1899: 749; Yarrell, 1843: iii, 513-515; Nelson, 1907: 762-764; Denton 1995: 90.

Cory's Shearwater *Calonectris diomedea*
(Mediterranean and Atlantic Ocean)
1933 Devon, at sea.   A (P)

Several earlier records were later dismissed as part of the Hastings rarities and the first record deemed acceptable was as recently as 10th September, 1933, when a flock of about 60 birds was seen by Mr Wynne-Edwards at sea, between the Casquets and a point, 23 miles off Prawle Point, Devon. Wynne-Edwards expressed doubts about his identification but Harry F Witherby thought them acceptable.

There was a lot of confusion regarding the identity of the larger shearwaters in the 19th Century (see Great and Sooty Shearwaters) and many Cory's Shearwaters were perhaps reported as Great Shearwaters. Large gatherings of shearwaters regularly seen off the Cornish coast in autumn would almost certainly have contained Cory's.

Birds later dismissed as Hastings rarities included a female of the Mediterranean race *C. d. kuhlii*, picked up on Pevensey Beach, Sussex 21st February, 1906, a male of the North Atlantic race *C. d. borealis,* found dead on the tide-line at Bulverhythe, St Leonards, Sussex on 14th March, 1914, with another there in 1920, and in 1946 William E Glegg reported the discovery by Mr J E Tandy, from the Tring Museum of a specimen of Cory's Shearwater *P. d. borealis* while the label read: "*Great Shearwater female washed ashore alive at Dungeness, Kent, Jan. 21, 1901, R. Johnson.*"

With the rejection of the Sussex bird the first record of this race concerned a corpse found at Salthouse, Norfolk on 29th January, 1966. It had been dead for about a week and was identified by RA Richardson, A Mannering and B Shergold among others.

Cory's Shearwaters are regularly seen from the coast in late summer and autumn chiefly in the southwest, as they move through British and Irish waters in large numbers. The most popular seawatching sites are Porthgwarra, Cornwall, and Cape Clear, Co. Cork.

References:
Hartert, 1912: 152; Yarrell, 1843: iii, 502-507; Witherby, 1945: iv, 361-363; Harrison, 1968: 118; Walpole-Bond, 1938: iii, 70; Penhallurick, 1969: 44; *British Birds* 1: 16; 3: 229; 33: 249; 34: 56-57; 60: 312.

Sooty Shearwater *Puffinus griseus* and **Great Shearwater** *Puffinus gravis*
(Atlantic and Pacific Oceans)   (Atlantic Ocean)
Sooty Shearwater: 1828 Yorkshire, Teesmouth.   A (P)
Great Shearwater: *c.***1838 Yorkshire,** Teesmouth.   A (P)

The two first British records of the Sooty and Great Shearwaters are inextricably linked and are treated here in the same account.

At a meeting of the Zoological Society in July, 1832, Arthur Strickland, of Boynton, Yorkshire, exhibited what he thought was Britain's first Great Shearwater. It had been found in August, 1828, early in the morning of a very stormy day, at the mouth of the River Tees, Yorkshire by George Marwood junior of Busby Hall. Sat on the water like a duck, Marwood shot it as it began to take flight.

This bird resembled an illustration of a specimen used in Yarrell's work (1843), obtained by D W Mitchell in Mounts Bay, Cornwall during autumn 1838. It is shown as a dark bird, and is in fact Britain's first example of a Sooty Shearwater (then thought to have been the young of Great Shearwater).

A pale bird (typical Great Shearwater) is also depicted in the illustration based on another found by Strickland soon after 1838, again from Teesmouth.

Yarrell's illustration was later used in Saunders' *Manual* (1899) to correctly illustrate Sooty Shearwater.

There was earlier confusion between the two species as Temminck pronounced that the dark bird (Sooty Shearwater) was the female and the pale specimens (Great Shearwater), males having only recently been distinguished from Manx Shearwater *Puffinus puffinus*.

The two specimens possessed by Strickland were the first Sooty and Great Shearwaters to be described in Britain. The Cornish Sooty Shearwater specimen used by Yarrell is often incorrectly claimed to be the first British record. Strickland's Sooty Shearwater specimen was said to be housed in the Yorkshire Museum.

Both species are regularly reported during autumn passage, often in large numbers. As with Cory's Shearwater *Calonectris diomedea*, Cornwall and southern Ireland receive the lion's share of records.

References:
Yarrell, 1843: iii, 502-507; Saunders, 1899: 737-741; Temperley, 1951: 197-198; Hartert, 1912: 152; Penhallurick, 1969: 44; Denton 1995: 11.

Mediterranean Shearwater *Puffinus Yelkouan*
(Mediterranean Sea dispersing into northwest Atlantic)
1874 Lothian/Fife, Firth of Forth. A (P)

E T Booth shot the first Scottish Mediterranean Shearwater at the mouth of the Firth of Forth on 19th August, 1874; it is probably also the first record for Britain and Ireland.

I have been unable to unearth any conclusive earlier reports as all birds at that time were recorded as Manx Shearwaters *Puffinus puffinus*.

An earlier report of a Mediterranean Shearwater in British waters' was a specimen in the collection of Mr E Hart. It was killed in Christchurch Bay, Hampshire in August, 1859 and was seen and identified by Mr Dresser. Unfortunately the identity of this bird was not confirmed and so remains in doubt.

Howard Saunders recorded specimens collected from Devon being present in the British Museum with another in the possession of John Hancock in Northumberland. Saunders and Col. Feilden also recognised two birds, in Pashley's shop that had been shot on the Bar, Cley-next-the-Sea, Norfolk on 22nd September, 1891. One was placed in the Cannop collection and the other sent to P Evershead of Norwich, later being sold to W R Lysaght and J B Nichols.

In 1908 Witherby examined several other records and the identification of several confirmed as Mediterranean Shearwaters. He listed 17 records from Yorkshire, the first of which was obtained near Redcar in the autumn of 1877.

In letters to Witherby, Mr W J Clarke, a wildfowler from Scarborough claimed that this was the commonest shearwater species off the Yorkshire coast in autumn and that specimens were shot from boats four to eight miles from land at dusk. Saunders had misidentified at least one Mediterranean Shearwater and so some confusion about early records has arisen.

Recognition and identification of Mediterranean Shearwater in British waters was proven in 1921 and re-examination of Booth's 1874 specimen resulted in it being confirmed as belonging to this subspecies (which was split from Manx Shearwater and given full specific status by the BOU in 1991).

Snow and Perrins (1998) go further and separate the two races of Mediterranean Shearwater as Balearic Shearwater *Puffinus mauretanicus* and Yelkouan Shearwater *Puffinus yelkouan*.

The BOURC currently does not accept any records of the nominate race *P. y. yelkouan* in British waters despite regular claims from seawatchers, while Snow and Perrins (1998) state that it has not been recorded in the Atlantic with any certainty.

Mediterranean Shearwaters are regularly sighted from the coast, usually during summer and autumn. The first Irish record of this species was identified in Belfast Lough, on 1st August, 1956.

References:
Ruttledge 1966: 37; Baxter & Rintoul 1953: 483; Pashley 1992: 23: 119; *British Birds* 2: 206-208; Snow & Perrins 1998: 53-55.

Little Shearwater *Puffinus assimilis*
(Atlantic south from Madeira and Caribbean, southern Pacific and Indian Ocean)

IRELAND
1853 Co. Cork, off Bull Rock.   A (98)

A bird that flew on board the sloop '*Olive*' late in the evening was caught on 6th or 11th May, 1853, while passing the Bull Rock, Co. Cork. It was taken to Valentia Harbour, Co. Kerry where it was given to Mr Bewicke Blackburn of that town who preserved it and later exhibited at a meeting of the Linnean Society the following June. Also examined by Mr Yarrell, it figures in his *History of British Birds*.

It is now at the Dublin Museum (P. Milne *in litt*), the bird was of the Madeiran form *P. a. baroli*.

BRITAIN
1858 Norfolk, near Earsham.

Like most early records involving seabirds, the first British Little Shearwater was picked up dead. A gamekeeper on the Earsham Estate, Norfolk, found it on 10th April, 1858. It had arrived during a gale and probably collided with a tree as it had a wound on one side of its head. Then called the 'Dusky Petrel', it was skinned and found to be a male, of the race *P. a. baroli*.

It was examined by Mr H Stevenson and exhibited by Osbert Salvin on 16th May, 1882, at a meeting of the Zoological Society and recorded by Saunders.

Stevenson recorded that the inner web of one foot had been nibbled away and the cased specimen appeared to have lost the distal half of the inner right toe. Although the web seems complete, taxidermists often fabricated them in wax. The specimen would need to be removed from the case to confirm this.

The specimen is presently stored at the Castle Museum, Norwich (Accession no. 38.944). The back of the case has a pencilled note in the hand of Thomas Gunn that reads: "*Copied from old label on glass. Dusky Shearwater. The only specimen of this species ever shot in England at Earsham April 15th 1856. Preserved by J. Sayer, Norwich. Cleaned by T. E. Gunn. March/86*"

An additional note in ink reads: "*Published accounts give the date as April 10, 1858 & state that the bird was found dead (not shot). E. A. Ellis*" (Dr A G Irwin *in litt*).

A bird of the Cape Verde race: *P a. boydi*, was allegedly found dead on the beach at Pevensey, Sussex, on 4th December, 1914, while the first live bird was found at West St Leonards-on-Sea, in the same county on 2nd January, 1915. These and further reports from the area were rejected as part of the Hastings rarity affair.

A Little Shearwater of the race *Puffinus assimilis elegans* was reported from Musselburgh, Lothian, on 9th December, 1990. The report was sent to the BOURC in 1995 and was still under consideration in December, 1999.

References:
Riviere 1930: 174-5; Saunders, 1889: 743; Seago, 1977; Walpole-Bond, 1938: iii, 68; Evans 1994: 9; *Ibis*; 23rd & 26th report; Kennedy, 1954: 18; Ruttledge, 1966: 37.

Wilson's Storm-petrel *Oceanites oceanicus*
(Southern oceans)
1838 Cornwall, near Polperro. A (31)

The first 'official' record came from Cornwall in 1838 when a bird was found during a mid-August wreck of European Storm-petrels *Hydrobates pelagicus*. It was picked up dead in a field near Polperro and examined by Mr H Couch prior to being sent to William Yarrell, who made a drawing of it.

It is possible that there was an influx of the species at this time as the following spring another bird was found in Norfolk, and two birds were also caught on a baited line dragged behind a ship in the English channel. Alternatively specimens may have been brought to Britain for sale to collectors.

Earlier in May, 1838, John Gould recorded seeing a Wilson's Storm-petrel from the deck of a ship that had just left Penzance and though his identification was not in doubt, as he had differentiated them from the European Storm-petrels, Gould's records were not accepted onto the British List as he was at sea.

Wilson's Storm-petrel is now seen annually from Irish headlands, and many others are reported at sea. The recent discovery of the 'Wilson's Triangle,' (an area just off the Cornish coast where Wilson's Storm-petrels are regularly attracted to fishing boats or bait laid down by birders) has given rise to annual pelagic trips.

References:
Ibis 1967, 157, Yarrell, 1843: iii, p 516; Penhallurick, 1969: 36.

White-faced Storm-petrel *Pelagodroma marina*
(Madeira, Canary and Cape Verde Islands)
1897 Strathclyde, between Kiloran and Kilchattan, Colonsay, Argyllshire. B (1)

After a southwesterly gale on 1st January, 1897 a White-faced Storm-petrel was picked up alive by a stream between Kiloran and Kilchattan, Colonsay, one of the Inner Hebridean Islands. It was sent immediately to Eagle Clarke at the National Museums of Scotland, Edinburgh. It was an immature female of the race *P. m. hypoleuca* from the Salvage Islands, near Madeira and the record was accepted.

In November, 1890, a severe gale caused a wreck of seabirds to be washed up on the northwestern shore of Walney Island, Cumbria. The bodies were picked up and taken to Mr Williams, a blacksmith at Barrow-in-Furness, who undertook taxidermy to subsidise his wages. Due to illness he had only skinned two petrels, a Little Auk *Alle alle* and another unrecognised bird. The rough skins had been placed in a glass-topped box as they were not fit for mounting. H A Macpherson visited Williams the following July and took the skin of the unidentified bird and one of the petrels, which he had recognised as a Wilson's Storm-petrel *Oceanites oceanicus*. The unknown bird was identified as a White-faced Storm-petrel.

Although accepted at the time, the validity of this record has been called into doubt: Barrow-in-Furness was a sizeable port at that time and the bird was in the company of a Wilson's Storm-petrel *Oceanites oceanicus*, itself a major rarity. In addition, nobody else had noticed a seabird wreck at the time and Williams must have been a lucky man to also receive a Greater Spotted Eagle *Aquila clanga*, washed ashore at Walney in 1875.

The 1897 bird remains the sole British record despite three further sight records rejected by the BBRC.

Reference:
Ibis; 1967: 157.

Leach's Storm-petrel *Oceanodroma leuchoroa*
(North Pacific and Atlantic Oceans)
1818 St Kilda.   A (SB)

Mr Bullock obtained the first British specimen of Leach's Storm-petrel on St Kilda in the summer of 1818; it was also the fourth known specimen from anywhere in the world. The specimen was sold to Dr Leach following Bullock's death and placed in the British Museum. In 1841, Sir William Milner discovered a nest and single egg under loose rocks near the summit of Dun, part of the St Kildan Islands. The first breeding site to be found.

Leach's Storm-petrel has been present around Britain's coast for a considerable time as a complete humerus bone was found in a 9th Century Viking settlement at Jarlshof, Shetland, during excavations in 1949.

Breeding in the Northern Isles and rarely on the Irish west coast, Leach's Storm-petrel is regularly seen passing west coast sites in autumn and early winter with smaller numbers reported from the east coast. 'Wrecks' of birds occur in times of severe weather with inland reports being the result of strong winds at sea.

References:
Montagu, 1862: 231-232; Venables & Venables, 1955: 246; Yarrell, 1843: iii, 520-523; Holloway 1996: 54.

Swinhoe's Storm-petrel *Oceanodroma monorhis*
(Northwest Pacific Ocean; winters western Pacific and Indian Ocean)
1989 Northumberland, Tynemouth.   A (3)

During night-time ringing sessions from the pier at Tynemouth, in July, 1989, European Storm-petrels had been successfully tape-lured. At 1.15am on 19th July, a large petrel called as it circled the trapping area. The tape was switched off and the calls of Leach's Storm-petrel *Oceanodroma leuchoroa* played, but the bird had gone. On 23rd July a large petrel was again attracted to the tape and trapped. In the hand, the ringers were amazed to see that the bird had a dark rump, but superficially resembled Leach's Storm-petrel. The bird was released after being ringed, photographed and measured.

On the evening of 26th July a second unringed bird, identical to the first was trapped. The ringing group including Mary Carruthers, Mark Cubitt, Adam Hutt, Keith Regan and Les Hall, began researching the possibility that the birds were Swinhoe's Storm-petrels or an undescribed close relative.

The following year a third individual was trapped on 6th July. It proved to be faithful to the site, being recaptured in five consecutive years. The dates are as follows: 6th July, 1990, 30th July, 1991, 29th July, 1992, 21st, 28th and 29th July, 1993, and 11th, 23rd and 25th July, 1994.

When the bird was captured in 1991, Dr David Parkin travelled from Nottingham to Tynemouth, and took a blood sample from the bird. The true identity of the birds took three years to sort out. Analysis of cytochrome-b mitocondrial DNA sequences taken from the blood sample proved that the birds were indeed Swinhoe's Storm-petrels. The 1991 bird was a female whose DNA sequences matched those taken from birds in Korea and Russia.

As well as Britain, records have come from France, Madeira, Norway and the Mediterranean coasts of Spain and Italy, some concerning birds in nest holes but without eggs.

References:
Birding World 2: 288-289, photo; 7: 271-273; *British Birds* 88: 342-348, photos.

Madeiran Storm-petrel *Oceanodroma castro*
(Azores, Madeira and Cape Verde Islands; separate population in Pacific Ocean)
1911 Hampshire, Milford.   B (2)

On 19th November, 1911, Roland Follett picked up a dead Madeiran Storm-petrel from the beach at Milford, Hampshire. The specimen was identified by W R Ogilvie-Grant and became Britain's first and sole record after the following previous claims from the Hastings rarities affair were dismissed.

They were: 1895 Kent Littlestone, female found dead on the beach after south-westerly gales, 5th December, 1905 East Sussex St Leonards, found dead, 26th November. Now in the Booth Museum, Brighton, 1906 Kent near Hythe, female found dead, 19th November.

The first of these was seen in the flesh while in George Bristow's taxidermist shop by Dr N F Ticehurst and Mr Boyd Alexander, who exhibited the bird in his collection at the BOC.

The second bird seems to have good credentials as it was seen by a constable who found the bird lying in the road on a stormy night. He gave the bird to Mr Farley, who mounted the bird. The only involvement by Bristow, the Hastings rarity taxidermist, was that he forwarded the specimen to Sir Vauncey Harpur Crewe.

IRELAND
1931 Co. Mayo, Blackrock Lighthouse.

The first Irish record was found dead at the Blackrock lighthouse nine miles off the coast of Co. Mayo, on 18th October, 1931. The corpse was sent by Mr D J Sullivan the assistant light-keeper, to G R Humphreys who identified it and added it to the collection at the National Museum, Dublin.

There have been at least three unproven claims of this species. Research in the Atlantic suggests that two populations breeding on the same islands in different seasons may be separate species.

References:
British Birds 5: 252; 25: 228; Harrison 1953: 70; Saunders, 1899: 731; *Ibis* 1967: 158; Walpole-Bond, 1938: iii, 61-62; *Dutch Birding* 21: 101-106.

Great Cormorant *Phalacrocorax carbo sinensis*
(Central Europe to India and China)
1873 Hampshire, Christchurch.   A (RB)

The first British record of this race (colloquially known as the 'Continental' Cormorant) concerned a bird obtained at Christchurch, Hampshire, in February, 1873. The specimen is now in the Natural History Museum, Tring. It was accepted by the BOU in 1931, just prior to conclusive proof that this race occurred in Britain. The evidence was provided when a bird found at Newhaven, Sussex, on 11th February, 1936, had been ringed in Germany, on 28th May, three years earlier.

A regular visitor in increasing numbers and now breeding inland.

References:
Harrison 1953: 86; Walpole-Bond, 1938: iii, 53; *British Birds* 24: 23.

Double-crested Cormorant *Phalacrocorax auritus*
(North America, south to the Caribbean)
1988 Cleveland, Billingham.   A (2)

On 8th December, 1988 a bird believed to be a Great Cormorant *Phalacrocorax carbo* took up residence on Charlton's Pond, Billingham, Cleveland. Martin A Blick told the warden, T J Williams, that a European Shag *Phalacrocorax aristotelis* was on the floating island. As European Shag had not been recorded on the reserve the warden checked, at a distance it looked right for European Shag but walking closer he found only the same Great Cormorant. Presuming a mistake had been made he left.

Following a subsequent report Williams took a closer look. Confused by its small size and unusually patterned underparts he returned with a scope. Noting the bright orange throat he made some rough sketches. The bird's features seemed intermediate between the Shag and Cormorant so was it a hybrid?

On 30th January, 1989, the bird followed a Great Cormorant while feeding, a feature of Double-crested according to Blick who watched the bird with Williams and M M Hallam. News was released when local BBRC member Dave Britton stated that it was indeed a Double-crested Cormorant.

A crowd of 170 birders gathered at dawn on 1st February, and saw the bird fly over at 8.25am. A couple of minutes later it returned to land. The identification was confirmed by at least 1,400 observers. It was last seen on 26th April, 1989 and was accepted by the BOURC as being present from 11th January, 1989.

Though the first Double-crested Cormorant had been found alive on 22nd December, 1963, in the hold of a Newfoundland cargo ship in Glasgow, Strathclyde, the bird had endured a period of confinement so the record is not acceptable.

The only other Double-crested Cormorant recorded in Europe was a first-winter found in Galway Harbour by Mr A G Kelly, from 18th November, 1995 to 6th January, 1996.

References:
British Birds 89: 163-170; 90: 458; *Birding World* 2:53-57, photo's; Evans 1994: 13.

Magnificent Frigatebird *Fregata magnificens*
(Tropical Oceans)
1953 Argyllshire, Tiree, Inner Hebrides.   A (1+ *5 Frigatebird spp*)

John Graham found a large exhausted bird in a freshwater lochan, near the south-west corner of the island of Tiree, Inner Hebrides at 10.30am on 10th July, 1953. He caught the bird in a landing net but it died at 8pm. The bird had a large "albatross" bill and the white head and breast typical of an immature frigatebird species. The remains were made into a cabinet skin at the National Museums of Scotland, Edinburgh.

Sir Norman Kinnear identified the skin as an immature female Magnificent Frigatebird of the Caribbean race *F. m. rothschildi*.

Despite five further frigatebird records, three in Ireland, the only other report to be specifically identified was a bird found exhausted on the Isle of Man in 1998 that remained in care until its death in the autumn of 1999.

Reference:
Sharrock, 1982: 33-34; Naylor 1998: 16.

American Bittern *Botaurus lentiginosus*
(North America; winters southern USA to Central America)
1804 Dorset, River Frome, Puddletown.   A (61)

In 1813 Montagu first described American Bittern from this British record, a year before it was first recognised in America by Edward Wilson. The bird was flushed from a ditch beside water meadows about half a mile from the River Frome during a pheasant shoot. It was shot by Mr Cunningham, of Puddletown, Dorset, in autumn 1804. The corpse was sent as a Great Bittern *Botaurus stellaris* to Colonel George of Penryn, Cornwall, and poorly mounted as a Little Bittern *Ixobrychus minutus* by a foreigner who did not note the sex. Later it was purchased by Montagu, who was astonished when the requested Little Bittern arrived. Montagu described the new species and named it Freckled Heron.

American Bittern was presumed to reach Europe by resting on the surface of the sea using outstretched wings!

During a visit to the Natural History Museum at Tring where this original type specimen is housed I found it was an immature bird.

The majority of American Bitterns found in Britain and Ireland have been sick, injured or shot. One individual captured on Bryher, Isles of Scilly in 1903 lived for three years in Tresco Abbey.

The majority of American Bitterns arrived between 1800 and 1945 when approximately 25% were found in the latter half of this century. 22 birds have been recorded in Ireland.

References:
Zool, 1890, p 183; Montagu, 1862: 173-174; D'Urban: 193; Naylor 1996: 10.

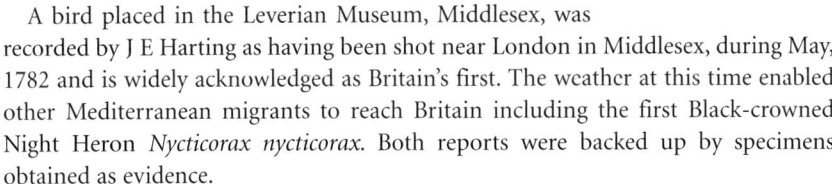

Little Bittern *Ixobrychus minutus*
(West Eurasia, Africa and Australia; winters Africa and Southern Asia)
1782 Greater London.   **A (350)**
A bird placed in the Leverian Museum, Middlesex, was recorded by J E Harting as having been shot near London in Middlesex, during May, 1782 and is widely acknowledged as Britain's first. The weather at this time enabled other Mediterranean migrants to reach Britain including the first Black-crowned Night Heron *Nycticorax nycticorax*. Both reports were backed up by specimens obtained as evidence.

Little Bittern was probably first mentioned as reaching Britain by Pennant who recorded it as having occurred in 1773. Under Bittern he wrote:

> "Mr Edwards mentions a small one of the size of a Lapwing shot near Shrewsbury. It answers the description of a kind frequent in Switzerland and Austria. We imagine it to be a strayed bird from these parts."

The report lacks the detail required for a first record.

Little Bittern is regularly reported and may have bred in the Norfolk Broads on several occasions. The first definite breeding record came in 1984 when a pair raised four young at Potteric Carr, Doncaster, South Yorkshire.

References:
Glegg, 1935: 112; Saunders, 1899: 381; Gurney 1921: 229; *British Birds* 82: 442-446; Pennant, 1761-1776., VII: 633-634.

Black-crowned Night Heron *Nycticorax nycticorax*

(South Eurasia, Africa and the Americas; European population winters in Africa)

1782 Greater London, (Middlesex).   A (573)

According to Pennant, the first British specimen was shot near London, Middlesex, in May, 1782 and placed in the Leverian Museum. This report was also mentioned by Montagu (1813) but at least three others had been shot before he wrote his manual. The records were from Ampthill, Bedfordshire (1791), Clivedon, Buckinghamshire (1797) and near Thame, Oxfordshire (*c.*1798).

The bird was considered an annual vagrant during the 19th Century and expected to breed; the Rev CJ Bulteel killed eight individuals during spring 1849, in Devon alone.

Two semi-captive populations of Night Herons fly freely around a site in Norfolk and Edinburgh Zoo. In 1997, a pair (race unknown) possibly bred in Somerset but proof was inconclusive.

There has been just one report of the American race that may have involved a genuine vagrant. It concerned the fresh corpse of an immature bird found floating in the mouth of the River Yealm, Devon on 30th October, 1936, following strong westerly winds in the North Atlantic. It was picked up by OD Hunt, but mention of it was omitted by both Witherby and the BOU.

References:
Glegg, 1935. 111-112; Saunders, 1899: 379; Montagu 1813: 175-176; *British Birds* 86: 610; 92: 177; Moore 1969: 54.

Green Heron *Butorides virescens*
(North and Central America, and West Indies)
1889 Cornwall, Penrice, near St Austell.   A (3)

In 1890, Mr Murray Mathew reported a small heron in the shop of Mr Foot, a Bath birdstuffer. He checked the museum skins at the South Kensington Natural History Museum and found it to be a Green Heron. Gamekeeper William Abbott shot it while searching for Woodcock at Hay Bottom, near Penrice, St Austell, Cornwall on 27th October, 1889.

Not recognising it he gave it to his master, Sir Charles Graves Sawle, who despatched it immediately to the birdstuffer. The bird was exhibited at 17th April meeting of the Linnean Society and accepted onto the British List as it was already known that herons could cross the Atlantic. The bird had been in at least its second calendar year and may possibly have been an adult, as it possessed adult-like crest feathers.

This record was later removed from the British List by Saunders (1899), Hartert (1912) and the BOU (1915) who doubted its ability to cross the Atlantic. Four days after this Green Heron had been killed, two American Bitterns *Botaurus lentiginosus* were shot in Ireland, surely not just a coincidence?

In 1971 the record was resubmitted to the BOURC which accepted Green

Heron onto the British List. Further visits to Britain have occurred since.

All British records were attributed to the American race *Butorides (striatus) virescens* which in 1993 was split from the African race *B. striatus* (Striated Heron).

The specimen is held at the County Museum, Truro.

The second individual was found at Stone Creek, North Humberside on 27th November, 1982 and was seen by over 800 people before its departure on 6th December.

References:
Zool, 1890: 105, 181; D'Urban: 194; Penhallurick, 1969: 64; Birding World 6: 161; British Birds 65: 424-427.

Squacco Heron *Ardeola ralloides*
(Southern Europe, Southwest Asia and Africa; winters Africa)

1775 Wiltshire, Near Boynton.   A (145)

Mr Lambert shot an adult breeding plumaged Squacco Heron near Boynton, Wiltshire, in 1775. The minutes of the *Linnean Transactions* mentioned that Lambert had sent a drawing of the bird in April, 1797, with a good description. This record was accepted by Pennant as Britain's first. The second record was in the following century and found near Ormesby Broad, Norfolk in 1820.

Remaining a rare vagrant the most popular months to find a Squacco Heron are May and June, with a south westerly bias.

References:
Montagu, 1862: 176; Gurney 1921: 229; Allard, 1990.

Cattle Egret *Bubulcus ibis*
(Almost cosmopolitan in tropics; nearest breeding in north of France)

1805 Devon, South Allington, near Kingsbridge.   A (101)

The Natural History Museum at Tring still houses the first specimen of Cattle Egret seen in Britain. It is an immature female, shot at South Allington, near Kingsbridge, Devon during late October, 1805 by Mr W F Cornish. Nicholas Luscombe of Kingsbridge sent the skin to Montagu who recorded it as the 'Little White Heron'. The bird had been present for some days feeding among cows where it characteristically fed on insects, several of which were later found in its stomach when dissected. Despite tolerating a close approach, Cornish bungled his first shot, only killing it with the second. Montagu announced the record in *Transactions of the Linnean Society.*

Cattle Egrets were a great rarity in Britain with the second acceptable record appearing over a century later in Norfolk during 1917.

There were only three Cattle Egret records prior to 1962.

References:
British Birds 11: 146-7; Moore, 1969: 53; Montagu, 1862: 175; Yarrell, 1843: ii, 462-465; D'Urban: 185-186.

Little Egret *Egretta garzetta*
(South Eurasia, west Central and southern Asia, Japan, Africa and Australia)
1826 East Yorkshire, near Paull.   **A (740** prior to 1971)

Despite many claims of Little Egrets in Britain and Ireland the species has had several different "first records" listed as officially accepted by various authorities. A bird shot near Paull, East Yorkshire, in March, 1826 is considered the first due to the fact that the specimen, a male, was available for examination at the Chester Museum. The bird was part of a large collection of British birds bequeathed to the museum by Thomas Potts of Chester with a label on the case giving the date and locality. The specimen was thought to have been destroyed in the 1950's.

To add some mystery to this report an unlabelled Little Egret specimen was sold at Southampton in a sale held in March, 1826 for £5 5s. It had probably been shot locally and J H Gurney suspected that it was the same specimen recorded in Yorkshire, as the date is exactly the same. Gurney claimed that the locality, recorded as Paull, Humberside, Yorkshire, may have been added to the label on the case at a later date, giving the impression that it had been killed in that county. Thomas Nelson checked the label and considered the handwriting to be the original work and in the same hand.

Montagu claims 1,000 Little Egrets were on the menu of a feast given by Archbishop Neville (1465). If this was correct they must have become extinct quite rapidly as no record of this species exists until 1792. In the same year, a bird was reportedly shot in Cork harbour, Ireland and placed in the Dublin Museum. This was recorded in Mr Templeton's *Catalogue of the Vertebrate Animals of Ireland* and repeated in Yarrell (1843).

The Rev Robert Holdsworth, of Brixham claimed the first British report, a specimen "shot on Flotoars, a shoal in the River Dart, dry at low-tide" in 1816. Montagu and D'Urban, who accepted the record, also described it.

In the *Manual of British Vertebrate Animals*, by the Rev L Jenyns, two Little Egrets were recorded from Penzance, Cornwall, in April, 1824. Both were killed but only one preserved.

Despite several reports by the early pioneering ornithologists, all records were dismissed by Howard Saunders until a bird shot at Countess Wear, on the River Exe, Devon, on 3rd June, 1870 satisfied him. Both Saunders and Harting accepted this as the first British record.

Little Egret remained a very rare vagrant to Britain with only 53 individuals recorded prior to the formation of the BBRC in 1958 but sightings are now expected during any visit to a suitable south coast location.

In 1996, a single pair nested on Brownsea Island in Poole Harbour, Dorset, successfully raising three young from a nest originally containing four individuals. This success was mirrored in Ireland when a colony of 12 pairs raised 24 young at a coastal site in Co. Cork, in 1997.

References:
Zool, 1901: 107; Montagu, 1862: 83-84; Yarrell, 1843: ii, 458-461; Saunders, 1899: 373-374; Harting 1912: 124; Nelson, 1907: 393-395; Mather, 1985: 98; D'Urban: 185; Kelsall & Munn, 1905: 199; Penhallurick, 1969: 60; Naylor 1997: 23-24; *Birdwatch* 66: 13; 69:16; *British Birds* 91: 273-280, photo of young birds; Fisher 1954: 18; *Birding World* 12: 304.

Great Egret *Egretta alba*
(Almost cosmopolitan, extremely local in Europe)
1821 East Yorkshire, Hornsea Mere.   A (112)

The first acceptable record was a bird present for several weeks in winter 1821 at Hornsea Mere, Yorkshire. The bird was caught and presented to Arthur Strickland. Strickland put forward a strong case for the acceptance of Great Egret onto the British List, at a meeting of the Natural History Section of the British Association, at Newcastle in August, 1838. Several authors had ignored the species but Strickland provided proof that the bird had occurred several times in Britain. The skin was incorrectly reported to be at York Museum.

A bird in the collection of Mr Foljambe at Osberton, Nottinghamshire, was shot nearby some time prior to 1838 but cannot be dated accurately to claim it as the first British record.

The Rev Kerr saw a white heron in the autumn of 1805 on the River Avon in Devon. It was with Grey Herons *Ardea cinerea* and although claimed to have been larger, was never proven to have been anything other than a mutation of that species. All attempts to shoot it failed. It was only accepted as a Great Egret by Montagu.

There were only ten records prior to 1974 but the colonisation of the Netherlands during the 1970s has resulted in Great Egret, appearing more frequently, mostly on the south and east coasts.

There have been several claims of birds belonging to the American race *E. a. egretta* including a bird at Billing Aquadrome, Northampton and later reported in Cambridgeshire between 27th November, 1997 to 14th March, 1998.

References:
Montagu, 1862: 174; Yarrell, 1843: ii, 454-457; D'Urban: 184; British Birds 92.

Purple Heron *Ardea purpurea*
(South-central Eurasia, north to Netherlands, and Africa)
1722 Greater London, (Middlesex).   A (701+)

The first report of a Purple Heron in Britain was shot near London, in 1722. Latham recorded the first published mention in 1787:

"This species inhabits Africa from whence a specimen has been received into the Leverian Museum. A second specimen is likewise in the same collection, which was shot in Ashdown Park, near Lambourn, Berkshire, belonging to Lord Craven".

Amazingly for what is now regarded as an annual vagrant to Britain the next record did not occur until 88 years later when a bird was shot in Norfolk. The species ceased to be considered by the BBRC in 1983, by which time 701 records had been accepted in Britain.

References:
Glegg, 1935: 111; Latham 1787: 237-238.

Black Stork *Ciconia nigra*
(Eurasia and Southern Africa; winters Africa)
1814 Somerset, West Sedge Moor.   A (139)

The first British record of Black Stork was in 1814, when an immature bird was shot near Stoke St Gregory, West Sedge Moor, Somerset on 13th May. The bird suffered an injury to its wing but was caught and kept in captivity, being fed on eels until it was taken to Robert Anstice of Bridgwater.

On 4th June, 1814, Anstice wrote to Montagu describing the bird. Montagu replied immediately saying that he was keen to obtain the bird, dead or alive. The stork was despatched to Montagu at Knowle, Devonshire, where it was released into a large walled garden with a big pan of water and kept alive. It gradually became quite tame coming for food when called.

Montagu reported that the stork began moulting in June and continued throughout the winter until it had attained its glossy breeding plumage by April, 1815.

When the bird died it was mounted and when examined at the British Museum, Tring, it still retained the dull brown neck typical of an immature.

About 20% of records were received prior to World War II and an expansion of the breeding population into France and more recently Belgium resulted in an upsurge of records during the 1990's.

References:
Somerset Orn. Club, 1988: 77; Montagu, 1862: 326-329.

White Stork *Ciconia ciconia*
(Central and South Europe, Southwest Asia and Northwest Africa)
1416 Lothian, St Giles Cathedral, Edinburgh.   A (490+)

White Stork was an annual visitor to Britain long before recording began, probably decreasing in regularity as the European population declined. The earliest record in the *Scotichronicon* concerned the first breeding attempt by this species.

"*In the year of our Lord 1416 . . . a pair of Storks came to Scotland, and nested on the top of St. Giles of Edinburgh, and dwelt there throughout a season of the year; but to what place they flew away thereafter no one knows.*"

An illustration in 1485 shows White Storks with nestlings on top of a chimney.

Willughby wrote of a specimen "taken on the coast of Norfolk" and recorded in a letter by Sir Thomas Browne to Christopher Merrett on 13th September, 1668 mentioning one bird shot from a watery marsh eight miles from another that he had yet to examine.

The next dated record came many years later when a bird was shot at Chollerford Bridge, Northumberland, in spring 1766. A large crowd of people gathered to see its skin after it was nailed to the wall of a local inn.

Although the above reports lack the accurate descriptions required by a modern day records committee there would appear to be no doubt about their authenticity.

References:
Baxter & Rintoul 1953: 333; Galloway & Meek, 1978: 25; Yarrell, 1843: ii, 489-492; *British Birds* 2: 160.

Glossy Ibis *Plegadis falcinellus*
(Almost cosmopolitan, nearest breeders in Balkans and irregularly Camargue, France)
1793 Berkshire, near Reading.   A (376+)

Two Glossy Ibis were seen flying along the River Thames, skimming the water between Henley and Reading, Berkshire, in September, 1793. Mr Lamb shot one bird, which he had mounted, and kept.

At the time, Glossy Ibis was recorded as three different species depending on which plumage stage it had reached: 'Bay' Ibis (perfect plumaged breeding adults), 'Green' Ibis (juvenile first-winter) and 'Glossy' Ibis (all other plumage states). The Berkshire birds were said to be midway between Glossy and Bay Ibis in plumage coloration so were probably adults moulting into non-breeding plumage. Examination of specimens like this allowed the three 'species' to be 'lumped' into one along with 'Brazilian Curlew' a name given to the bird claimed as the third record of a Glossy Ibis in Britain. This was a juvenile shot near Beaumaris, Anglesey in September, 1806 and described as 'Brazilian Curlew' in the *Naturalist's Miscellany*.

In the 20th Century, the Glossy Ibis population decreased considerably so that it is now a very rare vagrant no longer occurring annually.

References:
Montagu, 1862: 179-180; Radford, 1966: 52; Naylor 1996: 31-36.

Eurasian Spoonbill *Platalea leucorodia*
(Southern Europe and North Africa east to Japan and India)
13th Century Norfolk.   A (P)

Eurasian Spoonbill is treated as a regular but scarce annual migrant to Britain but was once a regular breeding species.

It bred in the heronries of Sussex, Middlesex and probably also in Kent; they were recorded breeding in at least three sites in Norfolk during the 13th and 14th centuries. The Eurasian Spoonbill was a popular bird at the tables of the rich with young birds regarded as a delicacy. They were reportedly hand-reared on the choicest kitchen scraps (new garbage and good meat), until ready to eat, a practise in common with the Common Crane *Grus grus*. The youngsters were compared to "fatted Gulls" which was a high complement as young Black-headed Gulls *Larus ridibundus* well fed on bullocks liver was a great favourite on the table.

Eurasian Spoonbill has never been recorded nesting in Scotland or Ireland and the date that the last native birds died out is not accurately known. It was first regarded as a vagrant or scarce migrant to Britain in 1774, when Pennant included it in his list. He noted that the Spoonbill "bred annually in Ray's time near Sevenbuys, near Leyden. A flock flew into Yarmouth in 1774."

This dated report is often quoted as the earliest British record.

During the 1980s and 90s the nearby Dutch population was thriving and Eurasian Spoonbill occurred as a regular migrant in Britain. A nest was built at Frodsham, Cheshire in 1996.

References:
Gurney 1921: 177-181; Pennant 1761-1776,. VII: 634.

Tundra (Whistling) Swan *Cygnus columbianus columbianus*
(North America and Eastern Siberia)

Once regarded as separate species, Whistling and Bewick's Swans are now treated as one and renamed Tundra Swan. The American race (Whistling Swan) has been recorded in Europe with Ireland holding the bulk of records. Prior to 1899, Whistling Swan had been noticed in the poulterer's shops of Edinburgh but evidence supporting this particular claim is flimsy.

IRELAND

1978 Co. Kerry, Lough Gill.   A (5)

With at least five (but probably six) records in Ireland prior to 1997, Frank King found the first at Lough Gill, Co. Kerry, present from 31st December, 1978 until 1st February, 1979 (P Milne *in litt*). Subsequent records in Ireland may have involved just three returning individuals.

BRITAIN

1986 Somerset, Curry Moor.

Only two birds have been recorded in Britain, the first at Hay Moor and Curry Moor, Somerset, from 5th to 25th January, 1986, also visiting Durleigh Reservoir on 26th January and 12th February. A J Bundy, J G Hole, D E and L Paull reported it. A different individual was present at South Slob, Co. Wexford, Ireland during the same period discounting thoughts that one individual could be involved in several reports.

The English bird returned to winter at Ibsley, Hampshire, from 31st December, 1986 to 25th January, 1987. It was again found at Curry Moor, Somerset for its third winter on 12th December, 1987 and remained until 31st January, 1988. This individual returned regularly until 1990.

References:
Birding World 9: 473; *Rare Birds* 3: 13; *British Birds* 81:545, photo; 90: 460; Evans 1994: 47; Saunders, 1899: 416.

Tundra (Bewick's) Swan *Cygnus columbianus bewicki*
(Northern Europe east to Siberia)

1823   A (WV)

This common winter visitor was first recognised as having visited Britain in 1829, when Yarrell recorded it as a new species.

In winter 1823-24, Yarrell was examining the corpse of a young swan shot in Britain, when he noticed that the trachea and bones were different to those of the usual wild swans (Whooper Swan *Cygnus cygnus*). He believed that this may prove to be a distinct species. In July, 1828, Yarrell purchased the sternum and trachea of a swan prepared by Dr Leach which appeared to be from the same species and had been taken from an adult. On 24th November, 1829, Yarrell presented the specimens to the Linnean Society and soon received further examples. Yarrell described the new species, Bewick's Swan in memory of Thomas Bewick. Richard Wingate of Newcastle had independently arrived at the same conclusion, at a similar time and as Bewick was one of his friends, accepted Yarrell's name. The type specimen (second British record) remains in the Hancock Museum, Newcastle.

It is an annual winter visitor to Britain in large numbers.

References:
Saunders, 1899: 415; Yarrell, 1843: iii, 104-114.

Pink-footed Goose *Anser Brachyrynchus*
(Greenland, Iceland and Western Europe)
*c.*1839   A & E (WV)

The specification of Pink-footed and Bean Geese *Anser fabalis* has been discussed for years and they are presently treated as two species. All birds occurring in Britain were regarded as Bean Geese until Mr A D Bartlett noticed differences. On 8th January, 1839, he exhibited specimens at the Zoological Society and published details of the distinction between them. Subsequent observation proved that Pink-footed was far more numerous in Britain than Bean Goose, indeed all the "grey geese" he observed at Holkham, Norfolk and around the Humber Estuary were found to be Pink-footed and not Bean Geese as thought.

Pink-footed Goose visits Britain in winter in large numbers, around 90,000 pairs. Some escapes and injured birds have bred.

References:
Saunders, 1899: 403; Yarrell, 1843: iii, 64-67; Cramp vol 1.

Lesser White-fronted Goose *Anser erythropus*
(Northeast Europe and Siberia; winters Southeast Europe and Southwest Asia)
1886 Northumberland, Fenham Flats.   A (136)

Alfred Chapman of Roker, Sunderland, had been shooting from a gunning punt at Fenham Flats near Holy Island, Northumberland since early morning on 16th September, 1886. While eating lunch he saw a goose coming towards him silently, alone and from the north about 20 yards above the water. At about 50 yards he lifted his gun and shot it as it swerved. The goose began to swim away when it hit the water so was shot again. Chapman was sure it was a rarity by the size of its bill and later identified it as a first-year Lesser White-fronted Goose.

The corpse was sent to Mr Cullingford the Durham taxidermist for mounting. Seebohm, Canon Tristram and Saunders later examined it.

Saunders did not recognise Lesser White-fronted Goose as a good species at the time and failed to include it in his 1899 *Manual of British Birds*. In 1908 he accepted the goose as a full species and it was added to the British List.

Approximately half the British records have been found in Gloucestershire among the large numbers of Greater White-fronted Geese *Anser albifrons* at Slimbridge.

References:
Galloway & Meek, 1978; *British Birds* 1: 14; *Field* 11th Dec., 1886.

Snow Goose *Anser caerulescens atlanticus*
(North America and northwest Greenland)

Two species/subspecies are involved here, Greater Snow Goose *A. c. atlanticus* and Lesser Snow Goose *A. c. caerulescens*. Although Snow Goose finds a place on the British List the true status of these birds is unclear because of escapes.

IRELAND
1871 Co. Wexford, Tacumshin:– *A. c. caerulescens.*   A (WV)
1877 Co. Mayo, Termoncarragh:– *A. c. atlanticus.*   A (WV)

The first Snow Geese seen in Britain and Ireland were two Lesser Snow Geese *Anser hyperboreus hyperboreus* found at Leadenhall Market on 9th November, 1871. The origins of the birds were checked by Sir Victor Brooke who found that they had recently been shot on the lake at Tacumshin, Co. Wexford, Ireland.

Several following Irish records included a flock of seven in Co. Mayo, in October, 1877. Two of these were shot at Termoncarragh, on the Mullet and a male paired up with a "tame" goose, living until 1884. It is now at the Dublin Museum and of the race *A. c. atlanticus.*

The first records of a Lesser Snow Goose *A. c. caerulescens* to be widely accepted involved two blue phase birds that were found by John Barlee and Robert F Ruttledge, on 8th January, 1946, with Greylag Geese *Anser anser* on the North Slob, Co. Wexford, Ireland. They appeared to the observers to look like Greylag Goose with abnormal head markings, but when described to Peter Scott, he immediately suspected they were 'blue' Snow Geese. The birds were not seen again until 18th April, when John Barlee saw one at North Slob. Ruttledge was "summoned by wire" and arrived on 20th April, when he confirmed the identification and also found the second bird. The birds were seen by a handful of observers before their last sighting on 22nd April. From sketches and descriptions of the head patterns it was clear that three individuals had been involved, one of which was a first-year bird.

The likelihood was that they were wild. The escape of some unmarked birds from Whipsnade Zoo in 1941 and 1942 precluded their admission to the British or Irish lists for a time.

BRITAIN
1917 Western Isles, Barra:– *A. c. caerulescens.*
1920 Kirkcudbright, Castle Douglas:– *A. c. atlanticus.*

Following the early Irish Snow Goose records, a series of reports came from Cumbria, Yorkshire and Northumberland but none were fully documented. The first dated and well described report in Britain came from Scotland, when in 1917 an adult Lesser Snow Goose was shot on 9th October, on the island of Barra, Scotland. Although accepted at the time this subspecies was still not officially added to the British List until the 1940s

In 1920, a flock of five Greater Snow Geese wintered near Castle Douglas, Kirkcudbright. One bird was shot in October before the remaining birds moved to the Solway where an immature bird was shot on 18th February, 1921.

The Snow Goose is tainted by the escape possibility, as there are feral flocks at large in Britain. True vagrants probably occur annually but the exact status is obscured by the large number of escapes.

References:
Baxter & Rintoul: 377-378; Saunders, 1899: 405-406; Kennedy, 1954: 84-87; *Birding World* 4: 139; *British Birds* 40: 44-47; 92: 178; *Field* Jan 30, 1904: 2666; Evans 1997: 51.

Canada Goose *Branta canadensis*
(North America; feral populations in Western Europe)

BRITAIN
1958 Argyll, Islay.   AC (RB)

Since 1958, individuals of races other than *B. c. canadensis* have been seen regularly in the Hebrides and Ireland. Their circumstances suggested they were probably genuine vagrants but any *B. c. canadensis* occurring cannot be detected among the feral flocks. The first report of a 'small race' bird was by J Shepperd on the island of Islay, Argyll on 5th April, 1958. It was described as a "small, dark, short-necked Canada Goose, distinctly smaller than the Barnacle Geese *Branta leucopsis* it accompanied". This is widely regarded as the first British record of a vagrant Canada Goose.

In addition P Anderson, a gamekeeper, poorly documented a Canada Goose shot on Tiree, Argyll some time before 1913. This remained the sole record on the island until 1958 and almost certainly concerned a genuine vagrant.

The second report concerned the first true vagrants to be recorded in Ireland and were two Lesser Canada Geese that wintered at the North Slobs, Co. Wexford in 1960-61, 1961-62; with just a single individual present during 1962-63 and 1963-64. Mr H Boyd, C J Cadbury and R F Ruttledge recorded the birds as being smaller than accompanying White-fronted Geese *Anser albifrons* and probably of the race *B. c. parvipes* or *B. c. taverneri*.

Willughby recorded both Canada Goose and Spur-winged Goose *Plectropterus gambensis* in 1678, among the King's Wildfowl in St James's Park. By 1785, Canada Goose was found on several ornamental lakes and towards the end of the 19th Century became widespread. A pair that nested on an island on the Hurstbourne in Hampshire until 1890 and a pair at Edgbaston Park Birmingham in 1885 may be the earliest feral breeding records relating to the origins of the British Category C population. It wasn't until the publication of Witherby's *Handbook* (1938-41) that Canada Goose was considered a feral species in Britain.

The first specimen taken in the wild was described and figured by Thomas Bewick, and was shot by Henry Mewburn of St Germans, Cornwall, but in 1813 Montagu did not regard the species as a British bird.

Various races of Canada Goose have been reported some are recorded below and are not necessarily accepted by the Rarities Committees involved:

The first record of a Canada Goose possibly belonging to the subspecies *B. c. hutchinsii* returned on at least three consecutive winters from 1994/95 with Barnacle Geese at Raghly, Co. Sligo, Ireland. It revisited each consecutive winter until at least 23rd March, 1998.

Two birds belonging to the race *B. c. minima* were found with Barnacle and Greenland White-fronted Geese from November, 1997 to March, 1998, on Islay, Argyll.

A small wintering flock of Greenland White-fronted Geese *Anser albifrons flavirostris* was present at Kilphedar, South Uist, Western Isles, from at least 21st February to 15th March, 1998, and held a bird considered to be of the race *interior*.

Migrant Canada Geese are rare vagrants to Britain and only the smaller race birds have generated interest due to their obvious differences from the established feral population. Much work on the identification and taxonomic status of the Canada Goose complex is required. The only proven vagrant was one of two birds together with a third, larger individual thought to be an 'Atlantic' Canada Goose *B. c. canadensis* that accompanied Pink-footed Geese *Anser brachyrhynchus* in Aberdeenshire from 17th November, 1992 until they were shot on 24th January, 1993. It bore a yellow neck collar that was traced to Maryland, USA where it had been trapped as a second year male in February, 1992. John Oates identified this bird as being a Lesser Canada Goose *B. c. parvipes*.

References:
Yarrell, 1843: iii, 91-96; Ruttledge, 1966: 69; Penhallurick, 1969: 92; *British Birds* 53: 162; 51; 92: 178: 50; *Irish Bird Report*, 1960: 9; Atkinson-Willes 1963: 265; Evans 4: 102; *Birding World* 12: 82-3, 124; Montagu, 1813: 124; Holloway 1996: 70.

Brent Goose *Branta bernicla*
(Northern Europe to Northwest Asia, North America and Greenland)
c.1678 Cleveland, Teeside. **A (WV)**

The earliest mention of Brent Goose as a British species came from Ralph Johnson of Brignall, Yorkshire, who showed the "Rat or Road Goose" to Willughby. Willughby published a description in 1678 separating it from Barnacle Goose *Branta leucopsis*. It is likely that the first reports came from the mouth of the River Tees, Cleveland.

Unlike other wildfowl, the Brent was said to be *"a very headless fowl, so that if a pack of them come into the Tees, it is seldom one escapes away, for though they be often shot at, yet they only fly a little, and suffer the gunner to come openly upon them."*

A common winter visitor to the east coast Brent Goose is a familiar sight on the Lincolnshire and North Norfolk coast with the Wash being Britain's most important site holding *c*.20, 000 birds.

References:
Nelson, 1907: 425; Willughby 1678: 361

Brent Goose (Black Brant) *Branta bernicla nigricans*
(Arctic North America and East Siberia; winters USA and East Asia)
1957 Essex, Foulness. **A (94)**

P J K Burton picked out a bird identified as a "Pacific Black Brant" among the dark-bellied Brent Geese *Branta bernicla bernicla* at Foulness, Essex, on 9th February,

1957. It was seen again at the same place on 17th February by five other observers but not seen again that year.

On 8th February, 1958 it was reported from the same place and was considered unlikely to be an escape as there were few in captivity and all were accounted for. The bird was accepted as the first record of Black Brant, which is considered a full species by some authorities.

Recorded annually especially among the well-watched Brent Geese in Norfolk, returning individuals probably account for many reports.

References:
British Birds 51: 132; 77:458-465; *Essex Bird Report* 1957: 12-13, sketch.

Red-breasted Goose *Branta ruficollis*
(West Siberia; winters Southeast Europe)
1776 Greater London, (Middlesex).   A (55)

Dr John Latham recorded the first British record, a bird shot at the beginning of a severe frost, early in 1776, near London. As Latham lived near the north Kent marshes it was possibly killed in that area but the exact location remains a mystery. The specimen was purchased by Marmaduke Tunstall and later passed to the Hancock Museum, Newcastle, where it was often mistakenly said to be a bird that was found later in the same year near Wycliffe-on-Tees, Yorkshire. This bird was kept alive on a small pond with Mallards *Anas platyrhynchos*, becoming very attached to one of them before dying in 1785.

In 1872, the collection of J E Harting then containing the London specimen came up for auction by Samuel Stevens, one of London's famous natural history agents. John Marshall wrote to Samuels stating: *"About lot 240 (the Red-breasted Goose), I wish to have it – Mr Gurney must not have it; I hope you understand. Of course should the British Museum bid for it, they must have it, but otherwise I must."*

The next acceptable record was not until 42 years later. There was however one dubious claim from Breydon, Norfolk, in 1805. A bird was identified from feathers left over after it had been cooked and eaten by Mr Wigg. Having purchased it from Yarmouth market he had wondered what this pretty bird might taste like.

As Breydon was a popular area for rare bird collectors to hunt, the man probably lost a considerable sum of money but only realised this after his meal.

Only 15 records existed prior to the formation of the BBRC in 1958. Since then it has become an almost annual vagrant with several recorded each winter.

References:
Zool, 1871: 2513; Mather, 1985: 130; Hancock: 148-149; Patterson; 1893; Glegg, 1935: 115; Temperley, 1951: 168; Naylor 1996: 37; Mearns 1998: 97; Taylor 1999: 158. [Harrison 1953: 211]

Egyptian Goose *Alopochen eagyptiacus*
(Africa; introduced to Britain)
pre 1841 Cornwall, Skewjack.   C & E (RB)

A number of Egyptian Geese were released by Augustus Smith on Tresco, Isles of Scilly, prior to 1845 and some local records may have been the result of his actions, the earliest being three birds obtained at Skewjack, Cornwall, in 1841.

In 1898, an adult male Egyptian Goose was shot at Beech farm, near St Albans, on 1st November. This was one of the earliest occurrences of a bird killed in the wild that could not be traced to a nearby collection.

From a British population of 906 in 1991, all but two breeding records came from Norfolk. By 1996, breeding attempts were made in seven counties as the established feral population spread from its East Anglia stronghold.

References:
Penhallurick, 1969: 93; Saunders, 1899: 412; *British Birds* 92: 179.

Ruddy Shelduck *Tadorna ferruginea*
(Southeast Europe and Central Asia)
Pre 1834 Southern England?   B

The first Ruddy Shelduck was shot at Bryanstone, Dorset, in the severe winter of 1776, the bad weather brought Britain's first Red-breasted Goose *Branta ruficollis*. Surprisingly only two records were noted prior to 1845. The specimen, a female belonging to Marmaduke Tunstall was placed in the Hancock Museum, Newcastle, where it was noticed by Mr G T Fox of Durham and recorded by Pennant as the first British record.

After being lost for 50 years the specimen was refound at Newcastle in 1995. It was identified as a Cape or South African Shelduck *Tadorna cana*. Publication of this error in 1999 means that the search is now on for an acceptable first record. Yarrell and Montagu state that the second record was a bird held in Selby's collection and obtained in Southern England. The third was killed at Iken, near Orford, Suffolk in 1834 and the property of Mr Manning of Woodbridge. Macgillivray mentions a bird shot in Sanday, Orkney by Mr Strang in October, 1831. Any of the above could now become the first record.

The prospect of single birds being wild is less likely than those involved with irruptions of the species. The first record that probably related to wild birds was on 8th September, 1884, when a group of four birds were found in Kent, one being shot. In 1886, a small influx into south and southeastern Britain involving parties of up to six birds took place. A larger invasion occurred in 1892, when a drought in southeastern Europe caused flocks of up to 20 birds to be reported in Britain and Ireland, with individuals reaching as far as Greenland. This movement of birds provided evidence of vagrancy for the species and all previous records were accepted.

The Ruddy Shelduck is placed in Category B by the BOURC, as it was believed not to have occurred in a wild state since 1950. However a review of records undertaken by Keith Vinicombe and A H J Harrop of birds involved in a massive influx into Europe in 1994 found that late summer records conformed to a pattern that indicated the arrival of wild birds. In time the BOURC may upgrade the species to Category A.

References:
Montagu, 1862: 302-304; Saunders, 1899: 421; Evans 1994: 52-53; Yarrell, 1843: iii, 136-140; Gurney 1921: 229; *British Birds* 92: 179; 225-255.

Mandarin Duck *Aix galericulata*
(North east Asia; feral populations in Europe)
1866 Berkshire, River Thames. **CE (RB)**

Mandarin Duck is on the British List as an established feral species descended from escapes. It was first brought to England before 1745 and placed in a private collection at Richmond, Surrey. The first bird found living in the wild was shot on the Thames in Berkshire in 1866.

Escapes from the 300 strong flock on the Duke of Bedford's estate at Woburn, where they were introduced in the early 1900s account for many early records including a bird shot at Radwell Mill, near Baldock, Hertfordshire on 21st December, 1916. The Mandarin's stronghold is now Surrey, Berkshire and Buckinghamshire, with approximately 7000 individuals in 1988. Up to nine pairs bred in Scotland during 1996 while a population of 20-30 pairs became established in Co. Down, Ireland.

References:
Marchant 1990: 60; Sage 1959; *British Birds* 92: 179-80.

American Wigeon *Anas americana*
(North America; winters USA and Central America)
1837/8 Greater London, Middlesex. **A (383)**

Notice of the first American Wigeon came from a large bustling market in London. Mr Bartlett purchased a drake thought to have been a 'variety' of Eurasian Wigeon *Anas penelope* at Leadenhall market from a row of its commoner cousins, in winter 1837/8. A possible female accompanied it, though this was not bought and the record remains unconfirmed. J H Gurney later obtained the male specimen for his collection.

The variety of plumage variation in winter between the sexes and different aged birds allowed the species to evade the collectors' attention, with the second British record of this species found much later in similar circumstances. An immature male was obtained at a game stall on 26th February, 1895 at a Leeds market, Yorkshire. Sent in a consignment from the coast it is now at Leeds Museum (accession No LEEDM.C.1962.1719).

The American Wigeon is one of the most frequently recorded Nearctic ducks in Britain with up to 20 individuals seen each winter.

References:
Mather, 1985; Saunders, 1899: 439; Yarrell, 1843: iii, 196-200.

Green-winged Teal *Anas crecca carolinensis*
(North America; winters west and south USA, West Indies and Central America)
***c.*1840 Hampshire,** Hurstbourne Park. **A (441+)**

No Green-winged Teal were held in captivity in Europe prior to 1900 so all records before this date do not have the 'of unknown origin' label that often accompanies wildfowl reports.

In *Zoologist* 1880, Arthur Fellowes of Burwood, Rotherfield, Sussex, stated that his father had shot a specimen in his possession "more than 40 years ago" at Hurstbourne Park, Hampshire. It was said that "the white crescent on its wing was very apparent and well defined." This became the first British record, but was claimed after one had been reported from Scarborough, Yorkshire, in 1851.

As was the case during the 19th Century, when one record was published previous claims of birds originally incorrectly identified often came to light.

British reports were no longer considered by the BBRC after 1990, by which time 441 birds had been recorded.

Green-winged Teal is given full specific status by the Dutch Rarities Committee.

References:
Saunders, 1899: 433; *Zool*, 1880: 70-71.

American Black Duck   *Anas rubripes*
(North America)

IRELAND
1954 Kilkenny, near Mullinavat.   A (26)

Frank Hudson of Carriganore, Waterford, visited Flanagan's poulterer's shop in Waterford where he noticed an unusual Mallard *Anas platyrhynchos*. The bird had already been sold but Hudson exchanged it and purchased it for the National Museum at Dublin. He visited a farmer named Croke of Listrolin, three miles west of Mullinavet, Co. Kilkenny, where the bird had been shot with another as they took flight from a marsh. The second bird, which he considered to be the same species, was only winged and escaped.

At the museum the duck was identified by P G Kennedy and P E Dunn, with later additional confirmation by Peter Scott as an adult female American Black Duck, the first European record.

The second bird avoided the guns and was seen alive by Dr James Cadbury on 18th February, 1961, with wildfowl in the west channel of the North Slob, Co. Wexford, and again on 20th February, by Major and Mrs R F Ruttledge. It was last seen 21st February.

BRITAIN
1967 Kent, Stoke.

The first American Black Duck in Britain was at Yantlett Creek, Stoke, Kent, on 18th and 25th March, 1967, probably a male. It was first seen by A Hutson, C E Wheeler and P J Oliver as it flew from the creek with a female Mallard and passed at a range of 300 yards. It was identified as a Black Duck as it landed briefly before heading out onto the Thames. Wheeler later found it on a nearby lagoon and took a description.

The record was accepted as there were few birds in captivity at the time, the escape possibility was regarded as low and there was two Irish reports.

Still rarely reported this side of the Atlantic, several long-staying individuals have paired with Mallard and produced hybrid young.

References:
Sharrock, 1982: 39-40; Evans 1994; *British Birds* 60: 482-483.

Blue-winged Teal *Anas discors*
(North America; winters south to Brazil)
1858 Dumfries and Galloway, Upper Nithsdale.   **A (240)**

In 1858, Mr W G Gibson from Dumfries wrote, " *a specimen of the Blue-winged Teal was shot here a few weeks ago".* The bird had been shot at Upper Nithsdale, Dumfriesshire by Mr Shaw of Drumlanrig. He sent it to Mr Hastings, birdstuffer of Dumfries before giving it to Sir William Jardine (who visited Shaw just before his death). Jardine later passed the specimen to the National Museums of Scotland, Edinburgh.

Some confusion existed over the sex of this bird, claimed by Saunders and Witherby to be a male when it was a female.

There is no question about the vagrancy potential of Blue-winged Teal as a male shot in Suffolk during 1971 had earlier been ringed as a juvenile in New Brunswick, Canada. The only breeding attempted in Britain concerned a pair nest building in Essex during 1996.

The second report claimed for this species in 1882, proved to be an immature Garganey *Anas querquedula.*

References:
Saunders, 1899: 434; Baxter & Rintoul, 1953: 399; Evans 1994: 62; Gray 1871: 373-375; *British Birds* 92: 180.

Red-crested Pochard *Netta rufina*
(Eastern Europe and North Africa, Central Asia and India)
1818 Norfolk, Breydon Water.   **AE**

The first Red-crested Pochard was a female, shot on Breydon Water, Norfolk, in July, 1818. It was in the possession of Mr Youell of Yarmouth when a drawing was made to feature in Hunt's *British Ornithology II.*

Hunt was *"informed that a male specimen was killed in Norfolk a few years since and is preserved in the London Museum."* There are no other details.

The female specimen was reportedly sold by the gunner for 21 guineas to Stephen Miller. Most of the specimens in his collection were in poor condition and later destroyed.

With over 200 reports in Britain especially in the Midlands each year, a large proportion must involve escapes. A proportion of these disperse from the feral breeding population established on the Gloucestershire/Wiltshire border.

References:
Paterson 1929: 115; Paterson1905: 190: 82; Hunt 1815: vol II: 333-6; *British Birds* 92: 180.

Canvasback *Aythya valisineria*
(Western North America; winters Southwest Canada, USA and Mexico)
1997 Norfolk, Welney.   **A (1)**

A bird with good credentials was found in Norfolk, by Carl Donner at Wissington Beet Factory Pools, Norfolk on 18th January, 1997 and was relocated in front of the main hide at the nearby Welney Wildfowl and Wetlands Trust Reserve by John Kemp on 21st January. Kemp telephoned Dave Holman and Richard Millington and the news was released onto Birdline with a cautionary warning of the hybrid or escape possibility. The bird had arrived with *c.*940 Common Pochard *Aythya ferina*. It was seen during the weekend of 25th and 26th January by about 2,800 observers who noted that it was fully-winged, wary and unringed.

It was seen daily at Welney or Wissington until 28th but was only seen on 6th and 22nd February and 7th-10th March before dispersing with the main Pochard flock.

The bird was a first-winter male with retained brown juvenile feathers and brown tinged tail feathers. However a small white area near the bill tip aroused suspicion, but was found on up to a third of all Canvasbacks checked.

An adult male found at Abberton Reservoir, Essex the following winter on 23rd November, 1997 was considered the same bird returning. It later returned to Welney in December.

It was later revealed that a possible drake Canvasback had been present at Cliffe, Kent on 7th December, 1996. It may have concerned the same individual but the report was withdrawn by the observer.

Having seen the Canvasback at Welney, Keith Vinicombe remembered a similar bird at Moreton Bank, Chew Valley Lake, Avon on 21st March, 1993, regarded as a Common Pochard x Canvasback hybrid on account of its apparently short neck, small size and the presence of a small white patch behind the tip of the bill. On 18th March, 1995 Vinicombe came across the bird again but it remained illusive.

Apart from anomalies with the bill pattern, other negative features originally noted on the Chew bird were dispelled when Canvasback was present in close proximity to Common Pochard, as at Welney. The Chew bird was again present intermittently from 19th April to 20th May, 1998, and was confirmed as a Canvasback by Vinicombe.

In a letter to *Birding*, the magazine of the American Birding Association, Vinicombe requested information about the British birds. General opinion was that they were Canvasbacks but the white bill marking indicated signs of damage or captive inbreeding, a feature present on half of the captive males at Slimbridge. Consequently further information about this bill-marking on wild American birds is required prior to any decision concerning the position of the Chew Canvasback on the British List.

Following at least four reported Canvasbacks that related to hybrids (Borders 1979, Merseyside 1988, Caernarfonshire 1989 and Cumbria 1991), two further reports concerned probable escapes. These involved a female with a drake Common Pochard at Fen Drayton, Cambridgeshire 9th and 26th-27th June, 1992, and a drake at Martin Mere Wildfowl and Wetlands Trust Reserve, Lancashire 5th-16th March, 1996.

References:
Rare Birds 3: 16; 82-83; 4: 59; 89-90; *Birding World* 6: 368; 11: 362; *Ibis:* 25th report; *Cambridgeshire Bird report* 1992: 59.

Redhead *Aythya americana*
(Western North America)
1996 Nottinghamshire, Bleasby.   A (1)

In the afternoon of Friday 8th March, 1996, Mark Dennis warden of Colwick

Country Park, Nottinghamshire visited the gravel pits at nearby Bleasby Village. Disturbing a group of Common Pochard *Aythya ferina* feeding near the bank he noticed a larger bird. Realising that the bird was possibly a drake Redhead he took notes and left to telephone county recorder John Hopper and his friend Bernie Ellis. Hopper also took a description before they agreed on the bird's identity, checking features against the *Wildfowl* guide (Madge & Burn 1988).

The next morning 20 birders visited the private site and the bird flew off onto nearby Gibsmere and the news was released nationally. About 2,700 birders visited the site over the weekend and the bird remained in the area until 27th March.

The North American population had increased by 36% to 888,000 birds in 1995 and the possibility of genuine vagrancy had therefore increased. The Nottinghamshire Redhead was formally accepted as the first Western Palearctic record in June, 1997.

A female found in Cheshire during 1996 had a green ring so was probably an escape, while a second drake was present at Rutland Water, Leicestershire from 4th-24th February, 1997, possibly the returning Nottinghamshire individual.

References:
Birding World 9: 93-97, photos; *Rare Birds* 2: 72; 3: 84.

Ring-necked Duck *Aythya collaris*
(North America; winters south to Central America)
1955 Gloucestershire, Slimbridge. A (379+)

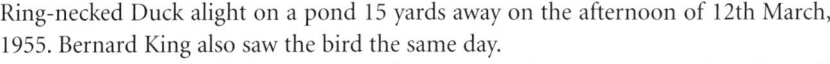

Watching from the studio window of her house at Slimbridge, Gloucestershire, Philippa Scott saw an adult male Ring-necked Duck alight on a pond 15 yards away on the afternoon of 12th March, 1955. Bernard King also saw the bird the same day.

On 13th March the duck was seen in the same place by Peter Scott and Hugh Boyd, and again the following morning as it flew over the Orchard Pen though not subsequently.

At the time the species was rare in captivity and had not bred in any European collection. It was therefore accepted onto the British List.

The second record in Gloucestershire came from the same site on 1st March, 1977, where it was caught and ringed. This bird was later shot in southeast Greenland. By December, 1993 there had been 379 British records.

NORTHERN IRELAND
1959 Co. Armagh, Lurgan Park.

An adult male spent most of the time asleep accompanying Tufted Duck *Aythya fuligula* from 20th March until 1st May, 1960 at Lurgan Park Lake, Co. Armagh. R W Culbert took notes that later allowed S Penney to identify it. It was seen each weekend attempting to avoid the activities of speedboat enthusiasts. Still partially moulting, the bird returned to the lake on 25th September where it was seen intermittently until mid-March, 1961.

Lurgan Park Lake held a Ring-necked Duck each year from 1962-1969, considered the same returning male. However, two birds were seen together in 1967 and 1968.

References:
Swaine, 1959; Sharrock, 1982: 68-72; Naylor 1998: 71-81; *British Birds* 54: 71-72.

Ferruginous Duck *Aythya nyroca*
(South and Eastern Europe, Central Asia and Iran)
pre 1771 Lincolnshire.　　　　　　　　　　　　　　　　　　　　A (*c.*300)

In the early days of ornithological discovery in Britain records of male Ferruginous Ducks were often reported. No females were discovered as the dull brown drake was considered to be the female of another species. Mr Foljambe of Osberton, Nottinghamshire found three specimens, one male and two females at London's Leadenhall Market on 6th December, 1812 (where birds frequently arrived from Holland), leading Montagu to announce Ferruginous Duck as a new addition to the British List. In fact the first record was an undated specimen recorded by Pennant in 1771. The drake had been killed in Lincolnshire, but there is no mention of this in *The Birds of Lincolnshire* (Smith and Cornwallis, 1955).

Once regarded as a regular visitor to Britain, with some records thought to involve escapes, Ferruginous Duck has become so rare that since 1999 reports were considered by the BBRC.

References:
Montagu, 1862: 60, 64.

Lesser Scaup *Aythya affinis*
(Western North America; winters south and east to Columbia)
1987 Staffordshire, Chasewater.　　　　　　　　　　　　　　　　A (33)

Stopping to look for a male Greater Scaup *Aythya marila* present at Jeffrey's Swag, Chasewater on the Staffordshire/West Midlands border, John J Holian pointed out a small immature Scaup-like duck to A D Barter and J J Oliver at about 9.45am, 8th March, 1987. They were unsure about the bird's identity so took notes and compared it to the Greater Scaup. They decided it was probably a hybrid Greater Scaup x Tufted Duck *Aythya fuligula*.

The bird spent a lot of time in willows or asleep and it wasn't until the evening of the 16th that John Fortey jokingly suggested it was a Lesser Scaup. He noted several features and after checking through books in the evening concluded that it was in fact an immature drake Lesser Scaup.

The following day, members of the West Midland Bird Club took descriptions, and confident of the identification, the news was released onto Birdline. Large numbers of observers converged on the site and were happy with the identification. The bird remained until 26th April and the record was accepted by the BOURC in 1989.

The second bird to reach Europe was found in Co. Down, Ireland, on 13th February, 1988 appearing for six consecutive winters until 1993, with the second British record again coming from the Midlands at Lound, Nottinghamshire, in 1990.

The first female was found in 1996 in Cornwall. Lesser Scaup is now recorded annually in Britain, with numbers steadily increasing.

The first report that had been given serious consideration was a drake found at Sutton Courtenay, Oxfordshire, in December, 1957 with three other Lesser Scaup reports at the time. Opinions were divided until on 3rd March, 1960, the bird was shot under licence and found to be a Tufted Duck x Common Pochard *Aythya ferina* hybrid. The other two and at least five more subsequent reports were all dismissed as *Aythya* hybrids.

References:
Twitching: 65-66; *British Birds* 51: 130; 85: 370-377, photo; *British Birds* 54: pl. 9, photo of the Berkshire hybrid.

King Eider *Somateria spectabilis*
(Circumpolar Arctic)
1832 Orkney, no locality.   A (163)

The first accepted King Eider record is of a bird present in Orkney during November, 1832, but no exact locality is given. Mr Bullock claimed to have found the nest of a King Eider in Papa Westray, Orkney, having six yellowish white eggs, smaller than that of a Common Eider *Somateria mollissima*. This was possibly a hybrid pairing as the female was poorly described. There was a widely held belief that King Eiders bred in Orkney.

In 1851, Joseph Duff of Bishop Aukland recorded a bird present at Bridlington, East Yorkshire and also listed a "*King Duck*" caught on the north bank of the Tyne at Bedlington, Northumberland during the early part of August, 1846. This is now regarded as the same, so the second British record.

A possible first recorded by the Paget brothers as being a female shot at Breydon, 25th July, 1813, lacked enough information for the record to be accepted. Thomas Southwell of Norwich doubted the word of Breydon shooter Lilly Wigg, and removed both King Eider and Harlequin Duck *Histrionicus histrionicus* from the Norfolk list.

The King Eider remains a rare but annual visitor to Britain, chiefly in the Northern Isles and Scotland. Few stray south to reach England and Wales, with only a handful recorded in Ireland.

References:
Patterson 1905: 195; Zool 1889: 383-5; 1851: 3036; 1900: 532; Mather 1986: 165; Montagu, 1862: 66; Macgillivray1852, vol 5: 161.

Steller's Eider *Polysticta stelleri*
(Arctic Russia to extreme North-western Canada)
1830 Norfolk, Caister.   A (14)

Britain's first Steller's Eider was killed on the 9th February, 1830. A boy named Alfred Harvey met George Barrow, a gunner returning from a days shooting, with a duck in his hand. Alfred ran home to fetch his father, Isaac Harvey, who bought the duck and mounted it. Both Alfred and Isaac Harvey became well known taxidermists in the Great Yarmouth area, known to lose rare specimens to rats or the pet cat. Harvey in turn sold the Steller's Eider unidentified, to the Rev George Stewart, Rector of Caister.

Stewart's collection was later presented to the Castle Museum, Norwich where the eider remains in good condition and has since been re-stuffed (Accession no. 47.31). It is on public display in the bird gallery (Dr A G Irwin *in litt*). This bird was figured in both Yarrell and Saunders' works.

Steller's Eiders reaching Britain probably originate from the wintering population in northern Norway, numbering *c*.5,300 birds (1991 count) or possibly birds travelling west to the Baltic. With Shetland closer to Norway it is surprising that Steller's Eider remains so rare there.

References:
Patterson 1905: 195, 83; Saunders, 1899: 463; Cotteridge & Vinicombe, 1996: 45.

Harlequin Duck *Histrionicus histrionicus*

(Iceland, Greenland, North America and East Siberia)
1862 North Yorkshire, Filey.   A (14)

Joseph Whitaker, a noted Victorian ornithologist, collector and author of *The Birds of Nottinghamshire* purchased an attractive drake Harlequin Duck from Alfred Roberts, a well-known naturalist, while visiting Scarborough, Yorkshire. He was told the bird had been shot ten years previously at Filey in the autumn of 1862. Saunders later claimed that the bird was picked up dead from the shore by fishermen. This is the first British record and the skin is retained with Whitaker's collection at Mansfield Museum.

Earlier reports of Harlequin Ducks in Britain had been dismissed, as examination proved most were young Long-tailed Ducks *Clangula hyemalis*. These included a "small flock in Torbay, Devon," a bird bought in a market by Lilly Wigg of Norfolk that was probably cooked and eaten, and a pair that bred on a pool in a Derbyshire garden.

A record still worthy of mention concerned a pair killed on the estate of Lord Seaforth, in Scotland during 1802. The pair were figured in Sowerby's *British Miscellany,* 1806, and possibly concerned genuine vagrants. The record was accepted without question by Montagu and Yarrell, but was relegated to "probably obtained in Scotland" by Saunders, and finally, "doubtfully authentic" by Witherby in 1939. The record is no longer accepted.

The first individuals to be 'twitched' in Britain were in 1987, when the keenest birdwatchers travelled to Shetland or Islay. The most popular was a long staying pair of immature females at Girvan, Ayrshire in 1996.

All but the first four records have been in Scotland.

References:
Zool, 1878: 135; Patterson, 1905: 194; Montagu, 1862: 66; Saunders, 1899: 457; Yarrell, 1843: iii 263; Witherby, 1945: iii, 326; Mather, 1986: 166.

Long-tailed Duck *Clangula hyemalis*
(Northern Europe, Asia and North America))
pre. 1762 Co. Durham, Barnard Castle.   A (WV)

The first mention of Long-tailed Duck in Britain was described by Mr Johnson who reported a pair that fed together for several days on the River Tees below Barnard Castle, Co. Durham. The two sexes were originally thought to have been different species. Francis Willughby published Johnson's description in 1762 calling the birds "Swallow-tailed Sheldrakes." The species had clearly gone unnoticed, as it is a common winter visitor averaging c.20,000 individuals.

It is found chiefly at sea in Scotland with a few occurring at inland sites further south each winter.

Reference:
Willughby 1676: 364.

Black Scoter *Melanitta nigra americana*
(North America and East Siberia)
1987 Lothian, Gosford Bay.   A (5)

The first accepted record was an adult male at Gosford Bay, Lothian, from 31st December, 1987 to 1st January, 1988.

Found by ex-BBRC member Alan Brown, the drake was watched between 3.35 and 3.50pm at a range of about 300m. At 12.25pm the next day he refound the bird much closer at about 150m. He was the sole observer and it was not seen again.

The earliest, but unacceptable report of an American Black Scoter was a bird killed near Rye, East Sussex, in 1915 and sold for £2 5s as part of the notorious Calke Abbey collection of specimens (lot 297) in 1925.

Another unacceptable report came from Spey Bay, Findhorn, Moray and Nairn on 29th December, 1979.

Though some regard 'American' Black Scoter as a full species, at the end of 1999 the BOURC had not officially 'split' the races. Most individuals are usually seen amongst distant scoter rafts and the earlier reports were unacceptable due to the bill shape and pattern being poorly described. Only adult males have been reported, as the separation of females in the field has not been dealt with in the popular British publications.

This race was added to the British List in 1994. There are five accepted records possibly involving returning individuals. There are no Irish records prior to 1999.

References:
British Birds 87: 243; Evans 1994: 83; Calke Abbey Auction Catalogue 1925: 18; Ian Dawson, *in litt.*

Surf Scoter *Melanitta perspicillata*
(North America)
c.1837 Lothian, Firth of Forth.   A (461+)

An old report from the Firth of Forth some time before 1837 is probably the first British record. Information regarding the report is scant, but the bird was apparently obtained by Mr Gould and recorded in Wood's *Naturalist* by Edward Blyth, curator of the Ornithological Society under the heading: "Rare birds killed in the winter of 1837-8":

"A few seasons ago Mr Bartlett received a recent Surf Scoter for the purpose of stuffing and he has also seen an immature Red-crested Pochard for sale".

The old records are poorly documented and the species has probably always occurred sporadically off the Scottish coast. Surprisingly there were only 42 accepted records prior to 1958.

In winter 1845 a decaying corpse of a Surf Scoter was picked up at Pendennis Castle, Cornwall, following violent gales. William Pennington Cocks described the remains as giving off a powerful "*noli-me-tangere-effluvia*".

Jardine, Selby and Temminck claimed Surf Scoter had been recorded in the Northern Isles. In March, 1845 (the same year as the Cornish record), three birds were seen between St Mary's Holm and St Margaret's Hope, South Ronaldsay, Orkney. Mr Ranken reported that the birds were "too wild to allow him close enough to shoot". Two years later Mr Moodie-Heddle saw a Surf Scoter at Longhope, Hoy, Orkney; he had previously seen three specimens.

Small groups of birds are presently recorded in Britain and Ireland each winter with many returning for several consecutive years. Although still considered by the IRBC, Surf Scoter was removed from the BBRC rarity list after 1990, when 461 birds had been recorded, 85% in Scotland with the Moray Firth and the Firth of Forth the most popular sites.

References:
Wood's Naturalist vol 3: 420; Baxter & Rintoul: 441-442; Yarrell, 1843: iii, 225-228; Penhallurick, 1969: 80; Booth 1984: 57; Naylor 1996: 41.

Bufflehead *Bucephala albeola*
(North America)

*c.*1830 **Norfolk,** near Great Yarmouth.   A (11)

In the records of Messers Paget, a specimen referred to as a "Morillon" (thought to be a type of goldeneye *Bucephala)* was in fact an old male Bufflehead shot at Great Yarmouth in 1830. Originally sold to Stephen Miller for 25 guineas, the skin was kept in his collection. On 22nd September, 1853 his specimens passed to Robert Rising, at Horsey, and on his death to Mr Colman for the Castle Museum, Norwich (Accession no. 22.85), on 17th September, 1885 for 25 gs. Since 1996 it has been on temporary loan to the BOURC cabinet at Tring.

The BOURC began investigating all pre-1958 Bufflehead records including the 1830 Norfolk record in July, 1996 following the submission of evidence indicating that it may be "unsafe", as two other specimens had since been found labelled as the Great Yarmouth bird.

Though rejected by Montagu it remains acceptable as Britain's first Bufflehead unless the BOURC decide otherwise.

An adult male in the Foljambe collection at Osberton, Notts, was said to have been shot at the mouth of the Humber in 1801, predating the Norfolk bird, but no accurate details are available.

The second acceptable record, an adult male shot by Richard Morris in the winter of 1864-65, on the Bessingby Beck near Bridlington, Yorkshire, is now in the Whitaker collection at Mansfield Museum.

This duck remains an extreme rarity in Britain with only ten records prior to 1998.

References:
Patterson, 1929: 115; Patterson, 1905: 193: 82; Seago, 1977; Allard, 1990; Riviere 1930; Cordeaux, 1872: 176; Montagu, 1862: 59-60; Taylor 1999: 188.

Barrow's Goldeneye *Bucephala islandica*
(Iceland, Southwest Greenland, Western Canada and the USA)
1979 Ayrshire, Irvine.   A (1)

It wasn't until 1991 that a long-awaited decision was made regarding Britain's first Barrow's Goldeneye.

The honour went to a bird at Irvine, Ayrshire, on 4th November, 1979 at the mouth of the River Irvine.

There had been a gale the previous day and the wind remained strong from the southwest with occasional showers. A male goldeneye landed in surf about 100m from five members of the Glasgow Birdwatchers' Club, swimming closer into calmer water about 75m away, at *c*.10.20am. Obviously not a Common Goldeneye *Bucephala clangula* it was identified by John T Knowler of Glasgow, as a drake Barrow's Goldeneye.

It was seen displaying to two female Common Goldeneye's and remained with Common Goldeneye, a few Greater Scaup *Aythya marila* and Long-tailed Ducks *Clangula hyemalis* on the sea between Irvine and Ayr. Later it moved to a large freshwater lake with the Common Goldeneye, Scaup and Tufted Ducks *Aythya fuligula*. It was last seen on 28th December, 1979.

This is the only record where the probability of it being a wild bird outweighs the likelihood that it had escaped, and is thought to have originated from the migratory North American population rather than the closer but sedentary Icelandic birds.

The first unaccepted record was mentioned in *Zoologist* by Mr Graham of York who reported a female shot in the River Mersey in 1864. His identification is suspect as he also found them "plentiful" in Ireland when he visited in 1844.

A second was shot in February, 1911 at Holy Island, Northumberland, the skin of which is held in the City of Stoke Museum. Following this, two drakes were shot on 18th March, 1913, at Scalloway, Shetland.

References:
British Birds 88: 104-106; Montagu 1813: 120-121; Zool 1864: 9038.

Hooded Merganser *Lophodytes cucullatus*
(North America)
1830/1 Caernarfonshire/Anglesey, Menai Straits.   A (2)

The first accepted record was described and figured in T C Eyton's *History of the Rarer British Birds*. Eyton received the first-winter male, which was killed in the Menai Straits, near Bangor, Caernarfonshire, in winter 1830/1. All subsequently accepted records are thought to have involved escaped birds and this species retains a precarious toe-hold on the British List.

 Four have reached Ireland, the first report involved two birds shot in Cork Harbour, Co. Cork in 1878 and the last in Co. Armagh in 1957. The latter bird is the only accepted Irish record.

An adult male Hooded Merganser was allegedly shot at Great Yarmouth, Norfolk, in winter 1829. Messers Paget recorded it and the specimen was placed in Mr Selby's collection. Professor Newton and Mr Stevenson in the *Transactions of the Norfolk and Norwich Naturalist's Society* discredited the record.

It was preserved as a skin, which was unusual for that period, as such a rarity would normally have been mounted. This specimen is not in the Castle Museum, Norwich as has been claimed.

An upsurge in recent reports are labelled 'of presumed captive origin; the most popular being a bird in Nottinghamshire in 1996.

References:
Saunders, 1899: 477; Yarrell, 1843: iii, 282-286; Eyton: 1836: 75; Stevenson 1890; Witherby 1938-46; Riviere 1930; Naylor 1996.

Ruddy Duck *Oxyura jamaicensis*
(North America, feral populations in Western Europe)
1949 Gloucester, Slimbridge.   C (RB)

First imported into Britain in the 1930s, Ruddy Duck is a native of North America that filled a niche in Britain's avifauna following the spread of birds from collections. In 1948, three hand-reared pairs and a single drake arrived at the Wildfowl and Wetlands Trust, Slimbridge, Gloucestershire from Salt Lake City, Pennsylvania. The birds began nesting the following year and several ducklings evaded the curator's attempts to pinion them, by diving. As each year progressed the number of fully winged birds grew and it was estimated that about 70 juveniles flew away between 1956 and 1963 (most in the harsh winter of 1962/3).

The first recorded breeding in Britain was at Chew Valley Lake, Avon, in 1960 and the species was admitted to Category C of the British List in 1971.

The first feral bird in Scotland considered not to be an escape was a male in Unst, Shetland on 16th May, 1974. The total British Ruddy Duck population reached 3,625 wintering birds in 1997 and was thought to be spreading to the continent.

Ireland's first record involved a male at Oxford Island, Lough Neagh, in March, 1973. During October, a female with four young was seen at the same site.

Ruddy Duck is believed to be a threat (through interbreeding) to the small European White-headed Duck *Oxyura leucocephala* population and experiments and studies are underway to prevent the latter's extinction including culling some of the feral Ruddy Duck population.

References:
British Birds 91: 337; 92: 180; Kear 1990: 184-5; Hutchinson 1989: 85; Thom 1986: 137.

Black Kite *Milvus migrans*
(Most of Eurasia, Africa and Australia)
1866 Northumberland, Alnwick.   **A (281)**

The first documented British record of a Black Kite is from Northumberland in 1866. Mr F Fulger, gamekeeper at the deer park at Alnwick trapped a Black Kite on 11th May, 1866. He thought it was just a "moor Buzzard" and sent it to Mr Bates, birdstuffer in Newcastle. It was taken in a rather bloody condition to John Hancock at Newcastle who skinned, dissected and mounted the bird. It was an adult male. The bird is in the Hancock Museum, Newcastle-upon-Tyne.

Kites were common throughout Britain during the Middle Ages and there is an illustration in *Hortus Sanitatis* (1485) which depicts one sat on a man's head. In 1684, Sir Robert Sibbald mentioned that the "black gled" was a former inhabitant of Scotland. Although these birds are often assumed to have been Black Kites, they were more likely Red Kites *Milvus milvus*.

Despite regular annual appearances Black Kite remains a difficult bird to see in Britain due to its nomadic nature.

References:
Hancock: 9; Gurney 1921: 80; *Zool*, 1869: 1598; Galloway & Meek, 1978: 44.

Bald Eagle *Haliaeetus leucocephalus*
(North America)
NORTHERN IRELAND
1973 Co. Fermanagh, Garrison.   **A (2)**

A farmer shot a juvenile eagle after it allegedly attacked poultry near Garrison, Fermanagh, Northern Ireland on 11th January, 1973. The specimen was thought to be a White-tailed Eagle *Haliaeetus albicilla* and placed in the Ulster Museum. In 1995, it was re-examined by Dave Allen who correctly identified it as an immature Bald Eagle (P. Milne *in litt*).

A review by the Irish Rare Birds Committee in 1997 accepted it as the first wild bird to be found in the Western Palearctic.

The second came to light following an article in the *Cork Examiner* dated 21st November, 1987. Killian Mullarney travelled to Kerry on 25th to check the identification of an eagle initially reported first as a Golden *Aquila chrysaetos* then White-tailed Eagle. He re-identified the bird as a juvenile Bald Eagle and raptor experts, Dick Forsman from Finland and Bill Clarke of the USA later confirmed this. The bird had been captured in an exhausted state at Ballymacelligot, near Castle Island, Kerry, on 15th November, 1987. It was taken into care and later released in the USA.

The Bald Eagle population has increased eight-fold since the 1960s when only 417 breeding pairs remained in the USA, no doubt increasing its vagrancy potential.

BRITAIN
1987 Anglesey, Llyn Coron.   **D [1]**

The first British record involved a bird seen by Anglesey birder John Wilkinson and his wife, over Llyn Coron, Bodorgan, Anglesey, on 17th October, 1978. A superb white headed-adult, it flew in from the west at 11am followed by an entourage of about 20 crows. It landed in the shallows of the lake where it was watched bathing and preening for some 45 minutes. The eagle departed soon after and it was not seen again (Ian Dawson *in litt*).

With the identification accepted, but the birds origin called into question, it was placed in Category D.

An earlier unaccepted report includes a mounted eagle presented to the Scarborough Natural History Museum from the collection of E P Brett of Sawdon in 1937 which Mr W J Clarke thought was in fact a Bald Eagle. Witherby refused to accept it was anything other than a White-tailed Eagle.

In 1950, P A Clancey found this specimen of the American Bald Eagle in the Scarborough Natural History Museum, where it remains. The label claimed that the bird had been captured at Long Pain, Bedale Wood, near Scarborough, 17th January, 1865. Although labelled as a White-tailed Eagle, Clancey confirmed Clarke's identification of a sub-adult Bald Eagle of the race *H. l. washingtoniensis*, but this was never accepted.

Documented in Nelson (1907) as White-tailed Eagle, Lady Downe sent it to David Graham of York for mounting. It was said to have been a fine male seen for several winters.

Later, John Mather agreed that it was a Bald Eagle but found no explanation for Brett's possession of it and the place of capture, Bedale was either spelt incorrectly or referred to a place elsewhere in the county. The collection had originally been owned by the Scarborough Archaeological and Philosophical Society and presented to the council in 1937. In 1950 it moved to new premises.

After all the changes of ownership, in 1953 Ralph Chislett, thought it likely that the Bald Eagle had been placed in the wrong case during storage or moving. There had been another killed fifteen years earlier in Sweden that is also no longer accepted.

References:
British Birds 43: 339; 48: 5; 339; 90: 466-467; Nelson, 1907: 336; Mather 1986; 189-190; Evans, 1994: 101; *Twitching:* 379-380, photo; *Birding World* 3: 81; Cottridge & Vinicombe, 1996: 48.

Egyptian Vulture *Neophron percnopterus*
(Southern Eurasia, India and Africa)
1825 Somerset, Kilve Cliffs, Bridgwater Bay. **B (2)**

An immature Egyptian Vulture was seen in a field near John Mathew's house at Chelvey (Kilve), near Bristol in October, 1825. The bird was feeding on a sheep carcass and so gorged that it was unable to fly any distance. Easily approached it was shot by a servant when it was half a mile away on the cliffs overlooking Bridgwater Bay, Somerset.

In the process of stuffing the bird, Bishop Stanley said it had an "extremely offensive smell," a character of this family. It was nevertheless preserved by Mathews and joined his collection of birds at Chelvey, and later recorded in Yarrell as being in the possession of the Rev A Mathew.

Another bird claimed to have accompanied it was actually a Grey Heron *Ardea cinerea*.

The second British record concerned an immature bird, shot while feeding on the remains of slaughtered farmyard geese at Peldon, Essex, on 28th September, 1868. It was auctioned for £38 17s in 1910 and was figured in John Gould's *Birds of Great Britain*.

The Egyptian Vulture continues to prove its vagrancy potential; an immature reached Denmark in May, 1993.

References:
Zool, 1876: 5000; Yarrell, 1843: i, 1-6; Evans 1994: 101; *Ibis* 140: 182-184. [Montagu, 1862: 360]

Eurasian Griffon Vulture *Gyps fulvus*
(Eurasia and Africa)

IRELAND
1843 Co. Cork, near Cork Harbour. B (1)

A Griffon Vulture caught on the rocks in Cork Harbour, Ireland, in spring 1843 was kept alive at the Earl of Shannon's property at Castlemartyr. The capture was published in the *Fauna and Flora of Cork* and the bird described as an adult, but after examination by Saunders it was said to have been an immature bird.

This record was dismissed by Montagu but now receives widespread acceptance.

BRITAIN
1927 Derbyshire, Ashbourne. E [2]

Hubert Hollick and his daughter Kathleen were at their home in Ashborne, Derbyshire, awaiting the return of their homing pigeons on 4th June, 1927. At 6pm two massive birds, obviously vultures, having pale ruffs around the neck and bald heads, circled low over them. The Hollicks went to Dr Earnest Sadlers house, where together they watched the birds at a distance of about a hundred yards. The birds headed into the strong northwesterly wind towards Buxton. One bird turned southeast heading towards Derby and after about 20 minutes both birds was lost from view.

Mr Hollick had previous experience of vultures in South Africa.

Eurasian Griffon Vulture has recently proven itself capable of vagrancy to Britain as an Italian ringed bird was found in Netherlands in 1992, while six birds were photographed soaring together in the Netherlands in June, 1998.

At the end of 1999 the BOURC removed Eurasian Griffon Vulture from the British List.

References:
British Birds 21: 96-7; Evans, 1994: 102; *Zool*, 1845: 934, 985; Saunders, 1899: 311; BOU, 1971; Hutchinson, 1989 states the wrong year; Montagu, 1862: 360-361; *Dutch Birding* 21: 314.

Pallid Harrier *Circus macrourus*
(Eastern Europe and western Central Asia, winters from southern Europe south to southern Africa and east to South-eastern China)
1931 Shetland, Fair Isle. A (9)

A male Pallid Harrier was seen on 24th April, 1931, on Fair Isle, Shetland. It was shot by George Stout on 8th May. The body was sent to the National Museums of

Scotland, Edinburgh where it was examined by Percy Grimshaw and Mr N B Kinnear, who said it was in its second summer plumage on account of some brown feathers on the nape, rear crown and wing coverts. Its stomach contained part of a Sky Lark *Alauda arvensis* and the remains of a Meadow Pipit *Anthus pratensis*, including the feathers.

The skin is at the National Museums of Scotland, Edinburgh.

The second record was a bird ringed as a nestling in Sweden in 1952 and shot in October, of the same year in Yorkshire.

In 1896, a female Montagu's Harrier *Circus pygargus* was obtained at Flamborough, Yorkshire. Though not acceptable at the time, a wing formula indicating Pallid Harrier was given. This report has never been officially recognised.

References:
British Birds 26: 8-11; Baxter & Rintoul 1953: 310; Mather, 1985: 193-194; Cottridge & Vinicombe 1996: 49.

Montagu's Harrier *Circus pygargus*
(Eastern Europe and Western Asia; winters Africa to India)
Pre-1734 Greater London. A (SB)

A popular misconception is that Montagu discovered Montagu's Harrier at the beginning of the 19th Century, but the first published notice of this species was in 1734 when Eleazar Albin's three-volume *A Natural History of Birds* contained an illustration of an adult male.

Albin's work lacked detail in the text, and the origin of his specimen is not known. At the time all adult male harriers were called 'Hen Harriers,' with females and immature birds named 'Ringtails.' Albin called his specimen "*The Ring tail-Hen-Harrier*" while the text described a female Hen Harrier *Circus cyaneuss*.

Dissection of specimens during the late 1700s resulted in the widespread acceptance that ringtails and 'grey' harriers were different plumages of the same species.

In 1795, a published description of a Montagu's Harrier was made by William Marwick in a paper on the birds of Sussex.

Montagu's first account of the 'Ash-coloured Falcon' was in his *Dictionary* published in 1802, which mentioned a bird from Wiltshire. He had not seen the bird in the field but separated it from Hen Harrier on account of its smaller size and longer more pointed wings, "*the third feather being much longer than any other.*"

Montagu was credited for proving that the grey male Hen Harrier developed from the ringtail plumage. He went on to describe an 'Ash-coloured Falcon' shot near Kingsbridge, Devon on 10th August, 1803: the first dated British record.

In his 1813 *Supplement,* Montagu had made further discoveries having observed birds in the field and remarked that he had not seen any later than October, raising the possibility that it was a migrant.

After contracting Lockjaw two years later, Montagu died and his specimens were sold to the British Museum, including his first specimen labelled "Wiltshire 1802".

The link between Montagu and his Harrier developed, until by 1840 the name Montagu's Harrier had become widely accepted both at home and abroad. Yarrell was the first to formally propose this recognition but only the English name was retained. In France, Viellot had referred to the bird as "Busard Montagu *Circus montagui*" but this Latin tribute was to be short lived and *pygargus* meaning 'White Rump' became the accepted scientific name.

At the northwest extremity of its range Montagu's Harrier is a very rare breeding bird in Britain.

Reference:
Clarke 1998: 6-17; 43; 57; *British Birds* 92: 133-4.

Northern Goshawk *Accipiter gentilis atricapillus*
(North America)

IRELAND
1870 Co. Tipperary, Galtee Mountains.   A (5)

An adult female American race Northern Goshawk in the Dublin Museum was shot in the Galtee Mountains, Co. Tipperary in February, 1870 before passing into the collection of Sir Victor Brooke. A second example was shot at Parsons Town, near Birr, Co. Offaly, during the same year. There have been five records of American Goshawk in Ireland with less than 25 records of the European Goshawk. The last, a bird seen on the North Slobs, Co. Wexford on 13th November, 1969 allowed the species to be upgraded to Category A.

BRITAIN
1935 Isles of Scilly, Tresco.   B (1)

The first and only acceptable British record concerned an adult shot on Tresco, Isles of Scilly on 28th December, 1935. The bird was part of Capt. Dorrien-Smith's collection, which is now in the Museum on St Mary's.

Robert Gray purchased an American Goshawk said to have been shot on the outskirts of Schiehallion, Perthshire in May, 1869 from a birdstuffer in Brechin, Forfarshire. Although in fresh condition, the head was stained and the plumage soiled by the person responsible for skinning it. He asked a Glasgow taxidermist to relax the specimen and was told that the brains and eyes had not been removed. Mr Harvie-Brown saw the specimen while in Gray's collection, and Saunders claimed that it was placed in the National Museums of Scotland, Edinburgh. The record was rejected by the BOU in 1915.

References:
British Birds 48: 5; Evans 1994: 104; Gray 1871: 39-40; *Ibis*: 292; Baxter & Rintoul 1953: 311; Saunders, 1899: 332; Kennedy, 1954: 106.

Common (Steppe) Buzzard *Buteo buteo vulpinus*
(Eastern Europe and Western Asia; winters East and South Africa)
1864 Wiltshire, Everley.   B (1)

A buzzard obtained at Everley, Wiltshire in September, 1864 and given to John

Gould was said to have been of the race *B. b. vulgaris*, though J H Gurney thought it was an immature of the race *B. b. desertorum*. Both races are no longer valid and collectively became Steppe Buzzard *B. b. vulpinus*. The skin was placed in the British Museum but no further details regarding the specimen are available.

Gurney also mentioned two examples killed near Newcastle, placed in the Hancock collection, which were never officially recognised.

There are also two unaccepted records from 1975: at Reculver and Chislet Marsh area, Kent, 12th January to 20th April and in the St Ives area, Cornwall, 27th October, to 2nd November.

References:
Saunders, 1899; 322; Evans 1994: 105; *Ibis* 1876: 366.

Greater Spotted Eagle *Aquila clanga*
(Eastern Europe across Russia and Siberia to northern Mongolia)

IRELAND
1845 Co. Cork, near Youghall. B (13)

Two eagles, present for several weeks on the estate of the Earl of Shannon, near Youghall, Co. Cork. were seen hunting low over the fields. One immature bird had killed a rabbit and was shot while eating it by a gamekeeper in January, 1845. The bird was then given to Samuel Moss who mounted it. Later the specimen came into the possession of the National Museum, Dublin, where it remains.

The other eagle was slightly paler but otherwise similarly marked. It was killed at the same site but not preserved. Following publication of these sightings it was thought that there had been several records of this "smaller eagle" in Ireland.

It is possible that another bird had been present for several years in the mountains above Cahirciveen, Co. Kerry, as a portrait of the eagle was shown to Mr Butler of Waterville and the Rev Bastable who recognised it instantly. Montagu thought a bird shot at Horn Head, Co. Donegal was a Greater Spotted Eagle after reading a description of it.

BRITAIN
1860 Cornwall, Hawks Wood, near Cheesering.

The granite hills that run through Cornwall to Lands End can reach an altitude of 1200 feet. Hawk's Wood is between two high peaks, and on 4th December, 1860 a shooting party approached a large raptor in a tree bordering the wood. Instead of flying off it scrambled down the tree to hide among some rocks. The bird was captured and found to be a male Greater Spotted Eagle, having the characteristic oval spots of a first year bird.

It was sent to Edward Hearle Rodd of Penzance and later dissected by his taxidermist, Mr Vingoe of Penzance. He said that the bird had suffered a recent accident to the elbow of the wing, preventing it from flying but the bird was still healthy. A large deposit of fat surrounded the gizzard, empty from a lack of food.

There was a claim by the Rev A Mathews that his friend Mr Heaven of Lundy had shot one three years prior to the Cornish bird but this report was unproven as the body fell over the cliff and could not be retrieved.
The last British record was in 1915.

References:
Montagu, 1862: 81-83; illustrated in Yarrell; *Zool*, 1861: 7311; Rodd, 1880: 3-6; Evans 1994: 105.

Lesser Kestrel *Falco naumanni*
(Iberia, Northwest Africa and southern Europe eastwards into Asia; winters Africa south of the Sahara)
1867 Yorkshire, North, near Green Hammerton.   **A (17)**
In November 1867, John Harrison of Walstrop Hall, near Green Hammerton, North Yorkshire, noticed a falcon flying around his farm for several days. He shot the bird, which was taken to David Graham of York, who preserved, and later identified it as Britain's first Lesser Kestrel, a second-year male.
Realising the importance of the specimen, Harrison placed it in the Yorkshire Museum, where it remains. The claws on the specimen are said to be relatively short possibly indicating a period in captivity, however Lesser Kestrel inhabits towns and cities where a raptor would soon wear its sharp talons on the hard brickwork.
Lesser Kestrel has declined considerably in recent years.

References:
Nelson, 1907: 372-373; Denton 1995: 115.

American Kestrel *Falco sparverius*
(North, Central and South America)
1976 Shetland, Fair Isle.   **A (2)**

Britain's first accepted record of American Kestrel was presumed to have been caught up in a front over Newfoundland that moved out to sea on 23rd May, 1976. It would have then been carried by westerly airstreams between Scotland and Iceland to arrive at Fair Isle on the 25th, when sightings of the unusual small falcon were thought to involve a Red-footed Falcon *Falco vespertinus*. That evening A M Taylor and Roger Broad went to search for the bird.
At 6.30pm in dull conditions they noticed an unsettled atmosphere among Common Starlings *Sturnus vulgaris* at South Reeva; walking towards them they flushed a small falcon, which landed on a cliff. A M Taylor moved closer and got a good look at its head pattern – it seemed wrong for Red-footed Falcon. Finally as darkness approached it was seen briefly in North Reeva.
That evening Taylor identified it as an adult male American Kestrel from the Peterson *Field Guide*.
The bird frequented the area between Malcolm's Head and Setter until the 27th, on one occasion sat on a post, eating a Meadow Pipit *Anthus pratensis*.
The second British record came three weeks later when Brian Mellow, Peter

Maker, H Deal and R Lee found a female American Kestrel at Bearah Tor, Cornwall on 13th June.

There is an early mention of an American Kestrel shot at Helmsley, Yorkshire, in 1882 but no other details were known until the skin of this adult female was found at the Yorkshire Museum. It bore a label that appeared to have been the original and not renewed at any stage indicating that it was indeed obtained at the aforementioned place in May, 1882. It was found to be of the nominate race *F. s. sparverius* or *F. s. phalaena*.

The original owner of the skin had identified the bird correctly but did not publicise the record. Fraudulent placing of an English site name on an imported skin is ruled out as there was no financial gain, claim of fame or kudos made. The condition of the plumage suggests that it was not held in captivity, as it is in pristine condition with the claws and bill undamaged and not overgrown.

A report was submitted to the BOURC but no decision had been reached by March 2000.

Additionally, a male shot in Bridlington Bay, East Yorkshire, in 1939, was procured by the Rev. Charles Hudson and sent to Mr Foljambe of Osberton Hall, Nottinghamshire, with papers regarding the birds authenticity. Still present in the collection, all documentation has been lost.

A third British record concerned a bird at Dungeness, Kent, during 1966-67. It was considered to be an escape.

References:
Dymond 1991: 25; Sharrock 1982: 208-211; Nelson 1907: 372; Denton 1995: 22-23.

Red-footed Falcon *Falco vespertinus*
(East Europe to Central Siberia; winters Africa)
1830 South Yorkshire, near Doncaster. **A (694)**

1830 was obviously a year when a considerable invasion of Red-footed Falcons took place and an adult male Red-footed Falcon was shot near Doncaster, South Yorkshire, in April. Although Yarrell and others often regard the Norfolk birds obtained in May as the first British records, the Doncaster record is prior to them. The April specimen joined the collection of Mr H S Foljambe, at Osberton Hall, Nottinghamshire and notice of the occurrence was reported to the Linnean Society. The specimen is retained at Osberton.

Three Norfolk specimens from Horning, Holkham and Great Yarmouth, obtained during 1830 have all been claimed to be Britain's first.

1. Of the Great Yarmouth bird, killed in Marshes behind Vauxhall Gardens, J H Gurney Jnr said "in all probability it was the first killed in Britain" and is the only specimen given an exact date (1st May, 1830). It is an immature male, presently in good condition and on public display in the bird gallery at the Castle Museum, Norwich (Accession no. 74.23(15)).

2. Southwell's copy of *Stevenson* contains a photograph with the caption "*The first British Red-footed Falcon. Killed at Horning May 1830 Gurney Coll*" with a cross placed under the male. Both male and female (Accession no. 15.935) are in good

condition at the Castle Museum. The label on the case reads *"Two out of three red legged Hobbies killed by Thomas Heath Esq. while feeding on earth worms after the plough & given by his son to Mr J H. Gurney. The third bird is now at Wymondham. X at Horning Erythropus vespertinus"*

Mr Lubbock said the Horning birds *"were observed during some very rough weather; four were in company, their actions and flight being peculiar, occasioned observation and pursuit,- they alighted upon the ground in a ploughed field, and when shot, the bills and legs were soiled as if they had been in the pursuit of worms"*

3. Riviere claimed that an immature male was killed at Holkham prior to 1830 but Southwell states that the birds at all three Norfolk sites were obtained in the same year.

Usually a dozen or so birds are reported each year with the occasional larger influx.

References:
Riviere, 1930; Saunders 1899; Paterson, 1905: 164; Yarrell 1843: i, 45; Cottridge & Vinicombe 1996: 51; Dr AG Irwin *in litt.*

Eleonora's Falcon *Falco eleonorae*
(Coastal Mediterranean, Canary Islands and coastal northwest Africa; winters Madagascar)
1977 Merseyside, Formby Point.   **A (3)**

At about 3pm on a hot and calm 8th August, 1977, K W Horton was overlooking an evaporating pool in the dune system of Cabin Hill at Formby Point, Merseyside. He saw a large dark bird approaching that he initially took to be an Arctic Skua *Stercorarius parasiticus,* but realised that it was in fact a falcon of similar size to a Peregrine *Falco peregrinus* but with a longer tail and sharply pointed wings. In direct comparison with a nearby Common Kestrel *Falco tinnunculus* he dismissed the melanistic possibilities of all regularly occurring British falcons. He then eliminated popular falconers' birds, including Lanner *Falco biarmicus* and Saker *Falco cherrug,* leaving dark-phase Eleonora's Falcon or Sooty Falcon *Falco concolor* as the only possibilities. Returning home after an hour he consulted field guides, the dark underwing-coverts clinching the identification as Eleonora's Falcon.

At 9.30am the following day in the company of A Copleston, M Garner and A Adams he again saw the bird as a Common Kestrel chased it into a nearby copse. The bird had alighted on a branch allowing them to see the underparts and head pattern. As Horton approached to about 50 metres the bird took off and began hawking insects. By 11.15am, as the falcon went to rest they were all confident of the identification but had doubts about the bird's origin. It was not seen again.

The BOU decided that the bird was in first-summer plumage as some immature spotting and barring remained on the underwing and tail. An investigation traced the only captive birds, which were still being held at the time.

References:
Sharrock 1982: 222-226, sketch.

Gyr Falcon *Falco rusticolus*
(Circumpolar Arctic)
c.1770 Shropshire, near Longnor.   A (380)

Generally accepted as the 'official' first, two birds were shot near Longnor, Shropshire, in *c.*1770, and described by Pennant as a "variety of Peregrine *Falco peregrinus*" that he called "*Spotted Falcons*." Montagu said that the superior size made it more likely that they were Gyr Falcons. Pennant's description fits Gyr Falcon, other than the iris coloration but this is presumably because he described the birds from mounted specimens with glass eyes fitted of the wrong colour.

The ancient sport of falconry in Britain dates back centuries, and an ancient illustration taken from a 10th Century manuscript depicts a Gyr Falcon used by a Saxon falconer. It was also often the case that fines were paid with livestock which included falcons and in 1139 the Exchequer fined a Lincolnshire man:

> "*One hundred Norway Hawks and one hundred Girfals: four of the hawks and six of the Girfals were to be white ones.*"

The "White Girfals" were almost certainly 'Greenland' Falcons and the "White Hawks" perhaps 'Iceland' Falcons, both races of Gyr Falcon.

Gyr Falcon has been known in Britain since accounts and records began. However there is no mention of it being a breeding bird or migrant to any part of Britain. In 1282, Edward I received Gyr Falcons direct from the King of Norway on more than one occasion, and sent four grey Gyr Falcons for Crane and Heron hawking, to the King of Castille, Spain.

As some falconers' birds undoubtedly escaped, Gyr Falcon was possibly the first British bird to carry the 'of unknown origin' caveat.

The first mentioned wild Gyr Falcon records was in 1762, in Halifax, Yorkshire, when a large falcon was shot. Mr Bolton sent a report and description of it to Pennant. It was a grey phase bird and then regarded as a variety of another species. Montagu described it as a male Gyr Falcon in immature plumage, but for some reason this record was not accepted as the first British record.

The vast majority of British records are from coastal locations.

References:
Montagu, 1862: 89-90, 95; *British Birds* 4: 251-252; Gurney 1921: 42, 50, 26.

'American' Peregrine Falcon *Falco peregrinus anatum or tundrius*
(North America)
1891 Leicestershire, Newbold Verdon.   B (2)

There has only been two accepted records of this race; the first was an immature bird shot by Mr W Whitaker at Newbold Verdon, Leicestershire, on 31st October, 1891, and the skin was held in Joseph Whitaker's collection.

It was exhibited by Mr E Bidwell at a meeting of the BOC held on 14th June, 1911 after having been examined and identified by Mr Ogilvie-Grant. It was in its second-year plumage and blacker than any other specimen held at the British Museum. It is now at the Mansfield Museum.

The only other record was an immature male caught in a net set to trap plovers at Humberston Fitties, Lincolnshire, on 28th September, 1910. It was given to Mr Caton Haigh who sent the skin to Dr Hartert who identified it. He also confirmed the identity of the 1891 bird.

The dark races of Peregrine Falcon *F. p. anatum* or *tundrius* are virtually inseparable, indeed they are considered conspecific by some authorities. *F. p. anatum* is found throughout Canada while *F. p. tundrius* breeds in Greenland so should not be an unexpected vagrant to Britain considering the frequency of Gyr Falcon *Falco rusticolus* records.

References:
British Birds 48: 6; 5: 219; *Bull.* BOC 27: 103.

Western Capercaillie *Tetrao urogallus*
(Northern Europe east to Siberia)
1837 Perth & Kinross. **BC (RB)**

The Western Capercaillie's range once covered a large part Britain since the last Ice Age as ancient bones were found in Teesdale and the species was used as rent payments to the Bishop of Durham in the 14th Century. Capercaillies were also mentioned as a quarry species in Wales.

Although an inhabitant of the pine forests of Britain and Ireland, Western Capercaillie declined until the last Irish bird was killed in 1760; Scottish birds were lost soon afterwards. The species had already disappeared from England.

The Western Capercaillie was absent from Britain and Ireland for about fifty years until re-introduction schemes started. At the end of 1827, Lord Fyfe took delivery of a pair of birds with a view to releasing them near Braemar, Perthshire when healthy young had been produced. The result was not recorded, but probably unsuccessful. In 1837 a successful release scheme at Taymouth Castle, Perthshire allowed the species to inhabit every suitable woodland in that county by 1879.

In 1994, the total Scottish population was estimated to be 2,200 birds but has since suffered a drastic decline.

References:
Saunders, 1899: 491; Yarrell, 1843: ii, 289-303; Kelsall & Munn, 1905: 267; *British Birds* 92: 180; Holloway 1996: 138.

Red-legged Partridge *Alectoris rufa*
(Western southern Europe)
***c*.1770 Suffolk.** **C (RB)**

Now an established part of the agricultural landscape of Britain, Red-legged Partridge was first introduced into the English countryside in about 1770. At this time domestic fowl were used to incubate large numbers of imported French eggs at two estates in Suffolk. The schemes were orchestrated by the Marquis of Hertford near Orford and Lord Rendlesham at Rendlesham. From there the species spread, aided by further releases of birds in other counties.

The first report of this species being brought to Britain was considerably earlier, but these were captive birds not involved with the eventual establishment of the British population.

An established and common breeding species with many birds released annually by gamekeepers.

References:
Saunders, 1899: 503; Gurney 1921: 203; Holloway 1996: 140.

Golden Pheasant *Chrysolophus pictus*
(Central China; introduced in Britain)
Pre-1880 Norfolk, Thetford.   C (RB)

There are two long established Golden Pheasant populations in Britain, one in Dumfries and Galloway and a larger one in East Anglia.

Golden Pheasant was first imported to Britain during the 18th Century but the first deliberate releases were not made until the 1880s. The earliest recorded population of feral Golden Pheasants in Britain stems from birds released at Elveden, near Thetford by Maharaja Victor Duleep Singh prior to 1880.

In 1905, a small population of Golden Pheasants established itself near Newton Stewart, Dumfries and Galloway, stemming from hybrid Golden x Lady Amherst Pheasant stock first liberated in 1895. The birds gradually outbred their Lady Amherst's genes to become a separate but well-established population.

Between 1,000 and 2,000 birds are estimated to make up the total British and Irish population.

Reference:
British Birds 92: 180-1; Holloway 1996: 148.

Lady Amherst's Pheasant *Chrysolophus amherstiae*
(Southwest China, Tibet and northern Burma)
Pre-1890 Bedfordshire, Woburn.   C (RB)

The existing British population that places this introduced species in Category C of the British List stems from birds released into Woburn Park, Bedfordshire in 1890, eventually spreading outside the parks boundary. 1991 estimates placed the number of birds present in that county at 100-200 birds, this dropped to 60 in 1995.

In 1825 while in Calcutta, Sir Archibald Campbell presented Lady Sarah Amherst with two pheasants from the King of Burma. Although the birds survived the journey back to England in 1828, they died a few weeks later.

Lady Amherst presented them to Benjamin Leadbeater who described and named them in her honour.

The first captive breeding was in 1871, with the first unsuccessful introduction of Lady Amherst's Pheasants by Robert Gordon of Bute at Mount Stewart, Argyll.

Bedfordshire remains the species British stronghold.

Reference:
Holloway 1996: 150; Mearns & Mearns 1988: 19-27.

Sora *Porzana carolina*
(North America; winters southern USA and Caribbean Islands, Central America and South America east to Guyana)
1864 Berkshire, River Kennet, near Newbury.   A (15)

At the 14th February, 1865 meeting of the Zoological Society held at Magdalene College, Cambridge, Professor Newton exhibited a specimen of "Carolina Crake". The bird had been shot the previous October (1864), on the banks of the River Kennet, near Newbury, Berkshire. Newton described the vagrancy potential of the rail family, stating that a previous extralimital record of Sora existed, when one was captured in Greenland. In 1897 two Soras boarded a yacht in the Atlantic and by taking food from the crew, at least one reached England alive.

Sora remains a very rare bird with only 15 acceptable records; of these two were at sea and two in Ireland.

References:
Saunders, 1899: 510; Radford, 1966: 84; *Zool*, 1865: 9540; Cottridge & Vinicombe 1994: 53.

Little Crake *Porzana parva*
(Central and East Europe and West Asia; European population winters in Africa)
1791 East Sussex, Catsfield, near Battle.   A (130)

The first proven report came to light in 1890, when Mr J E Harting showed that a Spotted Crake *Porzana porzana* illustrated in Marwick's *Aves Sussexienses* was actually a Little Crake. The bird had been obtained at Catsfield, near Battle, East Sussex, on 29th March, 1791, a hundred years earlier. Occasionally wrongly credited as being from Kent, it pre-dated all other reports and therefore became Britain's first record.

There was much confusion regarding the identity of small crakes and various birds had been claimed as Britain's first, including a female sent by Dr Tucker to Montagu from Ashburton, Devon in 1809.

Previous claims to the title included a crake sent from the Norfolk fens to a London poulterer's shop in early May, 1812. Mr Foljambe of Osberton Hall, Nottinghamshire, rescued it, while a second bird was obtained from the banks of the Thames. Both specimens were alike and announced to be a new species: the Olivaceous Gallinule *Gallinula Foljambei*.

They were in fact adult male Little Crakes, being blue-grey in colour, while previous records had been duller brown females or immature birds.

The peak months for vagrancy to Britain are March and early April, with an autumn peak in early November.

References:
Montagu, 1862: 109; D'Urban: 279; Walpole-Bond, 1938: iii, 332-335.

Baillon's Crake *Porzana pusilla*
(Eurasia, Africa and Australasia; European population winters in Africa)
Pre-1819 Suffolk, River Waveney, near Beccles.   A (76)

Baillon's Crake was a secretive but regular summer visitor to Britain before

accurate recording began. Before the fens and marshes of eastern England were drained it may possibly have been a regular breeding bird in Britain.

There are some inadequately described early reports but the first 'official' record of Baillon's Crake was a specimen obtained on the River Waveney, near Beccles, Suffolk in 1819. The mounted bird was seen by Rev R Sheppard and Rev W Whitear on 13th December, 1819. It was reported incorrectly as a Little Crake *Porzana parva* in the *Norfolk and Norwich Transactions., iii., p. 252.*

A bird trapped on ice at Melbourne, Cambridgeshire, in January, 1823, has also been claimed as the first British record.

Only two of the 76 records are from Ireland.

References:
Ticehurst, 1932: 458-459; Lack, 1934: 112; Evans 1994: 129.

Allen's Gallinule *Porphyrula alleni*
(Africa south of the Sahara)
1902 Norfolk, off Hopton.   B (1)

The wind had been blowing from the southwest in late December, 1901 and New Year's Day 1902 dawned with a sea mist in the Great Yarmouth area. On this day an immature Allen's Gallinule landed on a fishing boat off the coast near Hopton, Norfolk. The bird was caught by a member of the crew and taken to the local bird-stuffer, Walter Lowne.

Lowne identified the bird using books and skins borrowed from Prof Newton of the BOU. The bird was kept alive in a cage at his house, where it readily took mealworms. Although showing no signs of captivity, questions were asked about the bird's origin and some authorities, notably Riviere, still did not accept it. Enquires made by Arthur Paterson, who saw the bird when alive, revealed that a London dealer had advertised some for sale at thirty shillings and sixpence. He also considered it an escape and it remained so until accepted by the BOURC in 1974.

J H Gurney had accepted the record as the rail family is widely known for vagrancy and there are many instances of birds landing on ships. J B Nichols held the skin for 25 years, which was lost after being sold on 29th June, 1929. It remains the sole British record.

References:
Zool, 1902: 98; Saunders 1899; Paterson, 1905: 208; Paterson, 1929: 115; *British Birds* 2: 146; 67: 405; *Ibis* 1974: 578; Allard, 1990; Taylor 1999: 227.

American Purple Gallinule *Porphyrula. martinica*
(Southeast America to Argentina, West Indies)
1958 Isles of Scilly, Hugh Town, St Mary's.   A (1)

The gallinule family has suffered a confusing history in Britain and Ireland, with birds of a variety of species imported. The true number of American Purple Gallinules involved is therefore clouded with uncertainty. As a consequence only one relatively recent record from the Isles of Scilly is now recognised.

On the evening of 7th November, 1958, a tired Moorhen-like bird was rescued from a gutter in the High Street, Hugh Town, St Mary's, Isles of Scilly, by Margaret Hughes on her way to work. The bird was kept at the telephone exchange until the following evening, when she showed it to local ornithologist, P Z Mackenzie. He could not recall any species like it from his European guidebooks, and fed the bird mealworms at his home. Despite eating well the bird died on 9th November and the corpse was sent for preservation at the British Museum.

After examination, it was identified by J L F Parslow and accepted as the first and only American Purple Gallinule to reach Europe. It was an immature bird and the skin remains at the Natural History Museum, Tring (specimen number; 1958. 27.1).

Interesting early unacceptable reports include an undated record from the 19th Century in southwest Ireland. It was recorded as a "Martinique Gallinule" by Mr Thompson and later proved to be the first report of an American Purple Gallinule *P. martinica*.

Other possibles include a bird killed in August, 1863, by Mr Stares, in a marsh at Grange, near Gosport, Hampshire and a bird shot at Llandeilo, Dyfed in September, 1893.

References:
Sharrock, 1982: 101-102; Penhallurick, 1969: 103; Evans 1994: 131. [Saunders 1899: 518; Kelsall & Munn, 1905: 274]

American Coot *Fulica americana*
(North, Central and South America; winters southern USA, Central and South America)

IRELAND
1981 Co. Cork, Ballycotton.   A (3)

On 8th February, 1981, K O'Sullivan and Mr and Mrs D O'Sullivan returned to the lagoons and beach at Ballycotton where they had seen an unusual bird the previous day. It had shown characteristics of both Common Moorhen *Gallinula chloropus* and Common Coot *Fulica atra*. They mentioned it to C D Hutchinson and T C Kelly, who easily found the bird.

Hutchinson looked for previous hybrid reports in Cramp's *Birds of the Western Palearctic* on his return home only to be shocked by the plate showing the bird: an American Coot!

The bird remained until 4th April, 1981 and was seen by about 100 Irish and 112 visiting British birders.
Surprisingly a true hybrid Coot x Moorhen and nicknamed a 'Moot' was found in Suffolk less than three weeks after the American Coot was first discovered.

BRITAIN
1996 Kent, Stodmarsh.

The first accepted British record of an American Coot was possibly the eighth to reach the Western Palearctic. Chris Hindle found it during the afternoon of 16th April, 1996 while birding with his wife and son near the Lampen Wall, Stodmarsh,

Kent. Chris wanted to check the bill pattern of Common Coot *Fulica atra*, because he had just arranged to visit Morocco where he was hoping to see Red-Knobbed (Crested) Coot *Fulica cristata*.

The first bird he looked at did not have the characteristic Common Coot's white shield. He considered Crested Coot as a possibility but checking the undertail concluded that American Coot was more likely. Before releasing the news he dashed home to check literature and rule out the possibility of it being a hybrid. Chris returned to Stodmarsh where John Cantelo and Don Worsfold joined him. They agreed with his identification. About 50 birders saw the bird that evening with many more visiting until it was last seen on 30th April.

Britain and Ireland's only other report involved a bird present for just one day on 17th April, 1999 in Cumbria.

References:
Evans; *Rare Birds* 3: 19; *British Birds* 77:12-16, photos; *Birding World* 9: 137-140, photos.

Common Crane *Grus grus*
(Scandinavia east to Central Siberia; winters North Africa and Middle East to Southeast Asia)

IRELAND
12th Century   A (RB & P)

The earliest mention comes from 12th Century Ireland, when Giraldus

Cambrensis said that a hundred might be seen in a flock. It is possible that in various writings by 'non-ornithologists' Common Cranes may at times have been confused with Grey Herons *Ardea cinerea* but from the remains found in caves and lakes it is clear that Common Crane was once a widespread species in Britain and Ireland. Bones of this species have been found in an area near Thatcham Moor, on the Berkshire Downs, dating from *c*.8,000 *BC* to 5,000 *BC*.

Irish reports stated that "*The Crane was seen in this county* (Cork) *during the remarkable frost of 1739; but they do not breed with us,*" while in Co. Waterford "*The Crane* (Grus), *which is a bird of passage. During the great frost of 1739 some few cranes were seen in this county; but not since or before in any persons memory.*"

While this is the year that Common Crane was first properly documented in Ireland, the first may not have been in Cork. It is also known that the Grey Heron is often referred to colloquially as Crane (P. Milne *in litt*).

BRITAIN
1465

Possibly the earliest report of the species in Britain was at a banquet given in honour of Neville, the Chancellor of England, who was made Archbishop of York at Cawood in 1465; where the Bill of Fare stated that 204 birds were eaten. In the fifth Earl of Northumberland's Household Book (1512), it states:

"It is thought that Cranys muste be hadde at Crystynmas and other principal feestes for my Lordes owne Mees."

In January, 1526, nine Common Cranes were served at the wedding of Elizabeth, daughter of Sir John Neville, High Sheriff of Yorkshire, and Henry VIII passed an Act in 1534, prohibiting the taking of Crane eggs under pain of imprisonment.

Persecution led to Common Crane become a rare vagrant by the 1700s.

The BBRC recorded 1242 reports involving migrant birds in Britain and Ireland between 1958 and 1988. A tiny breeding population of up to 12 birds has existed in Norfolk since the 1980s.

References:
Nelson, 1907: 547; Mather 1986: 238-240; Kennedy, 1954: 126-127; Radford, 1966: 82, 25; Lack, 1934: 21, 110; Gurney 1921: 87, 164-172; Willughby 1678: 274; Yarrell ii, 439; Morris 1868; *British Birds* 92: 139; *Norfolk Bird & Mammal Report* 1997: 462.

Sandhill Crane *Grus canadensis*
(North America, Cuba and Northeast Siberia; winters southern USA and Mexico)

IRELAND
1905 Co. Cork, Galley Head. A (3)

In 1954, Mr Kennedy wrote *"An American Brown Crane recorded as shot in Co. Cork on 14th September, 1905 had probably escaped from captivity".* This was a Sandhill Crane killed near Castlefreke at Galley Head, Co. Cork that had been present since the 11th September. The taxidermist reported that it showed no signs of having being confined and was in "a very spent condition". This was the first to be reported from the Western Palearctic and its origin remained in doubt for years. In 1961, it enjoyed a change of fortune when the National Museum of Ireland admitted it to the Irish List (P. Milne *in litt*).

In 1971, D Goodwin and Dr D W Snow found the specimen showed characteristics of the most northerly and migratory race *Grus c. canadensis*. They also discovered that two of only four records of Sandhill Crane in eastern North America were on Prince Edward Island, Canada at the same time; in the autumn of 1905. This record was found to be acceptable and the species was added to the BOURC's then combined British and Irish List in 1971.

BRITAIN
1981 Shetland, Fair Isle.

The weather was poor on Fair Isle, Shetland on the morning of 26th April, 1981, with light snow flurries in the light northwest wind. At 11am, a crane flew over the observatory. Nick Riddiford, I S Rowley and I S Robertson were puzzled about the bird's identity having failed to see a striped neck pattern. D G Borton had watched the bird fly over Ward Hill an hour earlier and also failed to put a name to it.

As the weather brightened the crane was seen over Landberg. Robertson had suggested the possibility that the bird was a Sandhill Crane so everyone at the observatory made their way to a good vantage point to watch the crane as it soared over Busta and Field. It remained in the air for four hours allowing it to be identified as a Sandhill Crane.

At 7pm the first-winter bird landed at Homisdale where it gave good views before roosting at Easter Lother Water calling like a Canada Goose *Branta canadensis*.

The following morning the crane was present until the 9.30am plane flushed it and it headed northeast out of view.

The second British record came from Shetland, ten years later, on 17th September, 1991.

References:
Birding World 4: 322-323; British Birds 65: 427; 76: 105-109, photo; 65: 427. [Kennedy, 1954: 128]

Little Bustard *Tetrax tetrax*
(Northwest Africa, Iberia, east across South Europe, Asia; northern French population probably winters south to Iberia)
1751 Cornwall, no locality.   A (110)

A Little Bustard shot in Cornwall was sent to the Royal Society in London where it was exhibited in 1751. Unable to identify the bird it was dispatched to George Edwards for his opinion. In 1758, Edwards published Gleanings *of Natural History' vol. IV* which shows a coloured illustration of the specimen and this record was also mentioned by Pennant in his *British Zoology* (1761-1776) as the first British record.

Little Bustard has suffered drastic declines since the late 19th Century, which is reflected in the number of vagrants reaching these islands, only 17 records since 1958.

References:
D'Urban: 441; Rodd, 1880: 81; Gurney 1921:229; Pennant 1761-1776, VI: 286; Evans 1994: 135.

Houbara Bustard *Chlamydotis undulata*
(North Africa, Canary Islands, Central and southwest Asia)
1847 Lincolnshire, Kirton-in-Lindsey.   A (5)

While walking in a stubble field on Kirton Cliff, near Kirton-in-Linsey, Lincolnshire, on 7th October, 1847, Mr G Hanley flushed a large bird only 20 yards in front of him. He promptly shot the bird, which was in perfect condition. When skinned it was found to be a male, and its crop was full of caterpillars, beetles and snails.

Mr Roberts of Scarborough sent notice to *Zoologist* magazine that he had just obtained a Little Bustard *Tetrax tetrax*. When he became better acquainted with the bustard family he correctly identified it as a Macqueen's (Houbara) Bustard.

Mr G R Gray suggested the bird had been brought from Africa by a Mr Fraser and "allowed" to escape but, investigations proved that Mr Fraser's birds were all accounted for.

The cased specimen is presently held at Yorkshire Museum.

The last British record, a bird in Suffolk in November, 1962, was photographed stood in the centre of a country road close to the car of photographer Eric Hosking.

References:
Montagu, 1862: 25; Denton 1995: 95.

Great Bustard *Otis tarda*
(Eurasia east from Germany and Iberia to Western China, and North-western Africa)
1803 Moray and Nairn, Oakenhead.   A (*c*.105)

Great Bustard was once common throughout the south and East Anglia with populations recorded on the Yorkshire Wolds in 1391 and also as far north as Scotland. The species was even mentioned in an old recipe book dated 1413.

The last native Great Bustard was shot at Lexham, Norfolk, in May, 1838. By this time it was being recorded as a migrant with birds shot near Oakenhead, Morayshire, (1803), between Helston and The Lizard, Cornwall (March, 1843) and Savernalve Forest, Salisbury Plain, Wiltshire (9th August, 1849).

The Oakenhead bird (1803) being the first recorded vagrant Great Bustard in Britain.

Vagrancy to Britain is related to cold weather movements.

References:
Yarrell, 1843: ii, 363; Montagu, 1862:22; Baxter & Rintoul, 1953: 612-613; Lack, 1934: 110; Gurney 1921: 173-176; Holloway 1996: 433-434.

Black-winged Stilt *Himantopus himantopus*
(Southern Eurasia, Africa, the Americas and Australia)
1684 Dumfries and Galloway, near Dumfries.   A (319)

William Dalmahoy shot Britain's first Black-winged Stilt, at a loch near Dumfries, Dumfries and Galloway. He sent one of the two birds to Sir Robert Sibbald who illustrated and wrote of it in 1684, in *Scotia Illustrata*. The next occurrence was reported 32 years later when five arrived together at Penzance, Cornwall some time around 1718.

Black-winged Stilt bred for the first time at Nottingham Sewage Farm in 1945, when five adults reared three young from nine eggs. There has since been further attempts but only one, at Holme NNT Reserve, Norfolk in 1987 has been successful.

References:
Baxter & Rintoul, 1953; Saunders, 1899: 563; Naylor 1996: 125-126; Evans 1994: 141.

Cream-coloured Courser *Cursorius cursor*
(Southwest Asia, and North and East Africa)
1785 Kent, near Wingham.   A (33)

Killed by William Hammond near St Albans Court, Kent, Britain's first Cream-coloured Courser was an immature bird. Hammond found it very approachable and reluctant to fly. The bird would run swiftly, stopping only to pick up food from the ground. It called unlike any bird he had come across.

He sent for his gun and after a misfire the bird took flight, landing 100 yards from where it had taken off. The bird was not so fortunate the second time around and it was presented to Dr John Latham, of Dartford, a founder of the Linnean Society and an artist able to skin and mount his own birds.

Following an auction of his museum's contents in 1806, the specimen passed to one Donovan for eighty-three guineas despite interest from the Viennese Emperor.

Eventually it joined the collection at the British Museum at South Kensington only to be destroyed in a bombing raid during World War II.

References:
Montagu, 1862: 247-248; Harrison, 1953: 405; Evans 1994: 147.
A drawing made of the bird by Latham's daughter is figured in Harrison 1953: plate XLIII

Collared Pratincole *Glareola pratincola*

(South Europe, Southwest Asia and Africa; winters Africa)
1807 Cumbria, Bowness and **Lancashire,** Ormskirk. 	A (83)

William Yarrell quoted a report by Mr Bullock, of the London Museum, in the *Transactions of the Linnean Society* which said the first British specimen was shot near Ormskirk, Lancashire, in October, 1807. Mr J Sherlock preserved it and sold it to Bullock soon afterwards, later passing the specimen to the Earl of Derby.

The same bird had also been seen at Bowness, Cumbria, during the same month.

According to Montagu, a bird shot near Liverpool on 18th May, 1804 was taken immediately to Bullock who examined the corpse while it was still warm. The bird had been hawking insects, and the remains of winged beetles were found in its stomach. It was thought to have been a male and joined the collection of Lord Stanley, who sent a drawing and description to Montagu.

There is a possibility that the same specimen was involved in both Montagu's and Yarrell's reports with the date being incorrect in Montagu's work. The Bowness/Ormskirk bird from 1807 is widely regarded as the first British record.

References:
Montagu, 1862: 257; Yarrell, 1843: iii, 1-5; Hutchinson, 1986: 49; Evans 1994: 148-151.

Oriental Pratincole *Glareola maldivarum*
(South and East Asia; winters India east to Northern Australia)
1981 Suffolk, Dunwich. 	A (3)

On Monday 22nd June, 1981, David W Burns was walking among the coastal marshes between Dunwich and Walberswick, Suffolk when he spotted a brown tern-like bird flying towards him. Eventually it passed close enough for him to tell it was a pratincole with a chestnut underwing. Thinking he had found a Collared Pratincole *Glareola pratincola* he walked to where it had been lost from view and relocated it 20 minutes later on the ground. After 45 minutes of notetaking he fetched his camera, but the bird flew off as he returned.

The bird was back in the same spot when he returned from his walk. Getting to within 15m, he took a few photographs as it made several flights, always returning to its favoured spot. When he met John Grant, Jenny Berry and Zul Bhatia in a hide at Minsmere, he took them to see the bird.

The bird remained in Suffolk until 8th July, but it wasn't until 5th July that some observers began to question the initial identity. The white trailing edge to secondary feathers was presumed to have been worn off as the bird was in moult. Oriental Pratincole was suggested and was later accepted The same bird was re-found at Old Hall Marshes, Essex on 6th August, remaining to 11th October, allowing a steady procession of about 2,000 admirers to catch up with it.

The bird was accepted as a first-summer Oriental Pratincole as it retained some juvenile feathers when it arrived, moulting them out before it left Essex. All three British records have remained for long periods.

References:
British Birds 86: 115-120.

Black-winged Pratincole *Glareola nordmanni*
(West Asia; winters Africa)
1909 North Yorkshire, Reedholme, Danby Wiske, Northallerton. **A (31)**

On 17th August, 1909, Mr W S Charlton shot a pratincole feeding with a flock of Northern Lapwings *Vanellis vanellis* at Reedholme, near Danby Wiske, Northallerton, Yorkshire. Mr J Charlton sent notice of it to Witherby who wrote back asking him to check the bird's underwing colour. Further correspondence, including a photograph confirmed the identity and Dr Steward and Riley Fortune agreed. At that time it was considered to be Britains fourth Black-winged Pratincole, but the earlier three reports (below) were later rejected.

The three previous records in 1903 had come from Kent in May and June and East Sussex in July, but were investigated as part of the Hastings rarities affair, and rejected. The mounted Yorkshire bird is now at the Dorman Museum, Middlesborough.

All birds have arrived between July and November with two reports as far north as Northeast Scotland and Shetland, while there are only two Irish records.

References:
British Birds 3: 266; Mather, 1985: 253; Evans 1994: 153-4.

Little Ringed Plover *Charadrius dubius*
(Europe and North Africa east to Japan; south to the Philippines; West Palearctic population winters Persian Gulf, Arabia and northern tropics of Africa)
Pre-1835, Sussex, Shoreham. **A (SB)**

A specimen collected at Shoreham, Sussex and held in the collection of Mr Doubleday of Epping, had been killed some time before 1835. It was the first British record and involved a very young bird, presumably reared in the vicinity. Later authorities disregarded it, and several further records from the same locality during the 1850s.

In 1938 a pair successfully reared three young at Startops End Reservoir, Hertfordshire. The first confirmed breeding.

Little Ringed Plover has become a common summer migrant breeding at many inland sites. It remains rare in Scotland.

References:
Sage 1959; Yarrell, 1843: ii, 409; Montagu, 1862: 251; Walpole-Bond, 1938: iii, 132-134; *British Birds* 92: 140.

Ringed Plover *Charadrius hiaticula tundrae*
(Northern coasts from Norway and Sweden to Siberia)
1874, Sussex, Pagham Harbour.   **A (WV)**

In 1885, Henry Seebohm differentiated between the two races of Ringed Plover (*C. h. tundrae* and *C. h. hiaticula*) occurring in Britain, one obviously larger than the other. In 1934, G Carmicheal Low studied the races and concluded that *C. h. tundrae* was a good subspecies and found that it occurred in Britain.

He named eight records of this race in Britain, the first having occurred on 10th December, 1874; it was an adult female killed at Pagham Harbour, Sussex. The second specimen was killed in 1914.

This northern subspecies is an annual winter visitor and passage migrant.

References:
British Birds 28: 64-66.

Semipalmated Plover *Charadrius semipalmatus*
(North America; winters south to Patagonia)
1978 Isles of Scilly, St Agnes.   **A (2)**

At midday on 9th October, 1978, Paul Dukes and F Hicks heard an unfamiliar Spotted Redshank-like *Tringa erythropus* call near Porth Killier, St Agnes, Isles of Scilly. The call faded into the distance. Ten minutes later it was heard again as a bird thought to be an immature Ringed Plover *Charadrius hiaticula* flew by.

The following day other observers heard the call and thoughts turned to the possibility of a Semipalmated Plover. Reference books confirmed the call notes but field identification was impossible unless the partially webbed toes were seen. The bird was heard among the flock of about 70 Ringed Plovers gathered on Periglis Beach on the 11th but could not be isolated from them.

Late in the afternoon, the plover separated from the flock to feed among the seaweed of a cove below St Agnes Church. It was observed closely by Paul Dukes, A Dean, J Gregory, M Parker, J Ridley and D and J Sykes until dusk. The bird flew onto nearby rocks allowing the diagnostic palmations between the toes to be seen. It remained in the vacinity of Periglis Beach until 9th November and was watched by hundreds of observers.

At first the bird was harassed by the Ringed Plovers before establishing a feeding territory, which it defended.

Despite a report of a Semipalmated Plover at Ballycotton, Ireland that has never been accepted, there were no further records in Britain or Ireland until a long-staying first-summer bird was found at Dawlish Warren, Devon, in mid April, 1997, although it was not positively identified until mid June.

A female Semipalmated Plover that had been obtained at Rye, Sussex, on 8th April, 1916 was a 'Hastings rarity' and removed from the British List in 1962.

References:
Sharrock 1982:235-239, photo. [Walpole-Bond, 1938: iii, 132]

Killdeer *Charadrius vociferus*
(North America; winters USA and Central America to northern Chile)
1857 Dorset, Christchurch. **A (56)**

In April, 1857, the first example of a Killdeer to reach Britain was killed by Thomas Dowden, a keeper to the Salmon Association, in a potato field near Knapp Mill, on the River Avon, a mile from Christchurch, Dorset. It was taken to William Hart, birdstuffer of Christchurch and after being mounted and placed in a glass case, sold to Mr Tanner.

Dr P L Sclater later identified it as a Killdeer and investigated the circumstances surrounding the bird and published an account in *Ibis* with a recommendation that it be added to the British List.

The record was, and still is, acceptable. However, Saunders expressed reservations.

In July, 1904, Mr Pycraft discovered a specimen in the University Museum at Aberdeen labelled as shot at Peterhead in 1867. The Christchurch record was placed on the British List in 1912.

References:
Kelsall & Munn, 1905: 287-288; *British Birds* 2: 150; Hartert 1912: 168; *Ibis* 1862: 276. [Saunders, 1899: 543]

Kentish Plover *Charadrius alexandrinus*
(Europe and Africa, east to Japan, also USA south to western South America)
1787 Kent, Sandwich. **A (P)**

William Boys of Sandwich, Kent, an astute observer of natural history in his locality, shot three specimens of plover and sent them to Dr John Latham on 23rd May, 1787. Latham found them to be an unknown species and named them Kentish Plover.

At the time the species bred at Sandwich and was found in reasonable numbers along the Kent and Sussex coast.

An annual migrant in small numbers to Britain, about 40 birds are reported in an average year, mostly found on the south and east coasts with few inland.

References:
Harrison 1953: 316-324, The original plate from Lewin's *Birds of Great Britain* drawn from Latham's specimen is reproduced in Harrison 1953: plate 31.

Lesser Sand Plover *Charadrius mongolus*
(Central Asia to eastern Siberia; winters shores of Indian Ocean from South Africa to Australia)
1997 West Sussex, Pagham Harbour. **A (1)**

Lesser Sand Plover was a long overdue vagrant to Britain and on 14th August, 1997, John Bacon found a sand plover near Church Norton on the south side of Pagham Harbour, West Sussex. He called over three nearby birdwatchers including Timothy Edwards, but opinions were divided. News of the discovery was released and some of the first observers thought that the bird's feet projected beyond the tail when seen in flight; it was therefore pronounced to be a Greater Sand Plover *Charadrius leschenaultii* in almost full breeding plumage.

Having already seen this species in Britain, few high-listing twitchers visited Pagham, despite questions being asked about the identification.

Photographs of the bird were examined by Swedish sand plover guru Erik Hirschfeld after the birds departure on 16th August and he confirmed the identity as Britain's first Lesser Sand Plover, probably of the western race *C. m. atrifrons*.

In January, 1999 the BOURC accepted the Pagham Lesser Sand Plover onto Category A of the British List.

A summer plumaged bird present on the Don Estuary near Aberdeen from 18th to19th August, 1991 was considered by many to be a Lesser Sand Plover. Accepted by the BBRC at the time as a Greater Sand Plover, in 1999 they began investigating the possibility of it being a Lesser.

References:
Birding World 10: 294-297, photo; 11: 362; 4: 396-398, photo's; Ibis 140: 182-184; 141: 175-180

Greater Sand Plover *Charadrius leschenaultii*
(Southern Russia east to Mongolia; winters Africa, Southern Asia and Australia)
1978 West Sussex, Pagham Harbour.   A (12)

Tony Marr was shown a Kentish Plover *Charadrius alexandrinus* on the mudflats of Pagham Harbour, West Sussex, in the late afternoon of 9th December, 1978, but soon realised that the bird was far too big for that species. Suspecting that it was a sand plover he returned the following morning with A R Kitson and Richard Porter, and the bird was watched through telescopes feeding in a tidal creek. It was certainly a sand plover, but Lesser was not truly eliminated until the bird called. It was Britain's first Greater Sand Plover, probably a first-winter due to the buff fringed wing coverts.

It was only seen for one hour and 40 minutes on the 10th before being lost to sight in the harbour but was seen daily by about 1,000 observers in total until 1st January, 1979, showing a preference at low tide for the same creek. Towards the end of its stay it seemed weak and was thought to have died as a result of the freezing weather.

During 1979, a further two individuals were discovered in Orkney and Avon.

Tony Marr later became chairman of the BOURC, while Richard Porter was appointed head of species protection at the RSPB. He co-authored *Flight Identification of European Raptors*.

All but one of Britain's Greater Sand Plovers have graced coastal sites, there had been no Irish records up to December 1999.

References:
Sharrock 1982: 239-242, Photo.

Caspian Plover *Charadrius asiaticus*
(Central Asia eastwards from Caspian Sea; winters east and southern Africa)
1890 Norfolk, North Denes, Great Yarmouth.   A (5)

A pair of birds on the golf course, at the North Denes, Great Yarmouth in the morning of 22nd May, 1890, were the first Caspian Plovers to be seen in Britain. In the afternoon they moved to a market garden.

The palest bird, probably female flew off west as Arthur Bensley shot the brighter adult male. Getting them in line to kill them both was not possible, so he aimed at the brightest. The male was given to Mr Lowne the Great Yarmouth taxidermist, who placed it on top of a clock, out of the cat's reach, then sent it to Mr Southwell for identification and exhibition at a meeting of the Zoological Society.

It was later purchased for the Castle Museum, Norwich (Accession no. 39.90) where it remains in good condition. While the record concerning the female lacked full documentation it remains acceptable, and a new species of parasite was found on the freshly dead male.

A report that failed to receive acceptance was of a bird shot three years earlier near Rye, Sussex, on 21st August, 1887. Mr Gasson of Rye preserved it and some time later it joined the Harpur Crewe collection before passing to the Booth Museum, Brighton. The bird was originally thought to have been a Cream-coloured Courser and the record went unpublished until 1927, when it appeared in the *Catalogue of the Dyke Road Museum*, 5th Ed.

Caspian Plover was upgraded to Category A of the British List following the appearance of a fine adult male at Wingletang, St Agnes, on the Isles of Scilly on 21st May, 1988. Keith Pellow obtained a full description and several photographs.

There are no Irish records.

References:
British Birds 83: 549-550, photo; Riviere 1930; Allard, 1990; Saunders 1899; Paterson, 1905: 214.

American Golden Plover *Pluvialis dominica*
(Arctic North America and extreme Northeast Asia; winters South America)

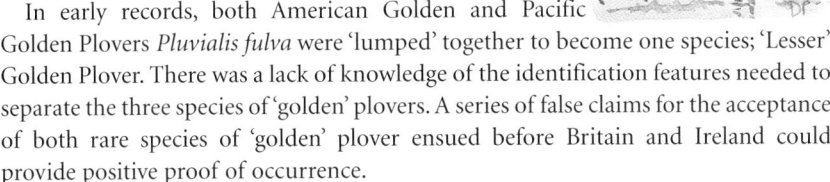

IRELAND
1894 Co. Mayo, Belmullet. A (238)

In early records, both American Golden and Pacific Golden Plovers *Pluvialis fulva* were 'lumped' together to become one species; 'Lesser' Golden Plover. There was a lack of knowledge of the identification features needed to separate the three species of 'golden' plovers. A series of false claims for the acceptance of both rare species of 'golden' plover ensued before Britain and Ireland could provide positive proof of occurrence.

In Ireland, an adult American Golden Plover (still retaining some summer plumage) was found at Belmullet, Co. Mayo by Mr E Williams among a consignment of European Golden Plovers *Pluvialis apricaria* sent to Dublin on 13th September, 1894. They were later placed in the Barrington Collection which is now at the National Museum, Dublin (P Milne *in litt*).

BRITAIN
1956 Shetland, Fair Isle.

Presently over 169 records of this vagrant exist but amazingly the first record was as recent as 1956. This was an adult seen on Vaasetter, Fair Isle, Shetland on 14th to 15th September, 1956. It was first presumed to be a moulting Grey Plover *Pluvialis squatarola* present in a small party of European Golden Plover but exhibited the typical brownish-grey axillaries of a Lesser Golden Plover. Skins held in the British and the Scottish National Museums were examined by F R Allison, George Waterston and M F M Meiklejohn who had seen the bird. They confirmed the identification of the "American race".

In autumn 1882, Mr J H Gurney found an American Golden Plover at Leadenhall Market. On 3rd August, 1883, Mr P D Malloch, fishing tackle maker of Perth shot a plover that crossed the road in front of him.

Two days later, Mr J Guille Millais visited him to purchase a European Golden Plover skin. Whilst staying with Mr Harvie-Brown, Millais met Mr Bidwell who discussed the dark underwing pattern of Pacific Golden Plovers. Returning home he checked his specimen and found the feature present, so sent it to Seebohm, who identified it as an American Golden Plover.

This record was later rejected by Bannerman and is no longer recognised.

The two 'Lesser' Golden Plovers were split into American Golden and Pacific Golden Plovers by the BOURC in 1986, at which time only seven records of Pacific had been accepted. By creating interest in the two 'new' species birders looked at golden plovers in more detail, leading to an upsurge in records.

Of the 169 American Golden Plovers recorded in Britain an additional 16 unidentified American/Pacific Golden Plovers have also occurred. About half of all reports have been from Cornwall, including the Isles of Scilly.

References:
Scot.Birds 1: 68; Dymond, 1991: 34; Baxter & Rintoul: 594; *Zool*, 1886: 26; FIBOT Bull Feb 1957: 112. [Saunders, 1899: 549]

Pacific Golden Plover *Pluvialis fulva*
(North and Northeast Asia, and Alaska; winters southern Asia, Australia and western North America)

1870 Surrey, Epsom.   A (46)

In October, 1908, Witherby and Ticehurst published the formal acceptance of a specimen held in the Charterhouse collection. It had been shot on Epsom Racecourse, Surrey on 12th November, 1870 and presented to Mr Stafford by Mr Aubrey, clerk at Nine Elms Station. Mr H L Popham later examined the specimen, which had been, labelled "*Plover (small like Golden)*"

This remains the first acceptable occurrence of what was at that time (together with American Golden Plover *P. dominica*) known as Lesser Golden Plover.

Surprisingly there were no further reports for almost 80 years until Steve Madge saw one briefly in the fields near Bempton, Yorkshire on 1st September, 1975.

An earlier, unaccepted record, was of a Pacific Golden Plover on display with European Golden Plovers *Pluvialis apricaria* at Leadenhall market, London in December, 1874, claimed to have been sent from Norfolk. Mr Dresser purchased the badly damaged bird and managed to make a skin and preserve the sternum, which he gave to Prof. Newton.

Saunders thought that the evidence was not good enough to include it on the British List.

Two further records followed: a bird shot at Loch of Stennis, Mainland, Orkney, during November, 1887, and a bird shot on the Thames at Shell Haven Point, Essex, by Mr H Nunn on 6th August, 1896.

References:
Evans 1994: 163; *British Birds* 2: 150; Bucknill, 1900: 283-4; *Zool* 1897: 330. [Saunders, 1899: 549]

Sociable Lapwing *Vanellus gregarius*
(Southeast Russia and Western Central Asia; winters Northeast Africa and Southwest Asia)

*c.*1860 **Lancashire,** near St Michael's-on-Wyre.   **A (40)**

An immature Sociable Lapwing was shot from a flock of Northern Lapwings *Vanellus vanellus*, near St Michael's-on-Wyre, Lancashire, during autumn 1860. The bird was mounted and, seen by candlelight, was duly recorded by Mr F S Mitchell of Clitheroe in *Birds of Lancashire* as a Cream-coloured Courser *Cursorius cursor*. Sociable Lapwing had yet to be recorded and described in Britain.

The cased specimen later passed into the possession of Mr Doeg of Manchester when it was correctly identified and exhibited, on 20th November, 1888, at the Zoological Society meeting, by Henry Seebohm.

Sociable Lapwing was officially accepted onto the British List approximately 28 years after its first arrival in Britain.

A record annual total of three birds were found in both 1968 and 1978, only two individuals have reached Ireland.

References:
Saunders, 1899: 553; *Zool*, 1888: 389; Evans 1994: 165.

White-tailed Lapwing *Vanellus leucurus*
(South Russia and Middle East, and West Central Asia)

1975 Warwickshire, Packington Gravel Pits.   **A (3)**

In 1975 there was an exceptional White-tailed Lapwing influx into Western Europe, with reports from Austria (March), Italy (April), Poland (April), Sweden (May), Finland (May), the Netherlands (July) and finally reaching Britain (July).

At 1pm on 12th July, 1975, while searching for migrants at Packington Gravel Pits, Warwickshire, J E Fortey, Mrs E Green and E G Phillips watched a strikingly patterned wader fly past. The bird alighted on a patch of shingle 30m in front of them. They quickly ruled out Sociable Lapwing *Vanellus gregarius* as it had a pale unmarked head and concluded it was Britain's first White-tailed Lapwing. A thorough description was taken before dark.

The bird was an adult male and remained in the area until 18th July, to the delight of hundreds of birders. An investigation proved that several birds had been imported into Britain but the European influx of 1975 and apparent range expansion of the species meant that White-tailed Lapwing was accepted onto the British List.

The second of only three British records concerned a bird filmed briefly at Chesil Beach, Dorset, on 3rd July, 1979 that was not seen again. The third bird was found at Cleadon, Tyne and Wear in 1984 but after constant harassment from Northern Lapwings *Vanellis vanellis* it moved to Telford, Shropshire.

References:
Sharrock 1982: 195-198, photo.

Great Knot *Calidris tenuirostris*
(North-eastern Siberia; winters India, China, Southeast Asia to Australia)
1989 Shetland, Scatness. A (2)

The first British record followed three reports of adults from Germany and Denmark in autumn 1987, and an adult in France in spring 1988. There is a possibility that these records concerned the same bird, finally reaching Shetland in 1989.

At 11.20am on 15th September, 1989, Pete Ellis was looking for waders roosting on the high tide at Scatness, south Mainland, Shetland. He was excited by an unusual wader with three Grey Plovers *Pluvialis squatarola*, a Red Knot *Calidris canutus* and two Dunlin *Calidris alpina* about 150m away. Grabbing his scope he was sure that it was a Great Knot, on account of its black chest. After noting several features, the small group took off and landed at the edge of a pool 60m away. The Great Knot fed briefly among the short grass but flew off with a Redshank.

Ellis telephoned Martin Heubeck, who arrived ten minutes later with Paul Harvey and they confirmed the identification using the *Shorebirds* guide. Harvey and Ellis checked the Pool of Virkie as the tide fell and found the bird on the far side where it remained until 3.40pm, allowing several local birders to see it. An hour later it returned and stayed until 6.30pm, when it left with two Eurasian Curlew *Numenius aequata* and was not seen again. The bird was photographed by Dennis Coutts.

Despite 30 hopeful twitchers flying into Shetland the following morning, the Great Knot moved on as a weather front brought gales and rain to the area.

A large number of observers, often at very long distance and in extremely poor light saw Britain's second Great Knot at Teesside in October, 1996. It became known as the "Great Dot" and several visits or a Questar telescope was needed before birdwatchers obtained acceptable views. At the end of its 24-day visit, the bird moved across the estuary to Bran Sands, approaching to within 10m of photographers.

References:
Birding World 2: 313-315, sketch; Evans 1994: 167-168; British Birds 85: 426-429, photo.

Semipalmated Sandpiper *Calidris pusilla*
(North America; winters Central and South America)
1953 Norfolk, Cley, Arnold's Marsh. A (89)

On 19th July, 1953 Peter Clarke found an adult Semipalmated Sandpiper on

Arnold's Marsh, Cley, Norfolk. It was observed by the warden and four others, for several hours at close range. The identity of the bird was a mystery and attempts to catch it or identify its footprints failed. Richard Bagnall-Oakley erected a small hide and took several photographs and 100 feet of cine film as the bird approached as close as 2m. Copies were sent to America, where the bird was identified by Roger Tory Peterson as a Semipalmated Sandpiper.

On 17th September, 1907 an immature bird was claimed to have been killed at Jury's Gap, Romney Marsh, Kent but was later discredited as a Hastings rarity.

It is now almost annual with about half of the records found in Ireland.

References:
Harrison, 1953: 386; Sharrock, 1982: 35-36, photos; Taylor 1999: 257.

Western Sandpiper *Calidris mauri*
(North America; winters southern USA and Central America)
1956 Shetland, Fair Isle.   A (9)

Kenneth Williamson and I I G Alexander saw a small bird, initially thought to be a Semipalmated Sandpiper *Calidris pusilla* at Kirkigeo, Fair Isle, Shetland, on 27th May, 1956. The bird was trapped on 29th May and remained until 3rd June.

I C T Nisbet of the BBRC suspected that the bird had been misidentified. Following research, he concluded that the bird was a Western Sandpiper, moulting into breeding plumage. The wader was accepted as the first record of this species in Britain.

The second record was of a brief one-day bird on the Isles of Scilly in 1969.

References:
Sharrock, 1982: 87-89; Dymond, 1991: 38; Naylor 1998: 141.

Red-necked Stint *Calidris ruficollis*
(Siberia; winters Southeast Asia and Australia)
1986 East Yorkshire, Blacktoft Sands RSPB Reserve.   A (5)

On an overcast and raining 23rd July, 1986, Brett Richards headed to Blacktoft Sands RSPB Reserve, Humberside (East Yorkshire). When he entered the Xerox hide at 10.30am he saw the 'Little Stint' *Calidris minuta* that had been reported the previous day and immediately suspected that it was a summer-plumaged Red-necked Stint. Brett took a description of the bird and confirmed his suspicions in a phone call with Steve James that evening.

On the 25th a Little Stint was present for comparison and Brett decided to inform birders countrywide via Nancy's Cafe at Cley, Norfolk.

Opinions remained divided until the stint was seen by several well known birders including Steve Gantlett, on Sunday 27th. At least 1,872 twitchers saw the bird before it departed on 29th when a low flying aircraft disturbed it. A total of £573 was raised for the RSPB.

A record concerning a bird at Brough Haven, Yorkshire from 14th to 19th September, 1973 was not accepted by the BBRC.

Ireland was graced by its first Red-necked Stint on 2nd July, 1998. It was an adult in breeding plumage found by Phil Davies at Ballycotton, Co. Cork and was seen by over 90 Irish birdwatchers during its three-day stay.

References:
Evans 1994: 1972; *British Birds* 82:391-395, photos. [Y.N.U. 1984: 35]

Little Stint *Calidris minuta*
(Northern Europe, east to northern Siberia; winters Africa and India)
18th Century Cambridgeshire.   **A (P)**

Thomas Pennant recorded the first mention of this diminutive wader in Britain during the late 18th Century, from a specimen killed in Cambridgeshire. In his work it was then named the "Little Sandpiper".

It is a common passage migrant.

References:
Yarrell, 1843: ii, 643.

Long-toed Stint *Calidris subminuta*
(Breeds Siberia; winters India, South-east Asia to Australia)
1970 Cornwall, Marazion.   **A (3)**

On 7th June, 1970, Philip Round visited Marazion Marsh, Cornwall to take a break from his A-level examinations, and saw a small, yellow-legged stint with an Ashy-headed Wagtail *Motacilla flava cinereocapilla*. Together with John Johns, he watched the bird for two hours, but could not make a firm identification. They returned following day when the bird was photographed down to 6m. Round and Johns concluded that it was a Least Sandpiper *Calidris minutilla,* which was accepted by the BBRC, as Long-toed Stint was not considered a potential vagrant at that time.

In 1974, Round read a paper in *British Birds* about stint identification. After examining photos, skins and finally first hand experience of Long-toed Stints in Thailand, he concluded that it had been a Long-toed Stint. He wrote to the BBRC to inform them in 1979.

Eventually the BBRC (in 1994) and the BOU (in 1995) reached a unanimous decision, that it was Britain's first Long-toed Stint.

This decision relegated a Long-toed Stint seen at Saltholme Pool, Teeside on 28th August, 1982 to Britain's second.

These are the only two British records with an additional bird found at Ballycotton, Co. Cork, Ireland in 1996, while a bird claimed in the Western Isles suffered from the same confusion with Least Sandpiper as the Marazion individual. The BBRC felt that the identification did not safely rule out the more common species.

References:
British Birds 89: 12-24; 85:429-436; Evans 1994: 172.

Least Sandpiper *Calidris minutilla*
(North America; winters southern USA and Central South America)
1853 Cornwall, Mounts Bay.   A (36)

On 10th October, 1853, Mr Vingoe, the Penzance taxidermist, shot an "American Stint" (Least Sandpiper) in a patch of wet grass near the sea at Mounts Bay, Cornwall. He took various measurements as part of a fine description and mounted the bird. It was then shown to the Cornish authority Edward Hearle Rodd, who in turn sent the details to Montagu. Rodd was the Town Clerk of Penzance, and Head Distributor of Stamps in Cornwall, his county avifauna was published in 1880.

This was the first European record of a Least Sandpiper.

Least Sandpiper records in Britain are widely scattered but the southwestern counties are responsible for the bulk of records. Ireland has recorded only seven individuals.

References:
Penhallurick, 1969: 138-137; Rodd, 1880: 108-109.

White-rumped Sandpiper *Calidris fuscicollis*
(North America; winters southern South America)
Pre-1839 Shropshire, Stoke Heath.   A (442)

An example of "Schinz's Sandpiper" (White-rumped Sandpiper), killed some time before 1839, was recorded by Mr Eyton in *Fauna of Shropshire*. It had been shot near Stoke Heath and placed in the collection of Sir Rowland Hill. Gould later examined the specimen and identified it as the bird named after a distinguished Swiss naturalist.

The second and third records were an adult pair shot at the Hayle estuary, Cornwall, in October, 1846. This was initially published as the first British record and the birds placed in the collection of E H Rodd.

A specimen in the Belfast Municipal Museum was believed by Thompson to have probably been killed in Belfast Lough, Co. Antrim, some time before 15th April, 1836. While it pre-dates the first British record it is no longer considered acceptable.

White-rumped Sandpiper is one of the most common Nearctic vagrants to Britain. Although an expected yearly average would be ten birds, in 1984 up to 29 reports made it a record year. About a quarter have been in Ireland.

References:
Saunders, 1899: 581; Yarrell, 1843: ii, 651-653; Naylor, 1996: 76-77; Rodd, 1880: 105-106. [(Kennedy, 1954: 198)].

Baird's Sandpiper *Calidris bairdii*
(North America and northeastern Siberia; winters South America)
1911 Western Isles, St Kilda.   A (216)

Britain's first Baird's Sandpiper was found along the rocky fringe of Village Bay St Kilda, Western Isles, on 28th September, 1911.

Eagle Clarke suspected the bird was something unusual so promptly shot it while it was wading in a small pool. It was found to be an adult female Baird's Sandpiper in winter plumage.

Previous records, consisting of an immature female killed on 11th October, 1900, at Rye Harbour, East Sussex and a bird shot at Hunstanton, Norfolk on 16th September, 1903 were later dismissed as Hastings rarities. The latter as recently as 1993.

In an average year about three Baird's Sandpipers are reported in Britain with a similar number in Ireland, the highest annual total attained in Britain is seven birds in 1983 and 1989 with 11 birds in Ireland in 1988.

References:
Riviere 1930; Clarke, 1912: ii, 233; Walpole-Bond, 1938: iii, 172-173; *Zool*, 1909: 124. [*British Birds* 1: 1586: 22; 199].

Pectoral Sandpiper *Calidris melanotos*
(North America and Eastern Siberia; winters southern South America)
1830 Norfolk, Breydon Water.   A (P)

A bird shot at Breydon Water on 17th October, 1830 proved eventually to be a female Pectoral Sandpiper. The bird was alone and its unusual call induced the shooter to kill it. Great Yarmouth Taxidermist Isaac Harvey preserved the specimen as a curious variety of Dunlin *Calidris alpina*.

Harvey possessed a poor reputation amongst sportsmen as their specimens often disappeared. He placed the blame on his cat, or having been nibbled by rats. It was suspected that he sold them on at an inflated price to other collectors.

The mounted Pectoral Sandpiper passed into J D Hoys' collection who suspected that it wasn't a Dunlin at all but probably an undescribed species of *Tringa*. He forwarded it to Yarrell mentioning his suspicions.

As the famous American naturalist James Audubon was visiting London at the time, Yarrell showed him the bird and the identification of this American species was confirmed.

A scarce but regular autumn migrant, Pectoral Sandpiper ceased to be officially rare in 1963.

References:
Allard 1990: 18-20; Riviere 1930; Yarrell, 1843: ii, 654-657.

Sharp-tailed Sandpiper *Calidris acuminata*
(Northeast Siberia; winters New Guinea and Australasia)
1848 Norfolk, Great Yarmouth.   A (25)

A man named Wilmot shot a lone wader at Great Yarmouth and took it to Thomas Knights, birdstuffer to the Castle Museum, Norwich during September, 1848. It was purchased by J H Gurney who recorded it as an American Pectoral Sandpiper *Calidris melanotos*. Seebohm examined the bird and identified it as an adult.

In 1892, the specimen was re-examined at Castle Museum, Norwich by Thomas Southwell and found to be a "Siberian Pectoral" or Sharp-tailed Sandpiper. It had been re-stuffed by Roberts of Norwich who said it had wounds to the neck and leg consistent with Wilmot's story though suspicions were aroused when Wilmot offered two freshly dead Red-winged Blackbirds *Agelaius phoeniceus* for sale, raising the possibility that he may have connections with visitors to America.

The record was accepted as the first British record and the skin is now on display at Castle Museum, Norwich (Accession no. 25.50).

Remaining a rarity in Europe, Sharp-tailed Sandpiper is unusual in that so few of the reports have involved juveniles. Only four are attributed to this age group.

There are only two Irish records.

References:
Riviere 1930; Allard, 1990; *Zool*, 1849: 2392; *Ibis* 1893, p. 181-185; Cottridge & Vinicombe 1996: 69.

Curlew Sandpiper *Calidris ferrugina*
(Northern Asia and Europe; winters sub saharan Africa, southern Asia to Australia)
1786 Kent, Sandwich. A (P)

Dr William Boys shot Britain's first Curlew Sandpiper at Sandwich Bay, Kent in 1786. The specimen, an immature bird, was figured in his *History of Sandwich*, 1789. The only previous European record was of a bird killed in Holland. It was called "Pygmy Curlew" and placed in the same genus as the Eurasian Curlew *Numenius aequata* on account of it's long de-curved bill.

After news of this discovery spread, Dr Leith thought he had seen the species in the marshes near Greenwich and soon found and shot a specimen. Realising that the species had been over-looked among Dunlin *Calidris alpina* flocks the collectors took their toll of migrating birds.

Mr Lenard at Holyavon, shot a "Pygmy Sandpiper" on 26th August, 1812. He passed it to Mr Weighton whom at the request of Mr Foljambe of Osberton, dispatched it to Montagu for examination. It appeared to be a moulting adult and comparing it to other skins and descriptions concluded that they were plumage variations of the same species now called Curlew Sandpiper. The misconception that waders in breeding plumage were a different species to the same bird in its winter dress was a common mistake at that time. Thus the Dunlin, Sanderling *Calidris alba* and Grey Plover *Pluvialis squatarola* were at one time 'split' into at least six different species!

Curlew Sandpiper can usually be found in good numbers during its autumn passage through Britain.

References:
Montagu, 1862: 48-49: 287-289; Harrison, 1953: 37: 384, Boys figure is reproduced in Harrison.

Broad-billed Sandpiper *Limicola falcinellus*
(North Eurasia; winters Asia and Australia)
1836 Norfolk, Breydon Water. A (202)

The first British record of Broad-billed Sandpiper was shot at Breydon Water,

Norfolk on 25th May, 1836, and recorded by Mr J D Hoy as a "Flat-billed Sandpiper" in breeding plumage. The record was mentioned in J H Gurney and W R Fisher's account of birds found in Norfolk.

When mounted, E M Cannop purchased the specimen and after his death W R Lysaght of Chepstow bought the collection. The Cannop collection is now housed at the Birmingham Museum.

Up to a dozen birds can turn up each year. It remains extremely rare inland.

References:
Zool, 1846: 1375.

Stilt Sandpiper *Micropalama himantopus*

(North America; winters South America)
1954 East Yorkshire, Kilnsea.   A (27)

On 31st August, 1954, Peter Waterton and Edward Jackson, two boys were staying at the Spurn Bird Observatory, East Yorkshire, found a wader on some marshy ground north of Kilnsea that they did not recognise. They saw it again the next day but it wasn't until 2nd September that R F Dickens accompanied them and saw the bird for himself. He alerted a handful of other birdwatchers who saw it the same day and the bird was also present on 4th September when at least a further eight observers managed to connect with it. This was the last time it was seen.

Independent descriptions were sent to Ralph Chislett who worked through the reports to ascertain the wader's identity. There were suggestions that it could have been a tattler *Heteroscelus sp.* or more probably a Stilt Sandpiper as the underwing and breast were barred. Dickens visited the British Museum of Natural History where he examined over 50 Stilt Sandpiper skins. He concluded that the bird was an adult in full breeding plumage but had lost the rufous colour to the cheeks. Chislett was shown a skin of the species and found the descriptions received from the observers matched it in every way.

The record was accepted as the first British occurrence.

Still a very rare bird, the longest staying individual visited various sites in Cheshire for six months in 1984 while there are no other records lasting more than a couple of weeks.

References:
Sharrock, 1982: 45-48.

Buff-breasted Sandpiper *Tryngites subruficollis*
(North America; winters southern South America)
1826 Cambridgeshire, near Melbourne.   A (713+)

Buff-breasted Sandpiper has long been known to be a regular visitor to Britain. The first example to be recorded in Europe was with a trip of Eurasian Dotterel *Charadrius morinellus*, near Melbourne, Cambridgeshire, where it was shot in early September, 1826. After being killed, the bird, an immature specimen, was preserved by Mr Baker of Melbourne. John Sims purchased it on behalf of Yarrell. An illustration of this specimen appeared in Yarrell's *History of British Birds*.

The first Irish record may have preceded the British report, it is not accurately dated but appears in the 1844-45 report of the Dublin Natural History Society. The specimen of this Buff-breasted Sandpiper is now at the National Museum, Dublin, having been shot near the Pigeon House Fort, Dublin.

About 20 birds are reported in Britain each year with the peak being 53 individuals in 1977.

References:
Saunders, 1899: 601; Yarrell, 1843: ii, 634-637; Lack, 1934: 99; Kennedy, 1954: 207-208; Evans 1997: 137-8.

Common (Wilson's) Snipe *Gallinago gallinago delicata*
(North America south to northern South America)

NORTHERN IRELAND
1991 Londonderry, Coleraine.   A (1)

A juvenile Wilson's Snipe shot by a wildfowler, Donald Curry, near Coleraine, Londonderry, Northern Ireland on 28th October, 1991 is the first accepted record. The bird was sent to Michel Devort a French researcher working for the international Snipe-shooters Club (CICB) who had requested the wings and tails of birds shot in various countries. Singling out the Coleraine bird, Devort realised that it was a Wilson's Snipe and informed the BTO. The remains were sent to Guy Mountfort who passed them to the IRBC for confirmation and acceptance. The wings and tail feathers were placed in the Ulster Museum, Belfast while the rest went into a very good 'Snipe soup' according to Curry!

Previous birds, later to be discredited, included a bird shot and exhibited by Colonel Meinertzhagen. He showed the bird, which had been shot on South Uist on 26th October, 1920, to the British Ornithologists' Club, where the identification was accepted at the time, and the subspecies placed on the British List.

An investigation of Meinertzhagen's records by Dr Alan G Knox found that the South Uist snipe was the earliest snipe specimen in his collection. Curiously written at a different time to adjacent entries, it had been placed at the foot of the first snipe page in his log, as if added on to the end of his list. In addition the method of skinning was not consistent with other specimens. All Meinertzhagen's records are now discredited

On 30th September, 1957, Stephen Brady delivered the corpse of a snipe to the Bolton Museum, found near Rumworth Reservoir, near Bolton, Lancashire. In poor condition, having been found on the 27th, the bird was preserved by Alfred Hazelwood who noticed its dark coloration. Following a close examination he contacted Meinertzhagen who confirmed the birds identity as a Wilson's Snipe. The Bolton skin was re-examined in 1993, and found not to belong to the American race at all.

BRITAIN
[**1985 Isles of Scilly,** St Mary's].   * [2]

When a Wilson's Snipe was found in 1998, Ian Lycett saw photographs of the bird and recalled a snipe he had photographed on 31st October, 1985 from a hide at Porthellick, St Mary's. At the time he had been struck by the bird's cold toned appearance and took some record shots, but despite alerting other birdwatchers little interest was shown in the bird.

After comparing photographs of the two birds he sent them to Killian Mullarney in Ireland who confirmed that there was a case for submitting the record. Some fourteen years after his sighting he began compiling a file to present to the BBRC and BOURC.

A decision is still awaited, but if not accepted, the honour of first for Britain will probably go to a bird seen in 1998 at Lower Moors, St Mary's, Isles of Scilly during autumn.

Bryan Bland, Jon Baker, Pete Milford and Andrew Chamberlin first noticed the bird when they searched for Jack Snipe *Lymnocryptes minimus* from the hide on Friday 9th October. The bird appeared much colder toned and more contrastingly black and white. Checking a Wilson's Snipe identification paper brought to Scilly by an optimistic Peter Poole they returned to the hide reasonably confident that they were indeed looking at Britain's first Wilson's Snipe.

On 28th October, Bland joined Peter Colston at the British Museum and confirmed the identification. A large selection of photographs, highlighting many detailed features, removed the need for an in-hand examination which was thought to be a pre-requisite for acceptance.

A full suite of characteristic feather detail had been noted and the BBRC and BOURC began the task of assessing its credentials. No decision had been reached by December 1999.

References:
Scot Nat, 1925: 11; Bull BOC 44: 58; *Birding World* 11: 227, 382-385, photos; 12: 56-61; *Birdwatch* 82: 23; *Ibis* 1993: 324; Paul Milne *in litt.*

Great Snipe *Gallinago media*
(Northeast Europe and Northwest Asia; winters Africa)
Pre-1787 Kent.   A (285)

The first record of Great Snipe, previously known as "Solitary Snipe" is rather vague. First recorded in Kent during the late 1700s, the species has been recorded almost annually since 1822 with over 500 records prior to the formation of the Rarities Committee in 1958.

According to Montagu it was first described by Pennant from a specimen taken in Lancashire and later placed in the Leverian Museum. Although undated this record is stated as preceding two Kent records, which involved two specimens obtained some time prior to 1787. They were mentioned by Latham in his three volume work *The General Synopsis of Birds, supplement I* and the dated reports were backed up by specimen evidence. One of these birds was presented by Latham to the British

Museum and is included in Leach's catalogue of specimens in the British Museum, 1816.

The fourth record, a bird shot near Horsham, Sussex on 1st October, 1793 is the first record presented with any details in addition to a skin. It was illustrated in Marwick's *Aves Sussexienses*.

Numbers occurring in Britain have mirrored a decline in the Great Snipe's European population.

References:
Montagu, 1862: 314-315; Harrison, 1953: 335; Walpole-Bond, 1938: iii, 226-229.

Short-billed Dowitcher *Limnodromus griseus*
(North America; winters southern USA, south to Peru and Brazil)

IRELAND
1985 Co. Wexford, Tacumshin.   A (1)

An hour before dusk on 30th September, 1985, Killian Mullarney noticed a dowitcher feeding among waders and ducks in a channel at the eastern end of Tacumshin Lake, Co. Wexford. At first he assumed it was the Long-billed Dowitcher *Limnodromus scolopaceus* which had been present for about a week, but realised that the upperpart coloration was not typical of a juvenile of that species. As the light was poor and the distance too great he attempted to get closer but the birds all took off and landed even further away; he decided to return the following day.

In the afternoon he found two dowitchers together in the same channel but shrouded in fog. Each time the birds took flight, due to disturbance by a Grey Heron *Ardea cinerea* and low flying swans, he drove closer to the shore to wait for the dowitchers' return. At 25m range he was able to recognise them as juveniles of each species and was able to make notes.

Later that evening the birds were also seen by P A Cummins, J F Dowdall and A Walsh, albeit distantly. The following day about 15 other observers obtained reasonable views before the onset of strong wind and rain.

Although the Long-billed Dowitcher remained until 4th October, the Short-billed was not seen after 2nd October.

There are 315 accepted dowitcher records that can not be assigned to either Long-billed or Short-billed; any one could be the first Short-billed Dowitcher.

BRITAIN
1999 Aberdeenshire, Rosehearty.   * [1]

In 1999, a bird found at Rosehearty, four miles west of Fraserborough, Aberdeenshire was Britain's first Short-billed Dowitcher. The juvenile bird arrived as part of an influx of Nearctic waders into Ireland and Scotland. It was first seen on 11th September, 1999 but was thought to have been a Long-billed as viewing had been distant and difficult.

Following a phone call from a mildly puzzled Paul Baxter, Dave Pullan and James

Smith began the process of positive identification from 11am on 13th September. It fed on the beach before about 30 birders obtained excellent views down to 30 feet as the bird roosted in Rosehearty Harbour. Here the diagnostic tertial pattern could be seen well and the Ruddy Turnstone-like call heard, allowing a confident and positive identification. Next day, about 500 birders perched in the dunes overlooking the beach and small rock pools where the bird fed unconcerned all day.

This individual, recognised by its missing tertial feathers on one side, then appeared at Greatham Creek, Cleveland where it toured the Tees Estuary throughout October, 1999.

At the end of 1999 the Rarities Committees were still looking at the report.

The first of a series of records that once held a place on the British List was a specimen acquired by the British Museum of Natural History in London in 1850. It was purchased by the museum from Mr Baker, taxidermist of Melbourn, Cambridgeshire and labelled "*Cambridgeshire 1843.*" Many of his specimens carrying British labels are of dubious origin and despite being described as a "reliable naturalist" which the best ornithological fraudsters' undoubtedly are, his specimens are now disregarded.

In 1993, a review by the BOURC overturned four remaining accepted records as there was a possibility the documentation was incorrect.

The first was a bird killed at Stonebridge, Middlesex in 1862. The specimen was said by Harting to have been shot in October, but Frank A Pitalka of the University of California who examined the skin in 1961 said it had certainly been shot no later than early September casting doubt on its authenticity.

Two specimens from Hampshire followed; the first being an adult male at Christchurch Harbour in September, 1872 and the second a juvenile female at Stanpit Marsh on 7th October, 1902. Again the evidence supporting these reports was questioned.

The fourth is a controversial record from Cley, Norfolk, still claimed by some, to have been Short-billed. It was found on 5th October, 1957 remaining in the Cley/Salthouse area until 3rd November. R P Bagnall-Oakley, M J Carter and P R Colston made field notes, DIM. Wallace made sketches and a number of photographs were taken. The bird clearly shows the tertial pattern of juvenile Long-billed Dowitcher *Limnodromus scolopaceus* but curiously has spotted undertail coverts more indicative of Short-billed.

References:
Bell, 1967: 38; *British Birds* 54: 340-357, photographs; *Irish Birds* vol. 3, 1985-1988: 596-597, sketch; *Birding World* 12: 364-370; 392, photos; 469. [Evans 1994: 192-193]

Long-billed Dowitcher *Limnodromus scolopaceus*
(North America and Northeast Siberia; winters USA and Central America)
1801 Devon. A (210)

Long-billed Dowitcher first occurred somewhere on the Devonshire coast in early October, 1801. It was a first-winter male and in poor condition, being very light, presumably having just crossed the Atlantic. The bird was apparently very tame allowing its captor to get close before killing it.

At the time it was named by Montagu as "Brown Snipe". Later named

"Red-breasted Snipe", the specimen was placed in the Natural History Museum, Tring where it has since been examined and found to be a Long-billed Dowitcher.

The number of Long-billed Dowitchers discovered in Britain has increased dramatically since 1975.

References:
Montagu, 1862: 313; Moore, 1969: 123.

Hudsonian Godwit *Limosa haemastica*
(North America; winters south to Argentina)
1981 East Yorkshire, Blacktoft Sands.   A (2)

At 7am on 10th September, 1981, RSPB Warden Andrew Grieve checked through the waders outside Xerox hide at Blacktoft Sands RSPB Nature Reserve, Humberside (East Yorkshire). He noticed a group of six sleeping godwits: five Black-tailed Godwit *Limosa limosa* and a smaller bird he thought to be Bar-tailed Godwit *Limosa lapponica* moulting out of breeding plumage.

The birds later took off to fly towards the River Humber and the smaller godwit was seen to have a similar tail and wing pattern to the Black-tailed. Grieve later checked his books and thought the bird was most likely a Hudsonian Godwit, but could not rule out the smaller, Icelandic race of Black-tailed Godwit.

The bird was seen for several days but the underwing pattern was not seen and its white undertail coverts, combined with the lack of white in the face, were at odds with the available descriptions of Hudsonian Godwit. Consequently it was presumed to be an eastern race of Black-tailed Godwit.

Determined to see the underwing pattern, Grieve watched the bird depart on the 27th and saw the diagnostic black axillaries, and was able to claim a Hudsonian Godwit.

On 1st and 2nd October a more detailed description was taken and on the 3rd hundreds of birdwatchers arrived. Unfortunately the bird only landed briefly before flying off never to return.

The godwit was considered to have been a male. It later emerged that Graham Catley (Lincolnshire recorder and BBRC member) had seen it at nearby Alkborough flats on 15th September.

What was presumably the same bird was present at Countess Wear, Exeter, Devon from 22nd November to 14th January, 1982, returning to Blacktoft in April, 1983. [A second was seen in northeast Scotland (1988).

References:
British Birds 80:466-473, sketch, 80: pl. 245-246 photos in Devon; Mitchell 1997.

Little Curlew *Numenius minutus*
(Central and Eastern Siberia, migrates south to Australia)
1982 Mid Glamorgan, Kenfig.   A (2)

At 3.45pm on 30th August, 1982, S J Moon and David E Dicks were walking along a track near Sker Farm, on the southern edge of Kenfig Pool and Dunes Local Nature

Reserve, Mid Glamorgan. Dicks called "Whimbrel" *Numenius phaeopus* as they flushed two birds from the dunes. One flew off while the second bird, which lacked a white rump and lower back, landed. After settling it began to feed.

At 100m the bird resembled an Upland Sandpiper *Bartramia longicauda* but as S J Moon looked through his telescope he was surprised to see that it more closely resembled a Whimbrel. As it had appeared smaller than the first bird they crept closer and Moon took a description while Dicks took photographs. Their first thoughts were that the bird was a Whimbrel *Numenius phaeopus* of the American race *N. p. hudsonicus* but the small size and bill suggested Eskimo Curlew *Numenius borealis*.

The bird was seen in the evening by other observers, but in the poor light the identification was not proven. The following day the bird was watched by J P Martin, D C Palmer, M C and N M Powell when it was identified it as a Little Whimbrel (now Little Curlew) from the available literature.

The Little Curlew was usually found on the dune-turf and adjacent pasture but also visited the golf course and Sker Rocks on the coast. It sometimes joined Northern Lapwings *Vanellus vanellus* and Common Starlings *Sturnus vulgaris* in a stubble field. The bird was last reported on the morning of 6th September having been seen by over a thousand observers.

Britain's only other record was a bird at Salthouse, Norfolk, in 1985.

References:
British Birds 76: 438-445, photos.

Eskimo Curlew *Numenius borealis*
(Northern Canada; winters South America. Possibly Extinct)
1852 Suffolk, near Woodbridge.   B (6)

Six British records exist; two birds shot near Woodbridge, Suffolk in November, 1852 were the first authenticated British records. At least one of the Woodbridge birds was seen and examined by J H Gurney (junior).

The first Scottish record was a bird shot by Mr R Cusack Smith at Durris, near Aberdeen on 6th September, 1855. It was preserved by Mr Mitchell of Aberdeen and identified by Mr J Longmuir who sent word of the event to Yarrell.

The only Irish record involved a bird from Sligo, purchased in a Dublin Market on 21st October, 1870.

Eskimo Curlew has had a tragic history being a common migrant easily shot due to its tameness. By 1895 the flocks had ceased to be seen and the species was presumed extinct in 1926. However one was reliably seen at Galveston, Texas in 1962, and there are hopes that it still survives.

The last report of the species in Britain was an adult in breeding plumage shot by Capt Dorrien-Smith on Tresco, Isles of Scilly, on 10th September, 1887.

References:
Ticehurst, 1932, p 378-379; Baxter & Rintoul: 542; Saunders, 1899: 631; Penhallurick, 1969: 125; Gray 1871: 290.

Premier Birding Sites in Britain and Ireland

St Mary's, Isles of Scilly. *P Palmer*

Spurn Point, East Yorkshire. *P Palmer*

Fair Isle, Shetland. *P Palmer*

Dungeness, Kent. *P Palmer*

Cley-next-the-Sea, Norfolk. *P Palmer*

Cape Clear, Co. Cork, Ireland. *R T Mills*

The Systematic List

Capped Petrel, Castle Museum, Norwich.

Yellow-billed Diver, Hancock Museum, Newcastle.

Bulwer's Petrel, (first and second record). York Museum.

Little Shearwater, Castle Museum, Norwich.

Swinhoe's Storm-petrel, Tynemouth.
M Cubitt

Swinhoe's Storm-petrel capture site, Tynemouth.

▲ White-faced Storm-petrel, National Museums of Scotland.

Double-crested Cormorant, Billingham, Cleveland.

A Tate

Magnificent Frigatebird, ▶
National Museums of Scotland.

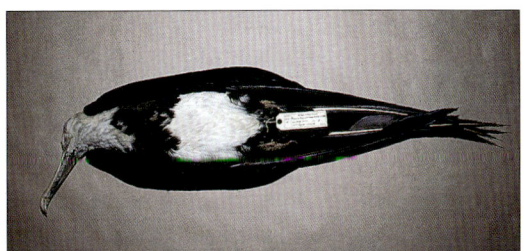

▼ Tundra (Whistling) Swan,
Curry Moor, Somerset.   *P Palmer*

Tundra (Bewick's) Swan, Hancock Museum.

Red-breasted Goose, Hancock Museum.

Blue-winged Teal, National Museums of Scotland.

The Canvasback twitch, Wissington Beet Factory Norfolk. *P Palmer*

Canvasback, Welney, Norfolk. *I Leach*

Redhead, Bleasby, Nottinghamshire. *I Leach*

Ring-necked Duck, *first Irish record*, Co. Armagh, Northern Ireland. *T Ennis*

Lesser Scaup, Chasewater, Staffordshire. *D Cottridge*

Steller's Eider, Castle Museum, Norwich.

Harlequin Duck, Mansfield Museum.

Pallid Harrier, National Museums of Scotland.

Bald Eagle, Ballymacelligot, Co. Kerry, Ireland.

R T Mills

Bald Eagle, killed, Garrison, Fermanagh, Northern Ireland.
A McGeehan

Black Kite, Hancock Museum, Newcastle.

Red-footed Falcon, Osberton Hall, Nottinghamshire.

Lesser Kestrel, York Museum.

American Coot, *first British record*, Stodmarsh, Kent. *A Tate*

American Coot, Ballycotton, Co. Cork, Ireland. *R T Mills*

Houbara Bustard, York Museum.

Oriental Pratincole, Dunwich, Suffolk. *J Belsey*

Oriental Pratincole, Dunwich, Suffolk. *T Loseby*

Semipalmated Plover, St Agnes, Isles of Scilly. *P Goriup*

White-tailed Plover, Packington Gravel Pits, Warwickshire. *P Clement*

Lesser Sand Plover, Pagham Harbour, West Sussex.   *I Leach*

Greater Sand Plover, Pagham Harbour, West Sussex.   *C Janman*

Great Knot, Scatness, Shetland.   *D Coutts*   **Caspian Plover**, Castle Museum, Norwich.

Semipalmated Sandpiper, Cley-next-the-Sea, Norfolk. *R P Bagnall-Oakley*

Greater Yellowlegs, Isles of Scilly Museum.

Sharp-tailed Sandpiper, Castle Museum, Norwich.

Red-necked Stint, Blacktoft RSPB, Yorkshire. *D Cottridge*

Baird's Sandpiper, National Museums of Scotland.

Long-toed Stint, Marazion, Cornwall. *J Johns*

Little Curlew, Kenfig, Mid Glamorgan. *R Smith*

Wilson's Phalarope, Rosyth, Fife. *SOC*

Pallas's Gull, Royal Albert Museum, Exeter.

Hudsonian Godwit, Exeter, Devon. *T Croucher*

▲ **Franklin's Gull**, Farlington Marshes, ▼
Hampshire. *J B Bottomley*

▲ **Elegant Tern**, Carlingford Lough, Co. Down,
▲ Ireland. *T Ennis*

Ross's Gull, Leeds Museum.

Aleutian Tern, Farne Islands, Northumberland.   *A R Taylor*

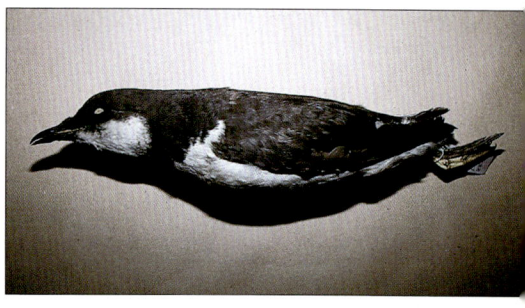

Brünnich's Guillemot, National Museums of Scotland.

Forster's Tern, Falmouth, Cornwall.   *J Johns*

Pallas's Sandgrouse, Chester Museum.

Ancient Murrelet, at sea near Lundy, Devon.   *D Atkinson*

Mourning Dove, Calf of Man.   *I Fisher*

Great-spotted Cuckoo, *first British record*, ▶ Hancock Museum, Newcastle.

Red-necked Nightjar, Hancock Museum, Newcastle.

Egyptian Nightjar memorial stone, Thieves Wood, Nottinghamshire.   *P Palmer*

Black-billed Cuckoo (left), *first British record* – Isles of Scilly Museum.

Common Nighthawk, Isles of Scilly Museum.

Egyptian Nightjar, Mansfield Museum.

Blue-cheeked Bee-Eater, Isles of Scilly Museum.

Pallid Swift, *first British record*, Stodmarsh, Kent.

J Pick

Chimney Swift, Porthgwarra, Cornwall. *T Loseby*

Pacific Swift, *first mainland record*, Cley-next-the-sea, Norfolk.

S Young

Yellow-bellied Sapsucker, Tresco, Isles of Scilly.

D Hunt

White-winged Lark, Booth Museum, Brighton.

▲ **Pacific Swift**, at sea, *photographed at Beccles,*
▲ *Suffolk.*

C Waller

Cliff Swallow, St Mary's, Isles of Scilly. *R Chittenden*

▲ **Tree Swallow**, St Mary's,
▲ Isles of Scilly. *A Tate*

Red-rumped Swallow, National Museums of Scotland.

Olive-backed Pipit, *first bird to be identified in Britain*, Fair Isle, Shetland, *R Dennis*

Pechora Pipit, National Museums of Scotland.

Horned Lark, Castle Museum, Norwich.

Buff-bellied Pipit, National Museums of Scotland.

Grey-headed Wagtail, Castle Museum, Norwich.

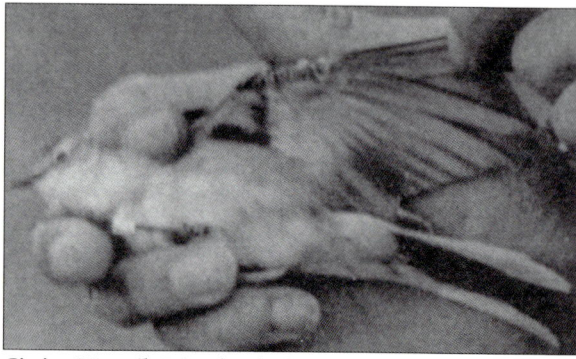
Citrine Wagtail, Fair Isle, Shetland. *G Mountford*

Cedar Waxwing, Noss, Shetland. *C McKay*

Cedar Waxwing, Noss, Shetland. *C McKay*

Brown Thrasher, Durlston Head, Dorset. *D Godfrey*

Grey Catbird, Jersey, Channel Islands. *R Long*

Siberian Rubythroat, Fair Isle, Shetland. *R A Broad*

Siberian Blue Robin, Sark, Channel Islands. *M Marsden*

Siberian Rubythroat, Fair Isle, Shetland. *S Cook*

Thrush Nightingale, National Museums of Scotland.

White-throated Robin, *first British record*, Skokholm, Pembrokeshire. *M Potts*

Pied Wheatear, National Museums of Scotland.

'Siberian' Stonechat, National Museums of Scotland.

Bluethroat, Hancock Museum, Newcastle.

Moussier's Redstart, Strumble Head. *M Barrett*

White-tailed Wheatear, Kessingland, Suffolk. *J Hewitt*

Desert Wheatear, National Museums of Scotland (first record of race *O d deserti*).

(Hudsonian) Whimbrel *Numenius phaeopus hudsonicus*
(North America; winters northern South America)
1955 Shetland, Fair Isle. **A (4)**
On 27th May, 1955 Kenneth Williamson, Valerie Thom and visitors to the Bird Observatory Fair Isle, Shetland, disturbed a flock of six Whimbrel *N. p. phaeopus* from an area of short-cropped turf. Thom noticed that one lacked the white rump.

Using dry-stone walls and dykes for cover they made observations of the bird for two days, convinced that the bird was an example of the American race of Whimbrel *N. p. hudsonicus.* The Whimbrel left the island on 29th May but the Hudsonian Whimbrel remained until 31st May when it became less approachable.

There are four records in Britain and Ireland: a second from Shetland and two Irish reports.

References:
British Birds 48: 379-381; Dymond, 1991: 46; Evans 1994: 200.

Upland Sandpiper *Bartramia longicauda*
(North America; winters south to Argentina)
1851 Warwickshire, near Warwick. **A (49)**
Hugh Reid, the Doncaster taxidermist, sent a description of an unknown wading bird to Yarrell in November, 1851. He had received the bird for preservation on 31st October from Mr RT Barnard of Kirton Hall, near Warwick and had been surprised when the man who shot it nearby recalled that he had found it *"so far inland sitting on a bean-stubble, and in a place where to which there is no water".* In February, 1854, Mr A G More visited Reid and, drawing his attention to *American Ornithology,* Reid immediately recognised the bird as a Bartram's (now Upland) Sandpiper. The specimen was placed in the collection of Lord Willoughby de Broke and is now at the City of Worcester Museum.

Most of the British records come from Cornwall, Isles of Scilly and South Wales with a much smaller number in Shetland.

References:
Montagu, 1862: 280; *Zool*, 1852: 3330: 1854: 4254.

Marsh Sandpiper *Tringa stagnatilis*
(Southeast Europe, West and East Asia; winters Africa, southern Asia and Australia)
1937 East Sussex, The Midrips, near Camber. **A (101)**
On 26th September, 1937, N F Ticehurst and Averil Morley were birdwatching at the Midrips and the Wicks, on the boundary of Kent and Sussex, just west of Dungeness. They checked a small pool and noticed two grey waders asleep about 30 yards away which they assumed to be Common Greenshank *Tringa nebularia*. While approaching closer the birds woke up and moved. Deciding the birds were too slender for Greenshank, Ticehurst and Morley dismissed the possibility of Green *Tringa ochropus* and Wood Sandpipers *Tringa glareola*. After viewing them for several minutes the two birds took off allowing the white back and dark wings to be seen,

eliminating the two 'yellowlegs' *Tringa melanoleuca/flavipes* and Redshank *Tringa totanus* as possibilities. Heading inland, the birds called, clinching the identity of Britain's first Marsh Sandpipers.

Walter Rothschild claimed a bird shot in October, 1887, near Tring Reservoirs, Hertfordshire was a Marsh Sandpiper but did not show it to any other authorities. It was later burned. There was a possibility of confusion with other species and the record was not officially recognised.

A run of records from Sussex and Kent were removed from the British List in 1962, as part of the Hastings rarities affair.

Marsh Sandpiper now appears on an almost annual basis.

References:
British Birds 31: 197-8; Shrubb, 1979: 152; Taylor, 1981; Naylor 1998: 172-3. [Saunders, 1899: 620]

Greater Yellowlegs *Tringa melanoleuca*
(North America; winters USA south to southern South America)
1906 Isles of Scilly, Tresco. A (35)

The first record of this species in Europe came from Tresco, Isles of Scilly, where Captain Arthur Dorrien-Smith shot one near the Abbey on 16th September, 1906. Mr A F Griffith exhibited the specimen at a meeting of the British Ornithologists' Club and he read out a letter from Dorrien-Smith describing the circumstances in which it was obtained.

References:
Penhallurick, 1969: 132; British Birds 1: 16; 14: 7.

Lesser Yellowlegs *Tringa flavipes*
(North America: winters southern USA, Central and southern South America)
1854/5 Nottinghamshire, Misson. A (275)

A bird shot by an un-named wildfowler at Misson, Nottinghamshire, in winter 1854/5 was sent to Hugh Reid a birdstuffer in Doncaster. Reid was an important natural history dealer whose records were included in various publications including *Ibis*. After mounting the bird he sold it to Sir William Milner of Nunappleton who exhibited it in London during spring 1855 before placing it in his collection.

As the only record at the time, Montagu said the bird had no place on the British List, but it was accepted and figured by both Yarrell and Saunders. The skin was placed in the Leeds Museum, where it still remains as a cabinet skin (accession No LEEDM.C.1962.1205).

Lesser Yellowlegs is a regular vagrant to Britain.

References:
Whitaker, 1907: 276. [Montagu, 1862: 296]

Solitary Sandpiper *Tringa solitaria*
(Northern America; winters Central and South America)
Pre-1870 Strathclyde, River Clyde, Lanarkshire. A (29)

A Solitary Sandpiper shot on the banks of the Clyde on the higher grounds of Lanarkshire was Britain's first record. It was killed some time prior to 1870 when it was passed to Robert Gray and was recorded by him in *Ibis*. The next two records were, from Cornwall, which together with the Isles of Scilly hold about half of the British records.

The peak arrival date for this rare Nearctic wader is September.

References:
Ibis 1870: 292; Baxter & Rintoul, 1953: 577.

Terek Sandpiper *Xenus cinereus*
(Northeast Europe and Siberia; winters Africa South Asia and Australia)
1951 East Sussex, The Midrips, near Camber. A (53)

A bird similar to a Common Sandpiper *Actitis hypoleucos* was watched by A H Betts hidden behind a low bank, while it fed below a foot-high mud bank at the Midrips, near Camber, East Sussex, on 30th May, 1951. The bird washed food items covered in mud before swallowing them. After excellent views down to 25 yards, he noted its most striking features, which were a long upturned bill and bright yellow legs. Leaving after 15 minutes he compared notes with *The Handbook of British Birds* and later skins at the British Museum confirming the identity of the first British Terek Sandpiper.

The second record occurred only three days later, in Suffolk, and was thought possibly to be the same individual.

There are three previous records, two Hastings rarities' and a bird at Christchurch Harbour, Dorset 16th May, 1925. All are unacceptable.

References:
Sharrock, 1982: 22-23.

Spotted Sandpiper *Actitis macularia*
(North America; winters USA south to Uraguay)
1849 North Yorkshire, Whitby. A (123)

This first accepted record was a tame bird shot while in the company of Dunlin *Calidris alpina*, by a sailor on the beach just north of the pier at Whitby, on 29th March, 1849. It was received the following day by Mr Graham, birdstuffer of York, who mounted it for Sir William Milner's collection and claimed that it was a female. E T Higgins of York, who saw the bird in the flesh, claimed that the sex could not be determined. The record was doubted by J H Gurney.

The second record concerned a female shot while feeding in a damp meadow near the river at Finea, Co. Longford, Ireland, by Frank Roberts on 2nd February, 1899.

The earliest records refers to a bird said by Edwards (1757) to have been shot in Essex and later described by him. The details are not sufficient to accept this record.

Other unaccepted reports included a bird killed in February or March, 1848. John Eyre, head keeper on the Earl of Manvers estate, shot a Spotted Sandpiper on the banks of the River Meden at Budby, Nottinghamshire. It was given to Mr H Wells of Edwinstowe, who identified and mounted the bird. Hugh Reid, taxidermist of Doncaster, purchased it, later selling it to Sir William Milner for his collection at Nunappleton.

In an attempt to trace the specimen Gurney wrote to Joseph Whitaker, who could vouch for the gentlemen involved but failed to trace the specimen.

Gurney had in his collection a specimen given to him by George Johnson which had been shot with a flock of five or six Common Sandpipers *Actitis hypoleucos* between Runton and Sheringham, Norfolk, about 26th September, 1839. Yarrell was the only person to accept this as the first British record; even Gurney doubted the species position on the British List, as unscrupulous dealers were at that time importing many skins.

On 2nd March, 1848, at Bridlington, Yorkshire, Mr Higgins claimed to have seen a Spotted Sandpiper on the beach. It was tame and allowed him to approach to within 15 yards.

Spotted Sandpiper is now an annual vagrant to Britain and Ireland with four or five reports annually.

References:
Sterland & Whitaker, 1879: 44; Whitaker 1907: 272; Saunders, 1899: 605; Yarrell, 1843, ii: 544-548; Nelson, 1907: 628; Harting, 1912: 180; Mather, 1985: 310; [Saunders, 1899: 606; BOU, 1971; Montagu, 1862: 293]

Grey-tailed Tattler *Heteroscelus brevipes*
(Northeast Siberia; winters Southeast Asia to Australasia)
1981 Ceredigion/Merionethshire, Dyfi Estuary.   A (2)

Reg Thorpe, a voluntary warden and 14-year-old Jeff Stenning, were at the Saltings Hide at the Ynis-hir RSPB Reserve on the Dyfi Estuary, (Gwynedd/Dyfed) Ceredigion/Merionethshire, on 13th October, 1981, when Thorpe picked out a smaller grey wader flying with two Common Redshanks *Tringa totanus*. Being unsure of the smaller birds' identity he later returned to the Saltings Hide where he obtained views at a range of 200m and raised the possibility that it was a tattler.

When he checked literature that evening he became convinced that it was a Grey-tailed Tattler, but to confirm his sighting he and R Q Skeen returned to the bird the following day.

The reserve warden suppressed the news as a delicate relationship existed between the RSPB and the tenant farmer, and there was the possibility of disturbing the wintering wildfowl. The tattler was watched daily on the high tide until chased by a Peregrine Falcon *Falco peregrinus* on 23rd October when it became more elusive, appearing only on the highest tides. The tattler was last seen on 17th November, 1981.

On 27th November, 1994, Jeff Stenning was leading a Scottish Ornithologists' Club field trip at Burghead, Moray and Nairn, when he identified a bird found by Kitty Macduff-Duncan and Isobel Grant as Britain's second Grey-tailed Tattler.

In February 1950, Mr W Robinson saw two tattlers at Back-sand Point near Sandwich, Kent and took a description which was confirmed by a friend. The record was not accepted. Harrison thought the birds were probably Wandering Tattlers *Heteroscelus incanus* and said identification of the two "races" (now separate species) in the field was not possible.

Two accepted Hastings records were later removed from the British List.

References:
Harrison, 1953: 368; *Birding World:* 7, 469-472; Walpole-Bond, 1938: iii, 206; *British Birds* 88: 255-262.

Wilson's Phalarope *Phalaropus tricolor*
(North America; winters South America)
1954 Fife, Rosyth.   A (275)

During the afternoon of 11th September, 1954, Frank Hamilton and Keith Macgregor were watching waders on two shallow pools, between Rosyth Dockyards and North Queensferry, Fife. A pale bird resembling a winter-plumaged phalarope was seen feeding with a group of Ruff *Philomachus pugnax*. The bird had yellow legs, no wing bar and a white rump and tail, features which were wrong for the two phalarope species encountered more frequently in Britain and Ireland. Realising that they had discovered something unusual the birdwatchers took a detailed description.

The bird remained until 5th October allowing at least a further 60 observers to visit. Using Peterson's American field guide D G Andrew named the mystery wader as a first-winter Wilson's Phalarope.

A summer-plumaged female Wilson's Phalarope, now in Mansfield Museum, Nottinghamshire, was claimed by the collector Mr J Whitaker, to have been shot at Sutton Ambion, Leicestershire, in 1886. The record was discredited by Montagu Browne in his *Vertabrate Animals of Leicestershire and Rutland* (1889) who stated:

> "*as I saw it before he* (Whitaker) *knew of its existence, I should not have failed to secure it for the Leicester Museum if I had the smallest grain of faith in its being obtained locally. I may say that being behind the scenes in this matter, I can emphatically state that the Wilson's Phalarope was not obtained in the county nor in Britain.*"

A bird sold at the auction of Sir Vauncy Harpur Crewe's collection in 1925, was said to have been collected at Scalloway, Shetland, on 10th June, 1911. However many of his specimens were of dubious origin and it was disregarded without acceptance.

A regular vagrant to Britain with three or four birds found each year.

References:
Calke Abbey auction catalogue; Saunders, 1899: 568; Sharrock, 1982: 49-50; Walpole-Bond, 1938: iii, 213 *British Birds* 48: 15-17; 190-191.

Red-necked Phalarope *Phalaropus lobatus*
(North America and North Palearctic; winters at sea off western South America, Arabian Sea and East Indies)
Pre-1676 Yorkshire, Brignall.   A (P & RB)

Ralph Johnson of Brignall, near Greta Bridge, Yorkshire, gave the first report of a Red-necked Phalarope in Britain. A description of this specimen by Willughby had appeared as early as 1676, entitled *"Mr Johnson's small cloven footed Gull"*. Willughby examined the mounted bird and at first thought it was a member of the coot *Fulica* family, on account of its lobed feet. After hearing an account of its feeding actions and call, he changed his opinion to place it amongst the gull *Larus* family.

This Red-necked Phalarope record was also known to Pennant, who wrote:

"*Mr Ray saw this species at Brignal in Yorkshire and one on the banks of a fresh water pool on the Isle of Stronsa, May, 1769.*"

Red-necked Phalarope is a scarce but regular passage migrant with a small breeding population primarily in Shetland.

References:
Nelson, 1907: 593-595; Gurney 1921: 229; Willughby 1676: 355; Pennant 1761-76: vol. II: 491-3.

Grey Phalarope   *Phalaropus fulicarius*
(North Holarctic; winters at sea off coasts of Africa and Chile)
1757 Yorkshire, Warley Clough.   A (P)

Only two records were known to Pennant, the first British record being described by George Edwards, who figured a winter-plumaged bird at Warley Clough, near Halifax, Yorkshire, killed by Thomas Bolton, a florist, in January, 1757.

At this time, the difference between the summer and winter plumage of several species of wading birds was not fully understood and early ornithologists regarded them as two different species. This was not so for Grey Phalarope, as Edwards also illustrated a bird in its red breeding dress in the same publication. His specimen had been collected in Hudson Bay.

Grey Phalarope is found on passage in varying numbers. Most are recorded along the coast but storms can drive large numbers inland.

References:
Yarrell, 1843. iii, 43-47; Nelson, 1907: 591-593 inc figure; figured in Mather 1986; Pennant vol. II: 491-3; Figured in Edwards 1757.

Pomarine Skua   *Stercorarius pomarinus*
(North Holarctic; winters chiefly in Atlantic Ocean north of Equator)
Pre-1819 East Sussex, Brighton and **Kent,** Dover.   A (P)

The first record of British Pomarine Skuas came to light after the sale of specimens from Mr Bullock's museum in April, 1819. In the catalogue of the auction it mentioned: page 32, lot 61, "*An undescribed Gull, much allied to the Arctic, but greatly superior in size, killed at Brighton*". lot 62, "*A second example of the same species, killed at Dover.*"

It is unclear which was the first record. Although the date and locality are not known, there would appear to have been no attempt of fraud.

As the differences between Pomarine and Arctic Skua *Stercorarius parasiticus* became known many specimens were later taken.

Regularly sighted on passage at coastal sites where up to 10,000 can be reported in a year: Pomarine Skua remains very rare inland.

References:
Montagu, 1862: 311; Yarrell, 1843: iii, 485-488; Walpole-Bond, 1938: iii, 298-300.

Pallas's Gull *Larus ichthyaetus*
(Southern Russia, west and central Asia; winters Persian Gulf, Arabian Sea and Bay of Bengal)
1859 Devon, Exmouth.   **B (1)**

William Pine and W Taylor of Bridgwater were fishing for bass from a small boat in the River Exe, off Exmouth, Devon, some time in late May or early June, 1859. A large gull amongst "ordinary gulls" attracted Pine's attention. Having his gun in the boat he shot it.

Taylor took the corpse to Mr F Ross of Topsham, Devon, who failed to put a name to the bird.

In October, 1859, he showed the specimen to W S D'Urban who had just returned from Canada and the Rev MA Mathew, later to become joint authors of *The Birds of Devon*. Still no positive identification was forthcoming so the skin was taken to Mr G R Gray on 1st November, at the British Museum. It was immediately recognised as an adult Great Black-headed Gull (Pallas's Gull) and was left with Gray for exhibition.

It was later presented to the Royal Albert Memorial Museum in Exeter, where it remains.

This is the only record where a specimen was collected and, following a review of records in 1993, all later claims of this species were removed from the British List. The first captive bird to reach Britain was brought to London in 1891.

References:
British Birds 86: 201-205, photo; Saunders 1899; D'Urban: 381-382.

Mediterranean Gull *Larus melanocephalus*
(Central and southern Europe, and Western Asia)
1866 Greater London, Barking-on-Thames.   **A (RB)**

Saunders identified the first British Mediterranean Gull in the British Museum in 1871. It was an immature bird said to have been shot in January, 1866, near Barking Creek on the Thames but because information regarding this specimen was lacking it was not widely recognised at the time. It is currently accepted as the first.

On Boxing Day, 1886, Charles Harwood went shooting on Breydon Water, Norfolk, and found the second Mediterranean Gull by accident. Unable to remove, a damp cartridge that had jammed from his gun, he fired at a gull just as he docked the boat 100 yards from the Bowling Green. On picking up his prize he thought it looked different, but Johnny Thomas dismissed it as a Common Gull *Larus canus*. Mr Quinton recognised it as a great rarity and sent for George "Hoppy" Smith, a well-known bird dealer in the area, an hour after it had been shot. On seeing the white wing tips Smith realised it was a rarity, so, hiding his excitement, bought it for five shillings.

He failed to find a description in Yarrell's *British Birds* so allowed it to be examined in the flesh by J H Gurney, Thomas Southwell and Major Feilden, who identified it as a Mediterranean Gull. Saunders exhibited it at a meeting of the Zoological Society.

Smith had a glass lidded box lined with cotton wool made for the Mediterranean Gull's skin and at each offer for the bird Smith increased the price; the highest being £300, from Lord Lilford. Eventually the collectors tired of him and it was sold for a much lower price of only two figures, to Robert Chase of Birmingham. The inflated price angered the original shooter of the bird and few gunners dealt with him afterwards.

When his collection was sold at his death many people boycotted the sale but the Norwich Museum benefited from this by gaining cheap exhibits. The bird is now held in the City of Birmingham Museum.

Mediterranean Gull is now a regular breeding bird.

References:
Zool 1887: p 69; Patterson, 1929: 177-179; Patterson, 1905: 251: *Birdwatch* 69: 16; Allard 1990: 77.

Laughing Gull *Larus atricilla*
(North America and Caribbean; winters USA to South America)
1923 East Sussex, Eastbourne.   **A (96)**

On 2nd July, 1923 Robert Morris had noted an unusual 'black-headed gull' at the side of a pool on the Crumbles, an expanse of shingle near Eastbourne, Sussex. He saw the bird again that evening and also on 3rd, 5th, 6th, 7th and 9th July. During this time he recorded a perfect description of an adult breeding plumaged Laughing Gull and made several watercolour sketches.

Morris, a loner, may have 'suppressed' news of his find to prevent it becoming a museum specimen. He sent a brief description of the bird to H F Witherby who wrote back:

"*There is no Gull exactly as you describe, that is to say, with a black head and entirely black primaries and deep blue-grey mantle*".

The description Morris sent to Witherby had lacked the details contained in his original notes and the report was dismissed.

After Morris's death his notes were given to R Gilbert who read the account and resubmitted it to the BOURC. The lack of white primary tips in the description was worrying but H G Alexander examined some adult birds in America during 1964 and found this feature variable with several birds also lacking white in these feathers. The report was accepted in 1968 as the first Laughing Gull to be recorded in Britain.

On 11th May 1966, W F A Buck and D W Taylor found an adult Laughing Gull in full breeding dress among Black-headed Gulls *Larus ridibundus* at Lade Pits, near Dungeness, Kent. The bird was in view for five minutes before flying off never to be seen again. At the time this was accepted as the first British record.

A flock of five "Laughing Gulls", including two with black heads, were seen feeding in a pool, among the shingle at Whinchelsea, by Montagu in August, 1774. One, an immature bird, was shot. The specimen was reportedly placed in the British Museum and was said to have compared favourably with American specimens. Unfortunately when examined later, the skin was found to have been that of an adult and not the immature supposedly obtained at Whinchelsea.

During a recent visit to the Natural History Museum at Tring I examined part of Montagu's collection and found two Black-headed Gull skins labelled by Montagu as Laughing Gulls.

British records have been at widely scattered localities.

References:
Yarrell, 1843: iii, 439-444; Walpole-Bond, 1938: iii, 267; Sharrock 1982: 138; *British Birds* 61: 213-214; 415-416.

Franklin's Gull *Larus pipixcan*
(North America; winters in South America)
1970 Hampshire, Farlington Marshes.　　　　　　　　　　A (37)
The first Franklin's Gull to be seen in the Western Palearctic was found at 4.40pm on 21st February, 1970.

As a small dark-winged gull approached 15-year-old David Cleal and Bob Perryman at the southern tip of Farlington Marshes, Hampshire, they soon realised that it was unusual. As it got closer Warden David Billet and friend John Smith also saw the bird and questioned its identity. They could see that it had an almost complete black hood and was presumably moulting into second-summer plumage. Billet and Smith later checked the identification against published material and were certain the bird was a Franklin's Gull.

The bird was eventually re-found on 1st March, settling down to a regular pattern of visiting a marsh lagoon prior to feeding on a nearby playing field and adjacent fields. It remained until 16th May, during which time it was visited by hundreds of birdwatchers and suffered damage to its upper mandible. Remarkably a second individual (with undamaged bill) was found at Arlington Reservoir, East Sussex, 55 miles to the east on 4th July the same year.

The upsurge of British records, which included six in 1991, is at odds with the species decline in its natural range.

References:
Sharrock 1982: 166-169, photo; *Birdwatch* November, 1997 65: 17; Cottridge & Vinicombe 1996: 81-2.

Little Gull *Larus minutus*
(Western Europe to Western Siberia also North America; wintering areas poorly known)
Pre-1813 Greater London, Chelsea.　　　　　　　　　　A (P)

An immature Little Gull shot on the Thames near Chelsea by Mr Plasted some time before 1813, was the first British record. It was first described by Montagu as a British bird and remained in Plasted's collection before passing into the hands of Mr Leadbeater. The species was presumed to be rare this far south prior to 1820.

Little Gull is regularly encountered on passage often in large numbers.

References:
Montagu, 1862: 163; Glegg: 166; Saunders, 1899: 663; Yarrell, 1843: iii, 426-429.

Sabine's Gull *Larus sabini*
(Arctic regions; winters Pacific coast of South America and South Atlantic off southern Africa)

NORTHERN IRELAND
1822 Antrim, Belfast Bay.　　　　　　A (P)

The first record of Sabine's Gull was an immature bird, shot on Belfast Lough, on 15th September, 1822. It was quickly followed by a second on the 18th and recorded by William Thompson after the first specimen was presented to the Natural History Society of Belfast, for the museum in 1833. This was four years after the species' discovery in Greenland by Sir Edward Sabine in 1818, and the first time that first-winter plumage had been seen.

BRITAIN
1839 Pembrokeshire, Milford Haven.

The first British record is a bird obtained at Milford Haven, Pembrokeshire in autumn 1839, the earliest record known to both Montagu and Yarrell.

Sabine's Gulls are seen in autumn from coastal headlands.

References:
Saunders, 1899: 658; Montagu, 1862: 164; Yarrell, 1843: iii, 421-425; Moss 1995: 91-2.

Bonaparte's Gull *Larus philadelphia*
(North America; winters USA to Mexico)

NORTHERN IRELAND
1848 Co. Antrim, River Lagan, Belfast.   A (116)

William Thompson was given a small gull that had been shot on the River Lagan, Belfast, Northern Ireland, on 1st February, 1848. He identified it as a Bonaparte's Gull, an almost mature male in winter plumage, before it was skinned. This was the first to reach Britain and Ireland and is now at the Belfast Museum.

BRITAIN
1850 Strathclyde, Loch Lomond.

Sir George Leith-Buchanan shot an adult Bonaparte's Gull at the end of April 1850 on Loch Lomond, Dunbartonshire (Strathclyde). It was exhibited in 1884, at the Zoological Society of London.

There is a strong March/April peak for vagrants in Britain.

References:
Zool, 1848: 2069; Kennedy, 1954: 242; Saunders, 1899: 661; Baxter & Rintoul: 634.

Slender-billed Gull *Larus genei*
(Northwest Africa, Southern Europe, Southwest Asia)
1960 Kent, Langney Point.   A (7)

The first record of a Slender-billed Gull came from Kent when D D Harber briefly saw an immature Black-headed-type Gull *Larus ridibundus* with a long bill at the sewage outfall, off Langney Point, on 19th June, 1960.

On 22nd June he saw the bird there again with R H Charlwood where they watched it at close range for the whole afternoon. The bird fed with Black-headed Gulls *Larus ridibundus* and the possibility of it being a Slender-billed Gull was raised. In correspondence with P A D Hollom they discussed gull identification. They saw the bird again on 6th and 10th July.

Harber visited the British Museum of Natural History in London to examine the skin collection and then entered into discussions with H P Medhurst who was familiar with the species.

The bird was subsequently identified as a first-summer Slender-billed Gull and accepted onto the British List.

Earlier unacceptable reports included an immature female at St Leonards, East Sussex, on 26th January, 1914, quickly followed by a male at nearby Bexhill, on 24th. Both specimens formed part of the Harpur Crewe collection and were later placed in the Church St Museum, Brighton. Mr A F Griffith the curator of the museum, thought that the accompanying data was too weak to allow the species a place on the British List and the records were found unacceptable.

References:
Sharrock, 1982: 105-107; Walpole-Bond, 1938: iii, 292.

Ring-billed Gull *Larus delawarensis*
(North America; winters southern USA to Mexico and West Indies)
1973 West Glamorgan, Blackpill.   A (614+)

While scanning gulls on Blackpill Beach, Swansea, West Glamorgan, at 1pm on 14th March, 1973, Rob Hume pulled out a paler bird. As he attempted to get a better view the birds took flight. Crows *Corvidae* and a Peregrine Falcon *Falco peregrinus* foiled his second attempt to get close. Eventually he watched the bird for an hour, joined by M Davies, noting the bird's relevant features and was sure that he was looking at a Ring-billed Gull.

After checking some books, they returned with Peter Lansdown and D R Waugh and found the gull, but by now the light was poor. The bird was not seen the following day but, on 16th Hume accompanied by D J Fisher found it again and in excellent light confirmed the identification.

The bird remained until at least 31st March and the BBRC received seven independent sets of sketches and notes. The bird was accepted onto Category A of the British List. A first-year bird was found at the same site less than three months later. Rob Hume and Peter Lansdown have been chairman of the BBRC

Ring-billed Gull is now found annually in good numbers.

References:
Sharrock 1982: 184-190.

Mew Gull *Larus canus heinei*
(From Moscow eastwards breeding Northern Siberia)
1984 Essex.   A (3)

There are only three accepted British records of the Russian race of Mew Gull *Larus canus heinei*: Essex, 18th February, 1984, West Sussex, 21st January, 1987 and Kent, 31st January, 1987. All trapped and identified from the biometrics sent to the British Trust for Ornithology's ringing office, the wing-length proving crucial. While accepting the records, the BOURC recommended that more work should be undertaken into the races of Mew Gulls.

References:
British Birds 87: 243; M. Rogers: *pers comm.*

Lesser Black-backed Gull *Larus fuscus graellsii*
(Breeds Iceland, British Isles, France and northwest Spain)
Mid 1700s Anglesey. A (SB)

The first Lesser Black-backed Gull to be recorded in Britain was shot from a breeding colony by Pennant in Anglesey in the middle of the 18th Century. Despite its small size he presumed it to be a Great Black-backed Gull *Larus marinus*. With a multitude of age related plumage stages large gull identification suffered from much confusion. As well as being linked to both Herring *Larus argentatus* and Great Black-backed Gulls the juvenile 'Lesser' was named by one author as a separate species: the "Wagel."

Both Pennant and Latham later claimed that the 'Wagel' was the young of the two previously mentioned species but still linked the adult 'black-backed' gulls together, while Lewin proclaimed that adult Lesser Black-backed Gull was a male Herring Gull *Larus argentatus*. Montagu sorted the mess out publishing details of the Lesser Black-backed Gull as a distinct species in 1802.

The subspecies *L. f. graellsii* is the race regularly found breeding in Britain and was found to be distinct from the nominate race *L. f. fuscus* by Dr Percy Lowe who named it *L. f. britannicus*. He realised the type specimen in the British Museum at South Kensington was a summer-plumaged male (No. 86. 7. 9. 1) collected in Caithness by Colonel Irby in 1886.

Unknown to Lowe, this subspecies had already been 'discovered' in Malaga, Spain and named as *L. f. graellsii* by Brehm in 1857. Lowe could not locate Brehm's type specimen and some measurements did not correspond with his own findings, so he dismissed *L. f. graellsii* as a race occurring in the Mediterranean or North African coast. This confusion was finally sorted out in 1930 and the name *L. f. graellsii* reinstated.

Lesser Black-backed Gull was clearly a common breeding species in Britain but earlier authors referred to it as *L. f. fuscus*.

There are estimated to be 83,500 breeding pairs of Lesser Black-backed Gulls in Britain and a further 5,200 in Ireland.

References:
British Birds 6: 2-3; 24: 24-25; Wingfield Gibbons *et al* 1993: 206-7; Yarrell 1843 iii: 663-4; Montagu 1813: 161; Holloway 1996: 210.

Yellow-legged Gull *Larus cachinnans*
(**Western Yellow-legged Gull** *L. c. michahellis* and **Eastern Yellow-legged Gull** *L. c. cachinnans*)
(Atlantic coasts from Netherlands south to West Africa; Mediterranean east to Kazakhstan and Persian Gulf)
1886 Norfolk, Breydon. A (P)

A bird shot on Breydon Water, Norfolk on 4th November, 1886, by Johnny Thomas was sold to J Cole who in turn showed it in the flesh to H Stevenson. It was sent to Mr E M Cannop to join his collection at Rollesby Hall. It was later found to be a male Yellow-legged Gull, Britain's first. The collection was catalogued by Thomas Southwell and consisted of 434 cases containing 336 species of birds.

This bird remains with the Cannop Collection at Birmingham and is of the race *L. c. michahellis* which is a frequent visitor to Britain, chiefly in late summer.

L. c. cachinnans is named Pontic Gull and given full specific treatment by the Dutch rarities committee and has alternatively been named Caspian Gull by others. It probably occurs in Britain on a regular basis but its true status is only just becoming clear. During a study of the plumage characteristics of Yellow-legged Gulls undertaken at a refuse tip near Mucking, Essex, from August, 1995, Martin Garner and David Quinn encountered birds on a regular basis. Their identification paper published in *British Birds* mentioned several individuals showing characteristics of 'Pontic' Gull' *L. c. cachinnans*. The earliest report was of a bird seen by artist Alan Harris in Hertfordshire during December, 1994.

Presently *L. c. cachinnans* is not on the British List and Yellow-legged Gull has yet to be split from Herring Gull by the BOURC. It is treated as a full species by the BBRC but to date only examples of *L. c. michahellis* have been accepted. Reports of the eastern race: *L. c. cachinnans* were still under consideration by the BBRC/BOURC in 1999.

References:
Patterson 1905: 83; 252; Saunders, 1899: 674, *British Birds* 90: 48; *Birding World* 11: 447.

(American) Herring Gull *Larus argentatus smithsonianus*
(North America)

IRELAND
1986 Co. Cork, Cobh.   A (26)

The first record of a Herring Gull of the American race *L. a. smithsonianus* was a first-year bird present at Cobh, Co. Cork, Ireland on 16th November, which remained into mid-December, 1986. It remained under consideration for some time allowing others to be recorded.

Killian Mullarney and Paul Archer visited the Cork city dump, Co. Cork, Ireland on 23rd February, 1990 in search of a reported Thayer's Gull *L. g. thayeri*. Mullarney pointed out a first-winter Herring Gull with an all-dark tail. His companion, Peter Leonard, suggested that it was of the race *L. a. smithsonianus*. Mullarney agreed, but the bird moved off towards the harbour before other observers could satisfy themselves. The bird was present the following day and was seen by several other observers. There was some discrepancy between the descriptions of the bird so Mullarney revisited the dump on 2nd and 3rd March. He found three different individuals, all first-winter birds.

Following the report of American Herring Gulls in Cork, two were discovered in Co. Donegal and one in Co. Galway, all during the same month. More than 20 *smithsonianus* gulls had been reported from Ireland at the end of 1998, while Britain had only four.

BRITAIN
1994 Cheshire, Neumann's Flash.

Despite an earlier claim, the first record to be officially adopted by the BOURC was a first-winter bird seen in Cheshire during 1994. It was found by artist David Quinn at Ashton's Flash and Neumann's Flash at 4pm on 24th February, whilst he was checking for white-winged gulls.

In the cold easterly wind he noted an obvious all-dark tail and suspected that it was an 'American' Herring Gull. He took notes and sketches until 4.50pm and again on 1st March at Witton Landfill Site.

The gull was also seen by Paul Kenyon and Paul Holt and was present in the area from 24th February, to 4th March, 1994. It was seen again briefly on the River Mersey by the Britannia Inn sewage outfall at Otterspool, Liverpool, Merseyside on 6th March by Mark Garner and Gavin Thomas.

A second-winter 'American' Herring Gull was reported by John Ryan and Ren Hathway on the Eastern Green Beach, Penzance, Cornwall, on 16th January, 1991. It stood out from the other birds on account of its uniform sooty grey upperparts, white rump and all black tail. A description was sent to Killian Mullarney in Ireland who thought it might be a first-year 'American' Herring Gull but further research was needed. This record has not been accepted.

With an increased interest in the racial identity of large gulls and publication of the relevant identification criteria of this race, the first months of 1998 saw an increase in the number of birds reported. Ireland receives the lion's share of acceptable reports.

References:
Birding World 3: 96-100, photo, *Rare Birds* 3: 88-89; *Cheshire Bird Report* 1995: 94-95, sketch 52; *Birds in Cornwall* 1991: 87.

Iceland Gull *Larus glaucoides*

(North America, Greenland, Northern Europe and the Baltic)

1822 Shetland, Baltasound, Unst.   **A (WV)**

Dr Lawrence Edmonston was known for finding white-winged gulls, having discovered the first Glaucous *Larus hyperboreus* and Iceland Gulls. It was at Baltasound that Edmonston killed an Iceland Gull on 22nd April 1822.

Dr Edmonston recorded many rare birds, creating a plantation at Halligarth in Baltasound, which still acts as a magnet to migrants today.

Iceland Gull occurs in Britain and Ireland in winter in small numbers with 70-80 individuals expected annually.

References:
Baxter & Rintoul 1953: 657-659; Venables & Venables 1955: 4.

Iceland (Kumlien's) Gull *Larus glaucoides kumlieni*
(Canada; winters North America)
1869 Shetland, Blackness.   **A (78)**

In 1997, the BOURC accepted an early Kumlien's Gull specimen found at the Natural History Museum at Tring. It was a third-winter female killed at Blackness, Shetland, on 24th November, 1869.

In 1995, the BOURC accepted a record of a bird photographed at Penzance,

Cornwall from 3rd to 15th March, 1979. At the time it became the first but is now the second British record.

A sight record from Portavogie, Co. Down, from 2nd to 4th January, 1981 became the first record for Ireland despite an earlier contender from Tralee, Co. Kerry, on 10th January, 1959. There were several other claims of immature birds in Britain and Ireland but problems with identification prevented acceptance at the time. As the plumage's of immature birds has become better known, gull enthusiasts have recorded this subspecies more regularly in recent years, with almost annual sightings since the first accepted reports in the 1980s.

An adult bird was discovered only a year after the first Irish record and watched by A J Merritt and Keith. Vinicombe, on 16th April 1982, at Chew Valley Lake, Avon. At the time this was the first British record.

References:
British Birds 53: 412; Ibis 133: 218-219; 90: 485; Evans 1997: 161.

Glaucous Gull *Larus hyperboreus*
(Circumpolar)
1809 Shetland, Unst.   A (WV).

Dr Lawrence Edmonston is credited with discovering the first Glaucous Gulls in Britain. He collected the first in autumn 1809 on Unst, Shetland, with another in 1814. He recorded a flock of up to 100 in Baltasound, Unst, during November, 1820, and the species became recognised as a regular visitor to Britain. Edmonston noted that the birds were always fat when they arrived in Shetland during autumn. They would linger around estuaries and bays, awaiting fishing boats.
Specimens were taken by throwing a hooked line that was baited overboard as Glaucous Gulls were attracted to carrion.

Glaucous Gull is a scarce but frequent winter visitor to Britain with at least 200 reported each year.

References:
Baxter & Rintoul 1953: 655; Lack 1986: 244.

Ross's Gull *Rhodostethia rosea*
(Arctic)
1847 Yorkshire, North Milford-cum-Kirby.   A (85)

An adult winter-plumaged Cuneate-tailed Gull (Ross's Gull), said to have been shot at Milford-cum-Kirby, near Tadcaster, Yorkshire, was preserved by David Graham, taxidermist of Spurriergate, York. In turn, he sold it to Sir William Milner of Nun Appleton who recorded it in a letter to *Zoologist* 1847 as having been killed on 22nd December, 1846 by Thomas Robinson of Saxton, a nearby village. Confusingly, the notes accompanying the specimen state that it was:

"*killed by Lord Howden's gamekeeper in a ploughed field at Grimston, near Tadcaster, Yorkshire in January 1847, and purchased by D. Graham, naturalist, York*".

This presents a different site, month and shooter, while William Milner's close

relative Henry Milner, clouded the issue further by stating that the bird had been killed by Homer the head keeper, in February, near Milford-cum-Kirkby.

Perhaps the confusion is explained as both sites were ploughed fields owned by Lord Howden and both fronted the River Wharfe yet the person named responsible for the bird's demise is not consistent.

This was the first time that the species had ever been seen and described in its non-breeding plumage, and though this record is still widely accepted it remains the only inland report from over 85 British records to date!

The skin was one of Milner's rarer specimens, initially placed in the Leeds Museum and thought to have been destroyed by a German bomb in 1941. Curator Adrian Norris found that it had been loaned to the Wakefield Museum some time around 1935 and returned it to Leeds in 1999 (accession No LEEDM.C.1922.1.1)

The opinion of several 'experts' was that the bird had the appearance of being mounted from a relaxed skin, rather than from a freshly killed specimen and Graham had a poor reputation as a taxidermist.

As records with Graham's involvement are currently under suspicion, it seems possible they will be removed from the British List. The following record is poised to take the 'first' crown should it ever fall.

The second British Ross's Gull was found at the more typical site between Whalsay and Skerries, Shetland almost 100 years later in 1936. It was a sick or exhausted immature caught in a scoop net dropped alongside a boat by John Irvine, a fisherman from Saltness, Shetland. Irvine was familiar with the locally occurring seabirds and noticed its small bill and wedge-shaped tail.

Following a period in care, it died. The skin was mounted before being presented to Mr G T Kay. Later it was obtained by John Simpson who, in 1970, described it as being in a poor condition. Presently the specimen cannot be traced.

Ross's Gull occurs annually in Britain with at least eight birds found in 1993 alone.

Reference:
Saunders, 1899: 659; Nelson, 1907: 665-667; Mather, 1985: 345-347; Naylor 1998: 201-2; Densley 1999: 3; 53-58.

Ivory Gull *Pagophila eburnea*
(Arctic)

*c.*1819 Somerset, Bridgwater.   A (120)

Britain's first Ivory Gull was an adult, shot some time around 1819 at Bridgwater, Somerset. It is now in the Woodforde Collection, in the City Museum, Bristol on loan from the Oxford Museum but not on public display. Little is known about the occurrence of this bird and there was no mention of it by either Yarrell (1843) or Saunders (1899).

However it may possibly be the bird mentioned in 1865 by Rev Murray Mathew as being caught by a local watchmaker who had baited a jar with a sprat at Weston-Super-Mare. He kept it alive as a pet for some time in his garden.

The earlier works of the 19th Century had all recorded the first as being an immature, shot on 13th December, 1822 by Dr Lawrence Edmonston at Balta Sound, Unst, Shetland, the skin of which was presented to the Edinburgh Museum. This is now regarded as the second record.

Ivory Gull has become a very difficult bird to find in Britain.

References:
Smith 1869: 598; Somerset Orn. Club, 1988; Palmer & Balance 1968: 193; Saunders, 1899: 685; Baxter & Rintoul, 1953: 664-665; *Zool*, 1865: 9470.

Gull-billed Tern *Sterna nilotica*
(Almost cosmopolitan, nearest breeding colony Denmark; European population winters Africa)

1813 Sussex.   **A (264)**

Montagu's Gull-billed Tern specimen from Sussex, taken some time during 1813, is the earliest dated British record and is now in the British Museum. At the time he was oblivious to the importance of the skin.

Early records of Gull-billed Tern are not well documented, as they were confused with Sandwich Tern *Sterna sandvicensis*. Indeed Sandwich Tern was only distinguished from Common Tern *Sterna hirundo* and named as a new species when a specimen from Kent was obtained in 1784 and published by Dr Latham. Gmelin first described the Gull-billed Tern five years later in 1789, from a bird collected in Egypt.

One of the earliest British Gull-billed Tern reports related to an example in Dr Latham's collection at Dartford. It concerned a specimen sent to him as the young of a Sandwich Tern, killed, he believed, near Sandwich, Kent, some time before 1824. Latham considered the adults (Sandwich Terns) to have developed a yellow tip to the otherwise all black bill exhibited by juveniles (Gull-billed Tern). He also mentioned other specimens from Sussex, particularly Rye but no dates or details were noted.

Montagu possessed one of the Gull-billed Tern specimens from Sussex mentioned by Latham; it had been collected in 1813. He had earlier published a description of the Gull-billed Tern under the name of Sandwich Tern, in his *Ornithological Dictionary* 1802, so presumably Montagu had not read Latham's description of the first Sandwich Tern.

Montagu later separated Gull-billed and Sandwich Terns when he was sent Latham's type specimen of Sandwich Tern collected in Kent and compared it with his Sussex Gull-billed Tern.

With the two skins side by side he realised they were two different species.

In the 1813 supplement to his *Dictionary*, Montagu published the differences between the two species and Latham's pre 1824 specimen, from Sandwich, Kent, was later accepted as the second British record.

The Gull-billed Tern has become scarce in Britain in recent years with the collapse of the small Danish breeding population.

References:
Harrison, 1953: 453: 472-473; Montagu, 1862: 343; Saunders, 1899: 639; Walpole-Bond, 1938: iii, 245-247.

Caspian Tern *Sterna caspia*

(Almost cosmopolitan except South America; European population winters Africa)

1825 Norfolk, Breydon Water.   A (255)

An immature Caspian Tern shot on 4th October, 1825 at Breydon Water, Norfolk was mentioned in Messers Paget's *Sketch of the Natural History of Yarmouth and its neighbourhood*. It was Britain's first report but unfortunately the specimen can no longer be traced.

A second undated specimen now at the Castle Museum, Norwich, was also collected in the vicinity of Great Yarmouth during 1830.

Both birds were recorded in *Zoologist* magazine in 1831 with one specimen in the collection of a "Norwich gent," while the location of the other was not known.

Surprisingly for such a regularly occurring vagrant, Cornwall only recorded its first Caspian Tern in 1997.

References:
Allard, 1990; Mag. Nat. Hist, 4: 117; *Zool* 1831: 117; *British Birds* 91: 482; Dymond 1989.

Royal Tern *Sterna maxima*

(Northwest Africa, North America and the Caribbean; winters south to Angola, Argentina and Ecuador)

IRELAND
1954 Dublin, North Bull.   D (4)

The first acceptable Royal Tern was found dead on 24th March, 1954. Mr R G Wheeler picked it up from the beach at the North Bull Bird Sanctuary, Dublin. The possibility that it had died in the open ocean and drifted to Ireland was investigated by Mr G M Spooner of the Marine Biological Laboratory, Plymouth. There was strong evidence to suggest that the tern had died in the Irish Sea and therefore was treated as a genuine vagrant. This remains the only bird to reach Ireland while four have reached Britain.

BRITAIN
1965 Kent, Sandwich Bay.   A (4)

Having dismissed the record of a male Royal Tern from Pevensey Marsh, East Sussex on 17th January, 1920 as one of the Hastings rarities, a Royal Tern seen by Ola Tunander, a Swedish ornithologist, on Shellness Point, Kent, on 28th July, 1965 became the first accepted record.

Having fetched P Newbound and M Davenport from the Sandwich Bay Bird Observatory, Tunander watched the bird and took notes. On 29th July additional observers watched the bird for a further 3½ hours.

A large amount of research was undertaken before the Rarities Committee were satisfied, as the other species of 'yellow-billed terns' had to be ruled out before acceptance. It was thought unusual for a bird to still have a black forehead in late July, although it is now known that un-mated birds can retain their summer plumage longer as they search for a mate.

A Royal Tern was found bearing a metal ring at Kenfig, Mid Glamorgan on 24th November, 1979. It had been ringed in North Carolina USA as a nestling some time during 1978/79.

References:
Sharrock, 1982:43-45; Naylor 1998: 211.

Lesser Crested Tern *Sterna bengalensis*
(North and East Africa, east to Australia)
1982 Anglesey, Cymyran Bay.   **A (8)**

C Hurford and John Chester were counting fledgling Arctic Terns *Sterna paradisaea* on the beach of Cymyran Bay, Anglesey, on 13th July, 1982, when Hurford saw a large yellow-billed tern among them. Chester suggested they took a description. The bird stood beside Arctic Terns on the beach before undertaking two short flights to settle near a Sandwich Tern *Sterna sandvicensis*. After ten minutes it took off towards Rhosneigr and was not seen again. The description fitted that of Lesser Crested Tern *Sterna bengalensis* and was submitted to the BBRC as such.

This caused some difficulties for the Rarities Committee, as the identification features were then not fully understood. Compounding this was a controversial tern in Norfolk during 1983, which was also a Lesser Crested Tern.

The Norfolk bird is presumed to have been the female bird called Elsie (from 'L-C' for Lesser Crested) that nested on the Farne Islands producing at least four hybrid young prior to 1998 at least.

A bird claimed to be of this species (or the less likely, Crested Tern *S. bergii*) was reportedly shot by Mr Lynch, of Cork Street, Dublin at the end of December, 1846, between Dublin and Howth. Two other birds were claimed to have been seen at the time but the record was not accepted.

Although there have been seven accepted records of Lesser Crested Tern in Britain and one in Ireland it is conceivable that only two birds may have accounted for all the reports, due to an overlap in the dates of records.

References:
Zool 1847: 1878; *British Birds* 82: 396-398. [Montagu, 1862: 348]

Sandwich Tern *Sterna sandvicensis*
(Western Europe and Africa to Northwest India, also Florida south to Brazil)
1784 Kent, Sandwich.   **A (SB)**

Sometimes referred to "Boys' Tern" *Sterna boysii* after its discoverer William Boys of Kent, Sandwich Tern was found breeding in large colonies on the Kent coast during the late 1700s. Boys noted that the bird had a shorter call than the Common Terns *Sterna hirundo* it associated with and obtained the first specimen at Sandwich, Kent in 1784. The following year, Latham published his description of the specimen under the name of Sandwich Tern. Latham's daughter, Ann, illustrated the specimen in Boys *History of Sandwich*.

The type specimen passed from Latham via a Mr Vaughan to Montagu along with the second British specimen, taken at a similar time at the end of August, 1784, on the banks of the Thames by Dr Leith of Greenwich.

Sandwich Tern is frequently seen around the British and Irish coast in summer.

References:
Harrison 1953: 472-473; plate XLIX; Montagu, 1863: 347: 343.

(American) Sandwich Tern *Sterna sandvicensis acuflavida*
(North America, Mexico and the Bahamas, south to Brazil)
1984 Herefordshire, Newhouse Wood.   A (1)

A bird picked up dead but still in a fresh condition on 8th November, 1984, at Newhouse Wood, Herefordshire, is the only British record of the American subspecies *S. s. acuflavida*. It is presumably easily overlooked, as separation of this form from the race commonly found in Britain is not widely understood in Europe.

References:
Naylor 1998: 405.

Elegant Tern *Sterna elegans*
(Pacific coast of tropical America)

NORTHERN IRELAND
1982 Co. Down, Carlingford Lough.   A (2)

There are only two records of Elegant Tern and both spent considerable periods in tern colonies. All reports have to be thorough to eliminate possibility of hybrid Lesser Crested Terns *Sterna bengalensis*, none of which have yet been described in adult plumage.

A single bird present at Greencastle Point, Carlingford Lough, Co. Down, from 22nd June to 3rd July, 1982, and at Ballymacoda, Co. Cork on 1st August, was in full breeding plumage with an obvious pink flush to the underparts. It had a typical shaggy crest and reddish bill fading to pale yellow at the base and was first found in a tern colony by Bill Laird, Jim Furphy and R E Scott but was later seen on 1st August at Ballymacoda, Co. Cork by Pat Smiddy. (P Milne *in litt*).

A second bird was watched displaying to Sandwich Terns *Sterna sandvicensis* at Lady's Island Lake, Co. Wexford in July, 1999. It apparently tried to feed sand eels to a juvenile Sandwich Tern present in a flock gathered in a nearby potato field. This record was under consideration of the IRBC in December 1999.

Elegant Tern is similar in appearance to Lesser Crested Tern and despite its unlikely vagrancy potential has been recorded in Europe on at least four occasions.

References:
British Birds 81: 567; photo 75: 478.

Roseate Tern *Sterna dougallii*
(Atlantic coasts and Indian Ocean, south to Northwest Australia)
1812 Strathclyde.   A (SB)

Roseate Tern was first discovered in Scotland on the Cumbrae's, two small rocky islands in the Firth of Clyde, by Dr Peter McDougall of Glasgow and two friends on 24th July, 1812. When McDougall picked up a tern *Sterna* shot by one of his friends, he noticed it was different. He began to take notes regarding the flying birds while his friends were instructed to obtain more specimens. McDougall distinguished the 'new' tern from Common Terns *Sterna hirundo* on the island but failed to distinguish between Common and Arctic Terns *Sterna paradisaea*, both present on the island but not recognised as separate species until seven years later. (J F Naumann scientifically 'separated' these two in 1819.)

McDougall arranged for one of his specimens to be sent to Montagu who published a description of the bird, and named it *Sterna dougallii*. The bird illustrated by Montagu is in an unnatural position, as the specimen was poorly mounted, having been shot in the neck.

McDougall mounted his own specimens and the type specimen sent to Montagu is retained in the British Museum.

Roseate Tern is an uncommon summer visitor, with breeding numbers at an all time low.

References:
Saunders, 1899: 645; Mearns 1988: 245-248; Fisher 1954: 26.

Aleutian Tern   *Sterna aleutica*
(Eastern Siberia and western Alaska; wintering grounds unknown)
1979 Northumberland, Inner Farne.   **A (1)**

At 1.30pm on 28th May 1979, R Haywood, a warden on Inner Farne, Northumberland, heard an unfamiliar call. He was surprised to see a dark tern *Sterna spp* with a striking white forehead unlike any of the terns regularly present on the island. After several minutes he contacted the other wardens: A E Dixey, A Ferguson, D E Mole and A R Taylor. Together they took field notes.

Consulting available books, the closest European tern was Bridled Tern *Sterna anaethetus* but the bird seemed to fit the unlikely Aleutian Tern much better. For the rest of the day they took more notes and photographs. The bird was seen down to four metres on one occasion and was still present the next morning. It then disappeared until early evening when it was last noted at 5.30pm. It was occasionally attacked by other terns and was rarely seen to land. This report was accepted as Britain's first Aleutian Tern and remains the sole record.

Little is known about the species, which has never been seen in winter, anywhere! In August, 1992, however, about 190 were found south-west of Hong Kong – presumably heading to unknown wintering grounds somewhere in the western Pacific.

References:
Sharrock 1982: 246-248, photo; *British Birds* 74: 411-416, photos; Cottridge & Vinicombe 1997: 88-9.

Forster's Tern   *Sterna forsteri*
(North America; winters USA and Mexico)
1980 Cornwall, Falmouth.   **A (28)**

Any tern in British waters during winter is worthy of a second look but a bird feeding offshore in the bay at Swanpool, Falmouth, Cornwall, at about midday on 29th January, 1980, did not fly close enough for B Cave to positively identify it.

On 20th February, he saw it again and thought it resembled a Sandwich Tern *Sterna sandvicensis* but the dark eye patch raised the possibility of it being a Forster's Tern. Despite searching by several observers it was not seen again until 9th March when Cave again found it, this time off Gyllyngvase, Falmouth. It eventually landed on rocks with gulls and allowed a better view, confirming that it was a first-winter Forster's Tern.

The bird was watched by hundreds of observers until it was last seen on 18th March and the record accepted by the BOURC.

Some individuals are believed to cross the Irish Sea moving between sites on the west coast of Britain and east coast of Ireland, accounting for several reports of what is presumably the same bird.

References:
Sharrock 1982: 248-251.

Bridled Tern *Sterna anaethetus*
(Caribbean east to Philippines and Australia)
1931 Kent, Dungeness.   A (22)

The decomposing corpse of a Bridled Tern was found near the Hoppen Pits, two miles inland from Dungeness, Kent on 19th November, 1931. It had a hole in its chest indicating that it may have been taken by a bird of prey. Although in poor condition it was preserved by the finder, Guy Mannering.

It was an adult male moulting from summer to winter plumage and thought to closely resemble the race occurring in the Red Sea, *S. a. anaethetus*.

A bird said to have been killed in September, 1875, on a lightship at the mouth of the Thames, is housed in the Booth Museum at Brighton. The bird was moulting from winter to summer plumage, so the autumn date must be wrong. Saunders and subsequent authorities rejected this record on account of the inconsistencies.

It wasn't until 6th August, 1979 that the first live bird was found in Britain. J Hamilton watched an immature Bridled Tern feeding near a light beacon just outside the entrance to Stromness harbour, Orkney. The bird was also seen by the same observer on the 7th and was the first Scottish record.

References:
British Birds 28: 90-4; 73: 513; Harrison, 1953: 466-467; Saunders, 1899: 654; Naylor 1996, 1998; C. Booth, *pers comm.*

Sooty Tern *Sterna fuscata*
(Tropical and subtropical islands in all oceans, also Red Sea)
1852 Staffordshire, near Burton-on-Trent.   A (26)

Edwin Brown of Burton-on-Trent, Staffordshire reported the amazing occurrence of the first Sooty Tern. The bird had been shot on the River Dove, at Tutbury; about four month's prior to 20th October, 1852 (recorded as December in some literature).

As the bird was reported to Brown as being a Gull-billed Tern *Sterna nilotica*, he was in no hurry to examine the specimen which had passed into the collection of Mr H W Des Voeux of Drakelow Hall.

Brown saw the specimen in December while visiting Drakelow Hall and then consulted Latham's work to find that it was a Sooty Tern. He claimed there had been no successful attempts to confine Sooty Terns in captivity and believed it to be a wild bird. As a result Yarrell exhibited the specimen at a meeting of the Linnean Society in February, 1853 and the species was placed on the British List.

The most celebrated occurrence of a Sooty Tern in Britain was an exhausted bird found at Ditchford Gravel Pits, Northamptonshire on 29th May 1980. It was picked up by John Ward and taken into care the following morning. It survived five months.

References:
Saunders, 1899: 653; Montagu, 1862: 348-349; *Zool*, 1853: 3755-6; Evans 1994: 261-2. [Frost. 1978: 159]

Whiskered Tern *Chlidonias hybridus*
(South Eurasia, Africa and Australia)
1836 Dorset, Lyme Regis.   A (126)

Mr T C Heysham was responsible for recording Britain's first Whiskered Tern. Along with a couple of friends, he had taken a boat from Lyme Regis, Dorset, in late August, 1836, to "amuse himself by shooting seabirds". Heysham selected the corpse from the group of birds killed that day and sent it to Yarrell for examination.

Whiskered Tern was added to the British List in an announcement published in the *Zoologist* (1843) and also figured in Yarrell's work as well as in Saunders' *Manual*.

In Britain a distinct peak of sightings, mostly adults, occurs in May and June indicating that migrants are overshooting normal destinations, while a smaller influx occurs from late July to early September.

References:
Saunders, 1899: 637; Moore, 1969: 170 Prendergast & Boys, 1983: 196; Yarrell, 1843: iii, 404-406; *Zool*, 1843: 80; Naylor 1998.

White-winged Tern *Chlidonias leucopterus*
(Southeast Europe, West and East Asia)

IRELAND
1841 Dublin, River Liffey, Dublin Bay.   A (743)

In 1866, Mr Harryblake-Knox reported that White-winged Tern had "occurred twice in Ireland, both times in the mouth of the River Liffey," Dublin Bay. The first was shot in October, 1841 by Mr M Coy.

This report was recorded in the ornithological notes from the City of Dublin but Kennedy (1954) recorded that a Mr Hill had shot the bird.

BRITAIN
1853 Norfolk, Horsey Mere.

Norfolk holds many records of White-winged Tern including the first in Britain. It was an adult shot from a flock of between 15 and 20 Black Terns *Chlidonias niger* on Horsey Mere on 17th May 1853, by Mr Risings' keeper. The shooter claimed there had been two birds present.

George Tredrick showed the bird in the flesh to Yarrell who confirmed the identification and the record was published in *Zoologist*. The specimen can no longer be traced.

White-winged Tern is an annual migrant with an average of less than 20 reports a year, mostly in autumn.

References:
Kennedy, 1954: 252; Riviere 1930; Montagu, 1862: 349-350; *Zool*, 1866: 306; 1846: 1375; 1871: 2829; Naylor 1998.

Brünnich's Guillemot   *Uria lomvia*
(Circumpolar Arctic)
1908 Lothian, Craigielaw Point.   A (35)

The first record of a Brünnich's Guillemot which remains acceptable was a female, picked up dead at Craigielaw Point, Lothian, on 11th December, 1908. Valentine Knight sent it to the National Museums of Scotland, Edinburgh, where it was considered to be an immature bird by Eagle Clarke.

Brünnich's Guillemot was incorrectly assumed by Yarrell to breed on the coast of Co. Kerry, Ireland, on the authority of Colonel Sabine who claimed that he had seen birds there in July. There are about 30 British records of this auk, the majority involving corpses found on the shore, and appear to be of the nominate race *U. l. lomvia*.

The first living individual was not found until 13th July, 1977, when a summer-plumaged adult was seen by three observers off Staple Island, Farne Islands, Northumberland: N Leeming, R Pimm and J B Ribbands.

There had previously been several false claims of this much sought after rarity:

Between Seahouses and Inner Farne, Northumberland a Brünnich's Guillemot was shot by Mr Cuthbertson while on route to the Farne Islands in winter 1883/4. The specimen remained in the possession of Mrs Cuthbertson, with Bolam (1932) and Harting (1912) considering the record good. It is not included in the lists of Hancock (1874) or the BOU (1971), so for the purpose of this work is not acceptable.

Following this, in 1847 Sir William Milner reported that a Brünnich's Guillemot and its egg had been taken on the Scottish Isle of Soay on 15th June, 1847. The claim was made by David Graham, a birdstuffer of dubious character from York, and Milner did not visit the site. This record never received acceptance.

Several early reports were winter plumaged Common Guillemot's *Uria aalge*, a fact brought to light following publication of Thorburns' painting of the species, which illustrated a Common Guillemot.

References:
British Birds 2: 425; Naylor 1996: 103. [Montagu, 1862: 145; Yarrell, 1843: iii, 348-350; Galloway & Meek, 1978: 99; Bolam 1932:663-664; Harrison 1953: 485; Handlist, 1912; Nelson, 1907: 724-725; Clarke, 1912: ii, 242; Mather, 1985: 373].

Razorbill *Alca torda torda*
(Scandinavia, North America and Greenland)
1937 Kent, Dungeness.   A

In 1937, after reading an article about Razorbill in the journal *British Birds*, Norman Joy went to retrieve some Razorbill carcasses that had been washed up at Dungeness, Kent, two months earlier. He picked up five, measured them and found one to be the larger northern race *A. t. torda*.

The 'Northern' race was newly described and added to the British List by the BOU in 1937.

The 'Northern' Scandinavian, American and Greenland *A. a. torda* is larger than the British and Icelandic *A. a. islandica* and are known to have reached Britain from a number of ringed Norwegian birds. They presumably occur in British waters regularly.

References:
British Birds 31: 90; 32: 2; *Birding World* 11: 229.

Ancient Murrelet *Synthliboramphus antiquus*
(Pacific seaboard of Alaska and Northeast Siberia)
1990 Devon, Lundy.   A (1)

While on an organised RSPB trip to see Atlantic Puffins *Fratercula arctica* on Lundy, Devon, on 27th May 1990, John Waldon noticed Keith Mortimer running towards him at 2.15pm Mortimer had been watching auks with Richard Campey near Jenny's Cove and at 1.45pm they had watched what they at first took to be a Puffin fly towards them and land on the water, 300 feet below in Jenny's Cove. Obviously something incredibly rare, they showed it to the group who reluctantly switched from watching the Puffins to assist with note taking.

Waldon and Stan Davies returned with Mortimer in time to see the mystery auk flying out to sea.

Luckily at 2.45pm, the bird returned to land on the water 200m away where it remained for 15 minutes before again heading out to sea with a Razorbill *Alca torda*. The identification of Ancient Murrelet was not confirmed until books were consulted on the boat returning to Bideford.

The news of this unlikely discovery was greeted with some scepticism but as it was seen in Jenny's Cove again the following morning birders made plans to twitch Lundy. The bird flew out to sea at 1pm but was found six miles east of the island at about 6pm by Phil Palmer, Ian Smith and a small group of Nottinghamshire birders. Despite realising that it would be dark when they reached Lundy, they set off and found the Ancient Murrelet at sea about halfway to the island. Swimming close to the boat at a range of only 2m in the company of a much shyer Razorbill, which appeared to have chosen it as a 'mate' it was recorded on film.

Over 3,750 birders travelled to see the bird, some made several unsuccessful attempts.

The murrelet remained faithful to Jenny's Cove until 26th June, 1990 and was best seen in early mornings, prior to feeding at sea. It would also hide in a rocky crevice 80m above the sea during the day as the species is primarily nocturnal.

It returned on 4th April 1991, staying to 20th June, and then again the following year from 30th March, to 29th April 1992. This early departure led to speculation that it may have died but during its stay had been seen by observers from all over Europe.

In 1989 larger-than-usual numbers of Ancient Murrelet were seen along the coast of California, with four venturing inland. (Prof. S. G. Sealy *in litt*).

References:
British Birds 87: 307-310; *Birding World* 3: 211-214, photos; Evans, 1994: 269; Cottridge & Vinicombe 1997: 92.

Pallas's Sandgrouse *Syrrhaptes paradoxus*
(Central Asia east to Manchuria and China)
1859 Caernarfonshire, Tremadoc.   **A (Many)**

An early event in the annals of ornithology that modern birdwatchers would love to be repeated was the irruptions of Pallas's Sandgrouse that took place in the latter half of the 1800s. The first birds to be seen in Britain arrived during early July, 1859.

At about 3pm on the 9th July, 1859, a party of three Pallas's Sandgrouse were seen running about making a chattering whistling noise on some sandy ground reclaimed from the sea near the River Glasslyn at Tremadoc, Caernarfonshire, by Owen Quin, a labourer who was "scuffling" turnips.

Fetching his gun, which he had brought to kill Rooks *Corvus frugilegus* on an adjacent potato field, he killed a fine adult male.

The labourer took the bird to Thomas Chaffers of Liverpool who held Portreuddyn Farm in the estate of T Madoc Esq, on whose land it had been killed. On 12th July

it was taken to Mr Butterworth a museum taxidermist who skinned and mounted the bird which was starting to smell. The contents of its gizzard were examined by Dr Collingwood, Lecturer on Botany at the Liverpool School of Medicine who found turnip seeds and "ripe furze seed" but no trace of any insects. This was accepted as the first British record and the specimen is now at Chester Museum.

At a similar time a male was shot at Walpole St Peters, Norfolk. This bird is occasionally claimed as the first British record but, lacking an accurate date, follows the Caernarfonshire record. The mounted specimen remains on display in the King's Lynn Museum.

On 21st May 1863, 14 birds were recorded in Northumberland and the following day 20 reached Staffordshire. After this date, birds were reported from almost every county and a small number were shot in Ireland.

In 1888, movements of Pallas's Sandgrouse took place on a massive scale and with up to 2,000 in Scotland alone it was inevitable that breeding would be attempted, and nests were found and robbed throughout the country. Despite an Act of Parliament passed to protect the birds, the sandgrouse population retreated from its temporary range expansion.

References:
Saunders, 1899: 488-490; Montagu, 1862:142; *Ibis* 1860: 107; Holloway 1996: 238.

Eurasian Collared Dove *Streptopelia decaocto*
(Europe, southern Asia and North Africa)
1955 Norfolk, Overstrand. A (RB)

In April 1955, a pair of Eurasian Collared Doves arrived in Overstrand, Norfolk and successfully fledged two young. These were the first wild-bred Collared Doves to be recorded in Britain. At least two of the birds wintered feeding on corn supplied by a resident. Also in 1955, two or three birds were present at a garden in Cromer.

P R Clarke had seen a fawn-coloured dove on the electricity wires above the coast road at Cley-next-the-Sea, Norfolk, during 1955, but dismissed it as there had been a similar looking hybrid dove in the area two years previously. This was probably also a vagrant Eurasian Collared Dove.

The species had undertaken a rapid range expansion from its homeland in central Asia with no European records prior to the 19th Century.

After hearing unfamiliar calls on 3rd July, 1956, Michael Seago saw a single bird in the trees of a large garden in Cromer, Norfolk. Consulting published material, he concluded they were Eurasian Collared Doves. The birds were regularly watched by Ralph Richardson and A C Church who found that two males and one female were present producing a single recently fledged juvenile on 29th July. A second clutch from the same pair produced a further two young that were ringed by Church, with a third brood reared successfully later.

It was reported that another pair had arrived in Overstrand, Norfolk, at the end of March, 1956, and reared two young. They reared at least one young in August, 1956.

Following these reports, a request was made for information about the origin of these birds to determine the status of escaped birds. They were found to have probably arrived from the continent as wild vagrants. As a result of the investigation, further earlier reports came to light.

A single bird was present at Manton near Brigg, Lincolnshire, from early May to September, 1952. The bird was reported to Reg May on 31st July, 1952 and he first heard it on 24th July. He saw the bird well on subsequent occasions accompanied by various observers, including James Fisher, and it was identified as a Eurasian Collared Dove. It reappeared during late April in the same area the following year and remained until October. The bird was almost certainly the first pioneer to visit Britain but despite this report the Norfolk Collared Doves remain the first acceptable records.

Presently the population is estimated to be about 200,000 with the species largely absent from western Ireland, highland Scotland, upland England and Wales.

References:
Sharrock, 1982: 72-77; *British Birds* 46: 51-55, 153-181, colour illustration, 50: 212; Wingfield Gibbons 1993: 238. [Smith & Cornwallis, 1955: 98].

Oriental Turtle Dove *Streptopelia orientalis*
(Urals, east to Japan, south to India and Southeast Asia)
1889 North Yorkshire, Scarborough. A (5)

James Backhouse submitted a specimen of Oriental Turtle Dove to the Zoological

Society. At the meeting held on 6th May 1890, Seebohm exhibited the bird which Backhouse claimed had been obtained by Mr Head, a local naturalist, while flying swiftly being pursued by small birds. It had been killed on 23rd October, 1889, at Nab Gutter, a small stream running from Olivers Mount down to the sea at Scarborough, North Yorkshire. Head, also shot a Red-breasted Flycatcher *Ficedula parva* on the same day.

Both Seebohm and Saunders examined the bird at the York Museum and found it lacking a neck patch and concluded that it was an immature bird of the race *S. o. orientalis*. This he compared to a specimen obtained from the Amur Delta, Siberia, held in the British Museum. The skin is widely stated to still be at the Yorkshire Museum, but has not been seen by an ornithologist for more than 20 years.

There has been only one record of a bird thought to be of the Himalayan race *S. o. meena*. This was seen by several birdwatchers, including warden Barry Spence, Tony Broome and John Cudworth, at Spurn, East Yorkshire from 11am to 3pm on 8th November, 1975. Only birds belonging to the nominate race form part of the British List.

Oriental Turtle Dove is a very rare vagrant.

References:
Saunders, 1899: 487; Evans 1994: 271-272; *Proc. Zool Soc., 1890*: 361; *Birding World* 5: 52, photo; Denton 1995: 42; Cottridge & Vinicombe 1997: 93

Mourning Dove *Zenaida macroura*
(North and Central America south to Panama)
1989 Calf of Man.   A (1)

After checking nets at the Calf of Man Bird Observatory on 31st October, 1989, Aron Sapsford removed three Common Blackbirds *Turdus merula* from a Heligoland trap and to his surprise also found a small dove of equal size. Presuming it to be a cage bird he put it in a bag and took it back to the observatory. After checking European guide books he showed the bird to Ian Fisher. He had seen the species in America and identified it as a Mourning Dove, which he confirmed by checking the National Geographic Society's *Birds of North America*.

The bird was ringed and released into the observatory garden as it seemed exhausted and had possibly only just arrived. It ate some grain in the afternoon but was found dead the next day. The bird was skinned and presented to the Manx Museum, where it remains.

It was examined by Dr Alan Knox and found to be a first-year bird, probably male. The bird's low weight indicated that it was probably not ship assisted so it was admitted to the British List.

Since this time, the Manx list has been separated from the British List.

BRITAIN
Outer Hebrides, Carinish, North Uist.   * [1]

The first British record concerned a tired looking individual at Carinish, North Uist, Outer Hebrides. Angus and Mairi MacPhail found it in their garden on 13th

November, 1999, and fed it with chicken food. It survived the night and late the following afternoon they telephoned Brian Rabbitts, joint recorder for the Western Isles, with news of "an unusual dove". Together with Brian Hill, Rabbitts saw the bird prior to dusk and released the news nationally. The following day 25 mainland birders saw it in the same garden, but reports about its health had persuaded many not to take a gamble.

The indication that it may not make it through the night were premature as it disappeared overnight. It was suggested that the bird had fallen victim to a cat but no feathers were found. This remains the only British record and if accepted will be the first.

A case of airborne assistance concerned a bird which arrived at Heathrow Airport Cargo Depot, Greater London during mid-morning on 9th February, 1998, in a consignment of freight from Chicago. Having survived the 12 hour flight, the bird eventually escaped into a warehouse on the site but access was denied to birdwatchers for security reasons. It eventually left the building and was not seen again.

References:
British Birds 89: 157-162; Birding World 12: 453, photo; Birdwatch 91: 61.

Rose-ringed Parakeet *Psittacula krameri*
(North-central and north-eastern Africa, through Afghanistan, Pakistan, India and Nepal to Burma; Established feral population in Britain)

1969 Kent, Gravesend. **C (RB)**

The first feral Rose-ringed Parakeets were seen in 1969, when a family party was present in the Gravesend area of Kent with a second in Croydon and Bromley. By 1973, the latter population had increased to 11 birds. A pair in the Claygate and Esher area of Surrey in 1970 produced young, and increased to six birds by February, 1972. A separate report from southwest Essex recorded Rose-ringed Parakeets in the Woodford Green area in 1971, rising to at least 22 birds in 1973.

By 1983, the British population centred in Kent and the Thames Valley was estimated at between 500 and 1000 individuals and the species was admitted to Category C of the British List. In 1997, the population was estimated to be about 1,539 birds.

New separate feral populations are establishing themselves in northern England.

References:
Rare Birds 3: 97-100; British Birds 92: 181-2.

Great Spotted Cuckoo *Clamator glandarius*
(South Europe, Southwest Asia and Africa; winters Africa)

IRELAND
1842 Galway, Omey Island. **A (40)**

After being "pursued by Hawks" an immature Great Spotted Cuckoo was captured alive but in an emaciated condition by two islanders at Omey Island on the Connemara coast, Galway in March, 1842. It survived for four days being fed on a diet of potatoes and water and on its death it was sent to the Museum of Trinity College, Dublin (P. Milne *in litt*). Mr A Crighton of Clifden, Co. Galway, provided an account of this record and Saunders examined it while at the museum where he confirmed the identity.

BRITAIN
1870 Northumberland, Bellingham.

An immature Great Spotted Cuckoo, possibly present since June, 1870, was shot in the Wark Forest, Clintburn, near Bellingham, Northumberland, on 5th August. It was presented to the Natural History Society of Northumbria and placed in the Newcastle (now Hancock) Museum by Mr W H Charlton of Hesleyside.

Vagrant Great Spotted Cuckoos occur early in the year. The earliest was on Lundy, Devon on 24th February, 1990 with most spring reports being on the south coast. Autumn records suggest that birds arrive from a different source as they favour the east coast.

References:
Saunders, 1899: 289; Kennedy, 1954: 283; Hancock: 27; Bolam: 244; Cottridge & Vinicombe 1997: 94-5.

Black-billed Cuckoo *Coccyzus erythrophthalmus*
(North America; winters northwest South America)

IRELAND
1871 Antrim, Killead. A (14)

In January, 1872, Mr H Blake of Dalkey reported that his birdstuffer in Belfast had mounted an American cuckoo, shot at Killead, Co. Antrim, on 25th September, 1871. The birdstuffer described it as being like a large Common Whitethroat *Sylvia communis* but smaller than a Common Cuckoo *Cuculus canorus*. Blake sent him the skin of a Yellow-billed Cuckoo *Coccyzus americanus* for comparison: it was not so yellow on the bill and had less white on the tail.

BRITAIN.
1932 Isles of Scilly, Tresco.

On 27th October, 1932, an American cuckoo flew into a shed on Tresco, Isles of Scilly and died. Mr A F Griffith exhibited it at a meeting of the British Ornithologist's Club in December, 1932 as a Yellow-billed Cuckoo *Coccyzus americanus*, a species that had occurred ten times previously. At the next meeting the bird was discussed by Dr P R Lowe, who proved that the bird was an immature Black-billed Cuckoo. He pointed out that the tail pattern was diagnostic of the species.

The specimen is now in the Isles of Scilly Museum.

Most vagrants arrive in poor condition with more than half of the records submitted to the BBRC concerning dead or dying birds.

References:
Kennedy, 1954: 284; *British Birds* 27: 111-2; 48: 7; *Zool*, 1872: 2943.

Yellow-billed Cuckoo *Coccyzus americanus*
(North and Central America; winters south to Argentina)

IRELAND
1825 Co. Cork, near Youghal.   **A (64)**
  An Irish gentleman shot a Yellow-billed Cuckoo near Youghall, Co. Cork, in autumn 1825. He immediately sent his butler with it to Mr Ball, of Dublin Castle; the bird still warm and bleeding on arrival. This record was first published in a letter to *Field Naturalist's* magazine in January, 1833, while Mr Thompson of Belfast, at the Zoological Society exhibited the specimen in June, 1835.
  The second Irish record from Old Connaught, near Bray, Co. Wicklow in 1832 was the same year as the first British records.

BRITAIN
1832 Pembrokeshire, Lawrenny.
  The Yellow-billed Cuckoo regarded as the first British occurrence was shot by the brother of James Tracey on the estate of Lord Cawdor at Lawrenny, Stackpole Court, Pembrokeshire (Dyfed), in autumn 1832, having been seen in the top of an ash tree taking insects. Tracey said:

  "*seeing it appeared nondescript, it was shot immediately and nothing more observed to its habits*".

  The skin was placed in the collection of the Zoological Society and is presently held in the Natural History Museum, Tring. Yarrell figured the specimen in his work.
  The first Yellow-billed Cuckoos were poorly documented as they were regarded as probable escapes. Yarrell mentioned a Yellow-billed Cuckoo killed in Cornwall, but gives no further information. He claimed that this bird followed the Irish records and was only described in a private communication.
  Harting (1901) recorded it as having been killed in 1825, while Hartert and later *British Birds* (1955) reported it or another as being killed in 1835, so it may have arrived during the same year as the first Irish bird or more likely confused with a Cornish record dated 1835.
  There was also a report from Poole Harbour, Dorset, prior to 1833, but the exact date is not known and the report not regarded as the first British record.
  Yellow-billed Cuckoos reaching Britain usually fail to find food and a large proportion of reports concern dead or dying birds.

References:
Yarrell, 1843: ii, 189-194; Montagu, 1862: 42; *British Birds* 48: 7; *Zool*, 1851: 3046.

(Dark-breasted) Barn Owl *Tyto alba guttata*
(Central Europe)
1937 Kent.   **A**
  In Kent, Major Powell-Cotton trapped an adult female Barn Owl in a gun tower on 8th December, 1937. Mr J Harrison saw the specimen in the Major's collection

while visiting in autumn 1947 and compared it to skins of the continental race *Tyto alba guttata*. He found a strong resemblance. This was the first British record of this race.

Reference:
British Birds 43: 54.

Eurasian Scops Owl *Otus scops*
(South Europe, Russia, West Asia and Northwest Africa; winters Africa)
1805 West Yorkshire, Wetherby.   A (90)

A bird in Charles Fothergill of York's collection had been shot in spring 1805, near Wetherby, West Yorkshire. There are few details about this record. The species was claimed to have visited many counties at some time prior to the 20th Century, frequently reaching as far north as Shetland.

Since 1910 it has become increasingly rare as a vagrant, generally attributed to a contraction in its northerly range.

References:
Montagu, 1862: 219; Nelson, 1907: 310-311; Mather, 1985: 392-393.

Snowy Owl *Nyctea scandiaca*
(Circumpolar Arctic)
1808 Shetland, Unst.   A (127 since 1958)

Travelling to Shetland in September, 1812, Mr Bullock was successful in procuring a bird killed by Lawrence Edmonston on Unst, where he claimed it had bred. Edmonston told Bullock of a specimen shot in Shetland in 1808. This earlier record was the first recorded in Britain.

On 3rd July, 1812, Bullock also visited North Ronaldsay and was told of a white bird as big as a goose with a head like a cat. The bird had been present for a month and favoured a rabbit warren called the Links. Bullock and two companions found the bird at the warren and approached to within 40 yards. Looking through a 'glass' the bird was found to be a pure white male Snowy Owl.

Bullock shot at it but failed to bring it down. It flew on for a mile and a reward was offered for its capture. Consequently the bird was harassed by poor marksmen but escaped by flying towards the island of Sanday. Bullock was informed that a female killed a few weeks prior to his visit had been plucked for feathers!

Regularly recorded on Unst during the last century, as word of the discovery spread, many birds were slaughtered for collectors in the south. Crofter, Robert Nicolson, accounted for at least thirty birds, while superstitious locals claimed: a cow would produce bloody milk if frightened by a "catyogle".

There have been 127 records since 1958. Snowy Owl was first discovered breeding on Fetlar, Shetland, in 1967, when five young fledged from seven eggs.

References:
Montagu, 1862: 222-223; Yarrell 1843: I, 134-138; Baxter & Rintoul, 1953: 266: Venables & Venables, 1955: 187-188.

Northern Hawk Owl *Surnia ulula*
(Boreal forests of Eurasia and North America)
1830 Off Cornwall, at sea. **A (10)**

A Northern Hawk Owl of the North American race *S. u. caparoch*, was found exhausted in the rigging of a collier a few miles from Looe, off the Cornish coast in March, 1830. It was easily captured alive by the crew and was presented by Captain Stacey to a friend of Dr Birkitt's when the vessel docked at Waterford, Ireland. Burkitt kept the bird alive for several weeks before it was mounted and exhibited at the June, 1835 meeting of the Zoological Society. Mr Thompson of Belfast gave an account of its capture and it was reported that it was also the first owl of any species to reach Ireland, albeit ship assisted.

In 1851, Mr E T Higgins recorded in *Zoologist* that a Northern Hawk Owl was shot at about 2pm on 25th or 26th August, 1847. The bird was hunting for prey in bright sunlight on Blackwell Hill, near the Yatton Station on the Bristol to Exeter Railway, Somerset. This was the first land-based Northern Hawk Owl record in Britain.

Mr Long killed the first British record of the European race *S. u. ulula*, at Amesbury, Wiltshire, in a period of severe weather during *c*.1830. Long gave the skin to Mr Rawlence of Wilton who placed it in his collection. The Rev A P Morres exhibited it at the Zoological Society in London on 4th April 1876, and the circumstances surrounding the discovery were somewhat vague.

Northern Hawk Owl is an invasive species but despite large numbers visiting Scandinavia during influx years they seem reluctant to cross the North Sea. It is perhaps surprising that at least three American birds have reached Britain, though ship assistance cannot be ruled out.

References:
Montagu, 1862: 218; Yarrell: i, 139-141; Rodd, 1880: 20; Smith 1887: 113.

Little Owl *Athene noctua*
(North Africa and Europe east to Tibet and northern China; south to Somalia)
1758 Greater London. **C (RB)**

The first published and dated record of a Little Owl concerned a bird caught alive in a chimney near the Tower of London. Edwards figured it in 1758. Another report concerned a bird shot in 1808, by the neighbour of Mr Comyns who lived in North Devon, both prior to the earliest published liberation date.

In Norfolk, one landed on a fishing boat ten miles off the Great Yarmouth coast. It was kept alive but died after refusing to eat, while in the same area a female was shot in the grounds of the Naval Hospital, Great Yarmouth, on 21st April, 1881. This was several years after the first release of captive birds, but the 'at sea' and coastal locations would indicate vagrancy attempts. They could just as easily have been leaving Britain rather than arriving however.

The resident British population of Little Owls are widely known to have originated from released birds, the earliest being in 1843, at Wakefield.

Various mentions of this species come from many counties including a note in an edition of Gilbert White's Selborne (1788), which recorded, *"the remains of a specimen of the rare Sparrow-Owl, Strix passerina, nailed up to a barn-door."*

Breeding Little Owls were established in Bedfordshire, Northamptonshire, Rutland and Kent by 1900, becoming a widespread resident in England and Wales by 1930. In Scotland, breeding first occurred in 1958; there has only been four records in Ireland.

The present population is estimated to be between 6,000 and 12,000 pairs. Despite reports of possible vagrants, the BOU do not currently include any records in Category A.

References:
Patterson, 1905: 157; Montagu, 1862: 219; Yarrell: i, 142-145; Saunders, 1899: 301; Wingfield Gibbons 1993: 248-9.

Tengmalm's Owl *Aegolius funereus*
(North Eurasia and North America)
1812 Northumberland, Widdrington.   A (47)

After the discovery of the first Tengmalm's Owl, the species was thought to have been overlooked and recorded as a Little Owl *Athene noctua*; a figure by Pennant in the plates for the first edition of *British Zoology* was a female Tengmalm's Owl. It was recorded as a breeding species at Castle Eden Dene, Co. Durham by Mr Hogg, in *Natural History of Stockton-on-Tees,* but this was doubted by Montagu. The first proven record was a specimen in Mr Selby's collection that was killed at Widdrington, near Morpeth, Northumberland in January, 1812.

There have only been seven records in the latter half of the 20th Century, with five from Orkney. The other two concerned a leg only (bearing a Norwegian ring) in County Durham and a bird in the Warren at Spurn, East Yorkshire from 6th to 27th March, 1983.

References:
Montagu, 1862: 225; Yarrell: i, 146-148; Naylor 1998.

Red-necked Nightjar *Caprimulgus ruficollis*
(Iberia and Northwest Africa)
1856 Northumberland, Killingworth.   B (1)

The only Red-necked Nightjar to reach Britain was thought to be of the race *C. r. desertorum*, the subspecies found in Algeria, Tunisia and the Sahara. It was shot at Killingworth, near Newcastle, on 5th October, 1856 and was recognised by John Hancock of Newcastle the next day, in the shop of a game dealer called Mr Pape. The bird was skinned and mounted by Hancock but could not be sexed by dissection. However, the white wing spots identified it as a male. The report was not published immediately as the specimen differed from an existing skin reportedly obtained in Hungary and held in his collection. After examining a skin in the British Museum he had no doubts about the identification of Britain's first and only Red-necked Nightjar.

It was subsequently placed in the Hancock Museum at Newcastle but on investigation by the author could not be found. Old photographs indicate it was removed from the main gallery c.1970s. In June 2000, it was found in a box of nightjar skins.

A nightjar at Bramford Speke, Devon on 26th March, 1991 arrived with early overshooting Mediterranean migrants and may have been this species but was not conclusively identified, while a dead bird allegedly found at the roadside near Camborne, Cornwall, on 16th September, 1998 was the subject of a hoax.

References:
Hancock, 1874: 83; Saunders, 1899: 269; *Birding World* 11: 328; Evans 1994: 292; *Zool*, 1862: 7936-7; *Rare Birds* 4: 356.

Egyptian Nightjar *Caprimulgus aegyptius*
(Northern Africa and Southwest Asia)
1883 Nottinghamshire, Rainworth.   A (2)

On 23rd June, 1883, gamekeeper Albert Spinks was in Thieves Wood, Rainworth, near Mansfield, Nottinghamshire. He fired at a rabbit on the edge of the wood and the noise flushed a nightjar from the side of the track. Noticing it was a pale looking bird he shot it. After keeping it at home for a day he decided that it was a young European Nightjar *Caprimulgus europaeus* and, as it had started to smell, threw it onto the ash pit. The following day his master, Joseph Whitaker, of Rainworth Lodge, visited. 'Fat' Spinks told him of the nightjar and went to fetch him the corpse. It was in poor condition and Whitaker, thinking that it was a "variety" (colour mutation) cut off the wings and tail prior to a few harsh words for Spinks.

After examination at home, he found it unusual that both wings should be symmetrical. His groom was despatched to fetch the remainder of the corpse and it was given to his birdstuffer, Samuel Hibbs of Ollerton. Despite the mutilation the bird was well mounted in flight, showing the undamaged upperside, with a small mirror on the back of the case to show the underwing pattern. Hibbs' work is relatively unknown outside the collections of Whitiker and Chaworth-Musters, of Annesley, Nottinghamshire.

Whitaker wrote to J H Gurney who identified the specimen as an Egyptian Nightjar. It was duly accepted as a genuine vagrant.

Whitaker, author of an early county avifauna, placed a stone with an inscription at the site where the nightjar was shot, to commemorate the event; it later suffered vandals. Part of his collection including the Egyptian Nightjar was sent to (and remains at) Mansfield Museum.

Britain's only other record was a bird that took off from Graham Walbridge's feet while he was walking through some rough pasture at Portland Bill, Dorset, at about 2.30pm on 10th June, 1984. The nightjar was flushed on a further two occasions, flying only short distances. On one occasion when the bird landed it was found to have walked 10-15 feet to hide behind a clump of thistles from which it took off. On the third attempt to see it on the ground, it made several circuits of the field before flying through a gap in the hedge. Happy that it was an Egyptian Nightjar Walbridge contacted other birdwatchers and after an hour returned to search the area without success. Despite using the lure of a tape-recorded Egyptian Nightjar song it was not found again.

The discovery of the Portland bird allowed Egyptian Nightjar to be upgraded from Category B of the British List to Category A.

References:
Whitaker, 1907: 141-142; Whitaker: personal notes; Frost. 1987: 107; *Ibis* 1932: 534; *Dorset Bird Report* 1984: 60-61; *British Birds* 92: 155-161.

Common Nighthawk *Chordeiles minor*

(North and Central America; winters South America)
1927 Isles of Scilly, Tresco.   A (16)

On 11th September, 1927, Major Dorrien Smith shot an American Nighthawk at Tresco Abbey, Isles of Scilly. Dr P R Lowe exhibited the bird, a female, at the November, 1927 meeting of the British Ornithologist's Club. This was the first example obtained in Europe and was said to be the typical form, *C. m. virginianus*.

The specimen is held in the museum at St Mary's, Isles of Scilly. These islands account for well over half of all British records, while unlikely locations have included Greater London and Nottinghamshire. Several have been found in poor condition or dead but one fortunate individual picked up at Moreton, Merseyside on 11th October, 1985 was eventually flown to Belize.

References:
British Birds 22: 98-100; 48: 8; Penhallurick, 1978; Naylor 1998

Chimney Swift *Chaetura pelagica*
(Eastern North America; winters South America)
1982 Cornwall, Porthgwarra.   A (6)

Stepping from his car at Porthgwarra, Cornwall, at 2.30pm on 21st October, 1982, L P Williams from nearby Hayle glanced upwards to see a 'dark bat' fluttering over the roof of a large house. Twenty minutes later, his companion G C Hearl watched a small swift flying towards him. Having been lucky enough to have seen a Little Swift *Apus affinis* in Cornwall the previous year, he could see that the 'jizz' was different and as it got closer noted the all black plumage and some small spines at the tail tip. Calling L P Williams over, they watched the bird flying around the houses and cliffs for two hours, during which time another birdwatcher and his wife joined them briefly. The swift then appeared to go to roost on the nearby cliffs.

They reached the conclusion that the bird was most likely a Chimney Swift and confirmed this later after consulting the literature.

The bird remained until the early morning of the 27th having been seen by hundreds of observers but amazingly a second individual joined it from the 23rd to 25th.

These Chimney Swifts constituted the first records of the species in the Western Palearctic and arrived during the best year ever for American landbirds in Britain. There were six records of this species prior to 1999 when possibly as many as 13 (not included in the totals above) reached Britain and Ireland. This was the product of a depression derived from Hurricane Irene.

References:
British Birds 79: 423-426, photos; 76: 47 photos; *Birding World* 12: 394.

White-throated Needletail *Hirundapus caudacutus*
(West Siberia to Japan, south to Northern China; winters Australia and New Zealand)
1846 Essex, Great Horkesley. **A (6)**

At 9pm on 8th July, 1846, Peter Coveney, a farmer's son from Great Horkesley, four miles from Colchester, Essex, shot Britain's first White-throated Needletail. Only wounded, it cried loudly as it fell, clinging so tightly to some clover when it was picked up, that it pulled stalks from the ground. He had first seen it on 6th July, when it was hawking insects over a small wood often flying to a great height.

It was thought that the bird, at the time called Spinetailed Swallow, was closely related to the nightjar *Caprimulgidae* on account of its late feeding habits.

Mr Catchpool recorded the occurrence and there was some suspicion about the report. It was proposed that the bird had been brought to England in the flesh from Australia so Messers Yarrell, W R Hall, Doubleday and Montagu examined it but accepted the record without hesitation.

References:
Zool, 1846: 1492-6; Cox, 1984.

Pallid Swift *Apus pallidus*
(Northwest Africa and Iberia to southern Iran; winters Africa)

IRELAND
1913 Co. Dublin. **A (14)**

A male Pallid Swift had been found dead at St John's Point, Co. Dublin, Ireland, on 30th October, 1913, preceding the first accepted record from Kent by 65 years. It had died while striking the lighthouse and was sent to R M Barrington who carried out migration studies at Irish lighthouses. He placed it in the Natural History Museum at Dublin labelled as a Common Swift *Apus apus*.

While researching some artwork, Killian Mullarney noticed the mistake and the identification of the specimen was confirmed prior to acceptance by the IRBC in 1994 (P Milne *in litt*). There are two Irish records.

BRITAIN
1978 Kent, Stodmarsh.

The first British record of a Pallid Swift was accepted as a bird found at Stodmarsh, Kent, in 1978. This followed at least nine other reports made since 1960 but none were proven.

As part of a sponsored bird count through the Stour Valley, W G Harvey and D Raine were watching Common Swifts *Apus apus* from the Lampen Wall at

Stodmarsh, on a cold and damp 13th May 1978. At about 10.30am they noticed a paler swift with a slightly different flight action. The bird fed close to the Lampen Wall occasionally passing as close as two metres. During the following 15 minutes they took field notes, before walking along the wall to meet C Clark, M Marsh, M Morley and P Murphy who had also been watching the bird. They all agreed that it was probably a Pallid Swift.

The news of its discovery was released and over the following days Stodmarsh was visited by hundreds of observers.

The Pallid Swift performed well from 7.30am to 4.30pm each day, remaining until 21st May with some unsubstantiated claims up to the 24th. The length of stay, prolonged views and over 500 observers enabled the species to be placed on the British List.

The bird had arrived with the main influx of Common Swifts.

Increased observer awareness has presumably led to the steady increase in reports with an influx in late 1999 (not included in the totals above) that may have involved up to 11 individuals.

References:
British Birds 88:526; Sharrock 1982: 230-235, sketch, and photo.

Pacific Swift *Apus pacificus*
(Asia east from Altai to Japan and Philippines; winters Indonesia, New Guinea and Australia)
1981 Norfolk, at sea.   A (3)

On 19th June, 1981, R Walden found a bird trying to land on his shoulder as he was on the deck of the Shell BT gas platform, on the Leman Bank, in the North Sea, 45km northeast of Happisburgh, Norfolk (*53 deg 06 min N 02 deg 12 min E*). At about 1.30pm he caught the exhausted bird as it clung to a wall and placed it on the next available helicopter ashore. At 7.30pm, Mrs S Irons telephoned Mike Parker from Beccles Heliport passenger terminal, Suffolk, to inform her work colleague that she had just received a tired swift *Apus*. Parker went to see if he could help and was surprised to see a white rump on the bird clinging to Mrs Irons' cardigan. He rapidly closed all the windows and after discounting Little Swift *Apus affinis*, due to its forked tail and scaly appearance, he telephoned Cliff Waller.

Waller took some photographs and a description, and discounted White-rumped Swift *Apus caffer* due to the bird's measurements. As the bird was looking better it was thrown into the air and released at 9pm to feed before dark. At this point the identification remained a mystery. The bird immediately began to take insects as it fed along the hedgerow surrounding the airfield but was lost as the light faded.

Independently, the two observers both identified the bird as a Pacific Swift after checking the literature that evening.

The following day the bird was seen briefly at Shadingfield, 4½km southwest of the heliport by Waller but was not seen again.

The in-hand measurements and photographs allowed the swift to be assigned to the nominate race *A. p. pacificus* and aged as a first-year individual.

Being in British waters, it was accepted as the first record for Britain and Ireland and placed in Category A of the British List. The first Pacific Swift to reach mainland Britain unaided was a bird found at Cley, Norfolk, by Alan Brown who had watched a strange swift with a white rump from the North Hide for ten minutes on the morning of 30th May 1993. While discussing it with Jackie and David Bridges in the coastguard carpark, Steve Gantlett, joined them. At 10.45am when he returned to the hide with Brown, the bird was still flying around with Common Swifts *Apus apus*. Realising it was either a White-rumped or Pacific Swift, Gantlett phoned Richard Millington who struggled with an injured foot to the hide.

After an obligingly close fly-past, Gantlett identified the bird as a Pacific Swift.

At 11am birders heard the news via the Birdline telephone service and about 650 birders managed to see the bird, which remained until 4.10pm.

The third and only other British report involved a bird at Daventry Reservoir, Northamptonshire on 16th July, 1995.

References:
British Birds 76: 503; 83: 43-46, photo; *Norfolk Bird & Mammal Report* 1993: 133; *Birding World* 6: 189-190, photo.

Alpine Swift *Apus melba*
(South Eurasia, Northwest and East Africa; winters Africa)

IRELAND
1829 Co. Cork, at sea.   A (570)

The first report of an Alpine Swift concerned a bird found eight to ten miles off Cape Clear Island, Co. Cork, Ireland. It was obtained and identified by William Sinclair in mid-summer, 1829. Because the record was 'at sea' very little importance was attached to it. Ireland's second record was at Dublin in March, 1833, the skin of which is in the Natural History Museum, Dublin (P Milne *in litt*).

BRITAIN
1830 Kent, Dover.

Britain's first Alpine Swift was found in the Dover Museum with a second specimen but lacked many details. It had been caught after flying into a room at Dover, Kent on 20th August, 1830 and having been mounted it was placed in the Thompson collection. It was destroyed in a bombing raid in October, 1943.

A bird killed at Kingsgate, Thanet, Kent, by the bailiff of Mr R Holford, in early June was used by Yarrell to figure in his book and claimed by him and Montagu to have been taken in 1820. Harrison, however, states that it was killed after the Dover bird and it is not accepted at all by some other authorities.

Of the 570 records less than 20 have remained for more than a few hours.

References:
Kennedy, 1954: 295; Harrison, 1953: vol 2. 28-30; Montagu, 1862: 337; Yarrell: i, 239-241; Evans 1994: 298-303.

Little Swift *Apus affinis*
(Africa, Middle East and South Asia)

IRELAND
1967 Co. Cork, Cape Clear.   A (16)

On the calm evening of 12th June, 1967, J T R Sharrock was watching a group of hirundines and Common Swifts *Apus apus* feeding near a ridge overlooking Cummer, Cape Clear Island, Co. Cork. Noticing a swift with a bright white throat he watched it pass several times at close range allowing him to record the bird's smaller size, shorter wings and more "fluttery" flight action. As it dropped lower he saw the square white rump and glossy upperparts. The bird was in view for about five minutes.

In later discussions with Major R F Ruttledge and I J Ferguson-Lees, it became clear that the bird had been a Little Swift and was accepted as the first and only individual to reach Ireland.

BRITAIN
1973 Denbighshire and Flintshire, Llanrwst.

On 6th November, 1973, a Little Swift was picked up exhausted on a school playing field at Llanrwst, Denbighshire. The bird was released the next day. The first British record was submitted by E Griffiths.

The first Little Swift to be seen fit and well in Britain was found by H P K Robinson among a mixed hirundine flock feeding over pools at Skewjack, Cornwall, on 16th May 1981. The bird had lost its secondaries presumably through moult and was seen by only a handful of observers fetched from watching a Woodchat Shrike *Lanius senator* at Porthgwarra.

References:
Sharrock 1982: 152-154; *British Birds* 68: 328-329; 77: 261-262.

Belted Kingfisher *Ceryle alcyon*
(North America south to Panama and Caribbean coast of South America)
1908 Cornwall, Sladesbridge.   A (4)

Britain's first Belted Kingfisher lay unrecorded for ten years until it was exhibited by Mr C Chubb at a meeting of the British Ornithologist's Union on 9th October, 1918. Mr G Thorne Phillips of Wadebridge, Cornwall had acquired the bird for the British Museum.

Accompanying the specimen was a statement from Mr F G Stevenson of Slades-bridge, Cornwall, who had shot the bird, in November, 1908. It said:

> "One day in November, 1908, the date of which I am not now certain, my attention was called by my neighbour at Sladesbridge, near Wadebridge, to a peculiar bird perching on the telegraph wires just outside my house. I took my gun and went out, but on my appearance it flew from the wires, alighting in a bush on the bank of the River Allen, I successfully stalked and killed it.

I sent the bird to a taxidermist in Plymouth, who stuffed it for me, but on making enquires failed to ascertain its name until in September of this year (1918) when visiting Wadebridge I made the acquaintance of Mr G Thorne Philips, of Polmorla Villa, who identified it as a Belted Kingfisher (Ceryle alcyon).

I handed the bird to Mr Phillips, who sent it to the British Museum, and it was exhibited at the meeting of the British Ornithologist's Club on October 9th 1918. This is the first recorded occurrence of this bird in England."

F. G. STEVENSON, NEWTON FERRERS.

By coincidence, a second British bird was found at the same site, 71 years later in 1979, where it remained until the autumn of 1981. There had been two fraudulent claims in between the two Cornish records; a male and female were obtained at Crowhurst, East Sussex on 17th and 18th March, 1919, respectively. Both formed part of the 'Hastings' records.

The discovery of a live bird in Ireland during 1978 initiated an investigation by the BOU and several earlier reports were reconsidered

Two earlier Irish claims were judged by Saunders (1899) to be unproven but following the Cornish report of 1908 the species was included in later editions of his *Illustrated Manual of British Birds.*

The 1908 Cornish specimen is presumed to have been destroyed by a bomb in 1940 but was formally accepted by the BOURC in 1980, following the Irish record in 1978.

IRELAND
1978 Co. Mayo, River Bunree.

The first accepted Irish record was found by John Donnelly while walking by the River Bunree, Co. Mayo on 10th December, 1978. Deducting that it was some kind of kingfisher he saw it the next day and 16th December. He subsequently wrote to J E Fitzharris, secretary of the Irish Records Panel who decided that the description could only fit one bird: Belted Kingfisher. On 3rd February, Fitzharris, Killian Mullarney and a small group of Dublin birders travelled to see it. They soon found the bird and obtained excellent views.

Although it seemed to have taken up residence this was brought to an abrupt end when a local man interested in taxidermy shot it! The offender was prosecuted and the specimen placed in the National Museum, Dublin.

A second Irish bird in 1980 was also shot

References:
British Birds 12: 160-1;55: 360; Sharrock 1982: 243-246. [Saunders, 1899: 280]

Blue-cheeked Bee-eater *Merops superciliosus*
(Africa and Middle East, east to Kazakhstan, and Northwest India)
1921 Isles of Scilly, St Mary's   A (8)

In June, 1962, J L F Parslow was examining the collection of birds belonging to T M Dorrien Smith at Tresco Abbey, Isles of Scilly and found a specimen of

Blue-cheeked Bee-eater labelled as an adult European Bee-eater *Merops apiaster*. Major A A Dorrien Smith had asked for the (European) Bee-eater reported from St Mary's, Isles of Scilly on 13th July, 1921, to be shot, as his collection lacked an adult. The corpse was sent to Messers Pratt and Sons, renowned taxidermists of Brighton, for mounting.

Soon after Parslow's visit, the collection was moved to the museum at St Mary's (where it remains). The face pattern of the bird was consistent with the migratory race *M. s. persicus*, which is found in Southwest Asia and northern Egypt.

This record pre-dated the previously accepted first report also from the Isles of Scilly, when Hilda Quick saw a strange bird while fetching milk on 22nd June, 1951. She had to return home so did not see the bird well. Lewis Hicks later called at the house and said he had also seen a beautiful bird, and together they returned to watch it catching bees and sitting on telegraph wires. It remained for just four hours.

Quick wrote to *British Birds*, as some features on the bird were not consistent with European Bee-eater. She was informed that the bird she had seen was in fact Britain's first Blue-cheeked Bee-eater, a position it held until Parslow's discovery.

References:
Bull., BOC, 92: 57-9; Sharrock, 1982: 24-25; *British Birds* 45: 224-227 colour painting.

European Bee-eater *Merops apiaster*
(Discontinuously in North, West, Southwest, East and Northeast Africa, Middle East, east to Kazakhstan and Northwest India)
1793 Norfolk, Mattishall.   A (666+)

The first report of this exotic looking bird was received in summer 1793, when a flight of 20 were seen at Mattishall, Norfolk. One was shot by the Rev George Smith in June and exhibited a year later by Sir James Edward Smith, then president of the Linnean Society. In October, 1793, what was presumed to be part of the same flock, returned to pass over the site.

Saunders claimed the year the birds were seen was 1793 not 1794 as often reported, as did Pennant, who included the species on the British List for the first time. The fact that Lewin's plate is dated 7th November, 1793 also supports this. Lord Derby was given the specimen, which eventually reached the Liverpool Museum (Dr A G Irwin *in litt*).

666 European Bee-eaters had been recorded in Britain prior to 1990 when the species was dropped from the BBRC's rarities list.

References:
Riviere, 1930; Montagu, 1862: 9; Saunders, 1899: 283; Yarrell, 1843: 200-201; Gurney 1921: 229; Naylor 1998.

European Roller *Coracias garrulus*
(South and East Europe, West Asia and Northwest Africa; winters Africa)
1664 Norfolk, Crostwick.   A (129)

Sir Thomas Browne accurately described the first European Roller to be seen in Britain in a note, which stated:

"On 14th May, 1664, a very rare bird was sent me killed at Crostwick, Norfolk, which seemed to be some kind of Jay. The bill was black, strong, and bigger than a Jays; somewhat yellow claws, tipped black; three before and one claw behind. The whole bird not so big as a Jay. The head, neck, and throat of a violet colour, the back and upper parts of the wing of a russet yellow. The fore part of the wing azure; succeeded downward by a greenish blue, then on the flying feathers bright blue; the lower parts of the wing outwardly brown; inwardly of a merry blue; the belly a light faint blue; the back toward the tail of a purple blue; the tail, eleven feathers of a greenish colour; the extremities of the outward feathers thereof white with an eye of green. – Garrulus argentoratensis."

Living in Norwich from 1636 he sent notes to Willughby, Ray and Merrett all pioneers in the ornithological world mentioned in an earlier chapter of this work.

The number of European Rollers visiting Britain has dropped considerably in recent years.

References:
Riviere 1930; Saunders, 1899: 281; *Zool*, 1876: 4840; Stevenson 1890, vol I: 312-313; Evans 1994: 307-311; Fisher 1954: 21.

Hoopoe *Upupa epops*
(Europe and Africa, east to China)
1666 Greater London   A (P)

The earliest dated record of a Hoopoe was mentioned in a book written by the physician-in-ordinary to Charles II. In it a life-size engraving accompanies a note regarding a specimen killed near London and given to the author in the winter of 1666.

A list of birds printed by Christopher Merrett in 1666 included Hoopoe, which had been reported by Sir Thomas Browne of Norwich. Browne has been credited with reporting the first Hoopoe but it is not clear whether these two records are connected. With the large gap in early ornithological knowledge and literature, it would appear the matching dates probably refer to the same individual. A bird with such a striking head-dress would possibly have received some degree of publicity at the time.

Hoopoe is recorded annually in Britain in small numbers, usually averaging 100 and occasionally well over 200.

References:
Rodd, 1880: xxii; *British Birds* 92: 18; Fisher 1954: 21.

Yellow-bellied Sapsucker *Sphyrapicus varius*
(North America; winters central and southern USA, Central America, Greater Antilles, south to Panama)
1975 Isles of Scilly, Tresco.   A (2)

At about midday on 26th September, 1975, David Hunt was leading a group of novice birdwatchers at the Great Pool, Tresco, where, checking the sallows, he spotted a woodpecker.

Hunt had no idea of its identity, so a description was taken and another group was called to see it. In the evening, Hunt checked the available literature, concluding that it was an immature male Yellow-bellied Sapsucker.

The following day after a mad scramble for transport at Penzance, Tresco hosted its first major 'twitch.' Hearing worrying tales of destructive hoards of 'twitchers' the Tresco estate's gamekeeper was dispatched, gun at the ready, to keep order.

The sapsucker was not considered to have been ship-assisted, as the autumn of 1975 was an extraordinary period for American landbirds in Britain.

Over 400 observers saw the bird before it was last seen on the 6th October. It was seen to make a series of holes in rings around tree-trunks, from which it drank the sap at hourly intervals in rotation.

A second individual identified as a first-year female was found on 16th October, 1988, by Dennis Weir on Cape Clear Island, Co. Cork, Ireland.

References:
Hunt: 149-150; Sharrock 1982: 202-205, photo; *Birding World* 1: 392-394, photo.

Great Spotted Woodpecker *Dendrocopus major major*
(Scandinavia and northern Russia)
1861 Shetland. **A (P)**

Saxby thought that a bird obtained in Shetland during 1861 was a Middle Spotted Woodpecker *D. medius*, while Gould illustrated the bird and thought it was a White-backed Woodpecker *D. leucotos*. Prof. Newton thought it was a slightly albescent Great Spotted Woodpecker.

Although never proven conclusively this was almost certainly the first British record of Great Spotted Woodpecker belonging to the Scandinavian race *D. m. major* which occurs regularly during migration in the northern Isles.

References:
Saunders, 1899: 276.

Eastern Phoebe *Sayornis phoebe*
(Eastern North America to southeast Mexico)
1987 Devon, Lundy. **A (1)**

Various visitors, including J Crook, had reported a possible Orphean Warbler *Sylvia hortensis* to the warden on Lundy, Devon as being present since 6.30am on 24th April 1987. Conclusive views had not been gained, however, and the bird lacked the characteristic white iris.

K J Mitchell, A J Wood and Colin McShane from Staffordshire were greeted with this information when they arrived on 25th April. Following a search of St John's Valley they set up mist-nets. At 4pm McShane saw the "Orphean Warbler" which was obviously some kind of flycatcher. After watching it for 15 minutes he fetched his two friends and over a period of about an hour they took plenty of notes. Despite their best efforts the bird refused to enter a mist-net, preferring to use it as a perch from which to make its fly-catching sallies. It wasn't until they left

Lundy that the identification of the first Eastern Phoebe for the Western Palearctic was finally sorted out; disappointingly it was not seen on subsequent days.

Two days prior to the Lundy bird, Alan Davies and Ken Croft had reported one at Slapton Ley, Devon.

The Lundy bird was accepted onto the British List by the BOURC while the BBRC and an American consultant rejected the identification of the Slapton bird.

References:
British Birds, 89: 103-107, sketches; *Ibis* 140: 182-184.

Calandra Lark *Melanocorypha calandra*
(Iberia and the Mediterranean region eastwards to Kazakhstan and Afghanistan)
1961 Dorset, Portland Bill.   A (7)

J S Ash heard a bird calling as it circled overhead with Sky Larks *Alauda arvensis* at 11.30am on 2nd April 1961, at Portland Bill, Dorset. The bird showed well as R J Jackson joined him and they watched it while making notes. It was obviously a Calandra Lark and remained in the area all day, during which time at least 23 observers saw it. This was the first acceptable record of the species in Britain.

In 1863 Mr J Gatcombe noticed a bird in the collection of Abraham Pincombe, birdstuffer of Devonport, Devon that he recognised as a Calandra Lark. The taxidermist thought it was a Horned lark *Eremophila alpestris* and assured Gatcombe that it had been killed locally at St John's Lake, by a man called Kendall, and then mounted by himself. The specimen was obtained by Gurney who said it did not look like a foreign skin, but later received a note from Mr Brooking saying that he should place no trust in anything said by Pincombe.

Gatcombe later reported another specimen but his records were never formally accepted.

On 16th May, 1916, a male Calandra Lark was shot from a party of five feeding on rough ground at Filsham Farm, St Leonards-on-Sea, East Sussex. The following day a female was killed at the same site and both specimens were seen in the flesh by Mr W R Butterfield. Neither specimen showed any signs of confinement and such a large number seen together would appear to have ruled out the possibility of escapes. While the records were accepted at the time, they were to later suffer the fate of their fellow Hastings rarities.

J A Stout shot a lark thought to be Calandra Lark at Setter, Fair Isle, Shetland in October, c.1928. Unfortunately the specimen was lost in transit to the Paisley Museum before being positively identified.

References:
Sharrock, 1982: 109-110 [Montagu, 1862: 189; D'Urban: 103; Walpole-Bond, 1938: i, 179-180; Dymond 1991: 75]

Bimaculated Lark *Melanocorypha bimaculata*
(Caucasus and Southwest Asia)
1962 Devon, Lundy.   A (3)

Michael Jones, warden on Lundy, Devon, saw a strange bird feeding with Common Linnets *Carduelis cannabina* on 7th May 1962. He fetched assistant warden Richard

Carden and they obtained poor views in the mist and rain. The lark remained on an area of short grass on the island, until 11th May, evading attempts to trap it. The bird was often seen being chased by Sky Larks *Alauda arvensis* so a size comparison was possible and the observers took a description of what they thought was a Calandra Lark *Melanocorypha calandra*.

There were no other visitors to the island during its five day stay and the report was sent to the BBRC. The committee recognised that the bird was in fact a Bimaculated Lark and a comparison made by Kenneth Williamson with skins proved this.

There are only three records of this species in Britain, the others being on St Mary's, Isles of Scilly in October, 1975 and on Fair Isle, Shetland in June, 1976.

References:
Sharrock, 1982: 117-120, sketch; Moore, 1969: 199.

White-winged Lark *Melanocorypha leucoptera*
(Southern Russia and Central Asia)
1869 East Sussex, near Brighton.　　　　　　　　　　　　　　　　　A (2)

The White-winged Lark has had a chequered history in Britain, several records from the Hastings rarities affair were later removed from the British List and a review in 1995, dismissed all but two of the rest.

On 22nd November, 1869, a birdcatcher near Brighton, East Sussex, trapped a female alive in a net, while attempting to catch 20 Snow Buntings *Plectrophenax nivalis*. It was shown to Frederick Bond of South Hampstead, London, who identified it as a young White-winged Snowfinch *Montifringilla nivalis* reporting it as such in *Zoologist*. He was convinced it was a wild bird.

Unknown to Bond, George Dawson Rowley had also seen the bird and correctly pronounced that it was a female Siberian Lark (White-winged Lark) before exhibiting it at a meeting of the Zoological Society.

A month later Bond wrote to the magazine again, correcting the identification.

The bird was placed in the collection of Thomas Monk of Lewes and later passed to the Booth Museum, Dyke Road, Brighton, where it remains cased with other specimens later rejected as part of the Hastings scandal.

The only other acceptable record concerned a bird (probably a first-winter male) that fed alongside King's Lynn sugar beet factory with a flock of ten Sky Larks *Alauda arvensis* on 22nd October, 1981. It remained until 24th October but news of its location was not released.

References:
British Birds 88: 365-371; Saunders, 1899: 257; Walpole-Bond, 1938: i, 177; Proc. *Zool* Soc., 1870: 52-3; Taylor 1999: 371.

Greater Short-toed Lark *Calandrella brachydactyla*
(South Eurasia; European population winters North Africa)
1841 Shropshire, near Shrewsbury.　　　　　　　　　　　　　　　A (512+)

In October, 1841, Henry Shaw, birdstuffer of Shrewsbury, wrote to Yarrell informing him that he had a Greater Short-toed Lark. The bird had been caught locally in a lark-net on 25th October. As the first record of the species in Britain, the skin was sent to Yarrell for examination and official confirmation of its identity.

Shaw, was a respected taxidermist with an expert ornithological knowledge. He became curator to the collection of Lord Hill (inventor of the penny post).

With about 18 records annually in Britain, spring overshoots are thought to involve southern birds, while greyer autumn birds are probably of eastern origin.

References:
Yarrell, 1843: i, 420-421; Zool, 1843: 80; Frost 1987: 125-128; Cottridge &Vinicombe 1997: 104.

Lesser Short-toed Lark *Calandrella rufescens*
(Spain and North Africa east to Manchuria; mainly resident and dispersive, but eastern populations winter south to Pakistan)

IRELAND
1956 Co. Kerry, Derrymore Island.   **A (43)**

About 40 Lesser Short-toed Larks were reported from Ireland in 1956 and 1958. The first was a flock of about 30 birds seen by Frank King on the salt marsh near Tralee Bay, Derrymore Island, Co. Kerry, on 4th January, 1956. Field notes were taken which described them as only slightly larger than Twite *Carduelis flavirostris* with the bill exactly like Greater Short-toed Lark *Calandrella brachydactyla*.

Just over two months later on 30th March, King visited Great Saltee, Co. Wexford, with P D Nolan, F O'Gorman and R G Pettitt. They found a group of birds that they described as five Lesser Short-toed Larks. These birds were identical to the 30 birds seen by King earlier that year. Only four birds were located the following day.

King discovered two more individuals with Sky Larks *Alauda arvensis* at Annagh, near Bellmullet, Co. Mayo, on 21st May, 1956, while with RG Wheeler.

The Irish records have been questioned in the past as the descriptions give no mention of some identification elements and other points such as the "lark-like bill" appear at odds with Lesser Short-toed features. These records have been reviewed by the relevant committees and remain acceptable.

BRITAIN
1992 Dorset, Portland Bill.   **A (1)**

Britain's first Lesser Short-toed Lark had been expected for years as Ireland had already recorded multiple sightings.

On 2nd May 1992, I R Dickie from Henley-on-Thames, Oxfordshire, accompanied a Young Ornithologist's Club group as assistant leader, to the top fields at Portland Bill Observatory, Dorset. He attempted to find a small pale bird that had flown into the limestone valley opposite the observatory at 10.10am without success.

At 5.40pm he returned to the fields with the group while its leaders prepared dinner. The pale bird flew up from the path and landed 400m away from him. He could see it was some kind of lark.

Discussing the bird's identity in the observatory, others dismissed it as a pale Sky Lark *Alauda arvensis*. Dickie returned to the field withAnna Hughes, another group leader who thought that it was possibly a Greater Short-toed Lark *Calandrella brachydactyla*.

When a Whinchat *saxicola rubetra* landed nearby for size comparison and the bird called she sent a YOC member back to the observatory to report it. The occupants ran to the field and Charles Wilkins the second group leader was the first to suggest that the bird might be a Lesser Short-toed Lark. Keith Vinicombe, member of the BBRC and later BOURC at first said it was a Greater Short-toed Lark but soon realised his mistake after looking through a scope. Again Lesser Short-toed was suggested and when it called, was recognised as such by Edwin Welland, an experienced birder. It eventually settled and gave good views to about 30 observers who managed to get there before 8.15pm when it flew to a distant part of the field out of sight.

About 400 birders searched the area the following dawn without success.

The record was accepted unanimously by the BBRC on its third circulation as Britain's first Lesser Short-toed Lark, in 1995.

There had been two previous unacceptable claims. Messers Swaysland and Borrer originally recorded a Greater Short-toed Lark netted near Brighton, Sussex on 15th November, 1873. Examination of the specimen in 1919 by Michael Nicoll revealed that it was a race of Lesser Short-toed Lark. In 1926, Mr E Hartert named it as *Calandrella rufescens kukunoorensis*, a sedentary race found only in Northwest China. The skin had been present in the Dyke Road Museum, Brighton since 1905 and was exhibited at a meeting of the BOC on 9th June, 1926. It was widely regarded as an escape and never gained official recognition.

A bird thought to have been a Lesser Short-toed Lark seen by warden Barry Spence at Spurn, Yorkshire, on 14th November, 1984, had disappeared when he returned with a mist-net. This record was not accepted by the BBRC.

References:
British Birds 88: 593-599; Mather, 1985: 421; Ruttledge: 141; *Birding World*: 5, 66, 179-180, sketch; Sharrock, 1982: 82-84. [Walpole-Bond, 1938: i, 180-182]

Crested Lark *Galerida cristata*
(Continental Europe south from the Baltic, South Asia, Northwest and upland Equatorial Africa)
Pre-1845 West Sussex, Littlehampton.   **A (20)**

Frederick Bond, founder of *Zoologist* magazine and a compulsive specimen hunter and egg collector, had in his collection the earliest British record of Crested Lark, obtained at Littlehampton, West Sussex, some time before 1845. It had presumably been netted by local birdcatchers who trapped larks *Alaudidae* and pipits *Motacillidae* for puddings and pies, while finches *Fringillidae* and buntings *Emberizidae* were sold into the cage bird trade.

Following Bond's death, the specimen was sold to Mr J Whitaker of Rainworth Lodge, Nottinghamshire, and later joined Sir Vauncey Harpur Crewe's collection at Calke Abbey.

The catalogue of the Calke Abbey auction in 1925, lists a case of larks including the Sussex bird. It sold for £4 5s.

Surprisingly for such a great rarity in Britain, two males were killed at Marazion, Cornwall the following year.

A report pre-dating the first 'official' Crested Lark record concerned a bird claimed to have been shot by Sir W H Russell, while a boy in Co. Dublin. This was never proven as the specimen was lost.

References:
Saunders, 1899: 255; Calke Abbey Auction; Kennedy, 1954: 303; Walpole-Bond, 1938: i, 182-183; Borrer 1891: 112.

Horned Lark *Eremophila alpestris*
(Holarctic)
1830 Norfolk, Sheringham.   A (WV)

In March, 1830, Britain's first Horned Lark was shot on the beach at Sheringham, Norfolk. John Sims of Norwich mounted it and sold it to Edward Lombe of Great Melton, Norfolk, where it joined one of Britain's largest collections of the time. A Horned Lark (Accession no. 18.73) presently in the Norwich Museum was the only specimen of this species in Lombe's collection. It is a male, possibly first-year, which was removed from its original case and is in poor condition. The broad pale fringes on the crown feathers resemble autumn birds but first-year males may still retain this feature into spring.

The second British record came from the same locality. Norfolk also claimed the third, a bird obtained at Great Yarmouth in 1850.

By 1880, the Horned Lark was a regular visitor and collectors regularly targeted it. Pashley, the Cley taxidermist, received dozens in the 1890s while a Great Yarmouth taxidermist received 50 in just four days. Influx years have been regularly reported with 800 found in Norfolk 1998.

References:
Yarrell, 1843. i, 403; Saunders, 1899: 159; Denton 1995: 51; *Birding World* 12: 8; *Birdwatch* 80: 22-3; Taylor 1999: 376.

Tree Swallow *Tachycineta bicolor*
(North and Central America)
1990 Isles of Scilly, St Mary's.   A (1)

Over 100 years after it was first claimed, Britain was finally graced with Europe's first acceptable Tree Swallow. Jeremy Hickman, a barman at the Mermaid Inn on the Isles of Scilly, found it after walking into the hide at Porth Hellick on 6th June, 1990. One of five hirundines flying over the pool, it looked like a House Martin *Delichon urbica* without a white rump. After a better view from the sluice, he ran to phone Carl Downing and Adrian Hickman to discuss the identification. Concluding that it was a Tree Swallow he returned to watch the bird and take notes.

The bird remained until 10am on 10th June when it spent the morning twittering from a fence post. Over 800 people saw it.

This remains the only accepted British record.

In summer 1850, John Evans was shown the skin of an unfamiliar swallow when he visited the shop of John Cooke, birdstuffer and museum-keeper in Derby. It had reputedly been shot in the company of 11 Sand Martins *Riparia riparia* at an area of common land named the Siddals, in a suburb of the city. Cooke thought it was perhaps a 'variety' and sought the opinion of Evans who purchased the bird for one shilling before sending it to John Wolley for examination. The skin was compared to other specimens in the British Museum and identified as a Tree Swallow (then called Severn Swallow). It was said to be in the Norwich Museum.

Following an investigation in 1993, Dr Alan Knox, chairman of the BOURC found that the specimen had never been at Norwich and was now lost. Alfred Newton had doubted the record in 1860, saying there was a possibility that the skins may have been muddled in the collector's shop. This record is therefore not acceptable.

References:
British Birds, 86: 188; 88: 381-384, photos; *Zool.* 1853, 3806-07.

Eurasian Crag Martin *Ptyonoprogne rupestris*
(Southern Europe, North Africa and the Middle East)
1988 Cornwall, Stithians Reservoir.   A (5)

Eurasian Crag Martin was expected as a vagrant to Britain for many years but the first arrived as recently as 22nd June, 1988. P Higson had driven to check the waders at the Golden Lion causeway at the north-western end of Stithians Reservoir, Cornwall, but, finding the water level too high, sat in the car to eat his lunch. He casually glanced upwards when he heard a loud burst of calls from a House Martin *Delichon urbica* flock and was surprised to see a brown martin with white tail spots only one metre above the car. Diving out of the car he picked the bird up over the west of the causeway with the House Martins and watched it for 10-15 minutes while taking notes. Realising that the bird was a Crag Martin he left at 1.30pm to telephone other birders. When he returned the bird had vanished.

The second British record followed 17 days later at Beachy Head, East Sussex, on 9th July. Again the bird was seen by one observer E D Urquhart, but it had vanished when he returned with another observer.

Both records were accepted by the BOURC in 1989.

References:
British Birds 83: 155-159; *Birding World* 12: 148-150.

Red-rumped Swallow *Hirundo daurica*

(Southern and Eastern Eurasia and Africa; European population winters in Africa)
1906 Shetland, Fair Isle.   A (329)

Large numbers of migrants had arrived on Fair Isle, Shetland on 2nd June, 1906. Among them, George Stout of Busta noticed three swallows with a red band across the lower back. They remained for several days before he succeeded in shooting one, but failed to locate the bird. Ten days later he found the corpse and sent it to Eagle Clarke for identification. The bird was found to be a Red-rumped Swallow of the race *H. d. rufula* and was the first British record of the species.

Annual totals have only exceeded double figures twice prior to 1987 when an amazing 61 individuals were reported, and since then the annual totals have been high.

References:
A.S.N.H., 1906: 205, 1908: 203; British Birds 1: 11; Thom, 1986; Dymond, 1991: 79; Clarke, 1912: 151; Naylor 1998.

Cliff Swallow *Hirundo pyrrhonota*
(North America; winters Chile, Brazil and Argentina)
1983 Isles of Scilly, St Agnes.   A (6)

An unusual hirundine was seen by several people on the islands of St Agnes and Gugh, Isles of Scilly, during the afternoon of 10th October, 1983. Paul Vautrinot saw it well enough to make a detailed description. He was unable to put a name to the unfamiliar bird and neither could M Opie, P Morrison and D N Smith as they saw it arrive at the Garrison, St Mary's, later that day. It flew past accompanied by Barn Swallows *Hirundo rustica* and after ruling out Red-rumped Swallow *Hirundo daurica* they presumed that it was a hybrid.

Michael J Crosby arrived to see the bird land, exhausted with drooped wings on a roof and recognised it as a Cliff Swallow from birds he had seen in the USA.

By late afternoon, several hundred birders had gathered to watch the bird feeding over the Garrison Wall. The following day, it moved to Lower Moors and before its departure on 27th October had visited several parts of St Mary's, favouring Higher Moors and Longstones.

This was the first Western Palearctic record with two subsequent reports coming from the East Coast: South Gare, Cleveland in 1988 and Spurn, Yorkshire in 1995. There has been one Irish record at Dunmore head, Co. Kerry in 1995.

References:
British Birds 81:449-452, photos; Naylor 1998.

Richard's Pipit *Anthus novaeseelandiae*
(Europe and Asia south to Australasia)
1812 Greater London.   A (P)

The first official record of what is now regarded as a scarce but annual visitor to Britain was captured alive in Copenhagen Fields, Middlesex, to the north of London, in October, 1812. The specimen was figured by Mr N A Vigors, MP in *The Zoological Journal*, v.1. 1831 and also used to illustrate the species in Yarrell's *British Birds*. The collection of birds belonging to Vigors was later presented to the Zoological Society.

A report exists of a bird of the race *A. n. dauricus* found by M Southam and D Lewis in recently mown grass on the edge of the runway at RAF Portreath, Cornwall. On Sunday 10th December, 1995. They spent one and a half-hours studying the bird. It was first seen in the company of four Richard's Pipits on 12th November when it was seen to have been noticeably smaller with an unusual call and jizz. This report was published in the *Cornish Bird Report* but not sent to the BBRC/BOURC (Tim Melling *in litt*).

There are remains (bones) of a Richard's Pipit dating back to the Middle or Late Pleistocene Age discovered in one of the Mendip caverns in Somerset. The species was once possibly widespread throughout Europe.

Just under a hundred migrants can be expected each year with the highest annual figure being 338 in 1994.

References:
Glegg 1935: 47; Palmer & Balance 1968: 180-182; Yarrell, 1899: i, 398-399; *British Birds* 92: 22; [*British Birds* 90: 164; Birds in Cornwall 1995: 159]

Blyth's Pipit *Anthus godlewskii*
(Southern Siberia, China and Northeastern India; winters India, Sri Lanka and Andaman Islands)
1882 East Sussex, Brighton. **A (9)**

While preparing a paper on the identification of large pipits in 1963, Kenneth Williamson discovered the skin of a juvenile Blyth's Pipit labelled as a Tawny Pipit *Anthus campestris* in the Natural History Museum, Tring. It had been obtained on 23rd October, 1882, at Brighton, East Sussex, but the species was not thought to be a potential vagrant to Britain and so not placed on the British List. It was only after a second bird turned up in Finland in 1975, that the record received more attention and admission to the British List, albeit on Category B. This specimen remains at Tring.

On 13th October, 1988, Paul Salaman and Arthur Livett had found a large pipit at Quoy, Fair Isle. The call sounded interesting but they moved away to check out a grey warbler at Shirva. The bird was not located again until midday on the 14th when David Russell heard it call overhead in a way that resembled Yellow Wagtail *Motacilla flava*, rather than Richard's Pipit *Anthus novaeseelandiae*. The bird landed and fed along the edge of a cabbage patch at Shirva where it was seen to lack the loral stripe of Tawny Pipit *Anthus campestris*. The structure and behaviour seemed untypical for Richard's Pipit.

In the afternoon, the bird moved to Quoy where Nick Riddiford decided that the bird was a Blyth's Pipit.

The bird remained in the area for three or four days and generally became more elusive before the last reported sighting on 23rd October. This record was pended BBRC awaiting further field notes, with the situation unchanged by December, 1999 (Tim Melling *in litt*).

A record of a first-winter Blyth's Pipit at Landguard, Suffolk on 4th November, 1994 was the first of the modern records to be accepted by the BOURC allowing Blyth's Pipit to be placed in Category A. It was killed by a Common Kestrel *Falco tinnunculus* after being trapped on the 10th.

A bird present at Skewjack, Cornwall, from 22nd October to 1st November, 1990 has been accepted as the second record.

Ireland has yet to be graced by the presence of a Blyth's Pipit.

References:
Birding World 1: 395-397, sketch; 3: 375-378; Naylor 1998.

Tawny Pipit *Anthus campestris*
(Northwest Africa and Western Europe east to Mongolia; the Western Palearctic population winters in the Sahel zone of Africa and in Saudi Arabia)
1858 West Sussex, Shoreham Harbour.   **A (P)**
   Occurrence of Tawny Pipit in Britain was first recognised by George Dawson Rowley who examined two birds from Sussex in 1862. Both had been shot in autumn and had been mistaken for Richard's Pipits *Anthus novaeseelandiae*. The first example of a Tawny Pipit had come from Shoreham Harbour, West Sussex, killed on 17th August, 1858. It belonged to Mr H Collins but was later purchased by Mr J B Nichols.
   The second bird had been obtained late on the evening of 24th September, 1862, near Rottingdean, East Sussex. A man called Wing took the bird to George Swaysland of Brighton to have it mounted. Swaysland recognised that it was unusual and possibly a Richard's Pipit so persuaded Wing to sell it. Swaysland then passed the bird to Dawson Rowley who realised that it was not a Richard's Pipit and discussed the matter with Alfred Newton. Newton suggested that it may be a Tawny Pipit.
   After notice of the event was published, Sussex and Kent regularly recorded this species.
   References:
   Saunders, 1899: 137; Walpole-Bond, 1938: i, 211-213; *Ibis* 1863: 37.

Olive-backed Pipit *Anthus hodgsoni*
(Northeast Russia to Central and East Asia; winters Southeast Asia)
1948 Pembrokeshire, Skokholm.   **A (209)**
   On 14th April 1948, Joan Keighly (later Joan Jenkins) and Peter Conder caught an unusual pipit in the garden trap on Skokholm, (Dyfed) Pembrokeshire. The bird was exhausted but was ringed and photographed before its release and a description taken. It was last seen on the island on the 18th April.
   Conder examined skins at the British Museum of Natural History later that year and thought that the bird was probably an Olive-backed Pipit. But the unusual time of year, coupled with little published material, placed doubt in his mind and the record was not submitted.
   In 1967, photographs of Olive-backed Pipits trapped on Fair Isle, Shetland, in 1964 and 1965, were published in *British Birds*, and the records were reported and accepted as the first British records. After reading this, Conder sent his record and photograph to I J Ferguson-Lees.
   At the time, the BBRC decided that there was insufficient evidence to accept the report but ten years later JTR Sharrock found the photograph among the *British Birds* files and investigated the report. It was resubmitted and this time was accepted by the BOURC as Britain's first Olive-backed Pipit.
   Remaining a great rarity until 1979, there has since been a massive shift in the species status. A further 293 were recorded in the next 18 years with 46 in 1990 alone. Fair Isle attracts the bulk of reports with Scilly and Shetland falling into second place. Ireland has only four reports.
   References:
   Sharrock, 1982:132-137; Naylor 1998; Cottridge & Vinicombe 1997: 108.

Pechora Pipit *Anthus gustavi*
(Northeast Russia to Central and East Asia; winters Southeast Asia)
1925 Shetland, Fair Isle.   **A (69)**

On 24th September, 1925, Surgeon Rear Admiral J H Stenhouse shot a pipit at Fair Isle, Shetland which proved to be a male Pechora Pipit. It had first been seen on 23rd, having been flushed from a turnip patch into a stook of oats and finally into some oat stubble. It had a call similar to Meadow Pipit *Anthus pratensis,* but generally the bird remained quiet. When examined, the contents of its stomach were said to have contained a large number of tiny black beetles.

The first and only Irish record was at Garinish, Firkeel, Co. Cork from 27th to 28th September, 1990.

Fair Isle remains the stronghold of this species in Britain.

References:
British Birds 20: 11-12; 91: 498; Scot. Nat., 1925: 141; Naylor 1998.

Red-throated Pipit *Anthus cervinus*
(Arctic Eurasia; winters India and Africa)
1854 Shetland, Unst.   **A (391)**

A specimen discovered in the late Frederick Bond's collection was labelled "*Unst, May 4th 1854.*" This bird had been captured in Shetland and purchased by Bond from the collection of Mr Troughton.

A report later removed as part of the Hastings rarities was of a bird shot by Walter Prentis at Rainham, Kent, in April 1880 while it fed among the freshly turned soil behind his plough. It was sent to Dover for preservation and exhibited by Dr R B Sharpe at the 1st April, 1884, meeting of the Zoological Society, along with a second Red-throated Pipit.

The second accepted record is a female collected from Fair Isle on 2nd October, 1908.

Many Red-throated Pipits fail to reach the criteria laid down by BBRC for acceptance, as they are frequent 'fly-over' only birds and observers with prior experience of the species must submit a full account of the call. Usually between six and ten birds are accepted annually.

References:
Baxter & Rintoul, 1953; Saunders, 1899: 135; British Birds 2: 423; 91: 500; Clarke, 1912: 122.

Water Pipit *Anthus spinoletta*
(South and Eastern Europe, east to northwest China)
1859 East Sussex, Brighton.   **A (WV)**

The first dated occurrence was made known by John Pratt, taxidermist of Brighton, when he received a locally killed bird in 1859. He also received a specimen from Worthing, Sussex at the same time and sent them to John Gould for examination and confirmation. Gould took five years to reply to Pratt and so the record was not published until 1864. One of the specimens was given to the Booth Museum, Brighton in 1903.

Due to confusion with Scandinavian Rock Pipits *Anthus petrosus littoralis*, the true status of Water Pipit in Britain is not easily unravelled. Henry Doubleday reported the first documented example to Yarrell and the addition to the British List was announced in *Zoologist* (1843). However the circumstances surrounding this discovery were not mentioned and it cannot be regarded as the first record.

Water Pipit occurs annually each winter probably numbering less than 100 individuals.

References:
Saunders, 1899: 141; *Zool* 1843: 79-80; Frost: 78; Lack 1986: 298.

Buff-bellied Pipit *Anthus rubescens*
(North America, western Greenland, eastern Asia)
1910 Western Isles, St Kilda. A (5)

Eagle Clarke and George Stout spent autumn 1910 on St Kilda, and found 35 new species of bird to the island. Clarke's best discovery was on 30th September when the wind was light, following strong westerlies the previous day. Attracted by an unusual call, Clarke found the culprit among a flock of Meadow Pipits *Anthus pratensis* and promptly captured Britain's first Buff-bellied Pipit, on a small burn, close to the village. It proved to be an immature male.

Previous claims in Edinburgh and London had been rejected by Saunders.

Ireland's only acceptable report was near Newcastle, Co. Wicklow on 19th October, 1967.

References:
British Birds 4: 285; Clarke, 1912: ii, 212, 200, 185.

Yellow (Blue-headed) Wagtail *Motacilla flava flava*
(Breeds Northern Europe)
1834 Essex, Colchester. A (P)

The fact that Yellow Wagtails on the continent differed from the British form (later called Ray's Wagtail) escaped the attention of ornithologists until 1832, when Gould pointed out the distinction. Two years later the first Blue-headed Wagtail was found in Britain, near Colchester, Essex in October, 1834. At the time it was called Grey-headed Wagtail, a name later given to another subspecies of Yellow Wagtail.

In a letter to Mr Heysham, Henry Doubleday said: "On 3rd October, walking with two friends on top of the cliffs at Walton-on-the-Naze, I had the pleasure of seeing two individuals of the Grey-headed Wagtail, one of which (a male) I shot. When I came to London I took it to Bruton Street (where the Museum of the Zoological Society was) and there I met with Bennett, Gould and Yarrell," all of whom confirmed the record.

Blue-headed Wagtail is the commonest of the continental migrant races to reach Britain and Ireland and breeding with British *flavissima* is recorded almost annually.

References:
Saunders, 1899: 127; Montagu, 1862: 363; Yarrell, 1843: i, 375; Wingfield Gibbons 1993: 495; Mays 1978: 20.

Yellow (Ashy-headed) Wagtail *Motacilla flava cinereocapilla*
(Breeds Southern France and Italy, east to the Balkans)
c.1842 Cornwall, Penzance. **A (P)**

A specimen of Ashy-headed Wagtail was said to have been obtained at Penzance, Cornwall. There are no other details.

Less than half-a-dozen are usually reported in Britain each year and the variety of hybrids or integrades prevent the correct identification of most. Most records are labelled as "showing characteristics of" rather than a definite claim being made.

References:
Hartert 38; Witherby I: 217.

Yellow (Grey-headed) Wagtail *Motacilla flava thunbergi*
(Breeds North-eastern Europe)
1842, Norfolk, Sheringham. **A (P)**

A male thought at the time to be an Ashy-headed Wagtail *M. f. cinereocapilla* obtained at Sheringham, Norfolk in 1842, was in fact the earliest Grey-headed Wagtail. The specimen (Accession no. 15.935(45)) is in good condition and currently held at the Norwich Museum. The entry in the museum's log reads *"Sheringham Norfolk, May 1842. J.H. Gurney Collection 15.935(45)"* (Dr A G Irwin *in litt*).

In spring 1901, a Grey-headed Wagtail was captured near Halifax, Yorkshire, with other records soon following. This race was officially recognised after the above examples and a pair with their eggs collected in 1906 was exhibited at the British Ornithologist's Club.

Grey-headed Wagtail is the second most commonly recorded migrant member of the 'blue-headed' wagtail races to reach Britain. About 40 can be expected annually.

References:
British Birds 1: 10; 91: 579; Hartert: 37; Witherby I: 216-7.

Yellow (Black-headed) Wagtail *Motacilla flava feldegg*
(Balkans east to Afghanistan and Iran; winters Northwestern India and East Africa)
1970 Shetland, Fair Isle. **A (7)**

In the 1990s, the BOURC looked at all Black-headed Wagtail records and found that many were unacceptable. Separation from some grey-headed race *M. f. thunbergi* was not as straightforward as first thought.

After thorough examination only a handful of records remained acceptable, the first being reported by warden Roy Dennis and J J Harris, among others, on Fair Isle, Shetland from 7th to 9th May 1970. It had been found by Julian Harris feeding among the short grass and stones on the shore of Easter Lother Water taking flies at ranges down to ten yards. The following day it flew to nearby cliffs at least twice and generally became more flighty. There were at least three other races of Yellow Wagtails reported on the island.

On the final day of the bird's stay it had moved to Byerwell pool in the middle of the island.

The first unacceptable report was a Hastings rarity seen by M J Nicoll, a well-known ornithologist who collected specimens in Sussex before taking a job at the Giza Zoological Gardens in Egypt. His specimens were sold to the Booth Museum, Brighton. Nicoll found and identified a male Black-headed Wagtail at Pevensey, Sussex, during May 1902. The bird was not obtained.

Until the BOURC review a male at Cley-next-the-Sea, Norfolk, on 17th to 19th June, 1910, had stood as the first record. It was seen by Mr J Rudge Harding who refound it two days later whilst out walking with a friend.

Black-headed Wagtail remains a very rare bird in Britain.

References:
Scot Birds 6: 215-216; Walpole-Bond, 1938: i, 253-254; Evans, 1994: 337-338; Frost 1987: 74; Seago 1967: 135; *British Birds* 4: 92; 64: 364; 88: 530.

Citrine Wagtail *Motacilla citreola*
(Northeast and East Russia, West Siberia, West and Central Asia; winters southern and Southwest Asia)
1954 Shetland, Fair Isle.   **A (118)**

A wagtail was captured at 5.45pm in the Gully Trap at Fair Isle, Shetland, on 20th September, 1954. Kenneth Williamson, H G Alexander, II Mayer-Gross, Miss M. Haydock, Mrs A W Thom and Miss V Thom examined the bird before it was placed in a roosting box in the laboratory. Although the light was poor the bird looked superficially like a young Yellow Wagtail *Motacilla flava*, but the mantle was too grey for the typical British *M. f. flavissima* or continental *M. f. flava* forms. The following morning the bird was re-examined and matched the published description of a juvenile Citrine Wagtail. It was released but the identification remained un-confirmed until juvenile Grey-headed Wagtail *M. f. thunbergi* could be discounted.

The bird was relocated by H G Alexander on Buness, 200 yards from the Observatory during the morning of 22nd. After watching it in the field he pronounced: *"Had I seen the bird in India, I should have no hesitation in calling it citreola."*

The wagtail was later found behind Williamson's laboratory where he took additional field notes while it fed. Six fresh observers arrived from Shetland on the *Good Shepherd* that evening but failed to locate the bird the following morning. It had been placed in the laboratory, having been caught for a second time by a staff member. Guy Mountford, I J Ferguson-Lees and DIM. Wallace were able to study and photograph the bird before its release. It had gained weight and was present all day. It was last seen on 24th.

Remarkably a second bird (unringed) was found hawking flies from the seaweed on the beach at the southern end of the island on 1st October. After being ringed and a description taken the bird was released, remaining to the 5th October at least.

On 26th November, Williamson, Alexander, Mountford and Ferguson-Lees met to examine skins at the British Museum of Natural History, confirming the identity of Britain's first Citrine Wagtails.

Publication of the relevant identification criteria has resulted in many more records.

In January, 1998, members of the Shetland Bird Club at the County Museum, Lerwick were viewing specimens collected between 1910 and the early 1950s by Sammy Bruce. Pete Ellis noticed that a skin labelled as a Blue-headed Wagtail *Motacilla flava flava* was in fact a Citrine Wagtail. The poorly written label dated the bird from sometime in the 1930s, predating the 1954 Fair Isle bird, but as the label provided no date or location it is unacceptable by the strict standards set by the BOURC.

The recent increase in sightings has been attributed to a number of birds now breeding in Scandinavia, while in 1976 a male was found feeding four young in Essex. Fair Isle receives the majority of records.

References:
Sharrock, 1982: 51-54, photo; Dymond, 1991: 85; *British Birds* 48: 26-9 photo; 91: 398; *Birdwatching* July 1997: 46; Cottridge & Vinicombe 1997: 110.

Pied/White Wagtail *Motacilla alba yarrellii/alba*
(Continental Europe throughout Asia, except peninsular India and southeast; also breeds Alaska and southeast Greenland)
1841 Greater London, Kingsbury Reservoir (Middlesex).   A (P)

While researching for his book *The Birds of Europe*, John Gould realised Pied Wagtail had never been described. He found it distinct from the White Wagtail *Motacilla alba alba* on the continent and in 1837 named it *Motacilla yarrellii*, after his friend William Yarrell. Following publication of this fact the search was on to find the first example of White Wagtail, in Britain.

Frederick Bond found two pairs in May 1841, at Kingsbury Reservoir, Middlesex, one of which was shot.

Yarrell in *Zoologist* (1843) announced its acceptance as a British bird.

References:
Yarrell, 1843: i, 362-370; *Zool* 1843: 79-80; Saunders, 1899: 123.

Bohemian Waxwing *Bombycilla garrulus*
(Holarctic)
1680 York.   A (WV)

The first record of Bohemian Waxwing in Britain and Ireland was mentioned in a letter to John Ray from Dr Martin Lister. He called the bird "Silk-tail" and drew a crude illustration of the waxwing. He said one or two had been shot in York during January, 1680.

The birds occurring in Britain are of the nominate race *B. g. garrulus* from northern Europe. The paler, greyer, American form *B. g. pallidiceps* has not been recorded here. In 1915, a third race *B. g. centralasiae*, midway in colour tones, was recognised. James identified this Siberian form in skins from the N F Ticehurst collection. The earliest specimen had been a female obtained on 18th January, 1895, from Cambridgeshire. Harrison exhibited six skins including the Cambridgeshire bird at the June, 1952 meeting of the British Ornithologist's Club.

Bohemian Waxwing remains a regular winter visitor in varying numbers from just a handful of individuals to thousands as in 1995/96, when probably *c.*10,000 birds arrived.

References:
Harrison 1953: vol 2. 299-300; Mather, 1985: 448.

Cedar Waxwing *Bombycilla cedrorum*
(North America; winters south to Northern South America)
1985 Shetland, Noss.   **A (2)**

A bird found tangled in netting in Oxfordshire in May 1985 was an escaped cage bird, so when a second individual was found a month later feeding among thrift on rocks on the island of Noss, Shetland it -was immediately put under suspicion. The bird was found in the afternoon of 25th June, 1985 by Mr and Mrs P Leward who returned to the visitor centre to inform NCC warden Clive McKay that they had seen a waxwing. McKay photographed it at a range down to 3m assuming it to have escaped. Despite attempting to contact local birders, the only other observer was Susan Crosthwaite. McKay watched it again the next day between 9.30am and 11.30am noting that it showed no positive signs of captivity (Ian Dawson *in litt*). At the time, this bird was accepted by the BOURC onto Category D as a possible escape.

Following a massive influx of Bohemian Waxwings *Bombycilla garrulus* into Britain, Peter Smith noted a build up of birds in the Sherwood area of Nottingham, where he worked, and after counting a flock of 160 he returned home for lunch. While looking at an American field guide he dreamily noticed the Cedar Waxwing plate, and after work at 3.15pm on 20th February, 1996, he returned to the waxwing flock.

Checking the undertail coverts on the first bird he saw from his parked car he was amazed to see that they were white. Nervously checking the various field characteristics of this Cedar Waxwing with the Bohemian Waxwings accompanying it, he went for reinforcements. He could only pursuade Eric Birkinshaw to join him and he was able to confirm the white undertail just before the flock departed to roost. The following morning it was located by Billy Simpson who confirmed the identification and alerted the 30 birders searching for it.

The streets of Nottingham were the scenes of mayhem for several days as birders searched for the Cedar Waxwing among the mobile flock of Waxwing. At their peak in March the total number there was thought to have exceeded 1,200 individuals.

The Cedar Waxwing remained in Nottingham until at least 18th March moving throughout the city with the Bohemian Waxwing flock with sightings up to nine kilometres apart. It had arrived at a time when large numbers of both species of Waxwings had been on the move in North America with birds arriving in Northwest Ireland thought to have originated from this source. This record was accepted onto Category A of the British List by the BOU in 1997 and the Shetland record was subsequently reconsidered. The species had become less common in captivity following an export ban of Mexican birds in the mid to late 1980s and the Shetland bird was upgraded to Category A in 1998 and therefore became the first British record.

Earlier unaccepted reports, included a specimen in the collection of Sir William Fieldon of Feniscowles, shot at Cambo, Fifeshire in 1841 and recorded by Robert Gray. Another undated specimen was recorded in 1851 and collected at Horseheath, near Linton Cambridgeshire, while, two birds killed at Stockton-on-Tees, Cleveland in 1850 were considered by Latham to be a race of Bohemian Waxwing *Bombycilla garrulus* then called the "Carolina Chatterer".

Curiously in 1871, Robert Gray recorded that a Cedar Waxwing which flew on board a ship leaving port in Canada, spent most of its Atlantic crossing perched on the rigging or figurehead from which it made frequent sallies. When approximately 15 miles from Ireland it flew to a passing ship returning to America. This was Ireland's only report of the species.

References:
British Birds: 86: 229; 91: 500;Montagu, 1862: 29; *Birding World* 9: 70-73, photo; 10: 360; *Zool*, 1851: 3277; Gray 1871: 109. [*British Birds* 48: 11].

Northern Mockingbird *Mimus polyglottos*
(Central and Southern North America)
1982 Cornwall, Saltash.   A (2)

After three failed attempts for this species to gain admission to the British List, (the first having been shot on a farm near Ashford, Kent, in 1851), a Northern Mockingbird in Saltash, Cornwall was finally accepted by the BOURC in 1996. E Griffiths first saw the bird at 7.30am on 30th August, 1982. It flew out of a conifer to avoid two Carrion Crows *Corvus corone* that had disturbed it. The bird called twice as it took cover in some small trees, while its flight was slow and the white wing flashes clearly seen. On hands and knees, Griffiths peered through a hedge to view the bird which was perched on the low branches of an apple tree 4m away. All relevant plumage details were noted in the four or five minutes before it took off, chased by Magpies *Pica pica*. It called again as it disappeared, battered by a force 7-8 north-westerly gale.

At the time the bird was seen there was an importation block on American species and a Black-billed Cuckoo *Coccyzus erythrophthalmus* and Black-and-white Warbler *Mniotilta varia* had been seen in the same county.

An earlier record at Blakeney, Norfolk in 1971 was discounted as an escape, as it had abraded feathers and a bald patch above the bill, while a bird at Worms Head, Glamorgan in 1978 split the BOURC and was thought to be of unknown origin.

Britain's second and only other record involved a bird at Horsey Island, Hamford Water, Essex from 17th to 23rd May 1988. Unfortunately the landowner refused to grant access and only local birdwatchers saw the bird, which frequented a grassy field and hedgerow of a coastal farm.

References:
British Birds 89: 347-356; Evans 1994: 341. [Harrison 1953: 239]

Brown Thrasher *Toxostoma rufum*
(Eastern North America)
1966 Dorset, Durlston Head.   A (1)

The only British record of this American bird remained in dense vegetation, in a wooded area above cliffs at Durlston Head, near Swanage, Dorset, from 18th

November, 1966, to 5th February, 1967. Its explosive "chat" call led Mr C S L Incledon to discover it. The bird fed on the ground at a range of about 25 feet and resembled a slim thrush with a tail equal in length to its body. It usually ate acorns that were repeatedly hammered, but was also seen to take earthworms. Returning home, Incledon checked various books and decided that it was a Brown Thrasher. The identification was supported in a telephone conversation with Mrs W G Teagle and various birdwatchers were informed. The bird was witnessed by observers on a path at the same time in the afternoon each day for two-and-a-half months. They included DIM. Wallace Dr J S Ash and M F Robertson.

At 4.15pm on 23rd November, the bird was trapped and ringed by F R Clafton while Dr D J Godfrey photographed it. This remains the only European record.

References:
Prendergast & Boys 1983: 210; *Birdwatching*, Nov. 1996: 14; Sharrock 1982: 146-148.

Grey Catbird *Dumetella carolinensis*
(North America and West Indies; winters south to Panama)

CHANNEL ISLANDS
1975 Jersey, St Brelade's Bay.   A (1)

A Grey Catbird had joined House Sparrows *Passer domesticus* to take crumbs in public gardens in St Brelade's Bay, Jersey, Channel Islands during the middle of October, 1975. Although appearing tired and hungry, the bird would not allow a close approach so the finder put bait below a paint tray propped up with a stick to trap it. Unable to name it, the captor contacted Frank Lawrence, a bird fancier who caught birds in the 1930s to supplement his low wage, and became an expert ringer with the Société Jersiaise. He identified it as a Grey Catbird.

The catcher placed the bird in his aviary and it was then taken to the Lawrence household in St Helier. Lawrence was the only person allowed to handle the bird for fear of its escaping whilst being photographed.

The catbird remained in the aviary for a further three or four years in reasonable health before dying of natural causes. The record was accepted onto the Channel Islands list as relating to a wild bird.

IRELAND
1986 Co. Cork, Cape Clear. A (1)

The only record on the British and Irish List concerns a bird found near South Harbour, Cape Clear Island, Co. Cork on 4th November, 1986. K Preston saw it perch for ten seconds beside a Song Thrush *Turdus philomelos* on the low roof of an outhouse whilst waiting for a Red-breasted Flycatcher *Ficedula parva* to appear. It then flew onto the fence and lawn of a nearby garden.

It flew towards South Harbour and was never seen again.

BRITAIN
[1998 Hampshire, Southampton].   [1]

On 21st October, 1998, a Grey Catbird was present on the *QEII* as it docked at Southampton. It had been found by crewmember Malcolm Draper soon after leaving New York and roosted each night behind the funnel on the helideck. It didn't leave the ship, which continued its journey through the Bay of Biscay with the catbird on board.

It had been provided with fresh water and various fruits only leaving the ship in Malta when feeding stopped.

A report from Cot Valley, Cornwall on 28th October, 1988, was rejected by the BBRC.

References:
Evans 1994: 342; British Birds 82: 1-3; 68: 9; 74: 526-7; Birdwatch 78: 16. [*Birding World* 5: 402; Birdnet; *Rare Birds* 5:57]

Hedge Accentor *Prunella modularis hebridium*
(Inner and Outer Hebrides)
1934   A (RB)

Resident in the Western Isles, the 'Hebridean' Dunnock (Hedge Accentor) is described as "at best very local and difficult to observe" in its range, the Inner and Outer Hebrides. This subspecies was described by Meinertzhagen who announced, on behalf of the BOU in 1934, that it was an accepted new race occurring in Britain.

This subspecies is resident and sedentary in Western Scotland and Ireland but some authorities (not BOU) separates the Scottish birds as *P. m. interposita* and the Irish birds as *P. m. hibernicus*; the latter was also described by Meinertzhagen.

References:
British Birds 28: 95-96; Wingfield Gibbons 1993: 296; Cramp 1988: 548-560.

Alpine Accentor *Prunella collaris*
(Mountains in Iberia and Northwest Africa, the Alps, east to Japan; winters at lower altitude)
1817 Essex, near Walthamstow.   A (40)

The 1832 edition of London's *Magazine of Natural History* contained a letter that read:

> "*Sirs, A few years since, I shot a small bird in a garden on the borders of Epping Forest, which I did not know, nor could anyone tell me what it was, till within a fortnight a gentleman requested me to allow him to take it to London. He accordingly went to Mr Gould, Naturalist, 20, Broad-street, Golden-square, who sends me an account of its being the Accentor Alpinus, or Alpine Warbler, the only one known to have been killed in England, with the exception of one in Dr Thackeray's garden at Cambridge. If any of your correspondents would like to see it, they can by calling at my nursery, Wood-street, Walthamstow.*
>
> I am, Sir, yours, & c. JAMES PAMPLIN. *Whips Cross, Walthamstow, January, 27th, 1832* "

This specimen had been shot while feeding with Chaffinches *Fringilla coelebs* at Forest House, Walthamstow, Essex in 1817. It predated the existing record of a pair of

Alpine Accentors feeding in the gardens of King's College, Cambridge, in 1822. The female was shot and preserved for Rev Thackeray on 22nd November. While the male was presumed to have been taken by a cat.

Alpine Accentor remains a very rare visitor averaging one record every five years.

References:
Yarrell, 1843: i, 219-222; Naylor 1996 and 1998.

Rufous-tailed Scrub Robin *Cercotrichas galactotes*
(South Europe, Southwest Asia and North Africa)
1854 East Sussex, Plumpton Bosthill.   A (11)

Brighton birdstuffer, George Swaysland owned a shop that was a meeting place for bird-netter's and shooters to take rare specimens. On 16th September, 1854, Swaysland was travelling on the south downs. When six miles from Brighton at Plumpton Bosthill, he saw a bird that appeared to be a pale Common Nightingale *Luscinia megarhynchos.* As he did not have a gun he proceeded for another four miles to borrow one. He returned to the original site and found it only 20 yards away. Describing it as "being like a young Red-backed Shrike" *Lanius collurio* he pursued the bird, which always hid on the opposite side of any bush that Swaysland approached. This is typical of the species. Eventually he shot at the bird and killed it at a range of 40 yards.

The bird proved to be a male Rufous-tailed Scrub Robin, then called Rufous Bushchat or Rufous Bush Warbler, of the western race *C. g. galactotes,* and was just starting to moult its wing feathers. The specimen was recorded by William Borrer of Cowfold, magistrate and collector, and examined by both Yarrell and Montagu who accepted the identification.

In 1907, Mr AL Butler wrote to Michael Nicoll questioning the racial identification as the bird depicted in Borrer's *Birds of Sussex* appeared to be of the race *C. G. familiaris.* The editors of *British Birds* upheld the original identification but some years later the specimen was accidentally incinerated.

Several Rufous-tailed Scrub Robin specimens of the eastern race *C. G. familiaris* passed through the hands of George Bristow and were thus rejected as part of the Hastings rarities.

Britain has produced eight records with Ireland receiving three.

References:
Montagu, 1862: 372; Saunders, 1899: 73; Walpole-Bond, 1938: ii, 54-56; Frost 1987: 79; Naylor 1998.

Thrush Nightingale *Luscinia luscinia*
(Scandinavia, East Europe and West Asia; winters Africa)
1911 Shetland, Fair Isle.   A (136)

The first proven occurrence of a Thrush Nightingale in Britain and Ireland was at Fair Isle, Shetland, on 15th May 1911. When a male arrived among a fall of 24 species of migrants, Eagle Clarke shot it behind the south lighthouse during one of his collecting expeditions. The bird had been found seeking food among rocks at the foot of the cliffs.

Mr Cullingford, taxidermist of Durham, presented a cased bird to Mr L A C Edwards in 1908. Although the label read: "*Savi's Warbler, Norwich, 1845*" it contained a Thrush Nightingale. It was thought that the bird had been killed at Norwich in 1845 and that a mistake had been made in the identification. However, the record was not accepted as the details written on the label may not have related to the specimen within.

The mounted and cased specimen of a Thrush Nightingale, known as 'Sprosser', was reported to have been obtained at Smeeth, Kent, on 22nd October, 1904. It was exhibited by Mr M J Nicoll but for a similar reason as the above record was not acceptable. Dr Hartert also suspected that it had been imported.

Thrush Nightingale was first distinguished from Common Nightingale *Luscinia megarhynchos* in 1831. Northeast Britain receives the majority of records with Fair Isle and Shetland sharing half of these.

References:
British Birds 1: 8; 5: 240; Riviere 1930: 82; Clarke, 1912: ii, 141; Naylor 1998; Fisher 1954: 26.

Common Nightingale *Luscinia megarhynchos hafizi/africana*
(Southern Russia to Afghanistan)
1971 Shetland, Fair Isle.   A (1)

This eastern race of Common Nightingale can only be safely recognised in the hand so not surprisingly there have only been two reports. The first was a first-winter bird found dead on Fair Isle on 30th October, 1971. A second bird was found alive at Spurn, Humberside, on 6th October, 1991. It remained until 14th, being trapped on the 9th. The report was in circulation with the BOURC at the end of 1999. At least two others have been claimed since the Fair Isle bird, which remains the only acceptable record.

References:
Birding World 11: 232; Evans 1994: 348.

Siberian Rubythroat *Luscinia calliope*
(Siberia: winters India to Southeast Asia and Philippines)
1975 Shetland, Fair Isle.   A (2)

On 9th October, 1975, A R Lowe, P J Roberts and S G D Cook found an unfamiliar robin-like bird at the North Grind, near the Sheep Cru, on Fair Isle, Shetland, while walking from the south of the island to the Observatory. After a few minutes, they concluded it was a Siberian Rubythroat. They were soon joined by Roger Broad and decided to trap the bird, which was examined at the observatory before being released into the garden. The bird was successfully twitched the same afternoon by Shetland birders. It was last seen at Setter on the 11th.

In the hand, it was seen to show traces of red on the throat and was considered to be an immature male.

The age of the bird and general appearance did not indicate a period of confinement, despite captive Rubythroats being available in Britain.

Following the BBRC's rejection of a bird found two years later at Donna Nook, Lincolnshire, on 14th October, 1977, the second record is of a male in Dorset present only for a day.

In October 1900, a pair of Rubythroats were seen and recorded by Joseph. Nunn of Royston at Westgate-on-Sea, Kent. Nunn was a competent observer who compared his notes with skins belonging to Alfred Newton. His sighting was reported in *The Times* but as no record was 'officially' published it was rejected by Saunders in the first edition of *British Birds* in 1907.

References:
Dymond 1991: 90; Sharrock 1982: 205-207, photo. [Harrison 1953: 158; *British Birds* 1: 8; Hartert 1912]

Bluethroat *Luscinia svecica*
(Europe east to China; wintering south to India and Africa)
1826 Northumberland, Newcastle.   **A (P)**

Thomas William Embleton of Methley, near Leeds, killed Britain's first Bluethroat on the boundary hedge of Newcastle Town Moor, in May 1826. The specimen was placed in the Newcastle (now Hancock) Museum and was of the red-spotted race *L. s. svecica*.

The first white-spotted bird *L. s. cyanecula* was caught in a Nightingale trap, near London, in May 1845. The bird was an adult male and was seen alive by John Hancock of Newcastle and Mr Hewitson while in the possession of its captor, James Green of City Road.

This specimen was not recorded until eight years after its capture and Green was a known importer of birds. Consequently this record was not accepted by Saunders, Newton or Ticehurst. However the next report of this race received a more favourable reception albeit temporarily: A workman named Gasson picked up the bird, an adult male, below the Dungeness lighthouse on 5th October, 1902 and it was recorded as the first British record. The specimen suffered one major drawback: it was handed to George Bristow, the taxidermist at the centre of the Hastings rarities affair. Despite acceptance at the October, 1902 meeting of the BOU it suffered the fate of all other vagrants that passed through the hands of Bristow: rejection in 1962.

A record from the previous century, deemed acceptable in Witherby's *The Handbook of British Birds*, states that a male white-spotted bird was seen near Scarborough, North Yorkshire on 12th April 1876, and so is the earliest known occurrence of this race.

A report that remains to be authenticated concerns a bird seen on the Isle of Wight from February, 1865 to September, 1867.

Bluethroat is a regular migrant on the British east coast in both spring and autumn. It remains rare in Ireland.

References:
Montagu, 1862: 366; trans Nat Hist Soc of Newcastle and Durham: 67; Harrison 1953: 160; *British Birds* 1: 8; Witherby 1945, ii: 198; Cottridge & Vinicombe 1997: 114.

Siberian Blue Robin *Luscinia cyane*
(East of the Altai through Siberia to Korea, winters south to Indonesia)

CHANNEL ISLANDS.
1975 Sark.   **A (1)**

The only European record of a Siberian Blue Robin comes from the island of Sark so for completeness is included here as the record was judged by the BOURC.

At 12.50pm on 27th October, 1975, Philip Guille extracted a bird from a mist-net placed in his garden under the sycamore canopy at the head of Banquette Valley on Sark. He had no idea what the bird was so it was photographed indoors and a feather by feather description taken. When released, the bird flew off low and undulating and was not seen again. Eventually it was identified as a first-year female Siberian Blue Robin as it lacked the breast-scales of an adult.

The record was accepted by the Sark Rare Bird Panel and due to its international importance also judged by the BOURC. This was the first record of this species west of Bengal.

References:
British Birds 70: 361-365, photo.

Red-flanked Bluetail *Tarsiger cyanurus*
(Northeast Europe across Asia to Japan; winters Southeast Asia)

1903 Lincolnshire, North Cotes.   **A (20)**

In January, 1954, an old report from coastal Lincolnshire was published in *British Birds*, prefixed by the word "probable". This record is now recognised as the first British occurrence of a Red-flanked Bluetail.

Mr G H Caton-Haigh of Grainsby, Lincolnshire, accompanied by his keeper Mr F Bacon visited North Cotes, Lincolnshire during a large movement of passerines on the 19th, 20th and 21st September, 1903. On one of these days they saw an adult male Red-flanked Bluetail but failed to shoot it. It had been seen first by Bacon who saw all the relevant features of the species as it moved along a hedge. Caton-Haigh was on the other side and noted all plumage details except the birds underparts. Although convinced of the identification and a description recorded in his unpublished *Birds of North Cotes* the lack of a specimen made Caton-Haigh reluctant to claim a British first. This was in line with the recording policy of the time.

Caton-Haigh regularly worked the north Lincolnshire coast. He added no less than three species to the British List.

An immature Red-flanked Bluetail of the race *T. c. cyanurus* shot by Samuel Bruce at Whalsay, Shetland on 7th October, 1947 was photographed and widely regarded as the first British record at the time.

The eastward expansion of the bluetail's breeding range is responsible for so many records being found in the last half of the 1990s. There are no Irish records.

References:
Venables & Venables, 1955: 172; Smith & Cornwallis, 1955: 39-41, 115; British Birds 61: 214-215.

White-throated Robin *Irania gutturallis*
(Asia minor, southern Asia and East Africa)

ISLE OF MAN
1983 Calf of Man.   **A (2)**

Following a day of dense fog on the Calf of Man, the wind was light south easterly as Adrian del Nevo, J R Calladine and M W Watson were walking to the observatory on 22nd June, 1983. A wheatear-like bird caught del Nevo's eye as it stood on a dry-stone wall 10m away. All three observers were puzzled by the bird, which lacked a white rump as it flew off. Watson left to fetch telescopes and open mist-nets nearby in the hope of catching it. The bird returned to the wall after a few minutes and the possibility of it being a White-throated Robin was suggested. It hopped about in some nettles and bracken before finally flying across a farmyard out of sight. Despite further searches the bird was not seen again. From the description taken, the bird was a striking male, the brownish primaries possibly indicating a first-year bird.

BRITAIN
1990 Pembrokeshire, Skokholm.

On 27th May, 1990, Britain's first White-throated Robin took up temporary residence on Skokholm. It was a female bird found by warden Michael Betts, J W Donovan, and D A Thelwell and remained present until 30th May. It was decided that due to the 35,000-plus incubating Manx Shearwaters *Puffinus puffinus* large numbers of birders could not be accommodated, though a small band of invited guests including author David Saunders successfully twitched the bird on the 28th. Margaret Potts and Michael Wallen also photographed it.

References:
Birding World 3: 208, photo; British Birds 87, p 83-86; 83: 543, photo: 84: 482; Cottridge & Vinicombe 1997: 116.

Black Redstart *Phoenicurus ochruros*
(Western Europe and North Africa to Northwest China)
1829 Greater London.   **A (SB & P)**

John Gould added Black Redstart to the British List describing the capture of a specimen near London in October, 1829. Frederick Bond also claimed the first record but his specimen from Brighton was killed in 1830. At the time it had been recorded as a rare migrant to the British Isles but I have been unable to trace conclusive information before this date.

With the establishment of *Zoologist* magazine in 1843, records were regularly submitted and this species was frequently encountered in southern counties during winter.

It remains a regular passage migrant and summer breeder.

References:
Yarrell, 1843: i, 241; Montagu, 1862: 270.

Moussier's Redstart *Phoenicurus moussieri*
(North Africa from Morocco to Tunisia)
1988 Pembrokeshire, Dinas Head.   A (1)

On Sunday 24th April 1988, Graham Walker was leading a group, which included Mike Barrett, at Dinas Head on the north Pembrokeshire coast. At 2pm Barrett noticed a colourful bird perched on a rock that resembled a Common Redstart *Phoenicurus phoenicurus*. He pointed the bird out to Walker who identified it as a male Moussier's Redstart.

After a minute it disappeared but was soon relocated, enabling the whole group to watch it for the next hour as it flitted among the rocks. The bird was harassed by a pair of Stonechats *Saxicola torquata* nesting nearby and after being photographed was lost at 3pm. Walker telephoned the county recorder but the bird was not seen again. It probably departed that evening, as it was a cloudless night.

Moussier's Redstart was accepted onto the British List without any problem as it is not known to have been held in captivity in Britain.

References:
Birding World 1: 160-161, photo; *British Birds* 85:108-111, photos; Cottridge & Vinicombe 1997: 113.

'Siberian' Stonechat *Saxicola torquata maura/stejnegeri*
(White Sea across Siberia: winters Iran, Southeast Asia, and Borneo)
1913 Fife, Isle of May.   A (272)

The honour of the first acceptable British record fell to an immature male of the race *S. t. maura*, collected by two famous Scottish ornithologists, Evelyn Baxter and Leonora Rintoul. The bird was obtained on the Isle of May, Fife, on 10th October, 1913 and was said to have resembled a Whinchat *Saxicola rubetra*. The specimen was sent to Dr Hartert for examination and confirmation of its identity. (In *British Birds* this bird was listed as a female).

A bird once credited as the first, but later removed from the British List concerned a male 'Indian' Stonechat *S. t. maura* (as it was then known) was shot by Mr E C Arnold, at Cley-next-the-Sea, Norfolk, on 2nd September, 1904 (Seago refers to it having been obtained at Morston).

Saunders accepted it after he had seen it in Pashley's taxidermy shop at Cley. At first he thought it was a melanistic Stonechat until he compared it with skins at the National Museum. The mounted specimen (Accession no. (479.966)) was held at the Eastbourne College Museum before being moved to the Castle Museum, Norwich in 1966 (Dr A G Irwin *in litt*).

In the 1970s Ian Robertson expressed doubts about the identification. Photographs were sent to Derek Goodwin at the British Museum and it was re-identified as an old male of the race *S. t. rubicola* or *S. t. hibernans*, occurring commonly in Britain and continental Europe. The bird is in extensive body moult with few remaining feathers on the rump and measurements also indicate *S. t. hibernans*. It was recommended in 1977 that the record be removed from the British List.

Colloquially known as 'Siberian' Stonechat, over 150 individuals have been recorded in Britain to date but only two have positively been identified as belonging to the race *S. t. stejnegeri,* the first being a male at Cley, Norfolk on 2nd May 1972.

Two birds have shown characteristics of the East Caucasus and North Iranian race *S. t. variegata;* the first was a male at Porthgwarra, Cornwall from 1st to 4th November, 1985.

References:
Riviere 1930; Pashley 1992: 111: 57; Baxter & Rintoul 1953, 1: 211; *Scot. Nat.*, 1913: 273-274; Evans 1994: 352-354. [*British Birds* 70: 237, 243].

Isabelline Wheatear *Oenanthe isabellina*
(South and Central Eurasia from Russia and Turkey eastwards; winters Northeast and East Africa and from Arabia eastwards to Central India)
1887 Cumbria, Aigle Gill.   A (17)

Thomas and Richard Mann were sowing corn at Aigle Gill farm, near Allonby, Cumbria on a fine but dull 11th November, 1887, when a pale 'Northern' Wheatear *Oenanthe oenanthe* perched on clods of earth allowed them to approach closely. The bird was easily shot, as requested by Rev H A Macphearson. He received it the next day and showed it to Saunders who compared it with skins in his collection and found it to be an Isabelline Wheatear. It was also examined before skinning by Messrs Seebohm, Sharpe, Harting and George Lodge who sketched it; Lodge's figure appeared in Saunders' *Manual.* When dissected it was found to be a female and the delicate barring on the breast indicated that it was a first-year bird.

The bird was exhibited on 6th December at a meeting of the Zoological Society of London and accepted onto the British List. Macphearson then presented it to the British Museum.

The next record of Isabelline Wheatear did not come until 90 years later, in 1977. This may have been because of its similarity to the female Northern Wheatear and the difficulty that surrounded their separation in the field.

The species remains very rare in Britain.

References:
Ibis 1888: 149; Saunders 1899: 21; Hutcheson, 1986: 88.

Pied Wheatear *Oenanthe pleschanka*
(Southeast Europe and South-central Asia; winters East Africa)
1909 Fife, Isle of May.   A (41)

Evelyn V Baxter and Leonora Jeffrey Rintoul were undertaking migration studies on the Isle of May, Fife, on 19th October, 1909, when at noon on the east side of the island, they flushed a dark wheatear that gave fleeting views between the rocks. They pursued the bird until a lucky shot (not for the bird) brought it down. Finding no description like it in Saunders' *Manual* they sent it to the National Museums of Scotland, Edinburgh, for examination by Eagle Clarke.

Still unsure of its identity, it was transferred to Dr Hartert at Tring, who pronounced that it was a female Pied Wheatear.

Pied Wheatear remained a great rarity until the 1970s when it became an almost annual visitor, mostly on the east coast in autumn.

References:
A.S.N.H., 1910: 2; *British Birds* 3: 296; *Scot. Birds* 8: 115; Thom, 1986.

Black-eared Wheatear *Oenanthe hispanica*
(Southern Europe, Northwest Africa and Southwest Asia, also Iran; winters West Africa)
1875 or 1878 Lancashire, near Bury. **A (59)**

Mr R Davenport shot an adult male Black-eared Wheatear near Bury, Lancashire some time around 8th May, 1875 or 1878. The bird had a fine black throat and was of the eastern race *O. h. melanoleuca*. He sent the specimen to be exhibited at a meeting of the Zoological Society.

The first specimen of the western race of Black-eared Wheatear *O. h. hispanica* was a male shot near Polegate, Sussex on 28th May 1902. This was the first of nine Hastings rarity records of Black-eared Wheatear and consequently later dismissed.

An earlier record of a bird seen and sketched at Spurn, Yorkshire, by Dr Henry Bendelack Hewetson, surgeon of Leeds, on 18th September, 1892 was of this race. At the time, it was published by J Cordeaux in *Birds of the Humber District* but as no specimen was obtained it was not taken seriously. However, it holds well by today's standards and is the first officially accepted British record of this race.

Black-eared Wheatear can be a difficult bird to see in Britain, with many moving on overnight.

References:
Saunders 1899: 23; Walpole-Bond, 1938: ii, 90-91; Mather 1986: 469.

Desert Wheatear *Oenanthe deserti*
(North Africa, Northwest Arabia, east to Mongolia; winters Saharan Africa, Arabia and Pakistan)
1880 Upper Forth, Alloa, Clackmannanshire. **A (73)**

A fine male Desert Wheatear was shot on 26th November, 1880, near Alloa, Clackmannanshire, Scotland. Mr J J Dalgleish, owner of the specimen sent it to be exhibited at a meeting of the Zoological Society in 1881, stating that the bird's stomach contained small flies picked up in a manner more restless than its commoner relative. The late date fits in with the now established pattern of vagrancy for this species, which during the 1990s became a regular and expected annual vagrant.

James Stout obtained a male Desert Wheatear at Fair Isle, Shetland, on 6th October, 1928, it having probably arrived on strong southeasterly winds the previous day. This bird was of the eastern race *O. d. deserti* while the four previous records had related to *O. d. homochroa*. It was accepted as the first British record of this subspecies.

The first Irish record was as recently as 1990.

References:
Saunders, 1899: 25-26; *British Birds* 24: 22-23.

White-tailed Wheatear *Oenanthe leucopyga*
(North Africa east to Saudi Arabia)
1982 Suffolk, Kessingland.   **A (1)**

Mr and Mrs R Tarry of Kessingland, Suffolk, saw a Black Wheatear *oenanthe leucura* in an area where farm rubbish and machinery was dumped near the local pumping station. At 6.15pm on 4th June, 1982, they telephoned B J Brown and the three of them visited Kessingland pumping station.

They soon located the confiding bird and still thought it was a Black Wheatear. There was however some discrepancies in the description, including a white feather on the head and no terminal tail band. Despite this, the news was released before they had chance to consult any literature. They soon realised the mistake when they compared notes taken over an hour's viewing with an illustration in Heinzal's field guide. It was Britain and Ireland's first White-crowned Black (now White-tailed) Wheatear.

The bird was watched by a large number of people. It was probably a first-year bird as the juvenile primaries had been retained and most likely the North African race *O. l. leucopyga*.

It was found during the hottest June for 35 years. There have been no further British records.

Following the surprising occurrence of this individual, all Black Wheatear records were reviewed and rejected by the BOURC as White-tailed Wheatear could not conclusively be eliminated.

References:
British Birds 79: 221-227, photo.

Rufous-tailed Rock Thrush *Monticola saxatilis*
(Northwest Africa and southern Europe east to Mongolia; winters Sahel zone of Africa to Kenya)
1843 Hertfordshire, Therfield.   **A (27)**

Joseph Trigg shot a male Rufous-tailed Rock Thrush at Therfield, near Royston, Hertfordshire, on 19th May 1843. Yarrell saw it in the flesh prior to its skinning by John Norman of Royston. It later joined the collection of Mr F D'Arcy Newcome, of Feltwell House, Norfolk, and was then presented to the Letchworth Museum by Lieutenant-Colonel T S N Hardinge. It is presently in the possession of the North Hertfordshire Museum, Baldock.

Yarrell figured the bird in his work and it also appears in Saunders' *Manual*.

Rufous-tailed Rock Thrush remains a rare visitor to Britain. Most are found in spring.

References:
Sage, 1959; Saunders 1899: 17.

Blue Rock Thrush *Monticola solitarius*
(Southern Europe, southern Asia and Northwest Africa)
1985 Argyll, Skerryvore Lighthouse.   **A (2)**

The BOURC investigated various records of Blue Rock

Thrush but, decided that, although having vagrancy potential, the probability of escape was too high as many birds were imported prior to 1980 from India. The first acceptable record for Britain involved a bird after this period, and as it was dead, made examination for signs of confinement easier.

A first-year male Blue Rock Thrush arrived at Skerryvore Lighthouse, Strathclyde, on 4th June, 1985. Although nervous when approached, it fed on insects on the rocks around the base of the lighthouse and helicopter pad. At night it seemed to be roosting in a crack in the rocks.

Although the weather was fine during the bird's stay, it was found dead on 8th June, by Mr A McConnell. It had possibly dehydrated as there was no fresh water present. Mrs Elizabeth McConnell wrote to the BTO on 14th June, enclosing the bird (it had been kept in a freezer until then).

John Marchant examined the bird, which had started to decay, and found that there was no evidence of wear to the feathers to suggest a captive origin. The skin was preserved by freeze-drying and kept at the Natural History Museum at Tring.

This record was accepted by the BOURC during a reassessment of records in 1991-92 and was considered to be of the eastern race *M. s. longirostris*.

A male found at Moel-y-gest, near Porthmadoc, North Wales on 4th June, 1997 was accepted as the second record but a female seen by David Hunt on St Martin's, Isles of Scilly on 18th May 1972 was never fully documented before his death. This would have pre-dated all other records and been Britain's first.

References:
British Birds 88: 130-132; *Birding World* 12: 412-413.

White's Thrush *Zoothera dauma*
(Northern and Central Siberia; winters southern India and Southeast Asia)
1828 Hampshire, Heron Court. **A (52)**

For many years, debate raged about White's Thrush, as it was thought either to be a colour variant of Song Thrush *Turdus philomelos* or the young of a Mistle Thrush *Turdus viscivorus*. The first British record concerned a male shot by Lord Malmesbury in January, 1828, on his estate at Heron Court, near Christchurch, Hampshire.

He said he had disturbed it while " *passing through a plantation, where it appeared to have established its haunt in a high furze break, as it returned to it repeatedly. Its flight was undulating, similar to that of a mistletoe thrush,*" of which Malmesbury thought was a variety. The bird was a plump and heavy female, alone at the time.

It was described by Mr Eyton in 1836 and named *Turdus whitei* in honour of Gilbert White of Selborne, who never saw White's Thrush, though the Latin name was later changed to *Zoothera dauma*. It figures in Yarrell's work and later Saunders' *Manual*.

During a visit to view the collection in 1894, Rev Mathew wrote: "*the Whites Thrush is in good condition, mounted with wings raised as in Yarrell's figure.*"

An earlier record came to light when Mr Bigge of Hampton Court produced a specimen that he had purchased from a Southampton birdstuffer in 1825. It was said to have been shot by one of the keepers in the New Forest. This specimen was lost after the sale of Bigge's collection in 1849, though it had been shown to Gould who doubted the bird's origin when he found the head to be stuffed with wool – a common practice among Australian taxidermists. Professor Newton also found the record unsatisfactory, as certain measurements were wrong.

References:
Zool, 1874: 4045; Kelsall & Munn, 1905:5-6.

Siberian Thrush *Zoothera sibirica*
(Central Siberia east to Japan; winters Southeast Asia)
1954 Fife, Isle of May.   **A (6)**

The first acceptable record of this striking thrush was as recently as 2nd October, 1954. The bird was trapped around midday, on the Isle of May, Fife, having been seen but not positively identified the previous evening. The bird's arrival coincided with a small movement of Redwing *Turdus iliacus*. The bird was seen in the hand by J A Nelder, D G Andrew and Mary Hawkes when a description was taken and the bird photographed. It was released and remained until 7th October being retrapped on the morning of 3rd October, when it had already began to put on weight. Though not a shy bird, it preferred to skulk among cover and under huts.

The bird was an unmistakable adult male, and despite having a slightly deformed bill having re-grown the upper mandible after the tip had been broken, was accepted into Category A of the British List.

A bird originally thought to be a melanistic Redwing shot between Guildford and Godalming, Surrey during winter 1860-61 and was later identified as a Siberian Thrush. Noting a similar underwing pattern to White's Thrush *Zoothera dauma*, it was placed in the collection of Frederick Bond. After being identified by Edward Blyth, who possessed considerable experience of eastern species, it was sent to the British Museum after Bond's death.

Contrary to the above, Gould claimed it had been a female shot by Mr Drewitt at St Catherine's Hill, near Guildford, in early February, 1855. Bond obtained the bird from Mr Smither of Farnham, Surrey, a retired gamekeeper.

The discrepancy in the dates is because Gould quoted the date it was shot (1855), while Bond labelled it when he purchased it (1860). Having been first identified as a Redwing, there would appear to have been no question of fraud.

Another specimen was picked up exhausted at Bonchurch, Isle of Wight, in winter 1874. Despite several records from the continent, neither reports were accepted by Saunders at the time and are presently unacceptable to the BOURC.

Siberian Thrush is a great rarity with only one record in Ireland.

References:
Sharrock, 1982: 59-61, photo; *British Birds* 48: 21-25, photo. [Saunders, 1899: 12]

Varied Thrush *Zoothera naevia*
(Western North America)
1982 Cornwall, Nanquidno. **A (1)**

Miss Philips of Nanquidno Farm, Cornwall, had seen a grey thrush feeding on the cotoneaster berries in her garden on 9th November, 1982. This was a week before the first birdwatchers found the Western Palearctic's first Varied Thrush.

At 2pm on 14th November, 1982, one of the ladies in an RSPB group at Nanquidno, Cornwall, reported seeing a grey thrush to E Grace, the leader. Consulting field guides, Dusky Thrush *Turdus naumanni* seemed closest to their bird. It was not seen again until the 17th when it was relocated by Bernard King and then independently by other Cornish birders, G C Hearl, S C Hutchings and L P Williams. Thoughts now turned to Siberian Thrush *Zoothera sibirica* or possibly an escaped Aztec Thrush *Zoothera pinicola* but still the features were incorrect. On the evening of the 18th Steve Madge was telephoned and the bird was placed in the 'escape' camp.

The following morning, several birdwatchers saw the bird and Steve Madge returned home realising that the underwing pattern fitted the *Zoothera* Thrushes. He soon realised that the bird was in fact an abnormally coloured Varied Thrush, lacking all the usual orange tones. Investigation revealed that the bird was probably a first-winter male but it was impossible to assign it to a particular race.

The bird remained until 24th November, but many thought that being an unlikely vagrant in an aberrant plumage, it stood little chance of acceptance by the BOURC. Although grey plumaged individuals have been rarely recorded in wild birds, it was even less likely for an immature bird kept in captivity to lack all orange tones. The escape likelihood of this species was considered to have been low as there had been no imports since 1975.

Varied Thrush was accepted onto Category A of the British and Irish List.

References:
British Birds 83: 187-194, photos.

Wood Thrush *Hylocichla mustelina*
(North America; winters from Texas south to Panama and northwest Columbia)
1987 Isles of Scilly, St Agnes. **A (1)**

Despite strong winds and showers, Paul Dukes and Rod McCann were birding the gorse scrub area at Wingletang, in the southern part of St Agnes, Isles of Scilly, on 7th October, 1987. Dukes flushed a bird from his feet that they thought was an American thrush, possibly a Veery *Catharus fuscescens*. It dropped into some gorse a few metres away.

They walked towards the bird only to see it take flight again. This time it was seen to be too large for any of the American thrushes already recorded in Britain and they discussed the possibility of it being a Wood Thrush and, after putting the bird up again, they were convinced that it was.

They alerted other birders on the island and 40 people gathered. Only one boat made it from St Mary's as the sea was too rough. The bird proved difficult to see as it made brief flights when disturbed, but was glimpsed under a bush by some lucky observers. Francis Hicks saw it on the ground in front of him. Although hundreds of birders searched for it over subsequent days, it was not seen again and was presumed to have perished in the appalling weather.

It was a composition of several observers' reports that finally placed Wood Thrush on the British List.

References:
British Birds 88: 133-135.

Hermit Thrush *Catharus guttatus*
(North America; winters southern USA south to Guatemala)
1975 Shetland, Fair Isle.   A (7)

Leaving Ralph A. Richardson and friends washing up at the observatory, Stephen Rumsey and Harold Nash set off at about 9am on 2nd June, 1975 to walk through Field Croft at Fair Isle, Shetland. Rumsey pointed out a Song Thrush *Turdus philomelos* to Nash, commenting that it was a new bird for his Fair Isle list. Realising that they were rare at this time of year, Nash took a closer look thinking it likely to be a Thrush Nightingale *Luscinia luscinia*.

Rumsey then realised that this small thrush with a red tail was clearly one of the American thrushes, so they took note of the salient features. The only members of the family to show rufous are Veery *Catharus fuscescens* and Hermit Thrush and so he concluded that it was the latter. After gathering other observers, including Roger Broad, Tom Francis, PJ Roberts and Ralph Richardson, they watched the bird for an hour.

It fed unconcerned in the recently ploughed furrows allowing an approach of nine metres and photographs to be taken. It frequently cocked its red tail, a characteristic feature of Hermit Thrush and whose description it fitted perfectly as they left to check available literature.

The bird remained all day, even bouncing several times out of the net erected to trap it. Later it was seen to tower up into the sky at dusk until out of view by P J Jackson and was not seen again.

There have been no Irish records.

References:
S Rumsey *pers comm*; Sharrock 1982: 193-195, photo; *British Birds* 48: 10.

Swainson's Thrush *Catharus ustulatus*
(North America; winters Mexico to northwest Argentina)

IRELAND
1956 Co. Mayo, Blackrock Lighthouse.   A (21)

On 26th May 1956, W P Roche, assistant keeper at the Blackrock lighthouse, Co. Mayo, found a freshly dead Swainson's Thrush, which had presumably flown into the light. The skin was examined in America where the eastern race, *C. u. swainsoni*, was identified. The bird was the first record of the species in Britain and Ireland. The specimen is now held at the National Museum, Dublin.

BRITAIN

1967 Pembrokeshire, Skokholm.

The first record in Britain was a bird found and trapped on Skokholm, Pembrokeshire on 14th October, 1967, remaining until 19th October. The observers were C K Britton, B Chambers and D A Scott.

The total number of birds ringed on the island that year was 16,616. This included eight species of bird new to the Island, including four American passerine species.

All but one of the British records has been on the west coast with almost half on the Isles of Scilly.

References:
Ruttledge, 1966: 156; Sharrock, 1982: 85-87; *British Birds* 48: 10; *Skokholm Bird Obs report,* 1967: 3, 13.

Grey-cheeked Thrush *Catharus minimus*

(North America and Eastern Siberia; winters eastern USA, West Indies and Central America)

1953 Shetland, Fair Isle.   A (44)

During late afternoon 5th October, 1953, William Eunson of Fair Isle, Shetland, saw a thrush feeding at the entrance to the observatory trap and secured the bird. It was identified as a Grey-cheeked Thrush by Kenneth Williamson using the Peterson field guide, but they kept the bird in a roosting box overnight to be sure. Confirming the identification criteria with Professor V C Edwards over the telephone, and after photographing the bird the following morning, it was released near the cliffs and disappeared. The bird was in first-winter plumage, and a tick larva, *Haemophysalis leporis-palustris* (also the first British record), was removed from its chin.

There have been multiple arrivals of Grey-cheeked Thrushes with at least 12 in 1986. Only four have occurred in Ireland.

References:
Dymond, 1991: 95; Sharrock, 1982: 37-38, photo; *British Birds* 48: 10.

Veery *Catharus fuscescens*

(North America; winters Central and northern South America)

1970 Cornwall, Porthgwarra.   A (4)

At 9.30am on 6th October, 1970, Giles Dunmore was surprised to see a small robin-sized thrush fly in front of him while watching a Yellow-browed Warbler *Phylloscopus inornatus,* feeding among the sallows growing at the bottom of the valley at Porthgwarra, Cornwall. He pointed the bird out to H P Medhurst whose first impression was of a large Thrush Nightingale *Luscinia luscinia* and they concluded that it must be an American thrush *Catharus.* After two minutes they informed other nearby birders and it was watched for a further 15 minutes before disappearing from view. For comparison, Medhurst then held up his copy of Peterson's field guide while the group looked at the thrush plate through binoculars. They concluded that the bird was a Veery, the first to be seen in Europe.

Keith Allsopp relocated the bird two hours later and watched it for half an hour feeding on elderberries, down to two metres.

It was then trapped and photographed, but after release the bird was not seen again.

E M P Allsopp checked the skins in the British Museum (Natural History) and concluded that the bird had been in its first-winter plumage but was unable to assign it to a particular race.

There had been just five records of this thrush in Britain prior to the millennium with the last bird seen for just one day at St Levan, Cornwall in October, 1999 and two on Lundy Island, Devon.

References:
Sharrock, 1982: 174-177, photo; *Birding World* 10: 184.

Eyebrowed Thrush *Turdus obscurus*
(Siberian and eastern Asia to Japan; winters China and Indonesia)
1964 Northamptonshire, Oundle.   **A (20)**

Eyebrowed Thrush had not been recorded in Britain prior to 1964, when no less than three were found. The first was in a Northamptonshire garden, the second in the Western Isles and the third, more traditionally, on the Isles of Scilly.

The first of this trio arrived at the garden of Mrs Winifred Smith and her son Martin in Oundle on 5th October, 1964, with an influx of Song Thrushes *Turdus philomelos*. They watched it from inside the house feeding on the berries of a yew hedge from 2.15-3pm, during which time a description was taken. It also drank and bathed with Song Thrushes *Turdus philomelos* in a small pool in the garden. The presence of pale tipped greater coverts indicated that it was probably a first-winter bird.

This record was accepted as the first occurrence of this species in Britain, half of which have occurred on Scilly.

References:
Sharrock, 1982: 129-132.

Naumann's Thrush *Turdus naumanni naumanni*
(Central Siberia, winters in Southeast Asia)
1990 Greater London, Woodford Green.   **A (2)**

Although there had been several records in Europe, the first Naumann's Thrush to visit Britain was in 1990, when Mrs Bridges saw a bird she did not recognise at Woodford Green, Chingford, Greater London/Essex, on 19th January.

The implications of this sighting were not realised at the time and it wasn't until 10.45am am on Saturday, 3rd February that Ken Murray, a near neighbour and birder saw the bird's red tail while recovering from a hangover in a chair near his kitchen window.

The bird was in an ivy hedge ten meters away and, realising that a red tail was not a feature of Redwings *Turdus iliacus*, he rushed upstairs with his binoculars. After confirming that the bird was still present, he began to take notes while his wife made phone calls.

Phil Vines was the first to arrive but the bird had disappeared after moving as close as five metres at one point. Fortunately after 15 minutes, it returned to feed on ivy berries. Various species were mused as candidates but the bird was tentatively identified as a Naumann's Thrush, although there was some discrepancies with the illustration in their field guide. They had also aged it as a first-winter male before the arrival of C Fentiman and T Wilson. Again the bird had flown but reappeared to allow the identification to be confirmed beyond doubt.

The bird was not found until 12.30pm the next day and, being on an open playing field with plenty of room for a large audience, the news was released onto the *Birdline* telephone service.

Considered perhaps almost too coincidental, Britain's only other Naumann's Thrush also visited Chingford, being seen only a few kilometres from Britain's first. It was present from 6th-11th January, 1997.

References:
Birding World 3: 50-53, photos; *British Birds* 91: 503; Evans, 1994: 376.

Dusky Thrush *Turdus naumanni eunomus*
(Northern and Central Siberia, winters in Southeast Asia)
1905 Nottinghamshire, Gunthorpe.   A (8)

On 13th October, 1905, a market gardener called Mills shot Britain's first Dusky Thrush. While walking by a dyke near his garden at Gunthorpe, Nottinghamshire, he heard a loud "chack, chack," call. A bird similar to a Fieldfare *Turdus pilaris* was sat in a willow tree. The bird, obviously not a Fieldfare resembled a Eurasian Jay *Garrulus glandarius* in flight and was shot with his second barrel. The bird was taken to Mr Bore (according to Whitaker and *Zoologist)* or Mr Rose (according to BOC) the Nottingham taxidermist who presumed it was a variety of Fieldfare. Joseph Whitiker of Rainworth and Mr P C Musters of Annesley Park examined it and after consulting Dresser's work on European birds, and found it to be a male Dusky Thrush in perfect plumage.

The bird was purchased and exhibited by Musters at the British Ornithologists' Club where it found acceptance.

On 21st March, 1973, on the second day of the Annesley Collection auction, lot 561 contained *"2 Mistle Thrushes, 2 Song Thrushes, 2 Redwing's, 2 Fieldfares, a Blackbird, a pied Blackbird, 2 Ring Ouzel's and a "Dusky Ouzle"* (Dusky Thrush), *Notts 1905."*
It fetched £11.

The majority of reports have fallen between November and February so probably involved wintering birds.

References:
Zool, 1905: 466; *Bull*, BOC 16: 45; Whitaker, 1907: 17-18; *Annesley Park Auction Catalogue*, 1973; Naylor 1998.

Dark-throated Thrush (Red-throated) *Turdus ruficollis ruficollis*
(Central Asia; winters northern India and China)
1994 Essex, The Naze. **A (1)**

It took 120 years and 28 British records of the Black-throated race *T. r. atrogularis* of Dark-throated Thrush before the first Red-throated bird was seen.

Arriving by bus from Colchester, Brian Smith walked from Walton-on-the-Naze, Essex, to the grass clifftop of Naze headland on 29th September, 1994. At 8.50am, he saw a thrush that resembled a Naumann's Thrush *Turdus naumanni* on the cliff below the cafe. He watched it for a few minutes before it flew into some bushes. Contacting Steve Beary from the nearest call box (who in turn rang a small local group), they watched the bird on the cliffs and an adjacent lawn before it disappeared. The identification was straightforward when good views were obtained and the news was released that it was Britain's first Red-throated Thrush. The bird was seen again on the lawn at 3pm and at dusk.

The bird remained faithful to the cliff-sides the following day often obscured by vegetation but later moved to a caravan site and adjacent hedgerows a kilometre to the south. It was aged as a first-year male on the strength of its coloration and two unmoulted juvenile greater coverts, and was seen by over 2,000 birdwatchers before last being seen on 7th October. It had probably been in the area some time as the wind was light westerly when it was first found.

A Red-throated Thrush seen at Easington, East Yorkshire, by N A Bell and G E Dobbs on 7th October, 1990 was not accepted by the BBRC. Both 'Red' and 'Black-throated' Thrushes remain conspecific but increasing fieldwork in breeding areas may lead to this view being revised.

References:
Birding World: 7, 392-395, photo, *British Birds* 92: 40-46, photos; YNU 1990: 65.

Dark-throated Thrush (Black-throated) *Turdus ruficollis atrogularis*
(Central Asia; winters northern India and China)
1868 East Sussex, near Lewes. **A (45)**

Thomas Monk of Lewes reported to *The Field* magazine that on Wednesday, 23rd December an immature male "Black-throated Thrush" had been shot near Lewes, East Sussex. Monk saw a bricklayer carrying the bird and purchased it for five shillings, though it was worth more than ten pounds. The bricklayer boasted to local friends that he had sold an old thrush to foolish Monk!

It was in excellent condition and preserved by Mr Swaysland of Brighton. This was the first British record.

Monk included the bird in his collection, which on his death joined Booth's famous collection at Dyke Road, Brighton.

There have been no Irish records.

References:
Zool, 1869: 1560; Walpole-Bond, 1938: i, 71-72; *Ibis* 1869: 128; Frost 1987: 74.

American Robin *Turdus migratorius*
(North America; winters USA south to Guatemala)

IRELAND

1891 Co. Dublin, Shankill.   A (32)

Following the acceptance of a bird on Lundy, Devon, there was a realisation that American landbirds were potential vagrants to Europe and the older records were subsequently reviewed. This allowed a bird shot at Springmount, Shankill, Co. Dublin on 4th May 1891 to precede the then first British record. It had been in good condition with beetles inside its stomach and had showed no signs of having been kept in captivity. The skin is now in the Dublin Museum.

This was the first of two Irish reports from the 19th Century. Three reports from Leicester, Shrewsbury and Kent followed but all were regarded as escapes even though the Shrewsbury report had appeared two days before a Common Nighthawk *Chordeiles minor* was found on the Isles of Scilly.

BRITAIN

1952 Devon, Lundy.

An American Robin was found on Lundy, Devon following a period of strong westerly winds that was responsible for a massive wreck of Leach's Storm-petrels *Oceanodroma leucorhoa*. It was present from the morning of 27th (but possibly since the 25th) October, 1952 until 8th November. When Peter Davis first saw the bird eating blackberries on the slopes of a gully on the eastern side of the island, it allowed him to approach to about ten yards. The bird was driven into a Heligoland trap and ringed at the Old Light before being shown to resident birdwatchers, F W and Miss Mary Gade, and John Ogilvie.

It was thought to be of the eastern race *T. m. migratorius* and had lost possibly as much as 40% of its body weight. It was photographed and released near the hotel.

It returned to the gully but later survived chiefly on earthworms found on the top of the island in the open grassland, where it regularly associated with Redwings *Turdus iliacus* and Common Blackbirds *Turdus merula*.

This record was predated when the Irish record was accepted.

The first mention of this species in Britain was from Dover, Kent, where a specimen was taken in April or May 1876. However, Harting considered that it had escaped from a passing ship.

A failed attempt by Lord Northcliffe, to introduce American Robin near Guildford, Surrey, was probably responsible for a bird that built a nest in Richmond Park in May 1912.

References:
Ruttledge 1966; Moore, 1969: 226-227; Harrison 1953: 137; Sharrock, 1982: 30-33, photos; *British Birds* 48: 10; Ussher *et al* 1900: 398.

Cetti's Warbler *Cettia cetti*
(Southern Europe and North Africa to Western Central Asia)

1961 Hampshire, Titchfield Haven.   A (RB)

On 4th March, 1961, Dr C Suffern heard a song he did not recognise, from an unseen bird in reeds at Titchfield Haven, Hampshire. The same song was heard again the next day and he saw the bird briefly with other birdwatchers. The bird remained until at least 10th April and was seen or heard by a large number of individuals including some of Britain's leading ornithologists. It was thought to have been Cetti's Warbler, and this was confirmed on 19th March when the bird flew into a mist-net. It was ringed by J A Miller and seen in the hand by about 25 people including P R Colston, I J Ferguson-Lees and M J Carter.

Montagu in his *Dictionary of British Birds* 1866, mentions two specimens of Cetti's Warbler as probably being a case of mistaken identity. They were in Gray's *Catalogue of British Birds in the British Museum* and the species was also mentioned in Jenyns *Manual of British Vertebrata*.

Three specimens of Cetti's Warbler obtained in Sussex were all rejected as part of the Hastings rarities affair. The first of these was a male shot at Battle on 12th May, 1904 and exhibited by M J Nicoll at the British Ornithologists' Club

Cetti's Warbler has colonised parts of Kent and expanded westwards into Cornwall with a few pairs in South Wales. In 1995, there were *c.*426 breeding pairs in Britain.

There has only been two Irish records.

References:
Sharrock, 1982: 107-109; Walpole-Bond, 1938: i, 366; *British Birds* 1: 9; Hutchinson 1998. [Montagu, 1862: 366-367]

Zitting Cisticola *Cisticola juncidis*
(Mediterranean, west and north France, also Africa and South Asia to Australia)

IRELAND
1962 Co. Cork, Cape Clear.   **A (4)**
An unfamiliar "tew" call attracted the attention of J T R Sharrock, on 23rd April 1962, leading him to a small bird in the sedges of the East Bog on Ballyieragh, Cape Clear, Co. Cork. He watched the bird for 20 minutes before it flew to another clump, in the tired or struggling manner typical of Fan-tailed Warbler (now Zitting Cisticola). The bird was then seen to start the species' characteristic bouncing display flight.

Having seen the species seven months previously in Spain, Sharrock was sure the bird was a Zitting Cisticola and took a description of it. He went to fetch other observers but failed to re-locate the bird when he returned 40 minutes later.

BRITAIN
1976 Norfolk, Cley-next-the-Sea.
In the early morning of 24th August, 1976, Nick Dymond saw a Zitting Cisticola in typical 'zitting' song-flight over a small pool near the East Bank at Cley-next-the-Sea, Norfolk. After clinching the identification he watched it fly west. Five days later, what was almost certainly the same bird was found at Holme NOA/NNT Reserve in hawthorns near the carpark where it remained from 29th August to 5th September, 1976.

Despite the close proximity of breeding birds to Britain, Zitting Cisticola appears reluctant to cross the North Sea.

References:
Sharrock, 1982: 115-117; Evans 1994: 380.

Pallas's Grasshopper Warbler *Locustella certhiola*
(Western Siberia and Central Asia to Japan; winters India and Southeast Asia)

IRELAND
1908 Dublin, Rockabill Lighthouse.   A (25)

At a meeting of the British Ornithologists' Club in 1908, Mr Ogilvie-Grant exhibited the skin of a Pallas's Grasshopper Warbler on behalf of Mr RM Barrington. Assistant light-keeper Martin Kennedy had picked it up dead on 28th September, 1908 at the Rockabill Lighthouse, five miles off the coast near Dublin. It was apparently in plump condition and not a wind-blown, exhausted bird. When dissected by Mr Pycraft it proved to be an immature male. The specimen remained in the Barrington Collection, which is now at the National Museum, Dublin (P. Milne *in litt*).

Ireland's only other record was a bird trapped on Cape Clear, Co. Cork on 8th October, 1990.

BRITAIN
1949 Shetland, Fair Isle.

A Pallas's Grasshopper Warbler was first seen at Leogh, Fair Isle, Shetland in a turnip and cabbage patch on 8th October, 1949, remaining until the 9th. When flushed, it was observed by Dr W H Bierman, R F Ruttledge, C I Murdoch, L P Samuels, George Waterston, T Yeoman, P Robertson and Kenneth Williamson. The party walked in a line to drive it to the end of a row of crops where the bird would sit before flying back into the turnips. On one occasion on the 9th, it remained in an open grass field allowing the observers to get a good view.

A description was written up from the notes of those attending a meeting during the evening of the 9th and Waterston, Williamson and Yeoman checked skins later. The identification proved conclusive and the record of Britain's first Pallas's Grasshopper Warbler was accepted.

Away from the Northern Isles, only Cley (Norfolk), Portland (Dorset) and the Farne Islands (Northumberland) have been visited by Pallas's Grasshopper Warbler, none remaining long enough to be widely appreciated.

References:
Kennedy, 1954: 354; *Bull., BOC*, 23: 18; *British Birds* 2: 230 photo; 43: 49-50; Dymond, 1991.

Lanceolated Warbler *Locustella lanceolata*
(East Eurasia from Central Russia to northern Japan; winters Philippines and Southeast Asia)
1908 Shetland, Fair Isle.   A (80)

On 26th October, 1910, a bird disturbed on the Pentland Skerries, Orkney, darted into a rabbit burrow. It did not evade capture, however, and was sent to Eagle Clarke. After examination he identified it as a Lanceolated Warbler. This jogged Clarke's memory and he checked his collection for an immature bird that he had shot at Fair Isle, Shetland on 9th September, 1908 as it took off from some rough grass.

With Dr C B Ticehurst he confirmed its identity as an immature Lanceolated Warbler, therefore pre-dating all other European records.

Lanceolated Warbler is an extreme rarity on the British mainland with the bulk of records (80%) found on Fair Isle.

There are no Irish records.

References:
A.S.N.H., 1911: 71; Clarke, 1912: 136.

River Warbler *Locustella fluviatilis*
(Central and Eastern Europe and West-central Asia; winters southeastern Africa)
1961 Shetland, Fair Isle.   **A (29)**

Shortly after midday on 24th September, 1961, a *Locustella* warbler was seen skulking in the "warbler-ditch" at Lower Leogh, Fair Isle, Shetland, by Peter Davis, P J Slater, G J Barnes and R M Nedderman. They watched the bird in tussocks and gained a brief view on a wire fence before erecting a mist-net. The bird was trapped within ten minutes and taken to the laboratory for processing. It was seen by about 15 observers and escaped from the hands of its captors during a photography session. After flying into a building ten minutes later, it was recaught and taken to Gilsetter Marsh for release. It had been identified as Britain's first River Warbler and showed well to the audience gathered at the marsh.

The bird was watched in a ditch the following day by the occupants of a croft at Lower Stonybreck.

References:
Sharrock, 1982: 112-114, photo; Cottridge & Vinicombe 1997: 126-7.

Savi's Warbler *Locustella luscinioides*
(Central and Eastern Europe to West-central Asia; winters possibly in sub-Saharan Africa)
1819 Norfolk, Limpenhoe.   **A (P)**

There was some early confusion regarding the identification of Savi's Warbler; the first example known to science was a specimen obtained during May, in the early 19th Century, in Norfolk. Rev J Brown killed the bird at Limpenhoe no later than 1819. It was submitted to Mr Temminck and mistakenly pronounced to have been an odd Eurasian Reed Warbler *Acrocephalus scirpaceus*. Following further confusion, the bird was incorrectly named as a Cetti's Warbler *Cettia cetti*.

This specimen was placed in the Castle Museum, Norwich and although lacking an accurate date of occurrence was undoubtedly the first British record of Savi's Warbler. If described and named at the time it would have been a new species.

In 1824, the Savi's Warbler was officially recognised by the Italian ornithologist of that name. Temminck's Norfolk specimen was subsequently reidentified in 1835 and several more specimens were then obtained from the Norfolk and Cambridgeshire fens. The first of these was collected by Mr Baker in Cambridgeshire in 1840 and described by Mr Gray in *Zoologist* (1843) as the first British record, though Brown's specimen (Accession no. 35.27) is clearly Britain's first record. It remains at the Castle Museum where it is in poor condition, the head being particularly badly damaged. It was originally mounted but has since been made into a skin with the accompanying label, dating from 1967/68, bearing derived information (Dr A G Irwin *in litt*).

Thought to be a regular but uncommon bird in Britain, the first nest was reported by Frederick Bond in 1846, at Milton, Cambridgeshire.

There were no further records of Savi's Warbler until a pair was found at Fair Isle on 14th May 1908.

By 1999, the species was so scarce that it was added to the BBRC's rarities list, while Ireland had only recorded four individuals prior to 1994.

References:
Saunders, 1899: 91; Yarrell, 1843: i, 268-269; Montagu, 1862: 372; Clarke, 1912: 135; Riviere, 1930: 60-61; Lack, 1934: 65; *Zool* 1843: 79-80; Cottridge & Vinicombe 1997: 127; *British Birds* 92: 24; Hutchinson 1998.

Moustached Warbler *Acrocephalus melanopogon*
(Mediterranean region, Eastern Europe and Southwest Asia; Eastern populations winter in Pakistan and northwest India)
1946 Cambridgeshire, Cambridge sewage farm. **A (9)**

Britain's first Moustached Warbler record involved a pair of birds that built a nest and reared young. By the time D E Sergent and R A Hinde noticed the first individual in Cambridgeshire on 3rd August, 1946, the youngsters had already left the nest and were hidden in undergrowth. The two observers briefly saw a single adult in a sallow bordering a large reed bed; it took flight and was not seen again that day despite searching for a further 30 minutes. The following morning, Hinde returned with C C Cox and A S Thom who found two adults in the reed bed. The pair returned regularly to some thick brambles ten yards from the waters edge and gave clear views at a similar range as they perched on route to the bush. It became obvious that they were feeding young at some distance apart within the brambles and therefore out of the nest.

On the afternoon of 4th August, Hinde again visited the site to take further notes. After about two minutes of calling, the male left the bushes and Hinde approached to find a young bird close to the top of the hedge. On the following days, single youngsters were seen with varying flying abilities and, on 8th August, Thom saw three juveniles together.

The observers agreed that the birds were probably Moustached Warblers but prior to this report there had only been one other record (later rejected). Confirmation of the discovery was needed and it was decided not to collect a specimen, but inform several expert ornithologists including James Fisher and Dr Thorpe to observe the birds. The species was also sketched and illustrated by the famous artist, Dr Eric Ennion while the Sedge Warblers *Acrocephalus schoenobaenus* in the area allowed good comparisons.

On 10th August, J A Gibb accompanied Fisher to the site and confirmed that the birds were identical to the Moustached Warblers he had seen in Malta.

There were no further sightings after 20th August. A decision was made to search for the nest, as the species would not usually choose bramble as a nest site. As no nest was located in the bush, even after it was cut down, the evidence for the record was overwhelming.

Prior to this, a rejected record had involved a bird killed at St Leonards-on-Sea, Sussex, on 12th April, 1915. It was shown to Mr H W Ford-Lindsay before skinning, and later passing to the Nichols' collection. The report was later dismissed with the Hastings rarities.

There are only four other records of Moustached Warbler in Britain.

References:
Sharrock, 1982: 13-18, *British Birds* 40: 98-104: 41: frontispiece illustrated in colour; 93: 29-38, colour sketches; Walpole-Bond, 1938: i, 367; Naylor 1998.

Aquatic Warbler *Acrocephalus paludicola*
(Germany eastwards to European Russia, including northern Italy and Hungary; winters Africa south of the Sahara)
1853 East Sussex, Cowfold.   **A (P)**

Aquatic Warbler can easily be overlooked and, at the time of the first British record, it was regularly breeding on the continent as close as the French and Dutch coasts.

At a meeting of the Zoological Society in May 1866, a specimen was exhibited labelled as a *"very bright Sedge Warbler".* Professor Newton had discovered it in the collection of William Borrer, of Cowfold, Sussex.

Borrer's Aquatic Warbler had been killed while crawling among grass and reeds in an old brick pit near Hove, East Sussex, on 19th October, 1853. Mr Harting examined it and then realised a second skin was in his own collection and that he had mistakenly overlooked it. A friend, who had killed it near Loughborough, Leicestershire in the summer of 1864 had sent the bird to him.

Borrer was a magistrate whose egg collection included all but four species then known to have bred in Britain. His county avifauna was published in 1891 and the Booth Museum at Brighton, later purchased his specimen collection in 1901.

Although the Sussex record stands as Britain's official first, Gould later pointed out that the bird figured in an earlier work: Hunt's *British Ornithology* as a Sedge Warbler *Acrocephalus schoenobaenus*, was in fact now obviously recognisable as an Aquatic Warbler. This record unfortunately lacks the supporting details required for a 'first' but was probably obtained in Norfolk, in about 1815.

By the time the BBRC had ceased to vet Aquatic Warbler reports in 1996, 1125 individuals had been recorded in Britain.
With its southwesterly bias, it is surprising that only 13 had been recorded in Ireland before 1994.

References:
Zool, 1867: 946; Saunders, 1899: 87; Walpole-Bond, 1938: ii, 19-21; Frost 1987: 74; Hutchinson 1998.

Paddyfield Warbler *Acrocephalus agricola*
(Southern Russia and Asia; winters Southwest Asia and India)
1925 Shetland, Fair Isle. A (45)

Following a light easterly wind on the evening of 25th September, 1925, Surgeon Rear-Admiral Stenhouse saw a small warbler the next day that he considered had just arrived at Fair Isle, Shetland. George and J A Stout also saw it.

What was presumed to be the same bird was subsequently shot in a field of turnips by George Stout on 1st October, 1925, and taken to Stenhouse, a keen collector of birds. He reported it as the first record for Britain.

Only four more records were received prior to 1974 and the recent upsurge in numbers may be linked to a westward range expansion.

Prior to 1994 only one had been recorded in Ireland.

References:
British Birds 20: 12-14; *Scot. Nat.*, 1925: 173; Thom, 1986; Dymond, 1991: 104; Cottridge & Vinicombe 1997: 128-9; Hutchinson 1998.

Blyth's Reed Warbler *Acrocephalus dumetorum*
(Eurasia eastwards from Finland; winters India and Sri Lanka)
1910 Shetland, Fair Isle. A (37)

While at Fair Isle, Shetland, on 29th September, 1910, the Duchess of Bedford observed a dull bird resembling a Garden Warbler *Sylvia borin* but unknown to her, skulking among turnips. The following day, it was found in the same place by one of Eagle Clarke's observers and captured following a "great hunt." Despite believing it to be just a Eurasian Reed Warbler *Acrocephalus scirpaceus,* the corpse was sent to Clarke who, with Dr C B Ticehurst, suspected that it was a Blyth's Reed Warbler and therefore new to Britain. It was despatched to Dr Hartert for confirmation, as they did not have any specimens for comparison.

Clarke believed it to be a new bird for Western Europe.

Before the formation of the BBRC in 1958, only nine records had been received, with four of the subsequent birds all found in 1912. In that year, there must have been a substantial influx of the species to the east coast as single birds were discovered away from Fair Isle at Spurn, Holy Island and on a light ship 18 miles north of Sheringham, Norfolk, at a time of comparatively few knowledgeable observers.

There had been just two Irish records prior to 1994.

References:
A.S.N.H., 1911: 70; Dymond 1991: 104; Clarke, 1912: ii, 135; Naylor 1996: 142; Hutchinson 1998.

Marsh Warbler *Acrocephalus palustris*
(Western Eurasia; winters Southeast Africa)
1863 Hampshire, Alresford. A (SB)

The earliest report quoted in recent literature comes from Alresford Great Pond, Hampshire in 1863. This pre-dated a report by Edward Blyth and became Britain's first record.

It is not surprising that Marsh Warbler was a late addition to Britain's avifauna as it has presumably never been common and is easily confused with the Eurasian Reed Warbler *Acrocephalus scirpaceus*. The species was first recognised in 1803.

Blyth found the Marsh Warbler near London in 1871. There was, however, strong speculation that it had bred at Christchurch, Dorset in the late 1860s and also nested in Hampstead in 1861-63 and 1865.

In the late 19th Century, Marsh Warbler was reported as a spring visitor in small numbers to Somerset, particularly near Taunton. The identification features were still relatively unknown for a while as the plates in the works of Gould and Lord Lilford carried illustrations of Eurasian Reed Warblers. The plate depicting Reed and Marsh Warblers in Dresser's *Birds of Europe* showed incorrect plumage tones and leg colour, while primary projection was an identification aid yet to be discovered.

Several nests were found from Bath to Oxfordshire before the turn of the century with uncertain reports from Norfolk and Cambridgeshire. The total British population peaked at 100-120 pairs and a small population flourished in the Avon and Severn Valleys. In 1995, possibly 29 pairs were present in Britain, dropping to 19 in 1996 with a shift from the Midlands to southeastern England. It remains extremely vulnerable at the fringe of its European range.

There had been no reports from Ireland up to 1994.

References:
British Birds 92: 150; *Essex Bird Report* 1997: 159; Saunders 1899: 81; Hartert 1912: 64; Holloway 1996: 328; Fisher 1954: 26; Hutchinson 1998.

Eurasian Reed Warbler *Acrocephalus scirpaceus*
(Europe, east to central Asia; winters in west Central and East Africa).
1785 Essex, Iver.   **A (SB)**

Rev John Lightfoot discovered Eurasian Reed Warbler and its nest, in reeds on the banks of the River Coln in 1785. The species was found to be present in a five-mile stretch of the river from Iver to Harefield Moor, Essex. Consequently Lightfoot wrote to Sir Joseph Banks and the letter was read out at the Royal Society. Notice of the discovery was printed in their *Transcriptions* for the year 1785, but the bird was not described in Pennant's *Zoology* until the 1812 edition.

Eurasian Reed Warbler was at first confused with Sedge Warbler *Acrocephalus schoenobaenus*, having a similar song and often sharing adjacent habitats. It was thought to be restricted to the southeastern counties of Kent, Essex and Surrey. By 1850, it had been found in the Norfolk Broads, with scarce reports from Staffordshire, Derbyshire and Lincolnshire.

The first Eurasian Reed Warbler found in Ireland was a bird that struck the Rockabill Lighthouse on 20th October, 1908. This followed a claim of a singing bird in a reed-bed on the River Shannon, near Portumna on 23rd July, 1904, by Mr A H Evans.

References:
Yarrell, 1843: i, 269-273; *British Birds* 2: 408; *Birdwatch* 69: 16; Wingfield Gibbons 1993: 334-5; Hutchinson 1998.

Great Reed Warbler *Acrocephalus arundinaceus*
(Europe, Southwest and East Asia and North Africa; winters Africa)
1847 Tyne and Wear, near Swalwell, Newcastle-upon-Tyne.   A (107)

On 28th May 1847, Thomas Robson of Swalwell, near Newcastle-upon-Tyne, shot Britain's first Great Reed Warbler near his village. The unfamiliar call had attracted Robson to the low vegetation beside a mill dam, where he found the bird skulking. The bird was called the "Thrush-like or Great Sedge Warbler" at the time and, after being shot, the specimen was placed in the Thompson Collection. It later passed into the hands of the Hancock Museum at Newcastle where it remains. Robson later became a well-known collector at Ortakoi, near Constantinople (Istanbul), Turkey.

Ireland had recorded only three individuals prior to 1994.

References:
Evans 1994: 389-391; Montagu, 1862: 373-374; Temperley, 1951: 96; Saunders, 1899: 83; Cottridge & Vinicombe 1997: 130; Hutchinson 1998.

Thick-billed Warbler *Acrocephalus aedon*
(Central and East Asia; winters India east to southern China and Vietnam)
1955 Shetland, Fair Isle.   A (2)

A large bird, resembling a Great Reed Warbler *Acrocephalus arundinaceus* with a rufous rump, was flushed from a turnip rig at Leogh, Fair Isle, Shetland, on 6th October, 1955. It immediately took cover but was flushed again and flew into dense vegetation on the bank of a nearby burn. A Yeoman trap was placed in a ditch and the skulking bird was manoeuvred towards the entrance, which was less than three feet wide. The bird was soon in the catching box at the end and after examination in the laboratory it was identified as a Thick-billed Warbler using Dresser's *Manual of Palearctic Birds* (1902).

It was seen by warden Kenneth Williamson and Valerie Thom, as well as I J Ferguson-Lees, editor of *British Birds* and H E Axell, warden of Dungeness RSPB Reserve. Dr Maeve Rusk, William Eunson and Williamson took photographs and after release near the Observatory Heligoland where it spent a short while, the bird flew to the craggy hillside above.

This was the first European record for the species and there has been only one other British occurrence, also in Shetland. It was trapped on 23rd September, 1971, but died two days later.

References:
Sharrock, 1982: 79-82; Dymond, 1991: 105; *British Birds* 49: 89-93; FIBOR 1955/56:11; 19.

Olivaceous Warbler *Hippolais pallida*
(Iberia and North Africa and the Balkans east to Pakistan and Kazakhstan; winters Africa)
1967 Fife, Isle of May.   A (12)

In 1999, all Olivaceous Warbler records were reviewed by the BOURC and several records failed to meet the required standard for acceptance. This included the previously accepted first. As a result the 'first' became a bird killed by a Great (Northern)

Grey Shrike *Lanius excubitor* on the Isle of May, Fife on 26th September, 1967. It was first seen and described as "a super skulker" by D A I Baty, W M Morrison, Andrew D K Ramsay, J J Dunbar and C F H Bruce on 24th September as they returned from the Low Light. After watching it creeping through nettles, it was trapped and detailed notes were taken before its release. The bird was retrapped a further three times before the decapitated body was retrieved from the shrike which had begun eating it.

The corpse was then taken to the National Museums of Scotland, Edinburgh where it was assigned to the eastern race *H. p. elaeica* before being pickled and the skin preserved flat (Reg. No. 1968.73). The first report of this taxon came from Portland Bill, Dorset, where Ken Smith trapped a bird on 16th August, 1956, but this was one of the records removed in 1999.

As the review was still ongoing in December, 1999 two earlier records from the Isles of Scilly were still in circulation; the first was present on St Agnes from 3rd to 4th October, 1961.

On the afternoon of the 3rd RE Emmett and D I M Wallace had brief views in poor conditions of a warbler in the tamarisks near Cove Vean. The following morning they refound it, with help from Peter Colston and Mrs Wallace, when they were able to obtain excellent views for over three hours at close range. Their notes and comparisons with a nearby Melodious Warbler *Hippolais polyglotta* allowed this report to be acceptable to the BOURC at the time despite being identified in the field, (all previous birds were found in observatory mist-nets).

For almost 50 years a record from Skokholm Island, Pembrokeshire had stood as Britain's first. At 1pm on 23rd September, 1951, an Olivaceous Warbler was trapped in a trammel-net. A description and photographs were taken and the bird was thought to be an adult. As the bird was probably tired it allowed an approach of about two yards as it perched on bracken at South Haven and was watched by Peter Conder, WG Bridges, David Boddington, Margaret Dun and John Peake. Gradually it became more illusive but was still present when the observatory closed on 3rd October. It was thought to be of the southern race *H. p. opaca*.

There had been two previous records in 1915 and 1920 that were later rejected as part of the Hastings rarity scandal. The first was obtained on 20th May 1915, between St Leonards and Hastings, East Sussex and after examination by Mr T Parkin, placed in the Nichol's collection before finally resting at the Dyke Road Museum, Brighton.

References:
Scot Birds 10: 24-25; Sharrock, 1982: 26-27, photo, *British Birds* 46: 191-192, photo pl. 27; 59: 195-7; 61: 350; Evans 1994: 391-392; Naylor 1998; Walpole-Bond, 1938: ii, 24.

Booted Warbler   *Hippolais caligata*
(Northwest Russia, east to Mongolia and south to Iran; winters India)
1936 Shetland, Fair Isle.   A (76)

On 3rd September, 1936, after south-easterly winds. George Stout obtained a bird he later identified as a Booted Warbler. The specimen, a female in worn summer plumage, was examined by George Waterston, H F Witherby, C B Ticehurst and N B Kinnear and found to be of the race *H. c. caligata*.

A bird of the race *H. c. annectens* was trapped on 12th October, 1980, at Theddlethorpe Dunes, Lincolnshire. The report was received by the BOURC in 1995 and in 1999 it announced that *H. c. annectens* was rejected as an invalid taxon (Tim Melling *pers comm*).

With only nine reports prior to 1977, the number of reports has risen dramatically, with 14 found in 1993 alone.

References:
British Birds 30: 226-7; 31: 7-8; *Ibis* 137: 590-591; Naylor 1998.

Booted (Sykes) Warbler   *Hippolais caligata rama*
(Northwest Russia, east to Mongolia and south to Iran; winters India)
1993 Shetland, Seafield.   **A (1)**

A *Hippolais* warbler was found at Seafield, Lerwick, Shetland, by Bill Jackson on 22nd October, 1993 and remained until 9th November. There was initial confusion regarding the bird's identity and thoughts moved from Booted Warbler of the race *H. c. rama* to Olivaceous Warbler *Hippolais pallida* of the race *H. p. eliaca*. The bird was trapped on 25th October, photographed by Kevin Osborn, and finally considered to be the *rama* race of Booted Warbler.

Little is known regarding the two races and more information is needed before a judgement regarding upgrading it to full specific status can be made. This record has been accepted by the BOURC but is currently treated as a race of Booted Warbler.

The southern race of Booted Warbler *H. c. rama* is separated by some authorities and named Sykes Warbler.

Reference:
Birding World 6: 437-438, photo; 492; Ian Dawson *Pers Comm*.

Icterine Warbler   *Hippolais icterina*
(Northeast France, north to Scandinavia, east to Western Siberia; also northern Iran; winters sub-Saharan Africa)
1848 Kent, Eythorne.   **A (P)**

Mr Plomley of Maidstone was the first person to report an Icterine Warbler in Britain. It was collected at Eythorne, near Dover, Kent on 15th June, 1848, having attracted attention by its loud melodious song. The skin was preserved by Mr Gordon of the Dover Museum and placed in the apparently "unrivalled" collection of John Chaffey of Doddington, near Exeter. The specimen suffered considerably after an insect attack and eventually disintegrated.

The record was mentioned in *Zoologist* and was accepted by both Yarrell and Montagu as a Melodious Warbler *Hippolais polyglotta*. However, they had not seen the specimen so there was a request for a more detailed description and the misidentification was rectified.

Usually over 100 are reported each year, with 276 in 1992 being the highest annual total.

References:
Harrison 1953: 181; Saunders 1899: 75; *Zool*, 1848: 2228; *British Birds* 92: 26; Cottridge & Vinicombe 1987: 132.

Melodious Warbler *Hippolais polyglotta*
(Northwest Africa, Iberia, France, Switzerland and Italy; winters West Africa)
1905 Cornwall, near Sandplace, Looe.   **A (P)**

With the removal of two Hastings reports, the title of Britain's first Melodious Warbler went to a bird killed near Sandplace, Looe, Cornwall, on 12th May 1905. In September the same year, Ireland also received its first record, at the Old Head of Kinsale Lighthouse, Co. Cork.

Several 'possibles' were reported in the 1800s, and the eggs of what was almost certainly this species or possibly Icterine Warbler was sent to Saunders in 1893, having been taken from a nest containing four eggs in an osier-bed in Croydon, Sussex in 1884. The finder was Major Mangles who unfortunately broke two eggs. The remaining two joined the collection of Mr F C Selous

The first positively identified bird concerned a male shot at Burwash, Sussex, on 30th April 1897. Having been sent by George Bristow for examination, NF Ticehurst reported the event in *Zoologist* and the record was duly accepted. It was, however, to suffer the fate of all Bristow's birds under the Hastings rarities affair.

Around 35 Melodious Warblers are recorded annually in the south and west.

References:
Zool, 1848: 2228; Saunders 1899: 77; Kennedy, 1954: 357; Walpole-Bond, 1938: ii, 23-24; *British Birds* 2: 408; 92: 27; Naylor 1996: 145; Montagu, 1862: 371.

Marmora's Warbler *Sylvia sarda*
(Southeast Spain and the West Mediterranean islands; some winter in Northwest Africa)
1982 Yorkshire, Langsett.   **A (3)**

G Lee of Barnsley telephoned J Lunn late on 15th May 1982, to tell him he had been watching a Marmora's Warbler on the Pennines at Mickledon Clough, near Langsett, Yorkshire. The next day at 7am Lunn found and watched the bird for 35 minutes in the steep-sided valley, cut from the gritstone by Mickledon Beck, before it disappeared. Later in the day it was discovered 500 yards down the valley by the first twitchers that had arrived to see it.

The adult male regularly sang from the top of heather on the steep east side of the valley, rising 20 feet into the air in a display flight not unlike a Common Whitethroat *Sylvia communis*. It held a territory in an area of heather, grass and bilberry about 400m × 50m where it was watched carrying nesting material. Remaining until 22nd July, it was seen by hundreds of observers.

This record was 2,100km north of its previously known range, during an exceptionally hot summer. Two further Marmora's Warblers have reached Britain: at Spurn, Humberside 1992 and St Abbs, Borders 1993, while records on the continent have also increased.

Birds reaching Britain are considered to belong to the race *S. s. sarda* found on Corsica and Sardinia.

References:
Mather, 1985: 496; *British Birds* 78: 475-481, photo.

Dartford Warbler *Sylvia undata*
(Southern England, France, Italy and Iberia south to North Africa)
1773 Kent, Bexley Heath.   **A (RB)**

It must come as no surprise to find that the first Dartford Warbler was discovered near the place it was named after. Dr Latham found the species on Bexley Heath, near Dartford, where he shot a pair on 10th April 1773. The discovery was conveyed to Pennant who published it in *British Zoology.* Confusion about the habits of this bird, which was thought to occur only in Britain, then followed.

Several specimens of this warbler were collected in southern England including some in winter 1783, near Wandsworth, Surrey. Ornithologists were confused by the fact that a bird appearing to be a winter migrant to Britain was found breeding in France. This contradicted the normal practise of birds migrating north to breed. When Montagu found the first nest of this species in the southwest of England early the following century, he solved the puzzle.

Britain's population was estimated to be about 1 679 breeding pairs in 1995. The majority breed in Hampshire and Dorset.

Ireland had enjoyed seven records prior to 1994.

References:
Montagu, 1862: 367-370; Harrison 1953: 187, illustration of type specimen; Hutchinson 1998.

Spectacled Warbler *Sylvia conspicillata*
(Southwest Europe, Middle East, North Africa, Madeira, Canary and Cape Verde Islands; winters northern Sahara and Northwest Africa)
1992 North Yorkshire, Filey.   **A (2)**

At 9.15am in the coastal mist of 24th May, 1992, Craig Thomas of Filey, North Yorkshire noticed a small bird flitting through Long Hedge on the Filey cliff-tops of the North Cliff Country Park. Excitedly, he called to Richard Harbird as the bird showed some features of Spectacled Warbler. Together they recorded all the salient identification features of this species as it fed in the open. Other birders alerted by their CB radios soon arrived and the bird began to sing.

Due to previous false alarms, Peter Dunn erected a mist-net and the bird was soon caught along with a Common Whitethroat *Sylvia communis* for comparison. After confirming it as Britain's first Spectacled Warbler, the fine adult male was released in the Arndale Ravine without a ring, it having been forgotten in the excitement! Despite a large band of hopeful observers gathering in the dense sea fog it was not seen after 10.30am.

The bird was refound in its original cliff-top hedgerow the next day where it proved difficult to see. About 100 birders had glimpsed it by noon when it went to ground until 3.30pm. It was then relocated and the panicking birders spent an agonising ten minutes following a shadow through the hedgerow before it settled down in the centre of the hawthorn. The bird sat still for about an hour allowing over 650 observers to train their telescopes on it.

It settled and seemed to be holding territory until it moved on with the arrival of a weather front on the evening of Friday 29th May.

The previously accepted records had just been removed from the British List, as the first (at Spurn) was found to have been a Subalpine Warbler *Sylvia cantillans*, while single Fair Isle and Cornish records could not be proven conclusively. An outstanding report from Lepe, Hampshire, on 15th April 1988 also just failed to gain acceptance.

One other record exists, a bird found at Landguard, Suffolk on 20th April 1997 remaining until 2nd May.

References:
Birding World: 5, 181-182, photo, 401; *British Birds* 91: 225-230, photo; 91: 506.

Subalpine Warbler *Sylvia cantillans*
(South Europe, West Turkey and Northwest Africa; winters northern and West Africa)
1894 Western Isles, St Kilda.   **A (430)**

On 14th June, 1894, a male Subalpine Warbler was shot by Mr J Steele Elliot of Dudley, on St Kilda. He had first seen it the day before, but due to its location in the Minister's garden and it being a Sunday, he was prevented from killing it. The bird was watched closely by several people as it fed along a row of young peas and a seeding parsnip that attracted insects. It had probably arrived in the southwesterly gales that ravaged the island on 12th June.

In the presence of Mr McKenzie and Mr Fiddies, the bird was shot and placed in spirits before being sent to John Cullingford of Durham for preservation. On 19th December, 1894, Dr R Bowdler Sharpe exhibited the bird at a meeting of the British Ornithologists' Club. It was of the race *S. c. cantillans*.

Subalpine Warbler is now a regular visitor with peaks of 32 in 1988 and 1995. Over a third of records are from Scotland with around 20% in south-west England. Presumably this reflects the distribution of the two races occurring in Britain: The Eastern *S. c. albistrata* is more likely to be encountered in the northeast, with the Iberian *S. c. cantillans* accounting for records in the southwest.

References:
Saunders, 1899: 53; *Zool*, 1895: 282; Evans 1994: 395.

Sardinian Warbler *Sylvia melanocephala*
(South Europe, Middle East and North Africa)
1955 Devon, Lundy.   **A (54)**

At 9.05am on 10th May, 1955, an adult male Sardinian Warbler was trapped at the Terrace on Lundy, Devon. It was examined and photographed by Barbara Whitaker, the warden, who showed the bird to F W Gade before its release into thick cover at mid-day. The bird was seen only briefly, its actions recalling a Dartford Warbler *Sylvia undata* but then disappeared never to be seen again.

A bird believed to be a Sardinian Warbler associating with a male Blackcap *Sylvia atricapilla* was seen by W S M D'Urban feeding among the ivy berries in his garden at Exmouth, Devon on 16th April 1890. The bird was described as smaller than the Blackcap "with a jet-black head but pure white throat." It was recorded in his book

The Birds of Devon under the name of Black-headed Warbler. The record was not fully accepted by Witherby.

A specimen taken in bramble bushes near Hastings, Sussex, on 4th June, 1907 was later dismissed as part of the Hastings rarities affair.

The species remains rare peaking at eight records in 1992. There were two Irish records in 1993.

References:
Moore, 1969: 244-245; D'Urban: 18-19; Sharrock, 1982: 77-78; Walpole-Bond, 1938: ii, 42.

Rüppell's Warbler *Sylvia rueppelli*
(Coastal regions of East Mediterranean: winters Northeast Africa)
1977 Shetland, Dunrossness. A (5)

At 6.15pm on 13th August, 1977, Rodney Martins saw a greyish warbler dive into the cover of a small willow in a garden between Skelberry and Boddam, Dunrossness, on Mainland Shetland. When he briefly saw the bird's head, he was immediately able to identify it as an unmistakable adult male Rüppell's Warbler.

Over the following 30 minutes, he gained brief glimpses and a flight view of the bird and at one point it perched in the open on top of a rose. He contacted Dennis Coutts and J D Okill and both saw the bird prior to dusk.

The warbler remained in three gardens joined by dry-stone walls where it foraged among the lichen. It remained secretive throughout its long stay and was last seen on 17th September. On 15th August, the bird was trapped and found to be in moult and renewing its primaries, so had probably been present for some time.

All but one of the subsequent reports has involved males, it was also the only mainland record and concerned a female at Holme, Norfolk on August Bank Holiday Monday 1992. The bird remained at Holme until Friday night.

Two male specimens of Rüppell's Warbler in the Dyke Road Museum, Brighton, which once belonged to Mr J B Nichols, had been shot in an old stone quarry at Baldslow, St Leonards-on-Sea, East Sussex, on 5th May 1914. These birds were dismissed as part of the Hastings rarities affair.

References:
Sharrock 1982: 226-229, photo; Naylor 1998; Walpole-Bond, 1938: ii, 41-41.

Desert Warbler *Sylvia nana*
(Middle East, Central Asia and Northwest Sahara)
1970 Dorset, Portland. A (11)

On 16th December, 1970, Grahame Walbridge flushed a small pale warbler from weeds near a building site as he walked to Portland Bird Observatory, Dorset. He noted its main features and promptly reported the sighting to F R Clafton and his wife. The three of them returned to the site and within 30 minutes had refound the bird. The warbler fed unconcerned on the ground and it was decided to trap the bird to identify it. On capture the bird was taken to the observatory where it was roosted overnight. The observers were satisfied that the bird was a Desert Warbler and it was released into the observatory garden in poor weather at 9am the next day.

The Desert Warbler remained present until 2nd January, establishing a regular pattern of feeding among nearby barley shoots and preening in an elderberry bush. It was seen by a large number of observers but was only seen once briefly between Christmas and New Year's day during a spell of severe weather. The barley field was ploughed on 3rd January and the warbler was presumed to have moved on.

Clafton examined skins and confirmed that the bird belonged to the nominate race *S. n. nana*, from the east of the species' range.

This record was not without precedent as Desert Warblers had been recorded in both Sweden and Finland while there have been a further ten occurrences in Britain prior to 1997, including a male singing and constructing a nest at Blakeney, Norfolk in 1993.

Reference:
Sharrock 1982: 178-181.

Orphean Warbler *Sylvia hortensis*
(South Europe, east to Turkestan, and Northwest Africa; winters Southern Sahara, India, Pakistan, Iran and Arabia)
1848 North Yorkshire, Wetherby.   **A (6)**

An attempt to collect a pair of Orphean Warblers which appeared to be nesting in a small plantation near Wetherby resulted in the female being shot on 6th July, 1848. The male was adequately described but managed to escape the hunter. The specimen was poorly mounted by the shooter who, from its general appearance, claimed that it had been incubating at the time. Mr Graham, purveyor of rarities and birdstuffer of York travelled to Wetherby, where he purchased the mount and contacted Sir William ME Milner who placed it in his collection and dispatched communication regarding the discovery to *Zoologist*. Milner's collection later passed to the Leeds Museum where the specimen remains (accession No LEEDM.C.1962.757).

There was no proof of any breeding attempt and it is now suspected that this statement was used to excuse the poor state of the mounted specimen.

The BOURC began to review this record in 1999 as the dealings of Graham recalls Bristow's Hastings reports (he also added an unlikely inland Ross's Gull *Rhodostethia rosea* to the British List). At the time of writing, the specimens are affectionately becoming known as the 'Tadcaster Rarities'.

The second specimen found in Britain was caught and kept alive for six months in Middlesex before being identified. This record is no longer accepted by the BOU along with the three others that followed it.

If the Yorkshire record is rejected, Britain's first would be a bird trapped at Portland, Dorset on the evening of 20th September, 1955. Dr J F Monk, K B Rooke, S R Hatch and Miss U Wall examined it in the hand when a description was taken. The consensus at the time was that it was a first-winter bird, perhaps male because of the dirty greyish-white iris colour and grey crown.

A J Bull and Alan Till also saw the bird prior to release, when it showed its white outer-tail feathers before diving into a large bramble. Unfortunately it was not seen again in the field.

Despite the close proximity of breeding birds in France, Orphean Warbler remains one of the most sought after *Sylvia* warblers in Britain.

References:
Montagu, 1862: 371; Saunders, 1899: 45; Mather, 1985: 499; Naylor 1998; *British Birds* 49: 180; 92: 523.

Barred Warbler *Sylvia nisoria*

(Central and Eastern Europe, west to Central Asia; winters East Africa).
1839 Cambridgeshire, Cambridge.   A (P)

A bird shot in a garden called Paradise near Queen's College, Cambridge was exhibited on behalf of John Robinson of Trinity Hall, Cambridge at a meeting of the Zoological Society on 4th March, 1879, by Professor Newton. It had been shot and mounted 40 years previously by Mr Germany, porter of Queen's College, who possessed a considerable collection. On his death in *c.*1859, it passed to his friend Elijah Tarrant. Robinson was an undergraduate of Tarrent's and bought the specimen in 1878 thinking it to be a variety of Common Nightingale *Luscinia megarhynchos*. It was seen by Frederick Bond soon afterwards and recognised as a Barred Warbler.

While remounting the specimen, Mr Doggett showed the bird to Professor Newton who made enquires about its origins.

Germany had shot the male bird in the spring or early summer of 1839 and showed it to Tarrant just after mounting. It was in poor condition, lacking some rectrices and feathers around the gape, having been shot at very close range due to its skulking behaviour. The date would appear unusual for this species in Britain and it could be argued that the skin might have been imported. However, there was no suspicion at the time and the glass eye in the mounted specimen was the correct colour of yellow; no birdstuffer would have known this had the specimen not been fresh.

By drawing attention to the species several more were soon obtained, with eleven records prior to 1896.

Becoming increasingly common in the 1990s, the peak year was 1994 with 230 reports, the average being *c.*150 individuals. Favouring the East Coast almost all have been immature birds in autumn.

References:
Saunders, 1899: 51; Lack, 1934: 66; Proc. *Zool* soc. 1879, p. 219; *British Birds* 92: 27.

Lesser Whitethroat *Sylvia curruca*

(Europe and Northern and Central Asia; European populations winter in arid country south of the Sahara)
1787 Buckinghamshire, Bulstrode.   A (SB)

Dr Latham of Dartford first recorded Lesser Whitethroat as a British bird in 1787, having received specimens and communication regarding the species from Rev John Lightfoot who had discovered it.

Siberian Thrush, Isle of May, Fife. *D G Andrews (SOC)*

Varied Thrush, Nanquidno, Cornwall. *T Croucher*

 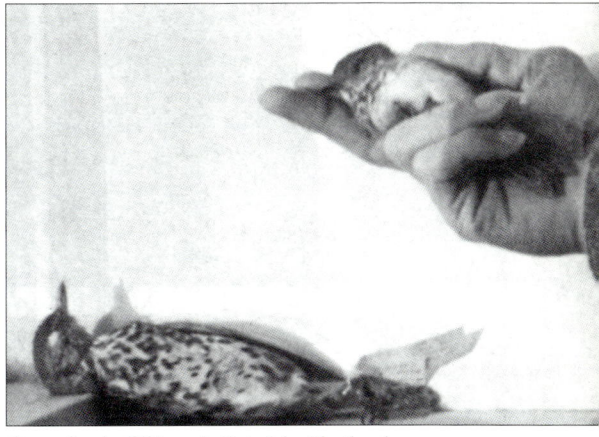

Hermit Thrush, Fair Isle, Shetland. **Grey-cheeked Thrush**, Fair Isle, Shetland.
S Rumsey *H A Craw (SOC)*

Veery, Porthgwarra, Cornwall. *K Allsopp*

Black-throated Thrush, Booth Museum, Brighton.

Red-throated Thrush, The Naze, Essex. *S Young*

Naumann's Thrush, Chingford, Essex. *D Cottridge*

River Warbler, Fair Isle, Shetland. *A Davis (SOC)*

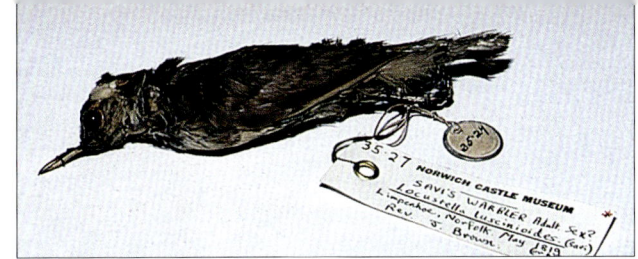

Savi's Warbler, Castle Museum, Norwich.

Great Reed Warbler, Hancock Museum, Newcastle.

Booted Warbler, National Museums of Scotland.

Booted (Sykes) Warbler *H. c. rama*, Shetland.　　*K Osborn*

Olivaceous Warbler, National Museums of Scotland.

Marmora's Warbler, Langsett, Yorkshire.　　*T Belsey*　　**Marmora's Warbler**, Langsett, Yorkshire.　　*T Loseby*

Spectacled Warbler, Filey, Yorkshire.
J Harriman

Spectacled Warbler, Filey, Yorkshire.
M Collar

Rüppell's Warbler, Dunrossness, Shetland.
D Coutts

Orphean Warbler, Leeds Museum.

(Two-barred) Greenish Warbler, Gugh, Isles of Scilly.
D Cottridge

Greenish (Green) Warbler, St Mary's, Isles of Scilly.
R Chittenden

Arctic Warbler, National Museums of Scotland.

Dusky Warbler, National Museums of Scotland.

Yellow-browed Warbler, Hancock Museum, Newcastle.

Red-breasted Nuthatch, Holkham, Norfolk.
D Cottridge

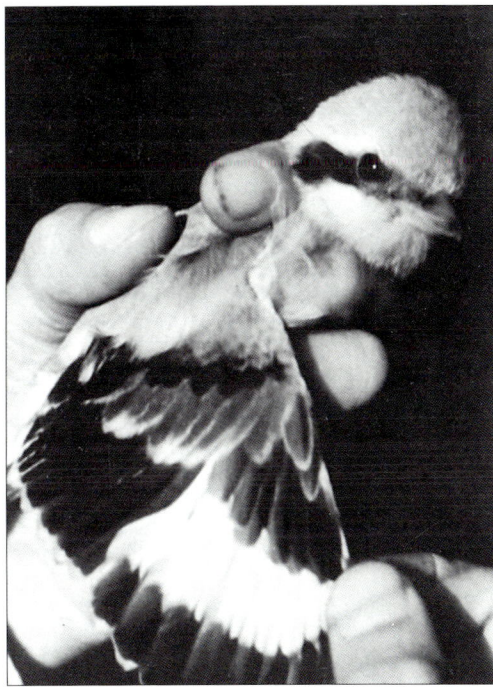

Southern (Steppe) Shrike, Fair Isle, Shetland.
K Williamson (SOC)

Brown Shrike, *first Irish record,* Ballyferriter. Co. Kerry
G Brinkley

Brown Shrike, Grutness, Shetland.
D Coutts

Philadelphia Vireo, Tresco, Isles of Scilly, *first British record.* *D Cottridge*

Philadelphia Vireo, Galley Head, Co. Cork, Ireland. *R T Mills*

Yellow-throated Vireo, Kenidjack, Cornwall. *D Cottridge*

Yellow-throated Vireo, Kenidjack, Cornwall. *A Tate*

Evening Grosbeak, St Kilda, Western Isles. *N Picozzi*

Arctic Redpoll, Hancock Museum, Newcastle.

Golden-winged Warbler twitch, Larkfield, Kent.
T Loseby

Golden-winged Warbler, Larkfield, Kent. *G Reszeter*

▲ **Bay-breasted Warbler**, Lands End, Cornwall.
Video grab by *Birding Plus/Otus*. *D Ferguson*

Wilson's Warbler, Rame Head, Cornwall.
K Pellow

Tennessee Warbler, Fair Isle, Shetland. *T Broome*

▲ **Northern Waterthrush**, St Agnes,
▲ Isles of Scilly. *R E Emmett*

Yellow-rumped Warbler, Exeter, Devon. *E H Ware (RSPB)*

Blackpoll Warbler, St Agnes,
Isles of Scilly. *H Miles*

Yellow Warbler, Bardsey, Caernarfonshire. *H Miles*

Black-and-white Warbler, National Museums of Scotland.

Summer Tanager, Bardsey, Caernarfonshire. *B Condry*

Lark Sparrow, Landguard, Suffolk. *D Cottridge*   **Lark Sparrow**, Landguard, Suffolk.

Savannah Sparrow, first record of race *P. s. oblitus* or *P. s. labradorius* Fair Isle, Shetland.   *T Loseby*

Savannah Sparrow, Portland, Dorset *('Ipswich' Sparrow P. s. princeps).*

D Cottridge   *J Hewitt*

White-crowned Sparrow, Fair Isle, Shetland.
R A Broad

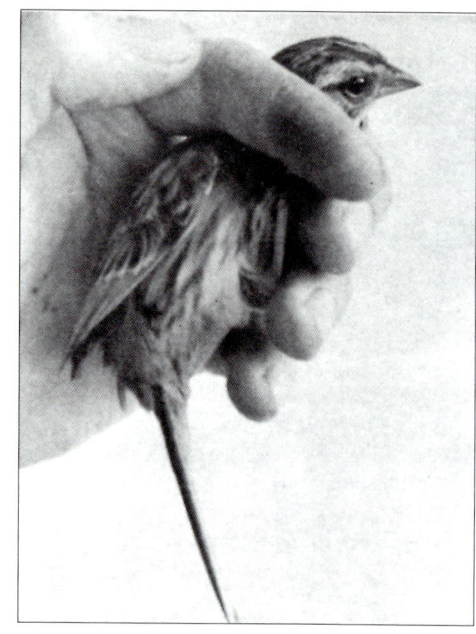

Song Sparrow, Fair Isle, Shetland. *A Davis* ▲
▼

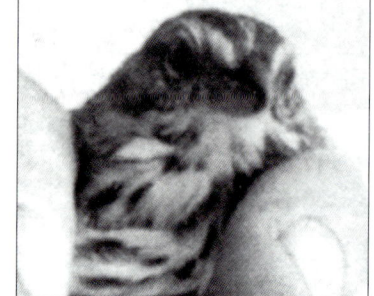

▲
▼ **Cretzschmar's Bunting**, Fair Isle, Shetland. *R Dennis*

White-throated Sparrow, National Museums of Scotland.

Black-faced Bunting, Pennington Flash, Greater Manchester. *S Young*

Pine Bunting, National Museums of Scotland.

Yellow-breasted Bunting, Castle Museum, Norwich.

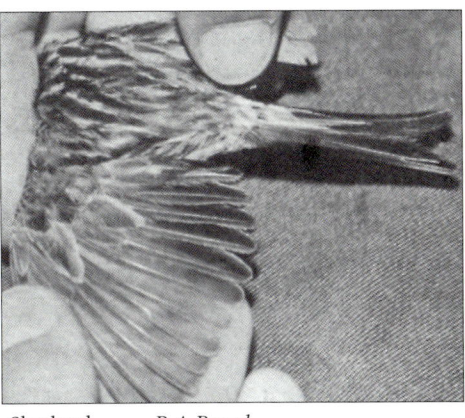

Pallas's Bunting, Fair Isle, Shetland. *R A Broad*

Indigo Bunting, *first British record*, Ramsey Island, Pembrokeshire. *A Tate*

Indigo Bunting, Cape Clear, Co. Cork, Ireland. *A McGeehan*

Reports under consideration in 2000 & Category 'D' Species

Booted Eagle, Drift area, Cornwall. *A Tate*

▲ **Booted Eagle**, Drift area, Cornwall. *A. Tate*

◀ **Booted Eagle**, Rogerstown, Northern Ireland. *P Kelly*

▲ **Short-toed Eagle**, Eastern Isles, Isles of Scilly. ▶
P Palmer

Slender-billed Curlew, Ayscoughfee Hall, Lincs.

Slender-billed Curlew, Northumberland.
J Harriman

Common (Wilson's) Snipe, St Mary's, Isles of Scilly.
I Leach

American Black Tern, Somerset. *M Collar*

Asian Brown Flycatcher, Fair Isle, Shetland. *J Hewitt*

Mugimaki Flycatcher Sunk Island, Yorkshire. *M Turton*

▼ **Short-billed Dowitcher**, Rosehearty, Aberdeenshire, *first British record.* *I Leach* ▲

Escapes and rejected records

Least Bittern, Dorman Museum.

Booth Museum, Brighton.   *P Palmer*

Brown Noddy, Chester Museum.

South Polar Skua, Castle Museum, Norwich.

Kermadec Petrel, Chester Museum.

Cape Shelduck (see Ruddy Shelduck), Hancock Museum, Newcastle.

Purple Gallinule, Sandscale Haws, Cumbria.
P Palmer

Andalusian Hemipode (left), Leeds Museum.

Cape Canary (see Citril Finch), Booth Museum, Brighton.

Ruby-crowned Kinglet, Booth Museum, Brighton.

Daurian Redstart, National Museums of Scotland.

Purple Martin, Booth Museum, Brighton.

Black Larks, Booth Museum, Brighton.

Pallas's Rosefinch, North Ronaldsay, Orkney.

D Tipling

Long-tailed Rosefinch, St Abbs, Lothian.   *P Palmer*

Eastern Meadowlark, Castle Museum, Norwich.

Rev Lightfoot found it to be relatively abundant during May and June near Bulstrode in Buckinghamshire where he obtained the first specimen. As Latham possessed specimens of Common Whitethroat *Sylvia communis*, he was able to distinguish it from that species and also figure the bird in *A General Synopsis of Birds*.

Lesser Whitethroat is a common summer visitor with an estimated population of 80,000 pairs in Britain between 1988-91.

The first proven breeding of Lesser Whitethroat in Ireland was recorded in the early 1990s.

References:
Yarrell, 1843: i, 293-296; Montagu, 1862: 377-378; *Latham Gen Synopsis of Birds*, 1st supplementary volume: 185-186; *Birdwatch* 69: 16; Wingfield Gibbons 1993: 338.

(Blyth's) Lesser Whitethroat *Sylvia curruca blythi*
(Siberia, Kirghiz Steppes and Mongolia)
1948 Yorkshire, Spurn. A (*c.*80)

A bird ringed during a heavy passage of migrants at Spurn, Yorkshire, on 29th October, 1948, was positively identified as belonging to this race as the second primary fell between the 6th and 7th in length. E Holmes, C A Milner and Ralph Chislet saw it. This was probably the first British record.

A second bird was trapped the following October and there have now been about 80 reports of this subspecies in Britain with 17 in 1994 being the best single year.

This subspecies has been suspected of being a good species and is colloquially known as 'Siberian' or Blyth's Lesser Whitethroat.

References:
YNU 1949: 13; *British Birds* 81: 383; Mather 1986: 502; Evans 1997: 257.

Garden Warbler *Sylvia borin*
(Europe east to Western Siberia; winters in Africa)
***c.*1800, Lancashire.** A (SB)

The first Garden Warbler was found in Lancashire by Sir Ashton Lever, who observed the bird's habits and collected specimens from all over Britain. He sent a specimen to Dr Latham, at Dartford, some time prior to 1800 who described it as a British bird. It was then found to be present in almost every English and Welsh county and numerous in Scotland.

Garden Warbler is a common summer visitor to Britain. During the BTO Atlas survey of 1988-91, an estimated 200,000 pairs were found in Britain, and 180-300 in Ireland.

References:
Yarrell, 1843: i, 285- 288; Montagu, 1862: 233; Wingfield Gibbons 1993: 342.

(Green) Greenish Warbler *Phylloscopus trochiloides nitidus*
(Northern Turkey east to Afghanistan)
1983 Isles of Scilly, St Mary's. A (1)

J H Ross found the first and only British record of a Green Warbler at 1.05pm, on St Mary's, Isles of Scilly on 26th September, 1983, while searching for an Icterine Warbler *Hippolais icterina*. He heard a call similar to that of a Greenish Warbler *P. t. trochiloides* along the southeast wall of the Garrison and looked up to see an unusual Greenish Warbler with a strong yellowish wing-bar. He called P T Bell, A G Ross, Paul Holt and D Richardson who all saw the bird well and assumed that the birds' bright yellow coloration could be attributed to a race of Greenish Warbler that they were unfamiliar with. They left to search for a Thrush Nightingale *Luscinia luscinia* while other observers including B Reed and A Davidson continued watching it.

The bird was subsequently identified as a first-winter Green Warbler (first-winters are more easily separated from Greenish Warblers in the field than the adults are). It remained until 4th October, by which time it was seen by hundreds of observers and both Arctic *Phylloscopus borealis* and Greenish Warblers had also been found for comparison.

At the time the first Green Warbler was found in Britain, it held full specific status and took its place in Category A of the British List for a short time before being regarded as a subspecies of Greenish Warbler *P. t. trochiloides*.

Green Warbler has a very restricted range and is most easily seen in the Western Palearctic by birders visiting the mountains beside the Black Sea in Turkey. It is reported to have interbred with Greenish Warbler.

References:
Isles of Scilly Bird Report 1983: 49, 63-64; *British Birds* 78: 576.

(Two-barred) Greenish Warbler *Phylloscopus trochiloides plumbeitarsus*
(Siberia, Mongolia and north-eastern China; winters Southeast Asia)
1987 Isles of Scilly, Gugh.   A (2)

A *Phylloscopus* warbler had been present on Gugh, Isles of Scilly since at least 21st October, 1987 and had been identified at various times as Greenish *P. t. trochiloides*, Yellow-browed, *P. inornatus* and even Arctic Warbler *P. borealis*. On 23rd, it was suggested that it was possibly a Two-barred Greenish Warbler, the first for Britain. On 26th October, Europe's three identification guru's Peter Grant, Lars Jonsson and Killian Mullarney paid a visit to the bird and after two hours of observation in continuous rain confirmed the identification.

Its place on the British List was short lived, as the species was regarded as conspecific with Green *P. t. nitidus* and Greenish Warbler *P. t. trochiloides* by the BOURC soon after its discovery.

The second British and fifth Western Palearctic record was seen by less than 30 observers, despite a large gathering at Wells Wood, Norfolk, on 15th and 16th October, 1996. It was most easily found by listening for a Pied Wagtail-like call *Motacilla alba*.

References:
Twitching: 333-336, photo; *Rare Birds* 3: 34.

Greenish Warbler *Phylloscopus trochiloides*
(Europe east from northern Germany; winters Pakistan, India and Indochina)
1896 Lincolnshire, North Cotes. **A (333)**

The wind had been blowing from the east since 3rd September, 1896, with heavy rain falling on the afternoon of the 4th – ideal conditions for a fall of migrants onto the Lincolnshire coast. Birds packed the hedgerows in considerable numbers and, with modern knowledge, a Greenish Warbler *Phylloscopus trochiloides* would seem almost predictable.

A bird feeding in a hedge near the sea bank at North Cotes, Lincolnshire was shot in the afternoon of the 5th September, 1896, by G H Caton Haigh of Grainsby Hall, Grimsby.

Saunders and Dr R B Sharpe examined it and accepted it as Britain's first Greenish Warbler, a female. It was then exhibited at a British Ornithologists' Club meeting on 21st October.

The second record of Greenish Warbler in Britain turned out to be the first Arctic Warbler *Phylloscopus borealis*, so it was decided to review the first report. The skin was sent to H F Witherby for re-examination and the identity confirmed using the wing formula. Lodge figured the specimen in Saunders' *Manual*.

Greenish Warbler is a scarce regular migrant found chiefly on the East Coast in autumn, peaking in late August.

References:
British Birds 3: 297-8; Zool, 1896, p 436-7; Saunders, 1899: 65; Naylor 1998.

Arctic Warbler *Phylloscopus borealis*
(Northern Fennoscandia east to Alaska; winters Southeast Asia)
1902 Orkney, Sule Skerry Lighthouse. **A (234)**

Thinking he had found an addition to the British List, Eagle Clarke located a specimen from Sule Skerry, Orkney, mistakenly labelled and previously reported by him as a Greenish Warbler *Phylloscopus trochiloides*. The bird was an adult male that had struck the lighthouse during the night of 5th September, 1902. After being sent in the flesh to Clarke it was at that time accepted as Britain's second Greenish Warbler. In 1909, Clarke corrected the mistake after examining a bird found on Fair Isle and it was accepted as the first British record of an Arctic Warbler.

On 28th September, 1908, Clarke flushed a bird from a patch of potatoes on Fair Isle, Shetland. Examination of the dark-coloured "Willow Warbler" *Phylloscopus trochilus* showed it to be an Arctic Warbler, then called 'Northern Willow Warbler' which had only been recorded in Western Europe once before: on Heligoland in 1854.

Fewer Arctic Warblers have reached Britain than Greenish Warblers, with which it is often confused. Both species have reached Ireland.

References:
Clarke, 1912: ii, 294, 131; British Birds 1: 82; 2: 310, 408.

Pallas's Leaf Warbler *Phylloscopus proregulus*

(Central, East and Southern Asia; winters Southeast Asia)
1896 Norfolk, Cley-next-the-Sea.   A (1112+)

On 31st October, 1896, Edward Ramm, a professional gunner from Cley-next-the-Sea, Norfolk shot a Pallas's Leaf Warbler in the long grass on the sea wall. After dissection by the local taxidermist, Henry Pashley, it proved to be a female, and when mounted it was sent to Thomas Southwell at Norwich.

Together with J H Gurney, he identified the bird and distinguished it from Yellow-browed Warbler *Phylloscopus inornatus*, which had already occurred in the county. It was sold for £50 to E M Cannop (his collection is in Birmingham) prior to becoming the possession of Mr W R Lysaght.

Mr Dresser (who announced that the species had only been found once before in Europe, on Heligoland, Germany) displayed the specimen on 1st December, at a meeting of the Zoological Society.

Amazingly Britain's second Pallas's Leaf Warbler was not found until 13th October, 1951. It was ringed at Monks' House, Northumberland. This species now occurs so regularly that reports are no longer considered by the BBRC.

By 1994, only 14 individuals had reached Ireland.

References:
Zool, 1896: 466; Pashley 1992: 37, 109; Saunders, 1899: 63; *British Birds* 45: 258-259; Cottridge & Vinicombe 1997: 139.

Yellow-browed Warbler *Phylloscopus inornatus*
(Siberia; winters Nepal, southern China and Southeast Asia)
1838 Northumberland, near Hartley.   A (P)

The first record of Yellow-browed Warbler in Britain (not accepted by Montagu) was an adult male, shot on the coast, near Hartley, Northumberland, on 26th September, 1838, by John Hancock. It was initially believed to be a Pallas's Leaf Warbler. It was described as feeding among umbellifers in a manner similar to a Goldcrest *Regulus regulus*. The addition to the British List was announced in *Zoologist* (1843).

The mistake in identification was corrected by Mr Swinhoe 25 years later in 1863. The skin was placed in Hancock's Museum, at Newcastle.

There had been *c.*310 records up to 1962 when Yellow-browed Warbler ceased to be considered by the BBRC. The annual average is now about 300 sightings in Britain alone.

References:
Yarrell, 1843: i, 316; Saunders, 1899: 61; 63; *Zool* 1843: 79-80; *British Birds* 92: 29; Cottridge & Vinicombe 1997: 139-40; Montagu, 1862: 390.

Hume's Leaf Warbler *Phylloscopus humei*
(From Sayan and Altai mountains south to the northwest Himalayas; winters mainly Indian Subcontinent from Pakistan to Bangladesh)
1966 East Sussex, Beachy Head.   A (30)

The true status of this warbler has been difficult to ascertain as Hume's Leaf

Warbler has only recently been separated from Yellow-browed Warbler *Phylloscopus inornatus*, with some previous reports presumably recorded as that species. The first individual to be accepted as a Hume's Leaf Warbler in Britain was present in Belle Tout Wood at Beachy Head, East Sussex from 13th to 17th November, 1966.

In the company of Roger Charlwood, R E Scott identified the bird the day after its discovery by Peter Clement, as it fed in the canopy of trees. It later moved down to almost ground level where it provided better views. It was also watched by Brian Metcalfe, Tony Quinn, Barry Cooper and Roger Charlwood who telephoned Scott the following morning.

Hume's Leaf Warbler usually arrives in Britain later in the year than Yellow-browed Warbler and some have wintered in Britain.

References:
British Birds 71: 464-465; 72: 124-125; 92: 96-100; *Birding World* 10: 360; *Sussex Bird Report 1966*: 45.

Radde's Warbler *Phylloscopus schwarzi*
(Central and East Asia; winters Southeast Asia)
1898 Lincolnshire, North Cotes.   A (174+)

At North Cotes, Lincolnshire, on 1st October, 1898 Mr G H Caton Haigh heard an unusual bird call from a hedgerow, which was then beaten until the caller was flushed out. It proved to be Britain's first Radde's Warbler, an immature bird. The specimen was lent to Saunders and illustrated by George Lodge in his *Manual*.

Caton Haigh regularly worked the hedgerows and sea walls of the Lincolnshire coast in search of vagrants.

The second British record was as recently as 1961, the same year as Britain's second Dusky Warbler *Phylloscopus fuscatus*.

The separation of Radde's and Dusky Warblers in the field was once considered extremely difficult and there are 363 accepted records not specifically identified to species level. With annual peaks of 24 Radde's Warblers in both 1988 and 1991 this eastern vagrant is surprisingly scarce on Fair Isle which is arguably the best site in Britain for eastern vagrants; the first record there was as recently as 1987.

References:
Saunders, 1899: 73; Naylor 1998: 321; Cottridge & Vinicombe 1997: 140.

Dusky Warbler *Phylloscopus fuscatus*
(Central and northeastern to southern Asia; winters northern India and Southeast Asia)
1913 Orkney, Auskerry.   A (198+)

Eagle Clarke, Dr C B Ticehurst and George Stout had spent the autumn of 1913 observing bird migration on Auskerry, Orkney. On 1st October, they obtained a small bird that had been skulking in a nettle patch. When it was compared to specimens at the British Museum of Natural History, Tring the bird was identified as a female Dusky Warbler, belonging to the nominate race. It was also found to be the first specimen obtained in Europe.

Radde's *Phylloscopus schwarzi* and Dusky Warblers share a similar history of vagrancy in Britain; both were only recorded once before the formation of the BBRC in 1958 and they have enjoyed an upsurge of records since the mid 1970s, preferring East Coast sites. Irish records had not broken double figures by December, 1999.

References:
British Birds 7: 220-3; Scot. Nat., 1913: 271, 1914: 7; Cottridge & Vinicombe 1997: 141; Hutchinson 1998.

Western Bonnelli's Warbler *Phylloscopus bonelli*
(Central, western and southern Europe and Northwest Africa; winters in tropical West Africa)
1948 Pembrokeshire, Skokholm.   A (55+)

Now an expected annual vagrant to Britain, the first record of a Western Bonnelli's Warbler occurred as recently as 31st August, 1948. A small *Phylloscopus* warbler was caught in the garden trap on Skokholm Island, Pembrokeshire at 7.30pm. John Keighly had noted a yellowish rump, striking white underparts and a *"hooeet"* call while in flight. Its captors were confused about the bird's identity and held it overnight. After further examination the next day, with no conclusion reached, the bird was killed.

The specimen was sent to Mr R Wagstaffe, Director of the Yorkshire Museum, who pronounced that it was a female Bonnelli's Warbler, most probably of the eastern race *P. b. orientalis*. However, the call would seem to rule out this possibility as the call of *P. b. orientalis* is a Crossbill-like 'chip' and so it was accepted as the first Western Bonnelli's Warbler.

P. b. orientalis was given full specific status by the BOURC in 1996 (see Eastern Bonnelli's Warbler).

There have been 55 accepted Western Bonnelli's Warbler records in Britain with an additional *c*.145 indeterminate Bonnelli's Warbler spp.

Reference:
Sharrock, 1982: 19-29.

Eastern Bonnelli's Warbler *Phylloscopus orientalis*
(Southeast Europe and Asia Minor; winters Sudan)
1987 Isles of Scilly, St Mary's.   A (3+)

J G T Hamilton and K R Lloyd first found a Bonnelli's Warbler at Salakee Farm, St Mary's, Isles of Scilly on the 30th September, 1987. Several other birders on the island went to see it but unfortunately no calls were noted. A week later, on 8th October, a bird was seen by T J Wilson, Charles Fentiman and M Reid at the same place, possibly the same individual.

Although they and other observers heard the typical *'tchip'* call, it was claimed that the *'hooeet'* call of Western Bonnelli's was also heard. This created a problem, as it could not have uttered the calls of both species.

The *'tchip'* call was noted by Chris Heard, then a BBRC member, who ascribed it to the 'eastern race' and it was also recorded as such in the *Isles of Scilly Bird Report*. With hindsight, the finders deduced that the *'hooeet'* notes were possibly from a nearby Common Chiffchaff *Phylloscopus collybita* and that a mistake had been made. The call remains the best aid to separate these two species in the field.

The BOURC began reviewing this 'new' species in 1995 and eventually the Scilly bird was admitted to the British List as the first record while one from Spurn, East Yorkshire on 15th October, 1970 was not.

It is possible that other birds previously accepted as Bonnelli's Warbler spp. might be upgraded, as there are currently *c*.145 records of Bonnelli's Warblers not assigned to either species.

Eastern Bonnelli's Warbler was only 'split' from Western Bonnelli's Warbler *Phylloscopus bonelli* by the BOURC in 1996 and while considering the taxonomic relationship an example of the eastern race *P. b. orientalis* was found at Whitley Bay Cemetery, Tyne and Wear. Dr David Parkin, at that time Chairman of the BOURC, visited the site fuelling speculation of an imminent decision and the warbler was seen by many for 'insurance'.

This individual was found on 20th September, 1995 and remained until the 29th, keeping high in the trees but frequently giving its diagnostic Crossbill-like *'tchip'* call. The bird was the first thoroughly documented occurrence of Eastern Bonnelli's Warbler in Britain. The report was submitted by M P Frankis, A S Jack and T J Tams and accepted by the BBRC in 1996.

References:
Naylor 1998: 326-328; *Rare Birds* 1995: 181; *British Birds* 90: 503; 89: 520; 92: 519-523; *Isles of Scilly Bird Report* 1987: 45.

Wood Warbler *Phylloscopus sibilatrix*
(West, central and Northeast Europe east to Altai; winters Africa)
1768 Hampshire, Selborne. **A (SB)**

During a period of great discovery among the common species found in Britain, Gilbert White separated Wood Warbler from Willow Warbler *Phylloscopus trochilus* and Common Chiffchaff *Phylloscopus collybita*. In correspondence to Pennant in 1768, he clearly described the three species yet Wood Warbler was not included in the 1776 edition of *British Zoology*. It was, however, included in White's *Natural History of Selborne*, in 1789.

In November, 1792, the Linnean Society published details regarding the species, supplied by Thomas Lamb, and in 1796, Montagu obtained specimens from various localities. The bird then rapidly gained recognition as a common summer visitor.

An estimated 17,200 singing males occur in Britain.

There are possibly up to 30 pairs in Ireland with numbers increasing during the 1990s.

References:
Yarrell, 1843: i, 297-301; Wingfield Gibbons 1993: 346-7; Hutchinson 1998.

(Siberian) Common Chiffchaff *Phylloscopus collybita tristis*
(Central Asia and Northern India)
1902 Orkney, Sule Skerry.   A (P)

The first accepted example of this race of Common Chiffchaff was a specimen collected from the Sule Skerry Lighthouse, Orkney, on the night of 23rd (*British Birds*) or 26th (Bull BOC) September, 1902. It was sent to Eagle Clarke but was not identified immediately as it had been immersed in methylated spirit.

He later exhibited it at the British Ornithologists' Club meeting of 21st November, 1906.

Tristis chiffchaffs, are recorded almost annually on the East Coast in autumn, some remaining for the winter. They are most often called Siberian Chiffchaffs with many birdwatchers of the opinion that the race deserves full specific status on account of plumage differences between *tristis* and nominate *collybita*.

References:
British Birds 1: 8-9; Bull BOC vol 29: 18.

Iberian Chiffchaff *Phylloscopus brehmii*
(Iberia, southwest France and northwest Africa)
1972 Greater London, Brent Reservoir.   A (1)

On 3rd June, 1972, a Common Chiffchaff *Phylloscopus collybita* with an uncharacteristic song was heard singing loudly at the top of a 15-20ft willow by J H Wood. Noting its black legs and describing the call as "like a young chicken" or just the 'chiff' part of a Common Chiffchaff's song. After making a recording, he contacted Dr Leo Batten who subsequently also tape-recorded the bird which was at Brent Reservoir, London (then Middlesex). Weeks later, the tape was compared to that of a chiffchaff belonging to the Iberian race *P. c. brehmii* and found to possess many similarities.

Following this, on 17th April 1983, a bird at Lodmoor, Dorset was also presumed to be this subspecies, as the song was very different from Common Chiffchaff and there were subtle plumage differences. The descriptions were insufficient at the time to allow acceptance of the subspecies onto the British List.

In 1998, the BOU looked at the chiffchaff complex and separated it into four species including Iberian Chiffchaff. The London record was re-examined and the tape recording of its song again compared to recordings of the 'new' species. The tape was also examined by Jochen Martens who agreed with the identification of Iberian Chiffchaff.

In April 1999, the BBRC announced that it would only consider records where a tape recording of the song was included with the description until such time that the field identification characters became fully understood. Almost immediately a chiffchaff with a very different song was found at the Verne, Portland, Dorset on 24th April. It was tape-recorded and attracted a large number of visitors who were struck by the songster, whose calls bore little resemblance to the *"chiff-chaff"* familiar to every British birder.

At the turn of the century the BOURC were investigating the possible occurrence of this species in Britain and the London record was accepted as Britain's first in January, 2000. The other reports were still under consideration.

References:
Morrison 1997: 142; Clement 1995: 64; London Bird Report 1972: 78; British Birds 92: 216; Birding World 12: 142.

Firecrest *Regulus ignicapillus*
(West central and southern Europe to Asia Minor)
1845 Cornwall, Penzance.   **A (P & RB)**

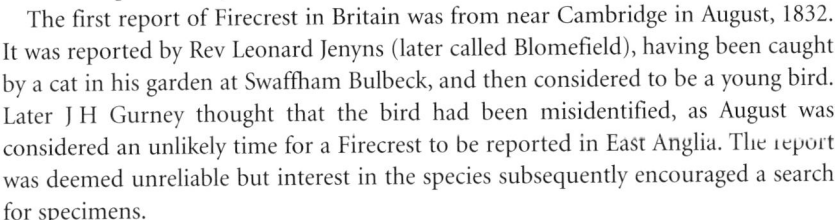

The first Firecrest seen in Britain was a bird killed during poor weather in Cornwall during March, 1845. It was shot in a low wet ditch, half a mile from Penzance and proved to be a female. A specimen described by Sir W Jardine and shot at Penzance on 6th March was presumably the same individual.

The first report of Firecrest in Britain was from near Cambridge in August, 1832. It was reported by Rev Leonard Jenyns (later called Blomefield), having been caught by a cat in his garden at Swaffham Bulbeck, and then considered to be a young bird. Later J H Gurney thought that the bird had been misidentified, as August was considered an unlikely time for a Firecrest to be reported in East Anglia. The report was deemed unreliable but interest in the species subsequently encouraged a search for specimens.

As a result, further records revealed that the bird had probably been overlooked in Britain. The Cambridgeshire report was often mistakenly recorded as the first British specimen despite rejection by Gurney, as was a "fire-crested Regulus in the company of some titmice [*Parus*]" caught by boys at Whitby, North Yorkshire, February, *c.*1850.

Firecrest spread westwards early in the 20th Century with breeding reported in the New Forest, Hampshire, in 1962. Spreading into Wales, Firecrest established a small breeding population in the 1970s, but so far it has not bred in Scotland or Ireland.

This southerly bias is reflected in the fact that the first Scottish record of the species was as recently as 1959 when a male was found on the Isle of May, Fife.

References:
Saunders, 1899: 59; Yarrell, 1843: i, 322-325; Rodd, 1880: 41-43, 195-196; Wingfield Gibbons 1993: 354; Thom 191986: 301; Lack, 1934: 62; *Zool* 1889 p. 172; British Birds 93: 84.

Red-breasted Flycatcher *Ficedula parva*
(Southern Sweden south to Austria and Bulgaria eastwards to Siberia; winters southern Asia)
1863 Cornwall, Carwythenick, near Falmouth.   **A (P)**

The first occurrence of Red-breasted Flycatcher in Britain was recorded by Edward Hearle Rodd in *Zoologist,* from a letter sent to him from Mr Gould:

"Strange to say, on the day I visited Falmouth one of the rarest European birds was shot for the first time in Britain. The bird in question is the Muscicapa parva, and you will find figures of it in my Birds of Europe, *which you have in the Penzance Museum. The plates will at once give you an idea of this pretty species (a robin amongst flycatchers). I certainly never expected this singular bird to have been added to our Fauna.*

"The specimen was sent in the flesh to Mr Grey, of the British Museum, and in this state I had it in my hands, so that there is no mistake about it. The bird was in good condition thanks to your genial climate. The bird was shot on the 24th of January, 1863, by Mr Copeland of Carwythenick House, in the parish of Constantine, near Falmouth, and is female. Unfortunately the specimen was placed in some insecure place, and the head was eaten by mice or rats, so that the body alone was sent to the museum. If you write to Mr Copeland, ask him to look out for the male, which will have a red breast."

The flycatcher had been seen for several days prior to being shot. Favouring a dead holly tree near the house it would skim the grass to take insects. A second bird was seen in a plantation 400 yards from the house. Despite attempts to obtain it the bird was not seen again.

The following November, a further example was found on the Isles of Scilly. The vast majority of birds are found from August to November, but a bird was present in Caithness on 6th January 1981.

Amassing a total of 228 records prior to 1958, the 'R B fly' is a regular passage migrant in Britain with up to 200 reported in 1984. A more typical average is 100.

References:
Montagu, 1862: 102-103; Rodd, 1880: 229-231, 26-28; *British Birds* 92: 30; Cottridge & Vinicombe 1997: 142-3.

Collared Flycatcher *Ficedula albicollis*

(Central and southeast Europe and West Russia; winters Africa)

1947 Shetland, Whalsay.   **A (21)**

On 11th May 1947, Samuel Bruce shot an adult male Collared Flycatcher at Skaw, on Whalsay, Shetland, after a week of strong southerly winds. It was the first acceptable British record following the dismissal of some Hastings birds.

A male "pied" flycatcher with a collar seen by Messers Pratt, taxidermists at Brighton on 24th April 1871, was ignored by the authorities of the day. Further records concerned two males obtained at Udimore Lane, near Wincelsea, East Sussex on 12th and 13th May 1911, with two more in 1916 and one in 1922. These were all rejected as part of the Hastings rarities affair.

The only female was found on the Out Skerries, Shetland on 25th May 1976.

References:
British Birds, 5. p 238; Baxter & Rintoul 1953: 148; Walpole-Bond, 1938: i, 344; Naylor 1998.

Willow Tit *Parus montanus*
(Northern Eurasia east to Japan)
1898 Greater London, Finchley, Coalfall Wood.   **A (RB)**

In 1897, German collector Otto Kleinschmidt and Dr Hartert found two Willow Tit specimens mixed up with Marsh Tit *Parus palustris* skins in the British Museum. The birds had been obtained at Hampstead and were the first to be reported in Britain. During the same year, Walter Rothschild received two specimens killed at Coalfall Wood, Finchley, Greater London, for his collection at Tring. One of these specimens became Hellmayr's type specimen and the first official record of a Willow Tit anywhere in the world, despite it being a common British bird.

In Saunders' *Manual of British Birds* (1899), there was no mention of the Willow Tit. At a similar time Dr Hartert in his work *Vogel der palaarktischen Fauna* (Birds of the Palearctic Fauna) included the recently discovered Willow Tit as a subspecies of *Parus atricapillus,* the Black-capped Chickadee of North America.

Kleinschmidt first mentioned the occurrence in Britain of the Willow Tit in German literature in 1898. It was named as a subspecies found in Britain but with no date or locality. In 1900, Mr Hellmayer gave it the subspecific name *Parus montanus kleinschmidti* as he separated two British taken specimens provided by Hartert, from the continental form *P. m. salicarius* found in West Germany. The British birds had been obtained in the "neighbourhood of London" and placed in the Rothschild collection at Tring.

Hartert later recorded Willow Tit as a subspecies of *Parus atricapillus* naming it *P. a. kleinschmidti* and recorded its typical habitat as being "Coalfall Wood, Finchley," with others reported from Tunbridge Wells and the Scottish valleys of the Tweed, Spey and Forth.

Some British ornithologists considered it to be a race of Marsh Tit *P. palustris kleinschmidti* but Mr P L Sclater argued that there was no room for two subspecies of the same species to live together in Britain and so it must be a new British bird, *Parus kleinschmidti.*

Once Willow Tit was recorded as a British bird, many disputes arose as to its validity, a similar situation having arisen with the separation of Marsh *Acrocephalus palustris* and Eurasian Reed Warblers *A. scirpaceus.* Many old ornithologists refused to accept the differences between Marsh and Willow Tit while others thought that it was a young Marsh Tit in its first-year plumage. Walter Rothschild published a convincing paper in the first volume of *British Birds* in 1907 and called for further specimens and information.

Willow Tit was the last regularly breeding British bird to be 'recognised', and during the BTO survey of 1988-91 there were an estimated 25,000 territories. There were only a few in Scotland and none in Ireland.

References:
British Birds 1: 23-24; 44-47; Wingfield Gibbons 1993: 366-7.

Northern (Boreal) Willow Tit *Parus montanus borealis*
(Northeast and East central Europe to Siberia)
1907 Gloucestershire, Tetbury.   A (3)

Following publication of a Fair Isle report, an earlier record came to light of a bird killed by J H Paddock at Tetbury, Gloucestershire, in March 1907. The bird was found to be a female typical of *P. m. borealis* and was presented to the British Museum of Natural History (registered number 1908. 10. 25. 6) where it remains. This was the first of only three accepted British records of birds showing characteristics of this race. The other two were from Minsmere, Suffolk on 15th and 16th September 1974 and Thorne Moors, South Yorkshire, on 8th February 1975.

On 3rd November, 1935 George Stout found a Willow Tit with brilliant white cheeks in a flock of three Continental Blue Tits *Parus caeruleus caeruleus*, on Fair Isle, Shetland. It was almost certainly the '*borealis*' race of Willow Tit and remains Fair Isle's only Willow Tit record, of any race to date. Although accepted at the time, the racial identity is no longer acceptable.

References:
Dymond 1991: 117; Evans 1994: 425; Nat 106: 75-76. [Baxter & Rintoul 1953: 137]

Red-breasted Nuthatch *Sitta canadensis*
(North America)
1989 Norfolk, Holkham.   A (1)

One of the most popular birds to reach Britain was the male Red-breasted Nuthatch found by Jean and Roy Aley at 1.30pm on 13th October 1989, at Holkham Meals, near  Wells-next-the-Sea, Norfolk. The bird fed on a grassy footpath before flying into pines. Wood Nuthatch *Sitta europaea* was immediately dismissed by virtue of its striking head pattern and it was thought initially to be a Corsican Nuthatch *S. whiteheadi*, but later dismissed. They failed to relocate it that day.

The following day it was seen in flight by Peter Hayman who heard its "toy trumpet" call. Dave Hatton and Paul Varney from Cambridge found it on the trunk of a pine by the summerhouse and confirmed its identity as Britain's first Red-breasted Nuthatch. The bird was seen again by the small group of birders present and the news put onto Birdline. The nuthatch was seen briefly and heard several times for the rest of the day. About 2,000 birders saw it in the first few days with possibly 5,000 throughout its seven-month stay. At first, viewing was difficult because of the narrow paths, but by its last reported sighting on 6th May 1990 it had become more obliging, regularly drinking from the gutter of the summer house at Burrow Gap.

During the September prior to its discovery in Britain, large numbers of Red-breasted Nuthatches were reported to be on the move in North America, as the species is sometimes irruptive. Red-breasted Nuthatch has been recorded on ships in the Atlantic and was a possible candidate for vagrancy. There had been a previous record from Iceland in May 1970.

References:
British Birds 88: 150-153; Birding World 2: 354-356, photo; Evans: 425.

Wallcreeper *Tichodroma muraria*
(Central-southern Eurasia, discontinuously from the Pyrenees to China)
1792 Norfolk, Stratton Strawless.   A (11)

While searching through letters written by Gilbert White, Thomas Bell found a letter from Mr Marsham, of Stratton Hall, Stratton Strawless, Norfolk, dated 30th October 1792. It read:

> "My man has just now shot me a bird which was flying about my house. I am confident I have never seen its likeness before. But on application to Willughby, I conclude it is the Wallcreeper or spider-catcher. I find he had not seen it in England. It is very beautifully coloured, though the chief is cinerous; but the shades of red on the wings, and the large spots of white and yellow on the quill-feathers are uncommonly pleasing."

His letter included a water-colour painting of two primary feathers.

Marsham was an accurate observer of natural history and wrote several papers on trees. This description of such a distinctive bird meant that the record was accepted almost one hundred years later, and pre-dated the then accepted first, of a bird at Sabden, below Pendle Hill, Lancashire in 1872.

References:
Zool, 1875: 4664; Riviere 1930; Naylor 1998.

Short-toed Treecreeper *Certhia brachydactyla*
(Central Europe and North Africa)
1969 Kent, Dungeness.   A (19)

Britain's first Short-toed Treecreeper was trapped in a mist-net at dusk on 27th September 1969 at Dungeness and roosted overnight before being released the next day. The bird was present until 30th September when it was retrapped and found to have increased its body weight from 7.5g to 8.1g. R E Scott of High Halstow, Kent reported the record.

The first treecreeper trapped at Dungeness Observatory, Kent on 10th October 1957 had been examined by H E Axell who claimed that it was "too grey" for a Eurasian Treecreeper *Certhia familiaris* and probably of continental origin. It may have been a Short-toed!

Kent holds the bulk of Short-toed Treecreeper records.

References:
Sharrock 1982: 165-166; *British Birds* 69: 508-509.

Eurasian Penduline Tit *Remiz pendulinus*
(Spain through central Europe to the Pacific coast of China)
1966 East Yorkshire, Spurn.   A (140)

Penduline Tit had been expanding its European range when the first British discovery was made. R J Raines and A A Bell saw a small bird in an elderberry bush just south of the Warren Cottage, at Spurn, Yorkshire, on 22nd October 1966. It was part of a flock engaged in mobbing a red fox. Positive that the bird was a Penduline Tit, they took notes before contacting other birdwatchers but after ten minutes the bird had gone.

A week later, on 28th October, 3km north of the original site, B Branson, M Densley and S J Kenyon relocated the bird in a patch of phragmites among the buckthorn, north of Kilnsea Beacon. Several observers saw the bird over a period of four hours, and an unsuccessful attempt was made to trap the bird which bounced out of the net twice, before finding a hole at the last try.

The second record was not until 1979 but by 1995 at least 60 birds had been reported and breeding suspected at least once.

References:
Mather, 1985: 538; Sharrock 1982: 144-45; Cottridge & Vinicombe 1997: 146-7.

Eurasian Golden Oriole *Oriolus oriolus*

(Europe east to central Asia; European population winters East and South Africa)
*c.*1761, no location.   **A (SB)**

Golden Oriole was added to the British List in the 18th Century. The earliest report of this species in Britain was published by Pennant between 1761 and 1776. He had "*only heard of one shot in Great Britain; in South Wales.*"

In 1787, Dr Latham wrote: "*Since the publication of my synopsis,* (1782) *this bird has twice been shot in England. One is now in my collection.*"

At the time Hunt's work was published, in 1815, only six British occurrences were known: one in Wales, two in Cornwall and three in Suffolk.

According to Dr Latham, Golden Oriole mentioned in Willughby's list (1676), did not refer to British specimens.

Golden Oriole was probably breeding in East Anglia during the latter half of the 19th Century.

Britain enjoyed an average of 143 migrants per year between 1990-95, excluding breeding birds.

References:
Gurney 1921: 229; Lovegrove 1994: 311; *Latham's Gen Synopsis of Birds*, 1st supplementary volume: 89; Pennant 1761-76: 626; Hunt vol II: 74; *British Birds* 92: 30; Cottridge & Vinicombe 1997: 147.

Brown Shrike *Lanius cristatus*

(Western Siberia to the Pacific, South Asia to China and Japan; winters from Pakistan and India to Southeast Asia and Philippines)
1985 Shetland, Grutness.   **A (1)**

In 1981, Mark Chapman found what he thought to be an Isabelline Shrike *Lanius isabellinus* at Kergourd, Shetland. The report was not accepted by the BBRC but they considered the bird to have probably been a Brown Shrike. On the 30th September 1985, he was given a rare second chance: as he was checking the garden at Grutness, Sumburgh, Shetland, he flushed a shrike. The bird perched on a post where it showed a black mask and bill with a bright supercilium, identical to his 1981 bird. Chapman realised that he was looking at a Brown Shrike and went to telephone various people, including the Fair Isle Bird Observatory. Despite deteriorating weather with heavy rain and the bird's reluctance to show for an hour, at least 12 people saw the bird before dusk, including Ron Johns, J D Okill, P Ellis and J Eames. It remained until 2nd October.

It is thought that the bird was an adult male.

IRELAND
1999 Co. Kerry, Ballyferriter.

When Jill Crosher described a bird she had seen on route to the Post Office at Ballyferriter, Co Kerry on 22nd November 1999, she was told it could be a Red-backed Shrike *Lanius collurio*.

But, chatting to Sinead McDonnell over the phone, she explained that the illustrations in Lars Jonsson's *Birds of Europe* did not seem to match that bird entirely. Seamus Enright reached the area by dusk but failed to see the bird and when showing Crosher his book she noted the similarity to Brown Shrike.

It wasn't until midday two day's later that birders confidently announced that it was indeed a Brown Shrike, probably adult male and the first Irish record. It possessed a grey cap with brown tones on the rear crown and could not be assigned with any certainty to a particular race.

It was last seen on 10th December 1999.

References:
British Birds 86: 600-604, photo; Cottridge & Vinicombe 1997: 148 Mitchell & Young 1997: 136; *Birding World* 12:483-486.

Isabelline Shrike *Lanius isabellinus*
(South Asia to China; winters northeast Africa)
1950 Fife, Isle of May.   **A (51)**

After a southeasterly wind on 24th September 1950 a few migrants arrived on the Isle of May, Fife. On the 26th, Miss Winifred, U Flower and Miss M I Kinnear saw a pale shrike fly into a small walled garden near the lighthouse. Using a burdock perch, it would drop to the ground in search of prey or make aerial sallies from the wall. Taking field notes in close proximity to the confiding individual they were unable to identify the bird. They later compared their records with the skins at the National Museums of Scotland, Edinburgh, and concluded that the bird was an adult male Isabelline Shrike in winter plumage. The bird was thought to be of the race *L. I. Phoenicuroides* and identifiable males occurring since have proved to be this race.

They sent their notes to B W Tucker at Oxford who accepted the record.

Until 1978, Isabelline Shrike was regarded a race of Red-backed Shrike *Lanius collurio* along with the Brown Shrike *Lanius cristatus*, and in 1980 the BOURC officially declared them separate species. Isabelline Shrike appears almost annually.

References:
Sharrock, 1982: 20-23; *British Birds* 44: 213-219, colour frontispiece; Cottridge & Vinicombe 1997: 148-9; *Birding World* 12: 236.

Lesser Grey Shrike *Lanius minor*
(South and East Europe and Southwest Asia; winters East and South Africa)
1842 Dorset, near Christchurch. A (158)

An adult Lesser Grey Shrike was shot during September 1842, at the same site as the first Whites Thrush *Zoothera dauma*, near Heron Court, Christchurch, Hampshire (now Dorset). The discovery was recorded by Rev Murray A Mathew in *Zoologist* 1894, who found the adult bird in Lord Malmesbury's collection, during a visit with Edward Hart of Christchurch. It had laid unnoticed in a case labelled "*Grey Shrike, shot Sept 1842*."

Prior to this discovery, a female Lesser Grey Shrike, killed on St Mary's, Isles of Scilly, during mid-November 1851, had been recorded as Britain's first. The specimen had been sent to Mr E H Rodd and mistakenly recorded as a Great (Northern) Grey Shrike *Lanius excubitor*. While checking his skin collection with Rev John Jenkinson, he noticed the differences and suggested that it was Loggerhead Shrike *Lanius ludovicianus*. Mr Gould eventually solved the bird's true identity.

There had only been five records in Ireland prior to 1994.

References:
Saunders, 1899: 149; Kelsall & Munn, 1905: 50; Rodd, 1880: 23-24; *Zool*, 1894: 345; Yarrell II: 619; Hutchinson 1998.

Southern Grey Shrike *Lanius meridionalis pallidirostris*
(Southern and Eastern Siberia; winters northeast Africa, Middle East and Pakistan)
1956 Shetland, Fair Isle. A (15)

On 21st September 1956, Kenneth Williamson and his daughter Hervor noticed a pale shrike alight on one of the poles supporting their mist-nets in crops on Fair Isle, Shetland. They watched the bird for an hour as it avoided capture by using poles and guys as vantage points. As it flew past a Heligoland trap it was mobbed by starlings at the entrance and forced into the trap. At least seven other observers saw the bird in the field or at the observatory where photographs and a description was taken. It was not reported subsequently. This taxon is often called Steppe Shrike.

References:
British Birds 50: 246-9, photo pl. 41; Naylor 1998.

Woodchat Shrike *Lanius senator*
(West, Central and South Europe, Southwest Asia and North Africa; winters North and West Africa)
1829 Norfolk, Bradwell. A (681+)

The Paget brothers recorded the first acceptable record of a Woodchat Shrike in Britain:

> "*a specimen shot at Bradwell, (Norfolk) April 1829, by Mr Adams, a farmer in that village, and in whose possession it now is.*"

The farmer reportedly had it preserved but no trace of the specimen has been found. Prior to this there had been an unacceptable report of an immature bird at Auton Stile, Co. Durham, in September 1824.

An immature bird of the Corsican race *L. s. badius* was obtained at Romney Marsh, Kent on 29th June 1909, by Mr W Horton and was the first and only British report of this race, but was later removed as a Hastings rarity.

Mr P A Clancy found a bird he thought belonged to the Iberian race *L. s. weigoldi* in the British Museum. Mrs E A Woods had obtained a worn male at Longfield, near Gravesend, Kent on 9th May 1934, while Mr D C Keef wrote in *The Times,* published on 12th May 1934, of a Woodchat he had seen despatching a beetle on a fence post, somewhere in Kent. Two days later, a box was sent to the newspaper containing the dead bird. Both reports probably referred to the same bird, which was the first confirmed British record of this race.

References:
Ticehurst: 129; Allard, 1990; Paterson, 1905: 128; Paget's 1829: 4; Hagemeijer 1997: 667; *British Birds* 55: 370; 92: 32; BOU 1992. [(Walpole-Bond, 1938: i, 322; Harrison 1953: 231)]

Spotted Nutcracker *Nucifraga caryocatactes*
(Eurasia from Scandinavia and the Alps to Kamchatka and China)
1753 Denbighshire and Flintshire, Mostyn.   **A (410)**

Pennant recorded the first occurrence in 1766; he took his description from the only specimen known in Britain, a Spotted Nutcracker shot on 5th October 1753, at Mostyn, Flintshire. The bird was described as being a link between the crows *Corvidae* and woodpeckers *Piciformes.*

A bird regarded as the second British record due to the lack of an exact date was mentioned by Latham as being a *"mutilated skin, now in the house of an acquaintance."* It was said to have been obtained in Kent some time prior to 1781.

Most of the vagrants to Britain have involved the race *N. c. macrorhynchus* known as 'Slender-billed' Nutcracker. Only two records are assigned to the nominate race *N. c. caryocatactes* ('Thick-billed' Nutcracker); the first was a male shot at Vale Royal, near Northwich, Delamere, Cheshire in 1860. Mounted by William Thompson of Chester it was later presented to the Grosvenor Museum, Chester where it remains. Mr R Newstead said *"there is no doubt what ever attached to this record,"* the first Nutcracker to visit Cheshire. The second was shot on 21st December 1900 at Chilgrove, West Sussex.

References:
British Birds 86: 358; Harrison, 1953: 93; Yarrell, 1843: ii, 122-124; Witherby 1938: 29-31; Bell 1953: 183; S. Woolfall, curator, Grosvenor Museum, Chester: *pers comm*; Naylor 1998; Hagemeijer 1997: 679; *Rare Birds* 4: 324.

Eurasian Jackdaw *Corvus monedula monedula*
(Scandinavia)
1911 Suffolk, Corton.   **A (P)**

It was presumed that Scandinavian Jackdaws reach Britain but this was unproven until Dr C B Ticehurst exhibited two specimens from his collection. They had been shot by Eric C Knight on 3rd March 1911, at Corton, near Lowestoft, Suffolk and had settled in his fields among a flock preparing to migrate. Ticehurst said that this race could only be reliably identified in the hand and recalled seeing some hung up as scarecrows in Suffolk.

Sight records of Jackdaws belonging to the eastern race *Corvus monedula soemmerringii* have been claimed in Britain on a number of occasions. In 1998, the BOURC examined literature and skins which indicated that plumage characters of Jackdaws were so variable that this taxon could only be accepted as new to Britain if a breeding bird or pullus ringed within its normal breeding range and showing characteristics of the race was recovered in Britain.

Continental Jackdaws arrive on the east and south coasts of Britain in October and November so true eastern race birds may be overlooked.

Ireland recorded its first bird relating to either *C. m. monedula* or *C. m. soemmerringii* at Lucan, Co. Dublin, between 25th February and 18th April 1997.

References:
British Birds; 28: 90; 92: 298; Ticehurst: 42-44; *Ibis* 141: 175-180.

Rosy Starling *Sturnus roseus*
(Southeast Europe and Southwest Asia; winters India)
1742 Greater London, near Norwood, (Middlesex).   A (514)

The first British record of a Rose-coloured Starling (now Rosy Starling) was recorded in G Edwards *A Natural History of Birds*, 1743-1750. He visited Salter's Coffee House, at Chelsea where the mounted specimen was kept and was permitted to draw it. The finished illustration was figured in his book.

Edwards gives no date for the occurrence and claimed that the bird had been shot at Norwood, near London. Bucknill included it in his Surrey list while Harting and Glegg placed the site in Middlesex.

Rosy Starlings reach Britain annually in varying numbers and peaked at 29 during 1994.

References:
Glegg, 1935: 21.

Spanish Sparrow *Passer hispaniolensis*
(Iberia, Northwest Africa, Sardinia and the Balkans east to Southwest Asia; mainly resident)
1966 Devon, Lundy.   A (6)

Observatory warden Cliff Waller from Blythburgh, Suffolk was about to commence a drive of the traps on Lundy, Devon, at about 11.20am on 9th June 1966 when he heard the call of a sparrow that sounded a little less harsh than the normal House Sparrow *Passer domesticus*. The previous day, I G Reynolds had reported an unusual sparrow so Waller searched for the bird and found a dark sparrow with strikingly white cheeks sat on a fence near Quarter Wall facing him about 30m away. He called John Ogilvie and they watched the bird, an adult male Spanish Sparrow, for five minutes, before inadvertently flushing it while trying to view its back. At 2.50pm it was relocated by F W Gade in the Tent Field but again soon disappeared.

The bird preferred to be alone and was difficult to find throughout its stay of about ten days. It spent most of its time in the Halfway Wall and church area, keeping away from buildings. It preferred to perch on fences and was seen by various people, but eluded Waller until 12th June when he took a detailed description.

In Autumn 1900, Arthur Rodgers was fishing in the River Trent, near Wilford, Nottingham, when he was attracted by the noise of a large chattering flock of sparrows that had congregated to roost in an ivy-covered hawthorn. He struck the tree with his pike rod to see how many birds were in it and knocked one down. Noticing that it was a strange individual he took it home and mounted it. He was a taxidermist in Nottingham who went out of business at the start of the First World War. It was a male Spanish Sparrow in excellent condition, showing no signs of captivity. Whitaker thought the record was good but may have involved ship assistance.

This record was found unacceptable; the chances of singling out a Spanish Sparrow among the other birds and then hitting it with a rod would seem beyond belief.

References:
Whitaker: 95-97; *British Birds* 74: 109; Frost. 1987: 107; Sharrock 1982: 141.

Rock Sparrow *Petronia petronia*
(South Europe and Northwest Africa, west and central Asia)
1981 Norfolk, Cley-next-the-Sea.   A (1)

On 14th June 1981, Europe was basking in the warmth of a high-pressure system. It is possible that Britain's first Rock Sparrow left Spain and headed for the cooler climate of the north Norfolk coast to be caught up with several other birds noticed on a day of strong visible migration.

At 8am, artist and twitcher Richard Millington checked two passerines beside the Eye Field fence at Cley-next-the-Sea, Norfolk. He gestured his companion Steve Gantlett to take a look at a stripy-headed sparrow accompanying a male Common Linnet *Carduelis cannabina*.

Lapland Longspur *Calcarius lapponicus* was quickly dismissed and Millington suggested Rock Sparrow. The bird flicked up onto the fence showing the diagnostic white tail spots confirming the identification to Gantlett who had previously seen the species in Europe.

They watched the bird feeding on the ground at a range of 50-100 metres, at times hopping up onto the fence.

Gantlett went to fetch other birdwatchers and J McLaughlin, M Eldridge and C Jones just made it before the bird flew off across the Eye Field at 8.30am. It was not seen again.

There is an earlier report concerning a cabinet skin held at the Yorkshire Museum bearing a label inscribed "*died at Lilford*" with no date. There is a Lilford in Greater Manchester but the origin is thought more likely to have been Lord Lilford's managerie at Lilford Hall near Oundle, Northamptonshire.

References:
British Birds 76: 245-247, sketch; Denton 1995: 84.

Yellow-throated Vireo *Vireo flavifrons*
(Eastern North America; winters in West Indies and from Southern Mexico to extreme north of South America)
1990 Cornwall, Kenidjack.   A (1)

A regular visitor to Kenidjack valley, near St Just, Cornwall, Andrew Birch checked the bushes at the bottom of the valley on 20th September 1990 and at 9am saw what he thought may have been a Pied Flycatcher *Ficedula hypoleuca* flitting among the foliage. After moving to the front of the bush it began fly-catching in full view. The bright coloration of the bird turned his thoughts to the American wood warblers *Parulidae*. He left to make phone calls to other birdwatchers and returned thinking it might be a vireo. Finally, he realised that he was watching Europe's first Yellow-throated Vireo.

The first local birders arrived at midday. It was two hours before the bird was seen again but it showed well into the evening. The vireo remained until 27th September giving excellent views to at least 3,000 observers. An on-site collection raised over £200 for the Mousehole Wild Bird Hospital.

References:
British Birds: 8, 362-365, photos; *Birding World* 3: 308-309, photos.

Philadelphia Vireo *Vireo philadelphicus*
(North America; winters Mexico south to Panama and northern Columbia)

IRELAND
1985 Co. Cork, Galley Head.   A (2)

On 7th October, 1985, J F Dowdall, J Adamson and P A Cummins saw an unfamiliar bird in sycamores and fuschias at Galley Head, Co. Cork, Ireland, accompanying a flock of Blue Tits *Parus caeruleus* and Goldcrests *Regulus regulus*. First impressions were that it was a Red-eyed Vireo, *Vireo olivaceus* until it turned to reveal lemon-yellow underparts. They had to leave the bird, as they were due to catch the ferry to Cape Clear Island. In the evening, after checking a photographic guide Dowdall was convinced it was a Philadelphia Vireo. The following day he returned to Galley Head with several other birders to confirm his suspicions. It remained in the area until 17th October and was the first Western Palearctic record; 56 birders saw it.

BRITAIN
1987 Isles of Scilly, Tresco.

Two years after the Irish record, the first British bird was found on Tresco, Isles of Scilly, on 10th October 1987. John Brodie Good watched a vireo hop into view at Borough Farm. He called to Richard Filby who identified it as a Philadelphia Vireo and confirmed it by checking the National Geographic field guide. The news was broadcast over the CB radio, but on St Mary's the confused message was ignored. Simon Harrop was the only other person to see the bird that day. That evening, boats were organised for the following dawn.

During the night possibly Britain's worst hurricane ever hit Scilly, but 984 birders were ferried to Tesco the next day. The bird remained until 13th October.

There have been no further European records.

References:
British Birds 76: 7, photos; 88: 474-477, photos; Evans: 452; *Twitching*: 301-302.

Red-eyed Vireo *Vireo olivaceus*
(North America and South America south to northern Argentina; all populations winter in South America)

IRELAND
1951 Co. Wexford, Tuskar Rock.   A (114)
On the 4th October 1951, a Red-eyed Vireo was killed when it struck the lighthouse, at Tuskar Rock, Wexford, Ireland. Capt C H B Grant examined it and found no evidence of captivity, while Mr J D MacDonald later confirmed the identification at the British Museum. Weather conditions at the time were favourable for trans-Atlantic vagrancy. There have been 25 records in Ireland.

BRITAIN
1962 Isles of Scilly, St Agnes.

The first Red-eyed Vireo to be seen alive in Britain was found on 4th October 1962. R E Emmett, I J Ferguson-Lees, D I M Wallace and his wife were checking the small fields near the Parsonage on St Agnes, Isles of Scilly, for migrants when they saw an unusual bird moving through the tamarisks. The observers watched the bird for almost two hours taking detailed notes. Referring to Peterson's American field guide, they decided it was a Red-eyed Vireo. The following day, Wallace and Ferguson-Lees were astounded when a second bird appeared. One was an adult, which was last seen on the 10th, the other an immature last seen on 17th.

A pair of Red-eyed Vireos were trapped by a birdcatcher known as Hatter Dick, at Chellaston, near Derby, in May 1859. Then called Red-eyed Flycatcher, the male was preserved and became the possession of Edwin Brown. He figured the bird in Mosley's *Natural History of Tutbury*. The female was not preserved.

F B Whitlock was happy with the identification but doubted their origin, Montagu accepted the report but it never gained widespread recognition. The location and circumstances were suspicious and the record was not accepted.

Red-eyed Vireo is the commonest vagrant Nearctic passerine, and in 1988 there were 11 reports including a couple in Ireland.

References:
Kennedy, 1954: 393; Sharrock, 1982: 28-30; *British Birds* 46: 378-379; Naylor 1988. [(Montagu: 103-104)] [Frost. 1978: 160]

European Serin *Serinus serinus*
(West, central and southern Europe)
1852 Hampshire, Portsmouth.   **A (SB)**

A male European Serin was obtained by Rev W Hazel in April 1852, from near Eastney Fort, Portsmouth, Hampshire. He recorded the event in *The Naturalist* magazine in 1853.

However the following record is often mistakenly quoted as the first British record:

Mr Pratt, taxidermist Brighton, had a female European Serin caught in a clap-net near Brighton, East Sussex on 20th June 1859. Though it was alone when it was trapped and appeared to be completely wild, at the time European Serin was widely thought to be a likely escape candidate.

Pratt mounted the bird and showed it to Mr Bond, who claimed it as a first for Britain and it was published as such by Montagu.

There had been *c*.431 British records and young raised in Britain prior to 1983 when the BBRC ceased to monitor reports.

References:
Montagu, 1862: 100; Saunders, 1899: 177; Kelsall & Munn, 1905: 60; *Zool.* 1860: 7105; *Ibis* 1861: 113; *British Birds* 91: 445; 92: 152.

Arctic Redpoll *Carduelis hornemanni*

(Circumpolar Arctic; spreads erratically south in winter)
1855 Tyne and Wear, Whitburn.   **A (751)**

A bird shot near Whitburn, Co. Durham, on 24th April 1855 was Britain's first Arctic Redpoll *C. h. hornemanni*. It is now at the Hancock Museum, Newcastle-upon-Tyne. There were only five more records before the turn of the century.

Prior to 1995, all but eight of the 305 British records were confined to the East Coast. In the winter of 1995/96 an unprecedented invasion of at least 391 and probably exceeding 500 individuals were recorded from almost every county except parts of the Southwest. There are no Irish records.

References:
British Birds 39: 150; Temperley, 1951.

Two-barred Crossbill *Loxia leucoptera*
(Northeast Europe, North-central Asia, northern North America and West Indies; winters south and west of breeding range)
IRELAND
1802 Co. Antrim, Grenville.   **A (122)**

A female Two-barred Crossbill was shot at Grenville, about two miles from Belfast, Ireland, on 11th January 1802. The report was forwarded by Mr Templeton of Orange Grove Belfast, but was thought to have been an escape or case of mistaken identity by Montagu, who claimed it was killed in June.

This record is now widely accepted and is the first of three birds to reach Ireland.

BRITAIN
1826 North Yorkshire, Plompton.

The first record of a Two-barred Crossbill in Britain came in 1826, as part of an irruption of the species into Europe. A single bird was shot at Plompton, near Knaresborough, North Yorkshire, some time during 1826.

In December 1904, on the death of J C Garth, in whose collection it had been housed, Riley Fortune of Harrogate purchased the specimen.

The second reports came in 1838, with two killed on the Isle of Wight and a single bird near Worcester that was considered to have been the American race *L. l. leucoptera.*

References:
Yarrell, 1843: ii, 38-43; Mather, 1985: 580; Naylor 1998. [Montagu, 1862: 136; *British Birds* 48: 13]

Parrot Crossbill *Loxia pytyopsittacus*
(Scandinavia and West Russia; mainly resident, also eruptive)
1818 Suffolk, Blythburgh.   A (576)

Following a note in Pennant's *British Zoology* (1776) of a male and female Crossbill of "the large variety" sent from Shropshire but which lacks other detail, a report concerning a female Parrot Crossbill obtained in 1818 at Blythburgh, Suffolk, is generally regarded as the first acceptable British record. The skin is now at the University Museum, Cambridge.

The species became better known to British ornithologists' in 1838, after the first influx of continental birds saw specimens reaching Leadenhall Market.

The first confirmed breeding in Britain was in Wells Wood, Norfolk in 1984, which followed an invasion of 104 birds present in the winter of 1982/83. This was eclipsed in 1990/91 when *c.*264 birds were found.

Scottish *L. scotica* and Common Crossbills *L. curvirostra* were recognised as separate forms in 1904, as a result all reports of crossbills in Scotland prior to this referred to just one species.

References:
Ticehurst: 83; Yarrell, 1843: ii, 34-37; Cottridge & Vinicombe 1997: 156; Holloway 1996: 412.

Trumpeter Finch *Bucanetes githagineus*
(North Africa, Middle East and western Asia)
1971 Suffolk, Minsmere.   A (8)

Trumpeter Finches were reported from southern Spain at the end of the 19th century and in 1971 two birds were recorded in Britain for the first time.

The first was found feeding among the sand dunes of Minsmere, Suffolk, by F K Cobb and Mrs A E Cobb at 10am on 30th May 1971. They were familiar with the species having seen them in Morocco but dismissed it as a cage bird. Miss A J Towns joined them but the bird flew off after five minutes.

Ten days later, on 10th June, it was refound at the same site by Dave Holman and Ray Turley and on the nearby cliff top on 15th by Ron Johns and others. The bird was assumed to have been a first-year male with the last confirmed sighting being on 19th June.

A second bird was found a week later on 8th June on Handa Island, Sutherland, remaining to the 9th.

The escape possibility was investigated by M D England and the three specimens known to be held in Britain were still safely behind bars. A Trumpeter Finch was also discovered on the Channel Islands in 1973. Additional reports from France and Germany assisted the British sightings to formal acceptance in January 1974.

References:
Sharrock 1982: 181-184.

Common Rosefinch *Carpodacus erythrinus*
(North and East Europe, across northern Asia to Kamchatka; winters Pakistan and India east to eastern China, Thailand and Burma)
1869 East Sussex, Brighton.   A (P)

A female Common Rosefinch was caught on the Downs near Brighton during the last week of September 1869. Mr Swaysland kept the rosefinch alive before placing it in the aviary of Thomas Monk of Lewes where it survived until June 1876. On its death the bird was preserved and placed in his collection. This is the first acceptable British record and was reported by Mr Bond in 1870.

A second specimen in Monk's collection, also killed near Brighton two years earlier was later found to be a hybrid.

An earlier report of a "Scarlet Grosbeak shot at Powick, Worcester, in December 1855 and preserved by Mr Brookes of Worcester" was included in R F Tomes *Birds in the Victoria County History* (1901). The evidence was not convincing and A J Harthan did not accept the record in his county avifauna (1945).

Common Rosefinch has become a regular passage migrant since its removal from the BBRC list in 1982, prior to which 2,410 records including *c*.45 in Ireland had been logged.

A single bird of the race *C. e. roseatus* was present at Amble, Northumberland from 27th February until 1st March 1994, was considered to be an escape.

References:
Saunders, 1899: 197; Walpole-Bond, 1938: i, 101-102; Harthan 1945: 26 *Zool*, 1870: 1984; Wingfield Gibbons 1993: 446-7; *British Birds* 92: 153. [Evans 1997: 334]

Pine Grosbeak *Pinicola enucleator*
(North Eurasia and North America; mostly resident but eruptive)
Pre-1831 Tyne and Wear, Pelaw.   A (14)

In 1877, J H Gurney reviewed the British records of Pine Grosbeak. He found only four of the 25 reports acceptable. The honour of first record was bestowed on a female shot at Bill Quay, Pelaw, near Newcastle-on-Tyne, Co. Durham, some time prior to 1831 (Bill Quay was once a mooring place for small, shallow bottomed vessels near a chemical works).

Gurney rejected the previous first, a sight record of a flight of birds over the Denes at Yarmouth, Norfolk on 22nd November 1822. The name of the observer is unknown although the Paget brothers (1829) recorded the event.

The species remains rare in Britain with records coinciding with Scandinavian invasions.

References:
Zool, 1877: 242-250; 1890: 125; Temperley, 1951: 59-60; Naylor 1996 & 1998.

(Northern) Common Bullfinch *Pyrrhula pyrrhula pyrrhula*
(Northern and Eastern Europe)
1894 East Yorkshire, Kilnsea.   A (P)

It is difficult to determine which records of the northern race of Common Bullfinch refer to genuine vagrants, but two birds killed in Yorkshire are widely regarded as the first British records. One was shot by Mr Craggs Clubley of Kilnsea in November 1894 and the second, a male, was shot in the same month nearby at Humanby. This specimen came into the possession of Mr Brown of Filey and Col Irby exhibited both at the Zoological Society's meeting in November 1895. The Kilnsea specimen was placed in the British Museum and the Humanby bird in the National Museums of Scotland, Edinburgh.

'Northern' Bullfinch remains a rare vagrant to Britain.

References:
Nelson 1907: 194-195.

Evening Grosbeak *Hesperiphona vespertina*
(Western and North eastern North America)
1969 Outer Hebrides, St Kilda.   A (2)

As a result of a major irruption in North America, Europe's first record came from Hirta, St Kilda on 26th March 1969.

At 10am, Nick Picozzi heard a metallic "jink" call from a bird perched on a drystone dyke 200 metres away. He watched the bird fly to the window of a Nissen hut where it attempted to land on the thin ledge. It allowed him to approach to within five metres when he snatched a photograph and noted the poor condition of the bird – it appeared to have some crown feathers missing. He did not see it again after it flew off. Picozzi identified the bird as an adult Evening Grosbeak and an investigation began to disprove the expected cagebird theory. There had been no Evening Grosbeaks imported into Britain for over 40 years and birds are known to lose head feathers at window ledge feeders in America. Together with the season's impressive movements, the record was formally accepted.

The second and only other record was a female feeding at a Nethybridge birdtable, Highland, from 10th-24th March 1980.

References:
Sharrock 1982: 162-164; Evans, 1994: 469.

Black-and-white Warbler *Mniotilta varia*
(North America; winters south to northern South America)
1936 Shetland, Scalloway.   A (15)

After a period of stormy weather during mid-October 1936, a Black-and-white Warbler was picked up dead at Scalloway, Mainland Shetland. Initially regarded as an escape, Mr Inkster sent the warbler to the National Museums of Scotland, Edinburgh, where it remains. The record is now accepted as the first British record.

The second record involved a live bird which graced trees on the Garrison, St Mary's, Isles of Scilly from 27th to 30th September 1975.

References:
Venables & Venables, 1955: 144; *Scot. Nat.*, 1937: 46.

Golden-winged Warbler *Vermivora chrysoptera*
(Eastern North America; winters Central and South America, from Guatemala south to Columbia)
1989 Kent, Larkfield.   A (1)

When Yorkshire born bird photographer Paul Doherty, went to post some letters at 3pm on 7th February 1989, he glimpsed a small bird as it 'flicked' out of a cotoneaster bush. He quickly found the bird again and was treated to stunning views of an adult male Golden-winged Warbler, although he did not realise the identification until checking an American field guide at home.

Rushing back to the site, with his camera, he failed to locate the bird before dark. Doubting his initial identification he gathered four local birders the following day to confirm or dismiss his report. By midday, Bill Jones, Tim Losebey, Terry Laws and Alan Woodcock had all given up and left as thick mist was hampering viewing. At 1pm Doherty tried again, this time taking his camera. He found the bird near Tesco in the first bush he approached. Positive about the identification and having got a record shot he telephoned some friends. The bird was only seen briefly by Andy and Jackie McKee at 3pm, before it retreated for the day.

The news was released via *Birdline* and 300 birdwatchers were present the following dawn, all connecting with it successfully in Tesco's carpark. The next day, the warbler spent the day in the local housing estate, where it remained for much of its three month stay.

The crowd of twitchers present during the first Saturday after its discovery was estimated to be between 2000 and 3000. Enterprising local Girl Guides cashed-in by selling cakes and coffee from a garage, while Tesco's supermarket opened its Coffee Shop for additional hours. On the Sunday at least 600 people saw the warbler as it worked its way from garden to garden and it remained until 9th April, at least.

It transpired that the bird had already been seen and photographed by Chris Miller after his wife told him of the bright bird she had seen in the garden on 24th January.

Golden-winged Warbler is a scarce species in the USA with a restricted breeding range and is considered an unlikely vagrant to Britain. This remains the only Western Palearctic record.

References:
Birding World: 2, 40-41, 48-52, photos.

Tennessee Warbler *Vermivora peregrina*
(Canada and northern USA; winters Central America to Venezuela)
1975 Shetland, Fair Isle.   A (4)

During the morning of 6th September 1975, Chris Heard and Graham Walbridge (later BBRC members), flushed a small bird uttering an unusual '*zit zit*' call from the dry-stone wall near the Double Dyke trap at Finniquoy, on Fair Isle, Shetland. The bright yellow and lime-green warbler stayed in the area for about two minutes and was constantly on the move. It then flew towards the south of the island and despite searching until dark, the bird could not be found and remained unidentified.

The warbler was relocated by the original observers in a small potato patch the next morning and agreed that they were watching a Tennessee Warbler. It was later seen by several observers including Roger A Broad and P J Roberts, who agreed with the identification.

The bird remained feeding in the standing crops until 18th September when it was trapped in a mist-net, ringed and photographed. It was not seen again until it was found for the last time at Field Croft on the 20th.

Roger Broad watched a calling Tennessee Warbler fly into the observatory trap four days later. It was unringed and 2.9g lighter, possibly reflecting a recent arrival. It was last seen later the same day at Buness.

References:
Sharrock 1982: 199-201.

Northern Parula *Parula americana*
(Eastern North America; winters Central America)
1966 Isles of Scilly, Tresco.   A (14)

Bernard King and his wife Marjorie, who were staying at the New Inn, Tresco, Isles of Scilly, in October 1966, described a mystery bird they had seen earlier feeding with Goldcrests *Regulus regulus* and hovering over the path near the Great Pool to David Hunt. Hunt rushed to the same spot on Pool Road on 16th October where he caught glimpses of the bird among the sallows. Hunt and King checked Peterson's *Field Guide to Western Birds*, where the bird closest to theirs was Olive-backed Warbler (Tropical Parula) *Parula pitiayumi*, a species from Central America and the Rio Grande Valley in Texas. As a footnote it mentioned the similar Northern Parula; and so the puzzle was solved.

The following day, after telephoning St Agnes, a handful of birders, including Ron Johns, braved a severe westerly gale to successfully see the bird, which was not seen after 17th October.

It was decided that the bird was a male moulting into winter plumage and was the first to reach Britain and Ireland. An earlier report concerned a tired bird caught on board the RMS *Mauritania* on 19th September 1962. Fed in captivity, it later died in Southampton, Hampshire, and the skin placed in the Liverpool Museum.

In Britain, the majority of reports have been from Cornwall and the Isles of Scilly, with three in Dorset and a dying bird at Wigan, Greater Manchester. There have been two Irish records.

References:
Hunt: 93-94; Sharrock 1982: 142-144; Naylor: 1998: 370

Yellow Warbler *Dendroica petechia*
(North and Central America; winters south to Peru)
1964 Caernarfonshire, Bardsey. A (5)

At 3.30pm on of 29th August 1964, Hugh Miles had just arrived at Bardsey Island, Caernarfonshire when a small bright yellow warbler on top of a hedgerow attracted his attention. He dismissed it as a bright Willow Warbler *Phylloscopus trochilus*.

What was almost certainly the same bird was seen two hours later by R F Durman while driving birds into a mist-net and he informed the warden, George Evans, who saw the bird briefly but well. The warden's thoughts also led him to think it was a variant Willow Warbler and instigated attempts to trap it. The bird entered the net at 6.20pm.

The bird was seen by all the visitors to the island and was photographed by Miles. Although suspecting it was a Yellow Warbler, the books in their possession lacked detailed information. The warbler was roosted overnight but died shortly after dawn on the 30th. Durman preserved the skin and Dr P M Driver dissected the carcass. The bird proved to be an immature male and the identification of Britain's first Yellow Warbler was confirmed by Derek Goodwin at the British Museum on 3rd September.

A Yellow Warbler of the eastern race *D. p. aestiva*, picked up near Axwell Park, Co. Durham, in May 1904 and exhibited at the BOC by Mr E Bidwell, is considered to have been an escape.

Two reached Ireland in 1995.

References:
Sharrock, 1982: 126-129; Naylor 1998; *British Birds* 1: 9; 48: 12.

Chestnut-sided Warbler *Dendroica pensylvanica*
(North America; winters Central America from Guatemala south to Panama)
1985 Shetland, Fetlar. A (2)

At 1.30pm on 20th September 1985, Michael Peacock was looking for migrants at the Burn of Feal, Fetlar, Shetland. It was a bright day with a north-westerly wind. While looking for a Garden Warbler *Sylvia borin* in a patch of thistles, he saw a second more brightly coloured bird, which flew onto a fence. Drooping its wings and cocking its tail, he noted its double yellowish wing-bars, bright yellow-green upperparts and white-grey underparts. The bird was watched feeding in a circuit, covering the iris patch and thistle bed. It would drop down from a vantage point to catch an insect before returning, or take prey by fly-catching.

He fetched his telescope for a better view after 30 minutes and at 3pm his wife Val arrived, the only other birdwatcher on Fetlar. The bird was last seen at 5.30pm that day and later, after telephone conversations, he concluded that the bird was the Western Palearctic's first Chestnut-sided Warbler, in first-year plumage.

The following day a group of Shetland birders searched the area, but the bird was not seen again.

Despite being one of the commonest warblers in eastern North America, Chestnut-sided Warbler remains one of the rarest of its clan in Britain, the only other report being a bird found at Prawle Point, Devon on 18th October 1995.

References:
British Birds 86: 57-61; Naylor 1998.

Blackburnian Warbler *Dendroica fusca*
(Eastern North America; winters Central America south to Peru)
1961 Pembrokeshire, Skomer. A (2)

On 5th October 1961, David Saunders had seen a number of migrants during his early morning walk on Skomer Island, Pembrokeshire (Dyfed), where he was warden. As he neared his house he noticed a bright yellow-breasted bird flitting among the ivy on a cliff above North Haven. He fetched Shirley Saunders and together they watched it, at times down to a range of ten metres. The bird remained active on the cliff all day but there was no-one else on the island to assist with identification. The bird was not seen the next day, having moved on in front of approaching bad weather. The record was submitted to the BBRC as a *"queer passerine,"* it was circulated twice and also shown to James Baird in the USA, with the conclusion that it was probably a Blackburnian Warbler.

As knowledge of trans-Atlantic vagrancy grew there was pressure to resubmit the record, and in 1990 it was accepted as the first Blackburnian Warbler found in the Western Palearctic.

A second bird was seen on 7th October 1988, on Fair Isle, Shetland. At 9.15am Jack Willmott and a party of five birders decided to work the north of the island and, whilst looking into North Restensgeo, Willmott saw a flash of yellow. Lifting his binoculars he caught a rear view of the striped bird and called out "Black-and-white Warbler" *Mniotilta varia* to Avery. The bird then flew to the other side of the geo showing its bright yellow head. Now not so sure of his initial identification, he called to the other three members of the group; his son Matthew, wife Margaret and Pete Massey. Together they mentally eliminated the American warblers known to them but were unable to put a name to it.

As other birders began to arrive, Chris Donald relocated the bird feeding on a neighbouring cliff at Furse where it was watched for an hour and identified as an immature male Blackburnian Warbler, the bird was seen to fly high towards Buness and never refound. Two unlucky birders staying on the island missed the bird.

One of the brightest of American wood warblers, the Blackburnian Warbler is named after Anna Blackburn (1726-1793) from Warrington, Lancashire, who established a natural history museum at Orford Hall.

References:
Birding World 1: 355-356; *British Birds* 85: 337-343, sketch.

Cape May Warbler *Dendroica tigrina*
(Eastern North America; winters in West Indies)
1977 Clyde, Paisley Glen.   A (1)

Alexander Wilson discovered the first Cape May Warbler in America around 1811, so it is fitting that the first to be found outside America should be within sight of his birthplace in Paisley, 15km from Glasgow.

T Byars was birdwatching in the ornamental parkland at Paisley Glen at about 2pm on 17th June 1977, when he was distracted by a burst of unfamiliar birdsong. As he investigated, he found a bright exotic-looking bird that he realised must be an American wood warbler *Parulidae* so for the next hour or so he took field notes. At 3.30pm he left to inform H Galbraith, returning 20 minutes later with a camera and tape recorder. The bird fed among the trees allowing an approach of about 4.5 metres and further field notes were taken by the two observers. The bird sang frequently until 7pm when it became more illusive in fading light as local birdwatchers arrived. It was not seen subsequently.

The bird was easily identified as an adult male Cape May Warbler from the plates of Peterson's *Field Guide to the birds of North America* on the evening of its discovery.

This record coincided with a large population increase in Cape May Warblers due to infestations of the spruce bud worm in America; its main food source.

References:
Sharrock 1982: 220-221.

Magnolia Warbler *Dendroica magnolia*
(North America; winters from eastern Mexico south to Panama)
1981 Isles of Scilly, St Agnes.   A (1)

Shane Enright and Alaric Sumner had seen nothing of note on 27th September 1981, as they walked along Barnaby Lane, St Agnes, Isles of Scilly, until a small bright warbler at the top of a pittosporum bush attracted their attention before dropping over the other side of the hedge. It had bright yellow underparts and a striking double wingbar. It was found again and fed almost constantly in the hedge top, hopping through the bushes working a circuit on either side of the lane. Its posture recalled that of a Red-breasted Flycatcher *Ficedula parva* as it dropped its wings and raised its tail.

The bird left the following evening allowing only 58 observers to witness the first and only Western Palearctic record.

The only other British report, although not acceptable, concerned the mummified corpse of a first-winter male found on a tanker at Sullom Voe, Shetland in mid November 1993. The ship had left Delaware, USA and travelled to Shetland via Mexico and Venezuela.

References:
British Birds 88: 107-108; Evans 1994; Naylor 1998: 371.

Yellow-rumped Warbler *Dendroica coronata*
(Northern and Central America; winters south to Panama)
1955 Devon, near Exeter, Newton St Cyres.   **A (14)**

An unusual bird call was noticed on 4th January 1955, as Mrs D Crook re-stocked the birdtable in her garden at the Old School House, Newton St Cryes, Devon.

On 5th January, Mrs Crook's son saw a bird feeding on the birdtable, less than three feet from the dining-room window and his mother recognised the call from the previous day. On 8th January, David showed the bird to his father, Dr D Crook who telephoned Mr F Raymond Smith.

Smith requested a more detailed description, and on 11th January, went to see the bird. Suspecting that it was an American warbler *Parulidae,* Smith visited the Royal Albert Memorial Museum, Exeter, where they examined skins under the guidance of Major A B Gay and concluded that the bird was a winter-plumaged male 'Myrtle' Warbler.

The bird became very tame during the heavy snow of mid January, allowing it to be photographed by E H Ware. It became territorial and regularly attacked the local Blue Tits *Parus caeruleus* from its favourite food of marmalade spread onto a slice of bread and butter. Though it did not show aggression to the House Sparrows *Passer domesticus,* several species including, Hedge Accentors *Prunella modularis,* Pied Wagtails *Motacilla a. yarrellii,* Great Tits *Parus major* and a Common Bullfinch *Pyrrhula pyrrhula* were all made un-welcome. Taking advantage of a nearby holly tree for roosting purposes, this remarkable event was witnessed by at least 60 travelling ornithologists before the bird was found dead after a severe frost on 10th February.

The warbler had probably arrived in the autumn of 1954, and been forced into the garden following bad weather. The skin was mounted and preserved in the Royal Albert Memorial Museum at Exeter.

References:
Moore, 1969: 266-267; Sharrock, 1982: 65-68, photo.

Blackpoll Warbler *Dendroica striata*
(North America from New York to Alaska; winters northwest South America)
1968 Isles of Scilly, St Agnes.   **A (35)**

At 12.30pm on 12th October 1968, R J Buxton noticed a small bird on a hedge near the post office on St Agnes, Isles of Scilly. He alerted Peter J Grant, P W and R J Burness and Paul A Dukes, and together they attempted to take a description of what they decided had to be an American wood warbler. Grant checked the books in his cottage and concluded that it was a Blackpoll Warbler and returned to double-check that it wasn't a Pine *Dendroica pinus* or Bay-breasted Warbler *Dendroica castanea,* the confusion species. The bird remained until 25th October and was seen by many other observers including Ron Johns, Dave Holman, F H D Hicks and Miss H M Quick.

This was the first European record apart from an unacceptable report of a bird on board RMS *Queen Elizabeth*, when it docked at Southampton on 12th October 1961. The next individual was found only ten days after the Scilly bird on Bardsey, Caernarfonshire and amazingly ten were recorded in Britain during autumn 1976.

Blackpoll Warbler is the most frequently recorded Nearctic wood warbler in Britain and Ireland.

References:
Sharrock 1982: 156-159; Naylor 1998.

Bay-breasted Warbler *Dendroica castenea*
(North America; winters Panama to Venezuela)
1995 Cornwall, Land's End.   A (1)

On 1st October 1995, David Ferguson and Jo Wayte found a brightly coloured American warbler while on holiday near Land's End, Cornwall. The bird was trying to find food among a vegetated stone wall near the 'First and Last House' along the coastal path. He managed to capture a small amount of footage of the bird on his camcorder at about 10.45am despite a strong westerly wind. The bird then took cover in a hole as a heavy shower approached but when the rain had subsided half-an-hour later, he could not relocate the bird.

Realising it was possibly a Bay-breasted Warbler, Ferguson released news of the discovery at 2.45pm but the bird was not seen again.

Later consulting a field guide, he identified the bird as a first-winter Bay-breasted Warbler, the first Western Palearctic record.

Examination of the video allowed two plants in the foreground to be identified by Dr John Richards proving that the bird had not been filmed in America. The record was accepted by the BOURC as the first British record.

References:
Rare Birds 1995: 198; *Birding World* 9: 318, photo; 8 369, photo; *British Birds* 90: 444-449, photo.

American Redstart *Setophaga ruticilla*
(North America, winters in Caribbean and Mexico south to Peru and northern Brazil)
1967 Cornwall, Porthgwarra.   A (7)

In the canopy of willows growing in boggy moorland above Porthgwarra, Cornwall, Keith Allsopp saw an unusual warbler flitting about on 21st October 1967. He called B Pattenden, N J Phillips and E M P Allsopp who were nearby and they were also joined by Bernard King and K L Fox. Excellent viewing became possible as the observers entered the sallows and stood quietly beneath it. The diagnostic yellow tail patches were noted as the bird was in view for about three hours before dark. Allsopp recalled that as the light faded a Sparrowhawk *Accipiter nisus* scythed through the bushes and the bird disappeared.

That evening they identified it as a first-winter male American Redstart from illustrations in Peterson's *Field Guide to the Birds of North America*, but it was not present the following day. It was assumed that the Sparrowhawk had found a taste for exotic food.

The first Irish record was at Cape Clear Island, Co. Cork, on 13th-14th October 1968.

References:
Sharrock 1982: 154-155; Lewington *et al* 1991: 399.

Ovenbird *Seiurus aurocapillus*
(North America; winters mainly Florida, West Indies and from Mexico south to Panama)
1973 Shetland, Out Skerries.   A (2)

Iain S Robertson was searching for migrants on Out Skerries, Shetland, on the afternoon of 7th October 1973, when he saw a Waterthrush-like bird *Seiurus noveboracensis* running among fallen rocks beside a dry-stone wall. After taking notes, he erected a mist-net but the bird initially ran underneath. It later flew into the net and Robertson took it home. He showed it to his wife and identified it as a first-year Ovenbird before releasing it into a nearby cabbage patch.

On 8th October, the bird was seen feeding on a grassy bank near the shore by visiting birdwatchers including Dennis Coutts a bird photographer, J H Simpson and Bobby Tulloch, tour leader and the RSPB warden of Fetlar.

They did not see the bird again but the crew of M B *Heather Bell* noticed a bird in the fish baskets on board as they left on 12th October. It left the boat as they passed Fetlar, from the description it was certainly an Ovenbird.

This was the first Ovenbird to reach Britain alive as previously R Wagstaffe had found a wing on the tideline at Formby, Merseyside, on 4th January 1969; another was found dead in Devon in 1985.

Ireland also has one dead specimen and one living record, a well-photographed bird on Dursey Island, Co. Cork in 1990.

References:
British Birds 63: 289; Sharrock 1982: 191-192.

Northern Waterthrush *Seiurus noveboracensis*
(North America; winters West Indies, Central and Northern South America)
1958 Isles of Scilly, St Agnes.   A (7)

While at Covean, St Agnes, Isles of Scilly, on 30th September 1958, G J Harris and Robert E Scott found a bird that they identified as a Northern Waterthrush. The bird was easily caught in a mist-net erected on the shore and examined at the observatory, where it was photographed before being released at Covean. The bird remained until 12th October, usually feeding on flies caught among piles of rotting seaweed washed up by the tide and dumped below a tamarisk hedge. When a high tide recovered the seaweed, the bird moved into a bulb field to feed on seaweed that had been scattered as fertiliser. The Waterthrush was seen by several additional observers during its stay as it fed wagtail-like, and bobbed its tail, in Common Sandpiper *Actitis hypoleucos* fashion. The record was Britain's first.

With over half of the records being found on the Isles of Scilly it was surprising when one was trapped at Gibraltar Point, Lincolnshire in October 1988.

References:
Sharrock, 1982: 95-98; Naylor 1998.

Common Yellowthroat *Geothlypis trichas*
(North America; winters south to West Indies and Panama)

1954 Devon, Lundy.   A (7)

A first-winter male Common Yellowthroat was trapped on Lundy, Devon on 4th November 1954. It was kept at the observatory overnight and, following a description taken by warden Barbara Whitaker, released the next day. The bird had probably been present for several days as it was in good condition when examined, though it had not been seen prior to being caught. Released into the cage of the Heligoland trap, the bird skulked wren-like among the vegetation from where it gave a characteristic "*chat*" call in disapproval at the human presence.

It was seen by several islanders including F W Gade, Fred Jones and John Ogilvie but the identity of the bird remained uncertain until confirmation by W B Alexander, who was sent some specimen feathers at the British Museum. Unfortunately it could not be ascribed to any particular race of this American species, of which there are 12.

The likelihood of escape for this species was very low and as its arrival coincided with Britain's first Yellow-rumped Warbler *Dendroica coronata*. Ornithologists recognised American passerines powers of endurance. The species was accepted into Category A of the British List.

References:
Moore, 1969: 267; Evans 1994: 481; Sharrock, 1982: 62-64.

Hooded Warbler *Wilsonia citrina*
(South eastern North America; winters chiefly Mexico to Panama)
1970 Isles of Scilly, St Agnes.   A (2)

Clive Totty and P G Williams flushed a large yellow/green warbler from the sedges beside the Pool, St Agnes, Isles of Scilly, at about 4pm on 20th September 1970, which they were unable to identify. Searches that evening and the following morning produced no further sightings, until K C Osborne refound the bird at 3pm while walking around the pool. The bird proved illusive and by 3.45pm was lost in the near-by bracken. He met G W and K D Edwards at the quay and they returned to quietly sit and wait. The bird eventually perched in the open among the bracken in sunlight for two minutes. They were able to eliminate the old world warblers and tentatively identified it as a female or immature Hooded Warbler.

It was next relocated on 23rd, when better views were obtained as the bird was driven into the bracken and base of some tamarisk bushes. By the evening everyone was happy with the identification of Hooded Warbler but they decided to check museum skins before submitting the report. The four original observers independently visited the British Museum and the Liverpool Museum, all reaching the same conclusion and the Hooded Warbler report was submitted.

This record was accepted in 1972 as a female. A second record for the Western Palearctic came 22 years later when an immature male was found in driving rain on St Kilda, Western Isles, on 10th September 1992.

References:
Sharrock 1982: 169-172; *Birding World* 5: 380-381; *British Birds* 65: 203-205, 351.

Wilson's Warbler *Wilsonia pusilla*
(North America; winters southern Texas, south to Panama)
1985 Cornwall, Rame Head.   A (1)

On 13th October 1985, Roger Smaldon, V R Tucker and R Burridge were birdwatching at Rame Head, Cornwall. At 10am Smaldon checked the hedgerows around Rame Church, and saw a small olive-green bird, obscured by foliage, at the back of a hawthorn. It turned to face him revealing bright yellow underparts and Smaldon knew he was looking at an American wood warbler but was unsure which one. The bird failed to reappear after dropping into some cover so he hurried to fetch his two companions.

They searched for two hours but the bird seemed to have disappeared. Burridge had earlier suggested that the description fitted Wilson's Warbler and he called out the bird's name when he found it in a small ash tree about 20 metres from the original sighting. After showing very well for a few minutes it went into the cover of an ivy clad hedge where it remained for most of the day only allowing ten local birdwatchers to see it. The Wilson's Warbler was watched taking insects from branches and flycatching. The bird showed a glossy black cap indicating it was an adult male in fresh plumage, as the species undertakes a complete moult prior to migration.

The bird was photographed and appeared to go to roost but was not seen again.

References:
British Birds 81: 590; 576, photo; 83: 404-408; *Birding World* 7: 108, photo.

Summer Tanager *Piranga rubra*
(Southern USA; winters Mexico to northern South America)
1957 Caernarfonshire, Bardsey.   A (1)

A bird resembling a bright European Greenfinch *Carduelis chloris* had been seen briefly by R Moss and R Stjernstedt at 7.20am on 11th September 1957, on the Island of Bardsey, Caernarfonshire. The views were inconclusive and the bird was lost in dense cover. At 12.15pm, J D Gay caught the bird in the Lane Heligoland trap. It was closely scrutinised by M R Buckley, R V Collier, E R Corté, A Cumber, R C Lee, A Morley and R W Arthur.

Provisionally identified as a Summer Tanager, the bird was released into brambles at the foot of a wall. It remained in the immediate vicinity feeding on blackberries but supplementing the diet with insects taken shrike-like in flight. Additional observers saw the tanager as it remained until 25th September, being re-trapped on 15th and 20th. On the latter date it had increased its bodyweight by 12g to 36.7g. At this time the bird was compared to the skin of an adult male Summer Tanager, loaned by R Wagstaffe of the City of Liverpool Public Museums.

Dr Charles Vaurie and Dr Eugene Eisenmann of the American Museum of Natural History later proved that the bird had been an immature male Summer Tanager as it possessed a bill too large for Scarlet Tanager *Pironga olivacea* and the Bardsey individual had a single reddish lesser covert feather (Scarlet Tanager's are black).

This remains the sole European record.

References:
Sharrock, 1982: 90-92, photo.

Scarlet Tanager *Piranga olivacea*
(Central and eastern North America; winters northwest South America)

IRELAND
1963 Co. Down, Copeland Island.   A (7)

On 12th October 1963, a female tanager, presumed to be a Scarlet Tanager, was trapped at Copeland Bird Observatory, Co. Down, Ireland. The bill measurements were considered at the time to be outside the normal range for this species and the possibility that it was a Summer Tanager *Piranga rubra* was not eliminated. This record is now accepted as a Scarlet Tanager following a review in 1985 and preceded the first report in Britain by seven years (P Milne *in litt*).

BRITAIN
1970 Isles of Scilly, St Mary's.

B D Harding noticed an unfamiliar bird perched at the top of a dead tree near Porth Hellick, St Mary's, Isles of Scilly, at midday on 4th October 1970. The bird had moved down into the foliage before David Holman, Ray Turley and others joined him. The bird soon flew out of the tree and was watched for ten minutes, during which time it was seen to make fly-catching sallies. The bird was not seen again but about 40 observers, mostly day-visitors from St Agnes had witnessed it.

Holman and Turley visited the British Museum and identified the bird as a first-year male Scarlet Tanager from the skin collection.

All but the first record occurred in the southwest with three on the Isles of Scilly, one in Cornwall and the other in Co. Cork.

References:
Ruttledge, 1966: 182; Sharrock 1982: 172-174.

Eastern Towhee *Pipilo erythrophthalmus*
(Eastern North America; northern populations move southward in winter)
1966 Devon, Lundy.   A (1)

Investigating reports from the residents of the Manor Farm Hotel, Lundy, Devon, on the morning of 7th June 1966, Cliff Waller and Miss J Mundy found themselves looking at an unfamiliar bird that resembled a large Dartford Warbler *Sylvia undata* with a finch-like bill. It fed thrush-like among the weeds and shrubs beside a dry-stone wall. After watching it for half an hour they returned to the observatory where it was identified as an adult female Rufous-sided Towhee from Peterson's *Field Guide to the Birds of North America*.

Quickly returning to the site, they trapped the bird and it was examined, ringed and photographed at the observatory. It remains Britain's only record and was found to be of the race *P. e. erythrophthalmus*, later given full specific status and named Eastern Towhee.

References:
Sharrock 1982: 139-140.

Lark Sparrow *Chondestes grammacus*
(North America; winters southern USA south to Central America)
1981 Suffolk, Landguard. A (2)

Trevor D Charlton and his wife Lesley visited Landguard Point, Suffolk, on the sunny afternoon of 30th June 1981. They flushed a flock of about 20 House Sparrows *Passer domesticus* and a Sky Lark *Alauda arvensis*, at 2.45pm from the short grass near the coastguard's cottage. Another bird had taken flight with them that appeared to be a bunting *Emberizidae* showing a lot of white in the tail. They walked to the shingle bank where the bird had landed and caught a brief glimpse of an unfamiliar face pattern as it moved around in the plants. Eventually the bird came out into the open to feed, permitting the Charltons to undertake some frantic note-taking. Realising that it was an American sparrow not already on the British List, Trevor Charlton telephoned Derek Moore, the Suffolk County Bird Recorder. Local birders arrived to see the bird and Arthur Westcott and Harry Lee produced a field guide as the bird proudly showed off its characteristic breast spot. This was Europe's first Lark Sparrow. The bird remained at Landguard until 8th July, occasionally feeding with House Sparrows and Common Linnets *Carduelis cannabina*. It was enjoyed by about 1,500 observers.

The report spent a period in Category D of the British List as the bird had possibly escaped from Holland or Belgium. It may also have arrived as a result of ship assisted passage. The race of the bird proved to be the nominate *C. g. grammacus* which is found in Texas as did a second bird in Norfolk in 1991. This seemed to rule out a captive origin in favour of ship assistance due to the site location near the container port Felixstowe.

There are no other records of this species in Europe.

References:
British Birds 88: 395-400; Evans: 485.

Savannah Sparrow *Passerculus sandwichensis*
(North America and northeast Siberia; winters North America south to Honduras and West Indies)
1982 Dorset, Portland. A (2)

While birdwatching at Portland Bill, Dorset, Gary Edwards and three companions found a mysterious passerine at 6.08am on 11th April 1982. Even at a range of 2.5m, they could not identify it before the bird disappeared. Ron King and Keith L Fox saw the bird briefly 12 minutes later and presumed it to be an unusual Meadow Pipit *Anthus pratensis*, although it also resembled Little Bunting *Emberiza pusilla*. Despite searching, they did not re-locate the bird.

Later that afternoon, Steve J Broyd saw a small streaky bird in the short turf of the cliff edge that he recognised as a Savannah Sparrow, having seen the species in America. Swiftly, he got his wife and J Tilbrook onto the bird before going to the observatory to inform other birders. Ron King recognised the bird as the same one he had watched earlier.

The bird remained until 16th April during which time it established a small territory marked by bursts of song from the top of limestone blocks, where it was watched by hundreds of observers. Mike Rogers trapped the bird on 12th April and, following correspondence with American ornithologist Professors J D Rising and Ian A McLaren, established that it was of the race *P. s. princeps*, known as Ipswich Sparrow. It was most likely a male from the small Sable Island population off Nova Scotia.

A first-winter bird present from 30th September to 1st October 1987, trapped on Fair Isle, Shetland considered to belong to either *P. s. oblitus* or *P. s. labradorius*, found in northeast Canada. It was first seen hopping out of a turnip rig by Peter M Ellis who thought it resembled a Little Bunting but with a better view realised it was most likely a Savannah Sparrow. After calling the observatory he was joined by Nick Riddiford, R J Johns and others, who all agreed with the identification.

The bird was soon trapped and although clearly not *P. s. princeps* the exact race involved was not clear. Investigations by the BOURC led Dr Jim Rising in Canada to conclude that it was most likely *P. s. oblitus* or *labradorius*.

These are the only British and European records of this species.

References:
British Birds 78:647-656, photos; 85: 561-564, photo *Birding World* 10: 143, photo.

Fox Sparrow *Passerella iliaca*
(Northernmost and Arctic North America; winters southern USA)

NORTHERN IRELAND
1961 Co. Down, Copeland Island.　　　　　　A (1)

On 3rd June 1961, John Wilde watched a bird slightly larger than a Rock Pipit *Anthus petrosus* mobbing a perched Common Cuckoo *Cuculus canorus*, while he was escorting visitors around the observatory buildings, at Copeland Island, Co. Down. Without his binoculars and looking into the sun, he was unable to identify the bird, which had disappeared when he returned with his bins. Miss E K Addy saw the same bird later in the day, still with the cuckoo, at the mouth of a Heligoland trap. Again the bird was unidentified but was successfully driven into the trap. The ringing team divided into two and took independent descriptions.

Following its release, the bird was difficult to observe and was not seen well in the field, even though it was present for a second day, when it found its way into the trap for a second time.

The group tentatively identified the bird as a Fox Sparrow but some additional features were later confirmed in correspondence with Kenneth Williamson, who compared the description with skins in the British Museum of Natural History.

It showed characteristics of the eastern race; *P. i. iliaca* which is occasionally treated as a full species and was the fourth record of this species in Europe.

References:
Ruttledge, 1966: 190; Sharrock, 1982: 111-112.

Song Sparrow *Melospiza melodia*
(North America)
1959 Shetland, Fair Isle. A (7)

On the evening of 27th April 1959, Roy H Dennis could not identify a bird skulking among the discarded barbed wire near a derelict radar-station on Ward Hill, Fair Isle, Shetland. It looked like a cross between a bunting *Emberizidae* and a Hedge Accentor *Prunella modularis*. He returned to the radar-station after fetching Peter Davis from the observatory and realised that they were looking at one of the American sparrows and caught the bird in a mist-net.

They identified it as a male Song Sparrow and roosted the bird overnight. The following morning, it was photographed and released at the observatory. It remained in the area until last seen at Vatrass on 10th May, and was seen by several ornithologists.

It was often difficult to locate but favoured the short grass at the cliff edge in South Haven and from 1st May would sing in the early morning. A group of American birders were amused by the interest in one of their back-yard birds.

The limited number of Song Sparrow records in Britain show a pattern of occurrences that favour northwest coastal sites in April or May.

References:
Sharrock, 1982: 102-104; *BirdWatching* April 1997: 45; Naylor 1998.

White-crowned Sparrow *Zonotrichia leucophrys*
(North America)
1977 Shetland, Fair Isle. A (3)

At 10am on 15th May 1977, J Potter found a large bunting with a striking black and white head at the entrance to the Double Dyke Trap, on Fair Isle, Shetland. He immediately drove it into the trap and it was locked in the catching box. Roger Broad and MA Peacock confirmed that it was an American sparrow before extracting it. The bird was examined and found to be an adult White-crowned Sparrow before its release at Shirva, where it was watched by several observers as it fed with House Sparrows *Passer domesticus* on recently sown seed. The bird was still present the next day.

The second record was found at the southwest end of Hornsea Mere, Yorkshire, later in the same month, at 2.15pm on 22nd May 1977.

Ray Hawley, D P Sharp and I G Howard found the bird perched and sunning itself on the low branch of a black poplar bordering a reedswamp. After 15 seconds it dropped briefly onto the ground before flying off and out of sight. The observers never saw it again.

At 3pm, R J Walker and G C M Yates saw the bird within 100 metres of the original sighting and watched it for a minute at a distance of 8m. After losing it in the vegetation, they could not relocate it. The five observers checked the literature at home and all concluded that it was a White-crowned Sparrow.

Both sparrows arrived during an exceptional spring for American vagrants.

The only other report involved a bird at Seaforth docks, Merseyside in October 1995.

References:
Sharrock 1982:217-219, photo.

White-throated Sparrow *Zonotrichia albicollis*
(North America)
1909 Western Isles, Eilean Mor, Flannan Islands. **A (22)**

An adult male White-throated Sparrow was shot near the lighthouse at Eilean Mor, Flannan Islands, Ross and Cromarty, Western Isles, on 18th May 1909. At the time it was considered by Eagle Clarke to have arrived at the wrong time of year for it to be a true migrant, but is now known to fit existing vagrancy patterns and was consequently accepted as the first British record.

In 1869, Mr W C Angus sent the skin of a female White-throated Sparrow to the Zoological Society for exhibition. Professor Newton read out a note regarding the report and chaired the meeting. The bird had attracted the attention of a Mr Mitchell by "*flirting its tail*" and calling from the top of a "*whin bush*" on 17th August 1867, near Broad Hill, on the Links of Aberdeen. He immediately shot it and took the corpse to Angus who examined it prior to skinning. The plumage was clean with no evidence of it being held in captivity. The stomach contained grass, sand, seeds and insects while further dissection proved that the bird was female. Angus compared the skin to a male specimen held at Marischal College, which had been sent from New Brunswick.

Mitchell presented the specimen to Angus for his collection, who in turn gave it to Dr Dewar of Glasgow. The specimen was eventually passed to the Glasgow Museum as part of Mr A B Stewart's collection. Kenneth Williamson and C Eric Palmer examined the bird (catalogue number 80-122 iy) in 1955 and found it to have no signs of wear, and concluded that it was a normal drift migrant.

A female caught alive in a birdcatcher's clap-net with Yellowhammers *Emberiza citrinella* at Bevan Dean, near Brighton, East Sussex, on 22nd March 1872 was exhibited by George Dawson Rowley FZS and recorded in his *Ornithological Miscellany*. On 13th February 1893, a third White-throated Sparrow was recorded from Holderness, East Yorkshire.

All British records prior to the 1909 report (less than six individuals) were considered to have been escapes, so the species had presumably been recorded as an imported species prior to 1900.

References:
Proc. *Zool* Soc., 1872, p. 681; 1870 52-53; 1869: 1547-1549; Lewington *et al* 1991: 407; *British Birds* 48: 14; 189; Clarke 1912: vol II,. 269.

Dark-eyed Junco *Junco hyemalis*

(North America)

IRELAND
1905 Co. Clare, Loop Head. **A (21)**

Mr R M Barrington acquired a specimen of "American Snowbird" (Dark-eyed Junco) shot at Loop Head lighthouse, Co. Clare, Ireland, on 30th May 1905. He reported it in *The Irish Naturalist* and exhibited the specimen at the Fourth International Congress.

At the time, 'Greenland' Redpolls *Carduelis flammea rostrata* had occurred in Ireland but the junco had never been recorded in Greenland and so was thought incapable of crossing the Atlantic. This bird, along with all early American passerine records, was dismissed as a cage bird. It is now accepted as the first and only record in Ireland preceding Britain's first by over 50 years. The skin is in the Dublin Museum.

References:
Ruttledge, 1966: 195; *British Birds* 48: 14; 1: 12.

BRITAIN
1960 Kent, Dungeness.

After hearing an unfamiliar song on the morning of 26th May 1960, R E Scott interrupted his ringing to find a finch feeding in a Robin-like manner. He summoned C J Booth and together they pushed the bird into a mist-net near the Dengemarsh sewer at Dungeness, Kent. Once in the hand, it was ringed and identified as a male Slate-coloured (Dark-eyed) Junco but they failed to re-locate it after its release.

The identification of the bird was accepted, but the junco was not admitted to the British List at the time because of the escape likelihood. In 1970, the BOURC began to reassess the record, as there had been three others beside the older Irish record, all in May; a vagrancy pattern had been established. In 1971, the Kent bird was accepted.

References:
British Birds 44: 367-368; 69: 452-453.

Lapland Longspur *Calcarius lapponicus*
(Circumpolar)
1826 Cambridgeshire.   A (WV)

In February 1826, a consignment of larks *Alaudidae* was sent from Cambridgeshire to Leadenhall Market and among them was Britain's first Lapland Longspur. It was purchased by George Weighton of City Road, who then placed it in the collection of N A Vigors, MP (see Richard's Pipit). It was recognised by Mr Selby who duly recorded the occurrence. The market, which sold birds which had been shot in Britain was very popular among the collectors, as many rare birds were discovered there.

The second British Lapland Longspur specimen was obtained near Brighton, a popular passerine-trapping centre. It passed into the collection of William Yarrell.

Between 200-250 Lapland Longspurs regularly arrive in Britain each winter favouring salt marshes, rough grass and arable fields on the east coast of England.

References:
Yarrell, 1843: i, 422; Saunders, 1899: 223; Lack, 1934: 58; 1986: 408; Eyton 1836: 95-96.

Black-faced Bunting *Emberiza spodocephala*

(Eastern Central Asia east to Sakhalin and Japan; winters south to Indochina and west to eastern Nepal)

1994 Greater Manchester, Pennington Flash. A (1)

On 8th March 1994, Peter Alker extracted five birds from a mist-net at Pennington Flash Country Park, Greater Manchester. One, at first glance, appeared to be a Hedge Accentor *Prunella modularis*, but when he saw the white outer tail feathers he rushed to the net and, on seeing the bird's pink bill, the possibility that it was a Pallas's Bunting *Emberiza pallasi* crossed his mind. He hastily took the net down and took the bird to show Anthony Whittle and Roger Wood in the park office.

The other birds were quickly processed and after glancing through Svensson's *Identification Guide to European Passerines* he telephoned his boss, Graham Workman and Kevin Baker at the BTO. As the bird was ringed and examined, it showed features of both Pallas's and Black-faced Buntings so a detailed description and photographs were taken before the still unidentified bird was released.

The news was telephoned to the Birdline North West Hotline and local birders were asked to watch out for the bird at the site which was baited with seed.

During the evening, Alker scoured his books but could only find a single photograph of Black-faced Bunting, which looked good but was not conclusive. He was put in touch with Julian Hough and after discussing bunting identification the pair agreed to meet the following morning.

Ted Abraham of Birdline North West was contacted, as Alker was now convinced that the bird was a Black-faced Bunting. The identification was confirmed early the next day when Abraham, armed with a copy of the *British Birds* paper on Bunting identification, found the bird in the baited area and the news was released nationally.

It was seen by several thousand birdwatchers during the first nine days and many made return visits as the bird slowly moulted into the breeding plumage of an adult male before last being seen on 24th April.

The BOURC accepted the identification and it was accepted into Category A of the British List.

A bird thought most likely to have escaped was seen at Hayle, Cornwall on 4th August 1985. No evidence confirming its identity has been submitted to the BBRC while a female/immature was present briefly at Woodhorn, Northumberland on 23rd October 1999.

References:
Birding World 7:94-97, photo; 494-495, photo; *British Birds* 90: 549-561, photo; M Rogers, *pers comm.*

Pine Bunting *Emberiza leucocephalos*

(Urals across Asia to Sakhalin; winters Middle East, India and China)

1911 Shetland, Fair Isle. A (37)

On 30th October 1911, a fall of migrants at Fair Isle, Shetland, produced Britain's first Pine Bunting. It was obtained by Jerome Wilson and despatched to Eagle Clarke, who identified it as a male. Most of Fair Isle's early rarities were captured by islanders to be despatched to mainland collections. It is now in the National Museums of Scotland, Edinburgh.

Pine Bunting remains rare in Europe.

References:
British Birds 5: 239-240; Dymond, 1991: 136.

Cirl Bunting *Emberiza cirlus*
(Southern Europe and North Africa)
1800 Devon, Kingsbridge.   **A (RB)**

Cirl Bunting was first recognised as a British bird by Col Montagu in winter 1800. He obtained several specimens from flocks of Yellowhammers *Emberiza citrinella* and Chaffinches *Fringilla coelebs* near Kingsbridge, Devon. In summer 1801, he found them breeding on the Devonshire coast, which remains their stronghold in Britain.

In all probability Cirl Bunting was present in England as an uncommon breeding species much earlier than this, overlooked among Yellowhammers. By 1837, Cirl Bunting had been obtained or reported from York, Doncaster and Edinburgh.

Gilbert White failed to mention the Cirl Bunting in 1788, so we can safely assume that it did not occur at Selborne, Hampshire. This would imply that Cirl Bunting established itself as a breeding bird in Britain approximately between 1788 and 1800.

Cirl Bunting remains an uncommon resident in southwest England.

References:
Yarrell, 1843: i, 448-449; British Birds 91: 146-148; 92: 153; Cole: 1-17.

Rock Bunting *Emberiza cia*
(Southern Asia, Northwest Africa and south Europe north to western Germany)
1902 West Sussex, near Shoreham.   **A (6)**

Two Rock (then called Meadow) Buntings present with a large finch flock were trapped near Shoreham-by-Sea, West Sussex, at the end of October 1902. One died soon after being netted and was not preserved, but Dr R B Sharpe of the British Museum saw the remaining bird alive, two months later. At the British Ornithologists' Club meeting on 21st January 1903, Sharpe described the event and the record was readily accepted. Howard Saunders thought that the species was an obvious candidate for vagrancy to Britain as Rock Buntings were regularly found in France and Germany, with records also received from Belgium and Holland. The Shoreham specimen was placed in the Dyke Road Museum, Brighton and was not subject to the Hastings rarities investigation as there was no involvement of the taxidermist at the centre of the scandal. This record remains Britain's first of only six accepted reports.

References:
Shrubb, 1979: 298; Evans, 1994: 494-495; Walpole-Bond, 1938: i, 162.

Ortolan Bunting *Emberiza hortulana*
(Europe, North Africa and Central Asia; winters sub-Saharan Africa and southern Arabia)
1828 Greater London, Marylebone (Middlesex).   **A (P)**

A specimen owned by the Newcastle Museum was exhibited on 15th January 1828, at a meeting of the Linnaen Society. It had been taken alive by a London birdcatcher in Marylebone Fields, Middlesex and figured in Brown's *Illustrations of Zoology* (1776). The illustration was drawn from the live bird while in the possession of Mr Moon in Hyde Park. It later joined the collection of Marmaduke Tunstall and then passed to the Newcastle Museum. This was the first recorded occurrence in Britain of a species that was regarded by some authorities to possibly be a female Yellowhammer *Emberiza citrinella*. At a similar time, Dr Latham described another new species, the 'Green-headed Bunting'. This was in fact the same bird and it had been described at a later date from Tunstall's mounted specimen, which had altered colour after its period in confinement. It remains athe Hancock Museum, Newcastle.

Despite declines in its European breeding range, Ortolan Bunting remains a regular passage migrant to Britain and Ireland.

References:
Yarrell, 1843:i, 455-456; Montagu, 1862: 16; Glegg: 43; *British Birds* 92: 34.

Cretzschmar's Bunting *Emberiza caesia*
(Southeast Europe and the Middle East)
1967 Shetland, Fair Isle.   **A (3)**

While on Fair Isle, Shetland, Roy H Dennis in the company of W N Landells and M Kristersson had suspected that a bird flushed from a field of rye-grass on the evening of 10th June 1967, may have been a Cretzschmar's Bunting. Despite searching, they failed to find the bird which was not seen again until the afternoon of 14th June, when Dennis again flushed it close to the original sighting. He watched it for 15 minutes, during which time he confirmed the identification of a male Cretzschmar's Bunting while taking a description and returned with G J Barnes and Landells to catch it in a mist-net. As it was dark, the bird was roosted overnight. It was released the next morning but not seen again until 18th when it was observed by several people feeding on seed heads. It was last seen on 20th.

Fair Isle was graced with the second bird almost 12 years to the day later, on 9th June 1979, while Britain's only other record was a bird on Stronsay, Orkney in May 1998.

A bird thought by Mr G Swaysland to have been obtained near Brighton, East Sussex, some time prior to 1875, was identified as an adult Cretzschmar's Bunting. Announcing this in *Zoologist* while describing an immature bird in his possession from the same place, Lord Clifton failed to convince his critics of its authenticity. The adult had no supporting data and the immature was considered by some to be a melanistic Yellowhammer *Emberiza citrinella*.

References:
Sharrock 1982: 148-152. [Walpole-Bond, 1938, i, 176]

Yellow-browed Bunting *Emberiza chrysophrys*
(Northeast Asia and east China; winters southeast China)
1975 Norfolk, Holkham Meals.   **A (5)**

During the afternoon of 19th October 1975, Mike Parker found what he thought was the Rustic Bunting *Emberiza rustica* that had been reported around the edge of a caravan site near Wells Wood, Norfolk. He found Dave Holman and John Kemp in the Dell at Wells Wood and the three returned to the area to split up and look for the bird. Holman found it sat six metres away in some tall weeds, giving the typical '*tic*' call of a rare bunting. Calling to his companions, notes were taken as he realised it was not a Rustic Bunting.

For 30 minutes, repeatedly they gently pushed the bird from the grass cover to perch on the weeds. It was not seen again despite searching the next day.

The three observers checked literature that evening, and later some museum skins sent from the British Museum, before being certain that they had found Britain's first Yellow-browed Bunting. There were some slight differences in the descriptions and the record would probably not have been proven but for a well-documented second individual on Fair Isle, Shetland in 1980.

The Norfolk bird had been accepted by the BBRC but did not receive the unanimous decision required from the BOURC for acceptance. The Fair Isle account was then published as Britain's first acceptable Yellow-browed Bunting and this allowed the original three observers to compare descriptions of the two birds. The file was unfortunately lost in the post but after it was reconstructed the record was unanimously accepted predating the Fair Isle bird.

R Kitson found the Fair Isle bird among the turnips at Setter on 12th October 1980. It was later trapped and released the next day, remaining until 23rd October. It was a male, possibly first-winter, and seen by only 20 observers, occasionally down to two metres.

Britain has enjoyed five visits of this far-eastern species with a bird on St Agnes, Isles of Scilly seen by hundreds of birdwatchers.

References:
British Birds 83: 430-432; 76: 217-225, photos.

Rustic Bunting *Emberiza rustica*
(Northeast Europe across to North Asia; winters Turkestan to China and Japan)
1867 East Sussex, near Brighton.   **A (414)**

Mr G D Rowley was shown a live bunting trapped on 23rd October 1867, in an area near Brighton, East Sussex, which was known for attracting rare birds. It was identified as Britain's first Rustic Bunting and the skin was placed in the collection of Thomas J Monk of Lewes before being housed at the Booth Museum, Dyke Road, Brighton, on his death.

The first Rustic Bunting to be found in Ireland was in 1959 on Cape Clear, Co. Cork, with records there just breaking double figures at the end of 1999.

References:
Saunders, 1899: 217; Shrubb, 1979: 300; Walpole-Bond i, 163; *Ibis* 1869: 128; *British Birds* 92: 82; Cottridge & Vinicombe 1997: 169.

Little Bunting *Emberiza pusilla*
(Northeast Europe and northern Asia; winters Turkestan to India and Southeast Asia)
1864 East Sussex, near Brighton.   A (676 +)

Several rare buntings were recorded for the first time in Britain during the late 1860s from the Brighton area. The first of them was a Little Bunting caught in a net by a local birdcatcher at the old naphtha works near the site of Roedean School. It was shown while alive to George Swaysland who then showed it to Mr G D Rowley on 2nd November 1864. After identifying it, he passed the bird to John Gould who exhibited it at a Zoological Society meeting on their behalf. It then joined Thomas J Monk's bird collection and the specimen was later purchased along with many of Monk's birds, by the Dyke Road Museum, Brighton.

The seventh record and Ireland's first was a bird picked up dead at the Rockabill lighthouse near Dublin, on 2nd October 1908.

During the 1980s, Little Bunting appeared annually in Britain, and in 1993 was dropped from the BBRC rarities list.

References:
Shrubb, 1979: 299; Saunders, 1899: 219; Walpole-Bond, 1938: i, 164-5; Bull BOC 23: 18; *British Birds* 92: 35, 82.

Yellow-breasted Bunting *Emberiza aureola*
(Northern Europe across northern Asia; winters India and Southeast Asia)
1905 Norfolk, Cley-next-the-Sea.   A (201)

Until Fair Isle was established as the site to see Yellow-breasted Buntings in autumn, the species was an extremely rare visitor to Britain. But the first three British records came from Norfolk, two of them shot by Mr E C Arnold at Cley-next-the-Sea. Of these, an immature female on 21st September 1905, was the first, and retained in Arnold's collection. The specimen was, according to its label, "*designed & cased by B Bates, Naturalist, Eastbourne*" and remains in excellent condition (Accession no. 479.966) at the Castle Museum, Norwich. The mount looks almost lost in a large case containing sea buckthorn, replica plants made of silk and coastal grasses, supposed to represent the habitat in which it was obtained.

The rear of the case is covered with sheets from the (London) Evening News dated Saturday 26th May 1906.

In *Notes on the Birds of Cley*, Henry Nash Pashley listed the specimen which he first thought was a female Cirl Bunting *Emberiza cirlus*. Pashley, a noted local taxidermist, mounted it (although it was sent to Bates to be cased). His shop, 'The Fishmonger's Arms' was used by the collectors of the day as a meeting place.

By further astonishingly good field craft or coincidence, Arnold found a third Yellow-breasted Bunting, this time in Sussex, but the views were not adequate for him to claim it as a county first.

Fair Isle has since attracted more than two thirds of Britain's Yellow-breasted Buntings with September being the favourite month.

References:
Riviere 1930; Riviere 1930: 27; Walpole-Bond. 1938: i, 144; Pashley 1992: 60, 105.

Pallas's Bunting *Emberiza pallasi*
(Central and eastern Siberia; winters Mongolia and China)
1976 Shetland, Fair Isle.   **A (3)**

At about midday on 29th September 1976, Roger A Broad began to check a small nondescript bunting that frustratingly only gave him brief flight views as it dived into the weedy margins of a potato field near Skerryholm on Fair Isle, Shetland. He had dismissed all the buntings on the Western Palearctic list and his thoughts turned to the American sparrows. J Watt joined him but the bird still proved difficult. It was discussed at the observatory over lunch and the American sparrows ruled out, as the bird was too dull. There were no further sightings and the cage bird possibility dimmed the enthusiasm slightly.

On 5th October, S D Cook, A R Lowe and Bill Oddie glimpsed the same bunting in a rape field at Tiang, where it was close enough to a Reed Bunting *Emberiza schoeniclus* for comparison. During that evening, Oddie concluded that it must have been a female Pallas's Bunting as it characteristically lacked a moustacial stripe.

The bird proved difficult to view or trap but it was finally mist-netted on 10th October. The bird was sketched by Ralph Richardson and roosted overnight. The following day, it was returned to Tiang but not seen again.

Ron Johns and Oddie later visited the British Museum at Tring and confirmed the identification as a female Pallas's Bunting that had suspended its moult. This first British and Irish record appeared during an excellent autumn for eastern vagrants.

The third British record was a bird trapped at Icklesham, Sussex, not recognised as such until the ringers checked their photographs against an identification paper two years later!

References:
Sharrock 1982: 212-216, sketch, photo; *British Birds* 87: 566.

Black-headed Bunting *Emberiza melanocephala*
(Southeast Europe and Southwest Asia; winters India)
1868 East Sussex, Brighton.   **A (123)**

Thomas J Monk of Mountfield House, Lewes found an adult female Black-headed Bunting near Mr Ballard's windmill on Brighton Racecourse, on or about 3rd November 1868. It was shot by Robert Brazenor in the company of his two sons while following a flock of Yellowhammers *Emberiza citrinella*. When skinned a number of eggs were found in the ovarium. Monk informed John Gould, who identified the specimen, which is now in the Dyke Road Museum, Brighton.

There have only been four Irish Black-headed Bunting records despite most British reports favouring the west. The majority arrive in late spring.

References:
Saunders, 1899: 205; Walpole-Bond, 1938: i, 142-143; *Ibis* 1869: 128; Naylor 1998

Rose-breasted Grosbeak *Pheucticus ludovicianus*
(North America; winters Central America to Peru)

IRELAND
1962 Co. Cork, Cape Clear. A (25)

At 1.30pm on 7th October 1962, M P L Fogden and J T R Sharrock found a first-winter male Rose-breasted Grosbeak near Trawkieran, Cape Clear, Ireland. The bird sat in bushes for about three minutes before disappearing, only to be re-found in exactly the same place three hours later. The grosbeak remained for 1¼ hours eating blackberries, during which time notes were taken. The bird was also present the following day in brambles at the "Waist."

H Dick and A J Tree saw an adult breeding plumaged male Rose-breasted Grosbeak at Shane's Castle, Co. Antrim, on 24th November 1957. The fact that a bird of this species should arrive in this plumage seemed strange. The escape possibility was raised and it was found that seven birds had been imported at a similar time but all were accounted for; they had been the first consignment of the species to reach Britain.

Ireland has been graced by the presence of six Rose-breasted Grosbeaks but a cloud of suspicion remains over this record and it remains unacceptable.

BRITAIN
1966 Isles of Scilly, St Agnes.

The first British record was a female seen by J R H Clements at midday near the Parsonage, St Agnes, Isles of Scilly on 6th October 1966. After flying off, it was re-found later by Peter Grant, Paul Dukes, Dave Holman and E Griffiths feeding among weeds. Disappearing again, it was eventually seen by all the birders on the island before being pushed into a mist-net at 6.15pm. The bird had already been identified in the field as a female Rose-breasted Grosbeak by Grant but a full description was taken in the hand while the bird was roosted overnight. During the same afternoon, a Red-eyed Vireo *Vireo olivaceus* had also been trapped and this was the first time that either species had been ringed on this side of the Atlantic. The grosbeak remained below the Parsonage until the 11th, feeding mostly on woody nightshade berries.

Dr Kenneth Parkes, curator of birds at the Carnegie Museum, Pittsburgh, Pennsylvania, commented that the weight of the grosbeak placed it on the threshold of emaciation, reflecting its recent journey.

Almost all reports have involved immature birds with the Isles of Scilly receiving the bulk of British records. Cape Clear, Co. Cork is the Irish hot spot for the species.

References:
Sharrock, 1982: 92-95; Ruttledge, 1966; *Irish Birds* 1957: 21-22; *British Birds* 53: 149-150; 61: 176-180.

Indigo Bunting *Passerina cyanea*
(North America; winters Mexico and Central America)

IRELAND
1985 Co. Cork, Cape Clear.   A (2)
The first record of this gaudy bird to be accepted as a genuine vagrant to Britain or Ireland was found by Anthony McGeehan and Dave Borton at Coosaneask, Cape Clear Island, Co. Cork, Ireland, on 9th October 1985. It moved around the island before being trapped by Dave Borton on the 11th at Trakieran where it settled down to stay until 19th October.

BRITAIN
1996 Pembrokeshire, Ramsey Island.
In 1996, an Indigo Bunting arrived in Britain with excellent credentials following several probable escapes. At 12.30pm on 17th October 1996, Darren Woodhead saw a small bird land on a nearby fence as he walked to the farmhouse on Ramsey Island, Pembrokeshire. It looked like a Common Rosefinch *Carpodacus erythrinus* but something was not quite right. He watched the bird in driving rain but soon left it to find shelter. The following dawn, he decided that the bird was definitely not a rosefinch and telephoned Ian Bullock, RSPB warden, who promptly took the small inflatable to the island.

Thoughts turned to the possibility that the bird was an Indigo Bunting, as four birders surrounded the garden to see it feeding Linnet-like on seed heads. The bird was soon confirmed as a first-winter male Indigo Bunting and the news released at midday.

On Sunday 19th, soaked birders waited by the Lifeboat Station at dawn but the force 7 wind made the crossing of Ramsey Sound impossible. At 3pm the wind direction had changed enough for the landing site on the island to be sheltered and the 360 waiting birdwatchers reached the site before dark and had excellent views of the bedraggled bird as it ate craneflys, sheltered from the rain in gorse bushes.

The bird was last seen on 26th October. This individual was widely regarded as having an excellent pedigree for acceptance onto the British List and following acceptance by the BBRC, the BOURC upgraded its status to Category A in January 1999.

Four previous reports were placed in Category D and another uncategorised, as large numbers of Indigo Buntings were imported between 1966-1978. The first was found on Fair Isle, Shetland on 3rd August 1964, remaining until the 7th. A second Fair Isle record, along with a report from The Naze, Essex, were placed in Category D as the escape likelihood could not be ruled out.

The fourth was found at Wells Wood, Norfolk, on Friday 21st October 1988. Michael J Saunt called to John R Williamson as he had seen an unusual bird that took flight showing its blue rump as soon as Williamson approached. They refound it after 45 minutes and suspected that it was an Indigo Bunting. Despite misgivings about its origin the news was released.

This bird exhibited unusual plumage and moult features indicating a probable period of confinement and was not placed in any category.

The fifth bird, a first-summer male at Flamborough from 23rd to 25th May 1989, was also placed in Category D as a likely escape, as it showed signs of an abnormal moult sequence.

References:
Cape Clear Bird Observatory Report 1985: 37; Birding World 1: 385-387, photo, 9: 398, photo; 11: 362; Evans 1994: 513; YNU report 1989: 78, 1991: 67; British Birds 85: 552; 90: 517; Lewington et al 1991: 421-2.

Bobolink *Dolichonyx oryzivorus*

(North America, winters Peru to southern Brazil and northern Argentina)
1962 Isles of Scilly, St Agnes.　　　　　　　A (21)

F H D Hicks found an unfamiliar bunting-like bird among bracken near the Pool on St Agnes, Isles of Scilly, on the morning of 19th September 1962. He ran to fetch M J Carter from the observatory and J A Burton joined the pair as they watched the bird. It remained in the bracken but would also make fly-catching sallies from the top of a dry-stone wall.

The bird was soon trapped in a mist-net and examined in the observatory where it was found to be in good condition and had probably crossed the Atlantic some time earlier. The mystery bird was presumed to have been a bunting and after processing was kept overnight before being released the next day. It was not seen again.

Carter realised the bird was a Bobolink after checking reference books on the mainland, but on 25th September he and Burton re-confirmed the identification when they examined skins at The British Museum of Natural History.

The Bobolink had been in its first-winter plumage and was the first accepted European record.

References:
Sharrock, 1982: 120-123.

Brown-headed Cowbird *Molothrus ater*
(North America; winters south to Mexico)
1988 Argyll and Bute, Islay.　　　　　　　A (1)

As part of his PhD project, Clive R McKay was checking the colour rings of Red-billed Choughs *Pyrrhocorax pyrrhocorax* at Ardnave, Islay on 24th April 1988, when he glimpsed a Common Starling *Sturnus vulgaris*. As he was concentrating he made a mental note check it out later as a lone bird in the area was unusual.

At 5.30pm, he finished the survey and called his companion Sue Crosthwaite on his CB radio to arrange a pick-up time. Walking back through the dune pasture he noticed the starling, which looked dark and spotless, in the same location.

He lifted his binoculars and saw it had a brown head and finch-like bill. He immediately radioed his partner to convey his discovery and then took a description over the next 30 minutes, as the bird fed between the legs of some cattle. While feeding, if it found itself more than 10m from a cow it would quickly fly back to feed beside it in a close relationship. It then crossed McKay's mind that the bird might be a cowbird. The bird ate barley or oat seeds in preference to insects and the cows were used as shelter or cover, rather than disturbing prey items in the manner of a Cattle Egret *Bubulcus ibis*.

At 6.15pm he contacted Pete Moore, warden of the RSPB Loch Gruinart Reserve, who refused to leave the house until he had eaten his Sunday dinner. An attempt to contact other birders on the island proved fruitless so, when a quick look at some books yielded no clues, McKay began the 26km journey to pick up Crosthwaite and return to the site. Arriving at 6.50pm they found the dunes quiet and the bird gone, Moore also arrived but despite a search until dark and again the next day, the bird was not seen again.

Consulting books belonging to Dr Malcolm Ogilvie a few days later, McKay identified the bird as a male, Brown-headed Cowbird probably in its first-year, second European record.

With the escape possibility being low, the Brown-headed Cowbird was admitted to Category A of the British List in 1993.

References:
British Birds 87: 284-288, sketch; *Birding World* 5: 401.

Baltimore Oriole *Icterus galbula*
(North America; winters Mexico to Venezuela)
1958 Devon, Lundy.   A (19)

A large yellow bird seen in flight, which had been flushed with a flock of Meadow Pipits *Anthus pratensis* from long grass on Lundy, Devon, attracted the attention of R H Dennis at 2.30pm on 2nd October 1958. It alighted on a dry-stone wall but then dropped into bracken in search of food. Dennis fetched W B Workman and together they watched the exhausted bird for about half an hour. After failing to catch it in a mist-net it was finally caught in the Garden Trap. Various people in the laboratory examined it at 3.15pm when photographs and a description were taken. The bird was identified as an immature female Baltimore Oriole and released into cover.

It remained until 9th October during which time it was re-trapped at 8am on 7th October when it was found to have gained 2.63 gm and seemed much stronger. This was the first acceptable record in Britain and Ireland.

Modern knowledge regarding the arrival of American vagrants in Britain led to a previous report coming to light. The bird involved was an immature male, caught alive in bushes, but in a weak state, by Andrew Anderson on, 26th September 1889 (or 1890), at Balta Sound, Unst, Shetland, and now in Chelmsford Museum, Essex.

It had arrived at the end of a week of stormy westerly winds and was kept alive for two days before dying on 28th. The corpse was passed to a H D Lloyd who forwarded it to T Edmonston. A second bird was possibly nearby at Haroldswick, Unst at a similar time although this was never proven and the report could relate to the same individual.

This oriole has good credentials for acceptance, as its plumage ties in with the published date and an arrival date in keeping with Nearctic vagrancy patterns. The specimen is in good condition showing no signs of damage that could be attributed to a period of confinement.

The downside of this report is that the skin was sent on 5th April 1894 (presumably already mounted) to George Bristow, the taxidermist at the centre of the Hastings rarities affair. Bristow then sent it to the Chelmsford Museum.

This record was investigated by the BOU in 1958 but as Baltimore Oriole was commonly imported at the time the record was rejected (Tim Melling *in litt*).

As expected of Nearctic vagrants, most arrive in autumn but at least two Baltimore Orioles have endured British winters. Both survived on a fruit diet provided at birdtables.

References:
Sharrock, 1982: 99-100; *British Birds* 48: 13; Cottridge & Vinicombe; *Birding Scotland* 1: 18-19.

Species Under Consideration

Reports of species submitted to the records committees where no decision had been reached by December 1999.

Short-toed Eagle *Circaetus gallicus*
(Southern Europe, east to Lake Balkhash, south to Iran and southern India; also Africa)
1999 Cornwall, Isles of Scilly.   * [1]

While searching St Agnes, Isles of Scilly, birders were surprised when a large raptor flew in from the sea. The first person to see it had probably been Paul Dukes who saw a large raptor flying in off the sea from the west at a height of about 50 feet just before 1pm on 7th October 1999.

The bird was named as an immature Short-toed Eagle by a loud and excited Ken Shaw while it neared the lighthouse. It soon moved off over Gugh and headed out over the sea to the Garrison on St Mary's. It departed from the northern end and on to St Martin's and White Island before setting up temporary home and roosting on Great Ganilly, one of the uninhabited Eastern Islands.

The bird appeared fit and strong making a few half-hearted attempts to reach mainland Cornwall the following day. By late morning the first mainland birders had seen the bird while those travelling on the *Scillonian* were able to see it almost overhead on one of its attempted escapes turning back as shower clouds loomed in the distance.

During its stay, the bird was airborne for much of the day hunting around the Eastern Isles and adjacent St Martins but it was never observed to take any prey.

The best views were obtained from boat trips and at times it flew low over the small boats or sat watching from crags on the islets. At about 11am on 11th October it circled high over Tresco. Crossing St Mary's it set off south-southeast towards France.

An earlier report had not received such a welcome: Peter Allard saw a large raptor hovering beside the Acle New Road, just after midday on 26th September 1998 near the village of Acle, Norfolk. He saw the bird at about 100m range and some 60m above the roadside marsh. Allard briefly considered the possibility that the bird was an Osprey *Pandion haliaetus* due to the very pale underparts. A combination of plumage features, shape and attitude in flight ruled out every large raptor on the British List with which he was familiar. The bird constantly hovered or hung in the wind with more regularity than even a Rough-legged Buzzard *Buteo lagopus* showing the broad underwings to be lacking any dark carpal patches and black fingered primaries. The brownish upperparts and a pale area near the rump were seen when it almost touched down and its large size was evident when mobbed by two crows *Corvidae*.

He contacted Dave Holman, informing him that the bird was probably a Short-toed Eagle. Unfortunately Allard needed to go to work and an hour passed before any birders reached the site, by which time it had moved on.

After reading through literature that evening Allard was, and still is convinced that the bird was a Short-toed Eagle. The timing was right for migration dates of Short-toed Eagle and the weather patterns suitable for vagrancy, however a single observer sighting without any optical aids combined with negative reports of an influx to neighbouring countries all induced Allard not to submit it to the BBRC.

Reference:
Birding World 12: 408-411; Birdwatch 77: 58; NBC Bull 32: 8-11.

Booted Eagle *Hieraaetus pennatus*
(Southern Europe, Central Asia and Africa)

IRELAND
1999 Co. Dublin, Rogerstown Estuary.   * [1]

At about 11am on 5th March, 1999, Sean Pierce watched a large raptor flying away from him over the golf course at Beaverstown that showed pale underparts not dissimilar to an Osprey *Pandion haliaetus*. He had searched the sky after waders, wildfowl and gulls took flight from in front of the hide overlooking the Rogerstown Estuary, Co. Dublin. Realising that the wing pattern resembled the Booted Eagles he had seen in Spain, he waited for the bird to return. When it did so the bird obligingly began quartering the fields just south of the hide allowing Pierce to conclude that he was almost certainly watching Ireland's first Booted Eagle. After about 30 minutes viewing during which time the bird visited Baleally dump he left to consult his field guides at home.

Two Common Buzzards *Buteo buteo*, a scarce species locally, had been present at the Rogerstown Estuary giving Sean cause to be careful as the identification pitfall presented by a pale Buzzard needed to be addressed. Discussing the relevant features over the phone with Killian Mullarney, Sean rushed back down Turvey Avenue to the hide where he relocated the bird at 2pm. The bird sat in an ivy-clad tree allowing further features to be noted but not all; these would need to be seen the next day.

After alerting Paddy O'Keefe and Jim McNally that evening, they clinched the identity the following morning and at least 30 birders watched it until 4pm. For most of the day it was presumed to be catching rats and mice before resting in trees where it attracted the attention of the local corvids.

A pale phase Booted Eagle was later reported from Dungarven, Co. Waterford, Broadway, Co.Wexford and over Bangor town in Co. Down into April but the bird failed to settle in one area long enough to attract a wide audience. In June it returned to the Rogerstown Estuary, and then seen for three days on Rathlin Island in July where it was thought to have been present for some time.

It is presumed that only one individual was involved and the identification of this bird is not in doubt. If accepted the record would constitute the first to reach Ireland and was still under consideration of IRBC in December 1999.

BRITAIN
1999 Kent, St Margaret's.

Despite a report from Kent in 1987 there had been no accepted British records of Booted Eagles prior to 1999. It would appear that the Irish bird making its way home or possibly another individual had crossed over the English Channel. A pale phase bird was claimed over St Margaret's, Kent just prior to midday on 28th September 1999 but after ten minutes it drifted northwest.

It was suggested that the Irish bird had made the short crossing from Rathlin Island to Scotland before moving south to Kent. In avoiding the English Channel it had then proceeded west un-noticed into Cornwall. Photographs obtained provided evidence of an Irish connection with it having similar features on worn flight feathers.

At 11.30am on 26th October 1999, it was seen over the Doctor's House at Porthgwarra, Cornwall by Stan Christophers, Gerry Bilbao, Jim Bryden, Terry Carne, Chris Sparks, John Wells and Martin Wightman. On view for more than 30 minutes it headed to St Buryan accompanied by a corvid entourage and was not seen again that day. It was then revealed that Jack Wilmot and Alan Bone had seen the bird at Drift Reservoir the previous day.

At 9.30am on 31st October, Dave Flumm stepped from his doorstep at Sancreed, and watched a distant raptor over the woods at Drift Reservoir. It was clearly a Booted Eagle. The bird remained close to the reservoir for the rest of the day by which time over 200 birders had seen it.

The following morning the rain stopped at midday and low cloud lifted allowing the eagle to resume hunting. It roamed over an area centred on Drift Reservoir reaching Lamorna, St Buryan, and Penzance, travelling to Hayle on 6th November. Becoming more elusive it was reported intermittently from Marazion and Plain-an Gwarry until 28th November.

It was aged as a 2nd calendar year bird. Dave Flumm Brian Mellow and three other birders believe they saw a Booted Eagle at Porthgwarra on 4th September 1975 but the views were too brief to claim it as a first.

References:
Birding World 12: 102-105; 347, 445-447, photos; *Birdwatch* 91: 60.

Slender-billed Curlew *Numenius tenuirostris*
(Ural region; winters North Africa and Middle East)
1998 Northumbria, Druridge Bay.   * [1]

On Bank Holiday Monday 4th May 1998, Tim Cleeves and his wife Anne entered the hide at Druridge Bay, Northumberland. They watched a Whimbrel *Numenius phaeopus*, *c.*150m away. Tim was confused when he scoped the bird to find it was a cold, pale grey looking curlew; "Perhaps it's a Slender-billed" he told Anne.

After some nervous note taking, Anne telephoned Tom Tams, who soon arrived, followed by Colin Bradshaw and Jimmy Steele. No definite conclusion was reached prior to dark.

Over the following three days debate continued about the bird's identity with many agreeing that it did indeed resemble Slender-billed Curlew and was most likely an immature female.

Controversy surrounded the Druridge bird and the BBRC were still investigating at the end of 1999.

Interest aroused by the Druridge Bay curlew brought to light an earlier British Slender-billed Curlew. According to reports Andrew McEwen shot the bird on No. 1 Beat at Edinample Castle, Lochearnhead, Stirlingshire in 1892 whilst employed as the keeper to Lord Bredalbane. The specimen is in case No. 18 in the A K Maples Collection, at Ayscoughfee Hall, Spalding, Lincolnshire having originally been moved from the Welsted Collection.

The bird is on loan from the Spalding Gentleman's Society and would appear to have reasonable credentials for acceptance as the position of Mr McEwen as a keeper was verified in 1984 by J Lyster at the National Museums of Scotland, Edinburgh.

There was unfortunately no mention of the bird ever being shot recorded in the game books of the Bredalbane Estate and so there is a possibility that it was one of the 'Hastings' specimens, however, more evidence needs to be unearthed.

Early records of Slender-billed Curlew in Britain occurred when the species was far more numerous in Europe than today. Six birds were shot between 1910 and 1919 in Kent and Sussex, although there is no doubting the identity of the specimens; the records were removed from the British List as part of the Hastings rarities scandal.

The first 'Hastings' report concerned a small party that arrived at the end of September 1910, at Brookland, near Romney Marsh, Kent. On 21st September two immature birds were shot from the flock, one of each sex. The male was examined by Mr M J Nicoll before being mounted by George Bristow. A third bird, also an adult male in worn plumage was shot two days later and also seen by Nicoll. This specimen later passed to the Dyke Road Museum, Brighton.

References:
Harrison 1953: 345; *Birding World* 11: 181-191, photos; 274; *Rare Birds* 5; 20.

Audouin's Gull *Larus audouinii*
(Mediterranean Sea)
1998 Cornwall, Portreath.   * [1]

In Cornwall, Mason brothers, Andrew aged 25, and Chris 18, had spent New Year's Eve 1997 gull watching at Falmouth and decided to check the North Cliff sewage outflow between Portreath and Hayle on the way home. To their astonishment at 3.40pm Andrew saw "a Herring Gull *Larus argentatus* with a red bill and black legs" flying at cliff top height; it was an adult Audouin's Gull. They watched it for ten minutes as it landed on the brown slick 200ft below them and then went to fetch their father Robin at the family home in Camborne.

Returning at 4.20pm, they watched the bird swimming with Herring and Black-headed Gulls *Larus ridibundus*, noting as many features as they could before it left with the Herring Gulls as the first locals pulled into the car park. It was presumed to have headed to the Carbis Bay roost but was not seen again.

This report was still under consideration with the BBRC in October 1999.

References:
Birdwatch 68: 55; British Birds 90: 522; 92: 609; Birding World 7: 264.

Iceland (Thayer's) Gull *Larus glaucoides thayeri*
(Central Arctic Canada)
IRELAND
1989 Co. Galway, Galway City.   * [4]

The first occurrence of this bird in Europe came from the city dump at Galway, Ireland in 1989. The bird had been found by Tom Kilbane of Dublin, while bird-watching at Nimmo's Pier in Galway City, with S Cromien and J F Dowdall on 17th March 1989. It briefly sat on nearby rocks where it resembled a first-year Iceland Gull *L. g. glaucoides*, but took flight before a positive identification could be made. The following day they watched the bird for several hours at the city dump at close range concluding that the bird was in fact a Thayer's Gull, despite some minor discrepancies.

On 21st March they examined their photographs and released the news of its presence. It was present until at least the 31st.

A second report soon followed when another first winter bird was found at Cork City, Ireland, on 21st February 1990, remaining until 5th March 1990.

Following a third record at Belfast's North Shore Dump, Ireland, on 1st and 7th March 1997, further interest in identification and taxonomy was fuelled and it was thought that the first report from Galway had probably involved a Kumlien's Gull *L. g. kumlieni.*

In February and March 1998 an adult Thayer's Gull with streaking to the head, neck and upper breast frequented the area around Killybeg, Co. Donegal. At least 10 Iceland, 10 Glaucous Gulls *Larus hyperboreus* and three first winter American Herring Gulls *Larus argentatus smithsonianus* were also present. It remained faithful to the roof of Gallagher's fish processors and the town's main pier until at least 10th March being enjoyed by over 100 observers.

A further report was received from Newport Dump, Co. Mayo in 1998 but the IRBC had not reached a conclusive decision regarding any of the reports by December 1999. Large gaps in the knowledge of the Iceland/Kumlien's/Thayer's Gull complex remained as the millennium closed.

References:
Birding World 2: 125-129, photo's; 3: 91-93, photo's; 10: 93-100, photo's; 11: 102-108, photo; *Dutch Birding* 19: 47-48; *British Birds* 92: 74; *Rare Birds* 5: 115. [*Birding World* 3: 94-95, photo's; 4: 82-83].

Little (Least) Tern *Sterna albifrons antillarum*
(North America, south to Brazil)
1983 East Sussex, Rye Harbour.   * [1]

A small tern showing characteristics of Least Tern appeared at Rye Harbour, East Sussex, in each breeding season from June 1983-1992. At first this individual was passed off as an odd-looking Little Tern *L. a. albifrons*, nicknamed 'Squeaky' on account of its call. It appeared between mid May and June each year until 1988, when a recording was made by warden Barry Yates and Howard Taffs. This was compared to recordings made of Least Tern by the *Audubon Society* and the identification confirmed.

The bird was only heard on four occasions in 1989 but as the news was released nationally the large number of birdwatchers visiting the ternery at Rye in 1990 reported it almost daily until 19th July. During this period the same individual was reported visiting a Little Tern colony at Colne Point, Essex, from 28th June to 1st July and at West Wittering, West Sussex on 4th July. The bird returned to Rye Harbour in May 1992 for its tenth and final season.

The BOU was still awaiting more information regarding the calls of other races of Little Tern before making judgement on the validity of this record, as of December 1999.

References:
British Birds 87, p 60; Evans 1994: 262; *Birding World* 3: 197-199.

Black Tern *Chlidonias niger surinamensis*
(North America; winters South America)
IRELAND
1999 Co. Dublin, Sandymount.   * [2]

A bird showing characteristics of the North American race of Black Tern with seven European race Black Terns *C. n. niger* was found by Peter Andriaens at Sandymount, Co. Dublin on 3rd September 1999. He first noticed its grey flanks while checking for White-winged Terns *Chlidonias leucopterus* and realised that this was a feature of Nearctic race birds.

It remained until the 7th September and was seen by about 15 Irish birders and was best searched for when the rising tide coincided with the terns roosting from 7-8.30pm.

BRITAIN
1999 Somerset, Bleadon, Weston-super-Mare.

Swiftly following the Irish report and possibly involving the same individual, a bird showing similar features was found feeding over pools adjacent the sewage works at Bleadon, near Weston-super-Mare, Somerset on 3rd October 1999. Rupert Higgins and John Martin noticed the unusual plumage of the juvenile tern whose plain upperparts were more reminiscent of an adult than a juvenile. As Richard Andrews joined them they began to consider the possibility that it was of the North American race recently reported from Ireland. After noting its features they alerted other nearby birders.

John Martin later discussed the bird with Peter Colston who checked skins at Tring confirming the similarities in plumage between American birds and the bird at Bleadon.

Being close to the M5 the tern attracted a steady trickle of admirers on route to the Isles of Scilly before its departure on 11th October. Each night it was presumed to have roosted with Black-headed Gulls *Larus ridibundus* on Weston beach.

The record was submitted to the BBRC and remained under consideration in December 1999.

References:
Birding World 12: 378-9; 416-418, photos.

Category 'D' Species

Species that would otherwise appear in Categories A or B except that there is reasonable doubt that they have occurred in a natural state. The species currently listed are placed here pending further information.

At present these birds do not form part of the British List.

Category 'D'

1. Great White Pelican *Pelecanus onocrolatus*
2. Greater Flamingo *Phoenicopterus ruber*
3. Falcated Duck *Anas falcata*
4. Baikal Teal *Anas formosa*
5. Marbled Duck *Marmaronetta angustirostris*
6. Bald Eagle *Haliaeetus leucocephalus*
7. Monk Vulture *Aegypius monachus*
8. Saker Falcon *Falco cherrug*
9. Asian Brown Flycatcher *Muscicapa dauurica*
10. Mugimaki Flycatcher *Ficedula mugimaki*
11. Daurian Starling *Sturnus sturininus*
12. White-winged Snowfinch *Montifringilla nivalis*
13. Palm Warbler *Dendroica palmarum*
14. Chestnut Bunting *Emberiza rutila*
15. Red-headed Bunting *Emberiza bruniceps*
16. Blue Grosbeak *Guiraca caerulea*

The subspecies Little Auk *Alle alle polaris* is included in Category D.

Great White Pelican *Pelecanus onocrotalus*
(Balkan region: Africa and Central Asia)
1906 Norfolk, Breydon Water. D [24]

At 5pm on 21st July 1906, during a warm spell, a Great White Pelican flew in from the sea and landed on mudflats at Breydon Water, Norfolk. The following morning, at 9.30am, it left, heading east. Later in the month, what was almost certainly the same bird was found at Seasalter Marsh, near Whitstable, Kent. It was present until the end of October.

This would seem to be the first credible record of this species in Britain. However, it and several similar accounts have all been thought to concern escaped birds.

Breydon Water has accounted for about 50% of the *c*.15 records of White Pelican.

An early reference to pelicans in Britain concerns a humerus bone found in peat at Feltwell Fen, Norfolk and some old bones also found in the peat at Burnt Fen, Littleport, Cambridgeshire.

Further bones were considered more likely to have been Dalmation Pelican

Pelecanus crispus: In *c*.200 BC the inhabitants of iron age Glastonbury left pelican bones following a meal and it is possible that the birds were caught locally in the Somerset Levels. Some were from a young bird, too young to have fledged.

A pelican shot at Horsey, Norfolk, on 22nd May 1663, was held in the collection of Sir Thomas Browne. As the species was rare in Britain, Browne concluded that it was one of the King's pelicans that had escaped from St James's Park, London. They were reportedly kept there from 1660-70.

References:
Riviere 1930; Lack, 1934: 91; Evans 1994: 13; *British Birds* 2:159-160.

Greater Flamingo *Phoenicopterus ruber*
(Old World race *P. r. roseus* breeds Mediterranean area, Africa eastward to India)
1881 Staffordshire, near Calke. D [23]

No species sparks debate over escapes like Greater Flamingo. Various records have been accepted only to be subsequently rejected.

An adult Greater Flamingo was present for a week in early September 1881, on the estate of Sir John H Crewe in Staffordshire. As the bird moved across the River Manifold to another estate it was captured for that landowner and later killed. The specimen became the property of Sir Vauncy Harpur Crewe, at Calke Abbey. On his death in 1925, the mount was auctioned for £32, the most expensive specimen sold from his large collection, the next being a Black Stork *iconia nigra* for £12.

Two years later, Lord Henry Scott recorded a bird on the muddy shore of the Beaulieu River, Hampshire. It had arrived after a strong southwesterly gale and after a fortnight he shot it on 26th November 1883. It had been wary, not allowing anyone chance to approach it to within shooting distance, but Mr Goff, a punt-gunner, was dispatched by Montagu and the bird was killed as it took flight at a range of 120 yards. The bird was housed at the Palace House, Beaulieu.

The following year, a further individual was seen at New Romney, Kent by Capt G E Shelley on 12th August 1884, and after a strong southerly gale, a Greater Flamingo arrived at the Traeth-bach Estuary, Merionethshire, on 28th September, 1898. Mr Caton Haigh shot the bird on 21st October and it showed no sign of captivity.

Investigation of establishments possessing captive birds failed to prove that they had escaped. The species was admitted to the British List on the strength of these reports and some may be genuine. Following further records the species was later investigated and subsequently placed in Category D.

There had been about 50 records of Greater Flamingo up to 1997, some escaped birds carrying rings, others perhaps originating from a feral flock established in Germany during 1987. Most remarkable, was a flock of 12 birds watched circling off the north Norfolk coast in 1980.

In July 1997, the BOURC began a review of migration and movements to assess likelihood of natural vagrancy from both western and eastern populations.

References:
Saunders, 1899: 395-396; 756 *Calke Abbey Auction Catalogue*, 1925: 19; Kelsall & Munn, 1905: 207-208; Evans 1994: 45-46.

Falcated Duck *Anas falcata*
(Eastern Siberia; winters North India, Japan, Korea)
1971 Cambridgeshire, Ouse Washes.   D [15]

There are several modern records of this exotic duck; although regularly kept in captivity this species has the potential to reach Britain by joining migrating Eurasian Wigeon *Anas penelope* which share its breeding grounds. Of the early reports, a single bird was shot on the Ouse Washes on 14th January 1971, and a male was present at Cropston Reservoir, Leicestershire from 27th December 1975 to 27th March 1976. Further birds were seen at Kingsbury Water Park, Warwickshire, on 25th October 1981, Potteric Carr, South Yorkshire, from 4th to 7th February 1984 and Lound, Nottinghamshire, in 1984, all records concerned males.

A strange duck caught the eye of John Kemp as it flew past the main hide at Welney Wildfowl and Wetlands Trust Reserve, Cambridgeshire at 11am on 9th December 1986. It landed 150 yards away, where it remained into the afternoon and was immediately recognised as an adult drake Falcated Duck. Later it flew to the far side of the reserve, where it mingled with the thousands of Eurasian Wigeon, with whom it fed until lost from view. Due to the vast area covered by the Ouse Washes, the bird was not seen again until briefly on 27th December. The bird did not come to the grain placed outside the hide for the wildfowl, where any usual escape would normally have booked its place early, and was considered to be a wild bird.

The species continues to be recorded annually. Falcated Duck was placed in Category D of the British List by the BOURC in 1994 as natural occurrences cannot be ruled out. In the Netherlands there were four accepted records prior to December 1998.

References:
Twitching: 21-23; 54; *Birding World* 5: 401; *British Birds* 87: 567; *Dutch Birding* 21: 313.

Baikal Teal *Anas formosa*
(North east Asia, China, Japan)
1954 Shetland, Fair Isle.   D [6]

During an influx of Siberian species, an unusual female/immature Common Teal *Anas crecca*, accompanied by two usual-looking birds, was seen on a small pool at Hestigeo, Fair Isle on 24th September 1954, by D I M. Wallace, his father and W J C Conn. They noticed the slightly different individual after flushing it from the same pool the following day. One bird was certainly larger and possessed the underbody pattern of a Eurasian Wigeon *Anas penelope*.

On 30th September, H A Craw, W Craw, Dr W J Eggeling, I J Ferguson-Lees and Kenneth Williamson who had also noted the unusual individual, found the three teal on the same pool. The bird was examined more closely on 1st October and described to Hugh Boyd at the Wildfowl Trust. It was undoubtedly a Baikal Teal.

The case for acceptance was strongly argued by the observers and Baikal Teal was accepted into Category D.

A long staying drake at Caerlaverock, Dumfries and Galloway in 1973 ate goose droppings in preference to the daily handout of corn giving supporters of the duck's cause the ammunition they needed. It was upgraded to Category A in 1980 but after a BOURC review of the ten Baikal Teal records on file in 1993 the species was replaced in Category D. The identification of five records, including the Fair Isle bird was unproven, while escape could not be excluded in the rest of the reports. The first of which was an immature drake shot at Marsh House Decoy, Tillingham, Essex.

References:
Montagu, 1862: 59; Yarrell, 1843: iii, 165-168; Sharrock, 1982: 55-59, photo; Saunders: 432; Cox: 74; *Ibis* 1993: 495.

Marbled Duck *Marmaronetta augustirostris*
(Mediterranean region of Europe, North Africa and Middle East; winters locally or south to Central and West Africa)
1973 Clwyd, Shotton. D [11]
During March 1973 an adult Marbled Duck was seen at Shotton rifle range pool, Clwyd moving to Belvide Reservoir, Staffordshire, on 29th April. This was the first of many reports for this duck. All records are considered to have involved escaped birds.

Reference:
Birding World 5: 401.

Bald Eagle *Haliaeetus leucoce* is accepted in Category A of the Irish List. The account can be found in the main systematic list.

Monk Vulture *Aegypius monachus*
(North Africa and Spain, through Asia to China)
1977 Radnor, Builth Wells. D [1]
On 29th November 1977, Mr Davies, a farmer, saw a massive bird "the size of a turkey with an enormous hooked beak" walking in his fields with the sheep. He telephoned Harold McSweeney of Aberedw. Together they dug up the carcass of a dead sheep and laid it out in the field, obtaining some poor photographs on 2nd December.

The bird was identified as a Eurasian Black (Monk) Vulture and remained in the area for several weeks with sightings also at Glasbury and Painscastle. It later moved to Llynheilyn, near Llanfihangel-nant-Melan; the total area covered being a 14 × 2 mile strip. It was last seen 27 miles away, at the RSPB reserve at Gwenffrewd, on 20th February 1978.

On the whole, the bird did not allow close approach and had no indication of feather wear consistent with a period in captivity.

Originally rejected, the record was later reviewed in 1994. The vulture was an adult and appeared at a time when the European population was in serious decline therefore the BOURC decided that it was possibly an escape.

Reference:
British Birds 87: 613-622, photos.

Saker Falcon *Falco cherrug*
(Eastern Europe eastwards to Siberia, south to Iran; winters Southeast Europe, South Asia from Turkey to China, East Africa)
1976 Shetland, Out Skerrie's.   D [3]

Saker Falcon is frequently used by falconers and is renown for disappearing when the urge to migrate takes hold. Several Sakers are lost each year. The species does have the potential to reach Britain naturally, but the escape probability precludes it from acceptance.

However, three Shetland reports are serious contenders. The first was an immature bird on the Out Skerrie's from 1st to 5th October 1976. The second was on Fetlar (27th-29th May 1978) and the third on Fair Isle (23rd October to 3rd December 1986).

A record concerning a female/immature over Gott, Shetland for five minutes at 12.15pm on 21st May 1998, before heading east is also worthy of mention. It arrived at a similar time as a Cretzschmar's Bunting *Emberiza caesia* on Stronsay, a Scops Owl *Otus scops* near Glasgow and a Black-headed Wagtail *Motacilla flava feldegg* in North Wales; all eastern European birds.

Reference:
Evans 1994: 116-117.

Little Auk *Alle alle polaris*
(Franz Joseph Land and Barents Sea)
1954 Shetland, Lerwick.   D (3)

All records of this race of Little Auk are currently placed in Category D, as they are all tideline corpses. The reports were: Two females found at Lerwick, Shetland, 5th January 1954 and 19th January 1956, specimens now at Bolton Museum; and an unsexed bird between the Blackwater and Rattray Head, Moray and Nairn on 29th April 1990.

As a result of Col Meinertzhagen's fraudulent activities, an early report of a male killed in the Firth of Forth, Scotland on 21st January 1912, was removed from Category D.

Reference:
Ibis 1993: 325.

Asian Brown Flycatcher *Muscicapa dauurica*
(Southern and eastern Siberia, Japan, China, Korea and India: winters southeast to Indonesia)

IRELAND
1953 Co. Wexford, Great Saltee.   [1]

An Asian Brown Flycatcher believed to be a first-winter male was found on 6th September 1953, at Great Saltee, Co. Wexford at the same time as a Barred Warbler *Sylvia nisoria*. Brown Flycatchers had been imported into Britain at the time and the record was not accepted.

In 1999, at the request of the Northern Ireland Birdwatchers' Association the BOURC began to investigate a record of an Asian Brown Flycatcher present on Copeland Island, Co. Down on 24th October 1971. At the same time they re-visited a Fair Isle record from 1992.

BRITAIN
1992 Shetland, Fair Isle. D [1]

With earlier records failing to reach the approval of the BOURC the first Asian Brown Flycatcher to be positively identified in Britain was a first-summer bird seen by Paul Harvey, warden on Fair Isle Shetland on 1st July 1992. As he entered the small clump of trees known as the plantation to flush birds into the Heligoland trap at one end, an interesting small greyish bird slipped through a hole in the wire mesh. After ringing two Rock Pipits *Anthus petrosus* he returned and saw the bird, obviously a flycatcher on a nearby heather bank along with Jack Keiser and John Lumsden. The bird re-entered the plantation where it was seen in the thick canopy and identified as an Asian Brown Flycatcher. At 8.30am, the bird landed on a post inside the trap and was flushed into the catching box. After ringing, taking a description and photographing the bird, it was released back in the plantation.

The flycatcher had retained a good reserve of fat so was presumed to have come from the near continent, presumably arriving with several Red backed Shrikes *Lanius collurio* and a Bluethroat *Luscinia svecica* present on the East Coast.

Despite two records from Scandinavia, the date of arrival for this bird did not fit the established pattern so it was placed in Category D.

T H Alder found a small plain bird sheltering in an elder bush as he walked through the sand dunes on the Eastern Shore of Holy Island, Northumberland, on 9th September 1956. A Blackett, J Bryce, A Childs, B Little and James Alder saw the bird briefly and as it had a white eye-ring was assumed to be a Red-breasted Flycatcher *Ficedula parva*. After the bird failed to show James Alder crept up to the bush and looked upwards to watch it at a range of about five feet. He noted the features of the bird, which he saw well, and the bird then began flycatching allowing the other observers to see it. From their notes they were sure it was an Asian Brown Flycatcher and this was later confirmed after consulting Witherby's *Handbook of British Birds*. The bird had arrived as part of a fall of Eurasian Wrynecks *Jynx torquilla*, Barred Warblers *Sylvia nisoria*, Red-backed Shrikes *Lanius collurio*, chats Turdidae and flycatchers Muscicapidae probably numbering thousands.

This record was accepted by the County Records Committee but failed to convince the British Birds Rarities Committee, as the possibility of confusion with similar Siberian flycatchers could not be ruled out.

A specimen shot at Jury Gap, in Romney Marsh, Kent on 21st May 1909, was exhibited at a BOC meeting five days later by Michael J Nicoll. Although seen in the flesh by Ticehurst and the identification accepted, it was one of Bristow's Hastings rarities.

References:
Ruttledge, 1966: 171; Evans: 421; *Birding World*: 5: 252-255, photo; *Rare Birds* July 1992: 10-11; Galloway & Meek, 1978: 149; Harrison 1953: 195; photo of Kent bird in *British Birds* 3: 112; 87: 248-249; 50: 125-126; Walpole-Bond, 1938: i, 339-340; *Ibis* 1998.

Mugimaki Flycatcher *Ficedula mugimaki*
(Central and East Siberia and Japan; winters Indochina, Indonesia, Malaysia)
1991 East Yorkshire, Stone Creek.   D [1]

As part of an excellent autumn's birding on the East Coast of Britain, Britain's first Mugimaki Flycatcher was found on a foggy 16th November 1991.

Roger Parish from Harrogate and John Ward were in the small wood at Sunk Island Battery, near Stone Creek, North Humberside (East Yorkshire) when at 2pm, Parish caught a glimpse of a small orange bird with creamy wing bars. After half an hour he saw it again with a tit flock *Parus spp.* and called to Ward. They were both able to watch the bird for about 30 minutes taking insects in a sycamore, at times within 15 feet. The bird was lost at 3.30pm and could not be relocated.

During the evening it was provisionally identified as a Mugimaki Flycatcher but after discussing the bird with Graham Speight things were not conclusive.

At dawn on 17th November, the two observers searched the wood and found the bird at 9.05am when it appeared with the tit flock. Speight, Mick Turton and Steve Exley joined them, but the bird was not relocated until 10.20am when it was on view for half an hour. They checked some books and released the news; it was indeed a first-winter male Mugimaki Flycatcher.

About 250 observers managed to reach the site before darkness fell with some missing it by minutes.

The bird was not seen again.

This species has a breeding range and migration routes similar to Pallas's Leaf Warbler *Phylloscopus proregulus* and at the time was expanding its range, so would seem a candidate for vagrancy. However, there are few records of westward movements even within Siberia. The species was placed in Category D, pending further information with a second review in 1999.

The only other Western Palearctic record involved a bird in Treviso, Italy on 29th October 1957.

References:
British Birds 87: 249-250; *Birding World:* 4: 392-395, photo; Evans 1994: 424.

Daurian Starling *Sturnus sturinus*
(Central and eastern Asia south to Northern China and Korea; winters Southeast Asia south to Sumatra)
1985 Shetland, Fair Isle.   D [2]

As a starling-sized bird showing a lot of white in the wing flew past the observatory window at Fair Isle, Shetland, on 7th May 1985, Paul V Harvey and Kevin B Shepherd bolted outside; Nick Riddiford saw their exit and followed. The unfamiliar bird was found on a crag above the observatory where Harvey suggested that it could be a Daurian Starling, a predicted Western Palearctic vagrant. A look in the observatory library confirmed the identification and the bird was watched fly-catching from the crag before it flew to Buness where it became much more flighty.

Later in the day, it was found at Gilsetter where it remained the following day, but was not seen again until 13th at Field Midden and Barkland. The bird preferred to feed by fly-catching in Bee-eater *Merops spp.* fashion most of the time, but also searched for leatherjackets and worms among the short-cropped turf. It was also observed to lift sheep droppings to locate invertebrates beneath and occasionally joined the local Common Starlings *Sturnus vulgaris* to feed on household waste. It stayed on the island until 28th May, having been trapped and sexed as a male on the 21st.

The identification was accepted by the BOURC but the species had not previously been recorded west of Pakistan. The species was very rare in captivity. A long-distance migrant and an immature bird had also been shot in Norway later the same year. This information allowed the species to be placed in Category A of the British List in 1989, however a review in 1994 found the report unacceptable as an escape origin could not be ruled out and it was replaced in Category D.

Two later records involved an adult male in a Newcastle garden in August 1997 and a first-winter bird at Balnakeil Craft village, Durrness, Highland from 25th to 27th September 1998.

References:
British Birds 82: 603-612, photos; *Birding World* 11: 332.

White-winged Snowfinch *Montyfringilla nivalis*
(Locally in Southern Europe, east through central Asian mountains to Tibet)
1969 Suffolk, Lakenheath. D [1]

A report of a White-winged Snowfinch feeding within an area controlled by the American Air Force at RAF Lakenheath, Suffolk from late July 1969 until July 1972 was, due to its unusually long stay and constant association with occupied buildings, placed in Category D. This is the only report other than Hastings records. These included an adult male among a large Sky Lark *Alauda arvensis* flock, seen by M J Nicoll at Rye Harbour, East Sussex, on 21st February 1905. The following day a bird was handed to taxidermist George Bristow from the same place. Nicoll who recalled the bird he had seen the previous day examined it in the flesh and the specimen was exhibited at the British Ornithologists Club.

Severe weather at the end of 1905 was instrumental in producing some of the most remarkable east to west daytime migration ever seen in southeast Britain. Many birds were picked up starving and frozen with two White-winged Snowfinches shot on 28th December, by Mr Playford from a flock of four in Paddock Wood, Kent. These specimens also passed through Bristow's hands and were accordingly later rejected. One of the Kent specimens purchased by Mr C J Carroll is in the Dyke Road Museum, Brighton. Others joined the collection of M J Nicoll.

References:
Harrison 1953: 290; Harrison 1968: 108; Walpole-Bond, 1938: i, 117; *British Birds* 1: 13; M. Rogers: *pers comm.*

Palm Warbler *Dendroica palmarum*
(North America)
1976 Cumbria, Walney Island.   D [1]

The headless corpse of an adult male Palm Warbler, was picked up from the tideline on Walney Island, Cumbria, on 18th May 1976, and submitted to the BBRC by D Satterthwaite and J Sheldon. Having lost its head, there is the possibility that the bird had been swept from the deck of a passing ship after colliding with the rigging earlier in the journey, probably outside British waters. The record was accepted into Category D.

References:
Hutcheson, 1986: 117; Naylor 1998: 413.

Chestnut Bunting *Emberiza rutila*
(Northeast Asia; winters Southeast China and Burma)
1974 Shetland, Foula.   D [7]

The first report of a Chestnut Bunting in Britain was a male present on Foula, Shetland from 9th to 13th June 1974. At the time, the species was held in captivity and all European records had occurred in autumn. As a result, this record did not appear to conform to the vagrancy pattern set by the European reports which were more likely to have involved wild birds.

A female that arrived at Out Skerries, Shetland on 2nd September 1994, was the first autumn record and the first to fit in with the continental vagrancy pattern. John Cooper obtained brief views of the bird, after a period of easterly winds brought a variety of eastern birds to Shetland, including Britain's first juvenile Red-necked Stint *Calidris ruficollis*. He identified it as a female or immature bird. It was trapped by Dave Okill and aged as an adult female. It remained until the 5th September feeding in roadside thistles. It is widely regarded by birdwatchers to have been a wild bird as there were fewer birds in captivity than previously.

A fine male was present in a Salthouse garden from 30th May to 1st June 1998. 800 people to queued for a brief glimpse of it, but the bird showed some feather damage to the forehead, a feature probably indicating a period of confinement.

References:
Birding World 7: 371-373; 11: 217-219.

Red-headed Bunting *Emberiza bruniceps*
(Central Asia; winters India)
1931 Orkney, North Ronaldsay.   D [333]

Mr and Mrs G Eardley Todd saw a bird new to them on the afternoon of 19th June 1931, feeding on arable land, on North Ronaldsay, Orkney. It was seen down to 15 yards for half an hour before flying out of sight. They consulted Gatke's *Heligoland* and identified the bird as a superb adult male Red-headed Bunting. They shot it later that day and the corpse was sent in the flesh to the British Museum, where it was skinned.

In 1910, a Red-headed Bunting was caught near Dover and examined in the flesh by Dr AG Butler, but the supporting evidence was considered flimsy and the record not accepted.

The species had been recorded in Europe five times prior to the Orkney record, in Belgium, Italy and Germany, while over 300 British records exist. This would seem excessive for a species that is not that common in captivity so the BOURC began to review reports in 1999.

References:
British Birds 25: 66-69; Harrison 1953: 276; *Ibis.*

Blue Grosbeak *Guiracea caerulea*
(Southern North America, Central America south to Costa Rica; winters Mexico south to Panama)
1970 Shetland, Out Skerries.   D [4]

A male Blue Grosbeak was found by RSPB warden Bobby Tulloch in a field of growing oats on Out Skerries, Shetland on 23rd August 1970, remaining until 25th. John Simpson from Whalsay saw it in the same field the next day but not subsequently, while locals claimed it had been present for "a week or two" (Ian Dawson *in litt*). It was considered an escape.

A second male was found at Kilterlity, Highland on 10th March 1972, with a third Scottish record in 1977, before England's first caught by a Gloucestershire cat in 1986. Two Norwegian records in 1970 and 1987 were considered to have involved wild birds.

References:
Birding World 6: 63; Naylor 1998: 417; Snow & Perrins 1998: 1688.

NEAR MISSES

"On 18th April 1910, the steamship Minniehaha ran aground on rocks near Bryher, Isles of Scilly. The consignment of cage birds destined for London Zoo were liberated and included four Northern Ground and six Inca Doves, four Sonoran Redwings, three Guyana Parrotlets, Purple and Bronze Grackles and six Columbia Crested Quail." [*BirdWatching* April 1997: 45]

Once acceptable records (now dismissed) rejections and possible escapes

The species in this section have at some time formed part of the British and Irish Lists or have been seriously considered as possible additions. In later reviews they were rejected or removed, i.e. Hastings rarities and species later thought most likely to be escapes.

Ship-assisted birds including those thought to have probably died outside British and Irish waters are also placed in this section, as are some reports where the proof of identification was not considered strong enough for a first record. They are species considered by some authorities to have the potential to reach Britain and Ireland in a wild state.

Many older records accepted at the time involved specimens that may have been imported to Britain and Ireland rather than occurring naturally. The Rarities Committees have undertaken investigations leading to the removal of some species from the lists. Understanding of migration, vagrancy patterns, and moult timings has allowed them to prove that genuine errors or fraudulent behaviour took place. The first reports of some of these species are mentioned in this section. They are no longer included in Categories A, B, C or D.

There is the possibility that individuals arrived as a ship-assisted vagrants, indeed records of the more unusual seabirds, such as Cape Pigeon, are thought to have been brought by sailors. Most birds found as tideline corpses are also suspected of having been thrown overboard near the British and Irish coast during deck cleaning rather than dying in local waters. For example, one of the most unusual experiences in Geoff Allard's career as a customs officer was when he had to report an Ostrich from the Isles of Scilly. The decomposing remains of its head, spinal chord and a few feathers were washed ashore on the beach at Bryher. The event was reported in the *Western Morning News*, in 1986.

The list of escaped bird species found in Britain and Ireland is long, and with little value placed on reporting cage birds at liberty, few were ever well documented, if at all. The first records of some may never be known. Consequently a section devoted to those species in Category E could form a work of their own. The BOURC accept that their list of escaped species is incomplete and so is not included here. These birds are said to be of 'unknown origin' and open to speculation, and only the most likely candidates spend a period of investigation in Category D, the majority are dismissed by observers long before reaching BOURC categorisation.

Many records slip through the net because the observer/s are not 100% convinced of their identification or do not believe their record stands any chance of acceptance. Such reports are now more frequently made known to the public via the various paging services and the Internet in an attempt to warn the public to be watchful.

Only the most noteworthy reports considered by some authorities to have involved genuine vagrants, despite being rejected by BOURC or IRBC, are mentioned below.

At present these birds do not form part of the British or Irish Lists.

Red-necked Grebe *Podiceps grisegena holboellii*
(North America and Northeast Asia)
1925 Rosshire, Aultbea. [1]

The American race of Red-necked Grebe is considerably larger than its European cousin (*P. g. grisegena*) with no overlap in measurements. Mr J MacGregor shot a bird of this race in a bay near Aultbea, Ross-shire, in September 1925. The bird had been present for several days. There was no doubt about its identity as it was a large bird with all measurements at the largest extreme of the range.

It was sent to the British Museum by Messers Betteridge and son of Birmingham, where it was examined and exhibited at the December 1927, meeting of the British Ornithologists Club by Dr P R Lowe.

Although originally accepted in good faith this record has been removed from the British List due to Meinertzhagen's involvement with it.

Reference:
Baxter & Rintoul: 501.

Wandering Albatross *Diomedea exulans*
(Southern Ocean)
1894 Orkney, at sea. [2]

At 6.45pm on 18th July 1894, John Harvie-Brown saw an albatross while at sea, 20 miles from one of the Orkney Islands, at first only 200-300 yards away then watched until at a range of least three miles. He described the bird as having "brown and mottled plumage of the back". He then reported:

"I watched a big bird. Gannets in several phases of plumage had been seen frequently. This bird was no Gannet. The flight petrel – or molly-like, seldom flapping; swinging and skimming from side toside, not flying straight like a Gannet; head low, and heavy bill, seen to be thick and short – a bird in what I would judge to be its second year's plumage. The captain, who stood close beside me at the time, said he had only seen one today (or the same) close to the ship, and that it was no Gannet."

Harvie-Brown, 1895.

The true identity of Harvie-Brown's bird cannot be proven from his description but Wandering Albatross is a strong candidate.

A dead Wandering Albatross hanging among Turkeys at Leadenhall Market, London, in December 1909, was possibly freshly killed as it was reported to have been dripping blood.

No complete data regarding any of these records are available and therefore this species is not admissible onto the British List.

References:
Ibis 109, p 145; *Birding World* 5: 382; Snow & Perrins 1998: 30.

Southern Giant Petrel *Macronectes giganteus*
(Southern Oceans)
1967 Cornwall, at sea. [3]

On 2nd November 1967, an adult Southern Giant Petrel was seen off the coast of France, this is the only record of the species currently accepted in the Western Palearctic. On 20th October 1967, thirteen days before the French report, Bernard King saw what was possibly the same bird off the Wolf Rock, Cornwall.

References:
Birding World, 5: 383; 6: 368;

Cape Pigeon (Pintado) *Daption capense*
(Southern Oceans)
1879 Merionethshire, Dovey Estuary. [2]

A Cape Pigeon reportedly shot on the Dovey Estuary, Merionethshire, in 1879, is in the collection of Sir Pryse Pryse at Gogerddau. No other information about the specimen is available and therefore remains unacceptable.

In 1894, a photograph of a Cape Pigeon shot at the Old Harry Rocks, Bournemouth, was sent from Thomas Cooper, the birdstuffer of Poole to Rev Murray A Mathew of Frome. It was said to have been killed while following a foreign steamer. It was identified as a Cape Pigeon and published in *Zoologist* (1894).

Cape Pigeon was easily caught by hanging a hooked line off the back of a boat, with many reportedly carried hundreds of miles before being liberated. Often the birds were kept alive and imported to Britain and in 1866, F W Hutton saw several released into the English Channel at the end of a voyage from New Zealand. While on board HMS *Bounty* during 1788, William Bligh took several on board and kept them alive, feeding them ground corn until they became fat. They soon lost their fishy taste and had "improved" to a point where they tasted like duck. As a result of this practice no records of this species are currently acceptable despite initially holding a brief position on the British List.

IRELAND

William Kelly shot a bird flying inland at Crumlin, west of Dublin, Ireland on 20th October 1881. It was reported by AG More to have flown off a passing ship. The skin is retained in the Dublin Museum.

References:
Ibis 1967: 150; Saunders, 1899: 750; *Birding World*, 5: 383; *Zool* 1894, 396.

Kermadec Petrel *Pterodroma neglecta*
(South-central Pacific)
1908 Cheshire, Tarporley. [1]

An adult dark phase Kermadec Petrel was picked up under a tree at Tarporley, Cheshire, on 1st April 1908. The bird's eyes had already began to sink when it was bought four days later at Chester Market by a person reported in various publications as either Alfred, Arthur or Robert Newstead. T A Coward also saw it in the flesh as it was drying out after mounting.

Mr C Oldham exhibited the specimen at a meeting of the BOC, held at Paganini's Restaurant, 42-48 Great Portland Street, London, on 20th May 1908. It had earlier been exhibited at the Zoological Society of London's meeting on 12th May 1908. Mr F D Goodman and Dr Bowdler-Sharpe of the British Museum confirmed the identification.

Tarporley is well inland and no named person saw the bird until it was purchased. The date (April Fools day) also raised questions.

The record was admitted to the British List at the time, but removed in 1971 as a result of an investigation into "long distance vagrancy in petrels" by Dr W R P Bourne.

References:
Ibis 1967: 154; 1971: 145; *Birding World*, 5: 385.

Collared (Gould's) Petrel *Pterodroma leucoptera (brevipes)*
(Tropical and subtropical Pacific)
1889 Ceredigion, between Aberystwyth and Borth. [1]

In late November or early December 1889, a strange seabird was seen flying slowly along the shore between Borth and Aberystwyth. It sat on the water where a long-shore shooter fired at the bird and missed. On a second attempt it was killed. The bird was taken to Rev J M Griffiths, vicar of Llanfihangel Geneu'r Glyn, who directed the shooter to Mr Hutchings, the Aberystwyth taxidermist.

Hutchings was well known for sending a mounted elephant to Chicago, where it was used as an urn. Tea ran down one side of its trunk and coffee on the other. He bought the bird and described it as a Sooty Shearwater *Puffinus griseus* before showing it to Mr Willis Bund QC in February 1890. Bund questioned the identification and eventually purchased it later that year. He then examined the skin closely and found it to be a moulting dark morph Collared Petrel.

During the Second World War, bombing destroyed the specimen, but there is no doubt about the birds' identity and the specimen was figured in Saunders *Manual*. The record is called into question however because there was a market in specimens collected in Fiji. Skins were sent home by missionaries and collectors to supply European museums from 1850-1888. Despite holding a place on the British List for almost a century, it was struck off by the BOURC in 1971.

References:
Ibis 1967: 155; Saunders, 1899: 747; *Birding World*, 5: 385; Frost 1987: 121.

Audubon's Shearwater *Puffinus iherminieri*
(Tropical oceans)
1936 East Sussex, Bexhill-on-Sea. [2]

At Galley Hill, Bexhill-on-Sea, East Sussex on 7th January 1936, Mr W E Dance saw a small seabird being harassed by gulls *Laridae* on the beach. The bird seemed tired and just spread its wings and collapsed in a vain attempt to fly. Dance took the bird home but it died half-an-hour after being picked up. He then took it to George Bristow for preservation where it was thought to be an Audubon's Shearwater, the first report of the species in Britain.

James Harrison who visited the finder and put him before a Commissioner for Oaths later confirmed the record, which is no longer acceptable as it was part of the Hastings rarity scandal.

Reference:
British Birds 30: 48.

Matsudaira's/Markham's Storm-petrel *Oceanodroma matsudairae/markhami*
(Subtropical western Pacific, migrating to Indian Ocean)
1988 at sea. [1]

A series of trips on board the *M.V. Chalice* was organised by seabird expert Peter Harrison during the late 1980s. These journeys proved that Wilson's Storm-petrels *Oceanites oceanicus* occurred annually off the southwest coast.

As the M V Chalice and 12 observers approached a French trawler during a pelagic trip off the Cornish coast on 3rd August 1988 a dark petrel flew to within 20m of the vessel. The forked tail ruled out Bulwer's Petrel *Bulweria bulwerii* and Swinhoe's Storm-petrel *Oceanodroma monorhis* seemed unlikely on account of the bird's large size. Markham's Storm-petrel *Oceanodroma markhami* seemed possible.

On 1st September Peter Harrison examined photographs of the bird taken by John Hall which showed obvious white primary shafts and decided that the bird was a Matsudaira's Storm-petrel and it was submitted as such to the BBRC.

The BBRC and Seabirds Advisory Panel members decided that the identification was not 100% certain and the bird could have been either a Matsudaira's or Markham's Petrel. W R P Bourne of the Dept of Zoology at Aberdeen University considered the bird to probably be an immature Bulwer's Petrel moulting its central tail feathers.

A second bird present at Ferrybridge, Dorset at various times from 14th to 29th May 1989, was also thought to have been a Matsudaira's Petrel as were two birds seen flying east at St Aldhelm's Head, Dorset on 10th May 1993.

There have been various sightings of dark rumped storm-petrels from a number of sites off the British coast but it is difficult to identify members of this group at sea.

References:
Birding World 5: 386-387; 1: 285, photos, 348, 405; 6: 368; *British Birds* 90: 305-313; 329-335, photo; 339-342; 90: 527; Morrison 1997:14.

Red-billed Tropicbird *Phaethon aethereus*
(Caribbean, Cape Verde Islands, Red Sea, Arabian Sea and Persian Gulf)
1854 Worcestershire, Malvern. [2]

A bird found dead on the farm of Mr Yapp, of Cradley, near Malvern, Worcestershire, in c.1854, was mounted by Mr Pitman and presented to Mr Walcott of the Malvern Museum. Through a variety of transactions it eventually reached J H Gurney in 1894. The specimen is now at the Norwich Castle Museum and is of the race *P. a. aethereus.*

Nigel Odin found the corpse of a slightly oiled Red-billed Tropicbird on the tideline at Landguard point, Suffolk, on 17th February 1993. It was sent to Ipswich Museum where on examination was found to be a female of the race *P. a. indicus* that occurs in the Persian Gulf and Arabian Sea. The bird had presumably boarded a ship in the Red Sea possibly flying into rigging at night, when they actively take fish and squid attracted by the lights. The body was probably then washed overboard near Felixstowe docks.

Neither reports were accepted as their origins are uncertain.

An additional report concerned a sub-adult flying west past Prawle Point, Devon on 7th August 1999.

References:
Rare Birds in Britain 1993, 23; *British Birds*: 87, 480-487, photo; Saunders, 1899: 366; *Birding World* 12: 301.

Cape Gannet *Morus capensis*
(Afrotropical region)
1852 Lothian, Bass Rock. [2]

In 1852, William Macgillivray described an adult Cape Gannet that had been given to him by William Stables and said to have been caught on the Bass Rock, Lothian in May 1831. The bird possessed the black gular stripe typical of the species and its measurements were compared to those of his British-taken Northern Gannet *Morus bassanus* specimens and those of his American specimens preserved in rum.

Unfortunately Stables had shipping interests in Leith so the possibility of it having been imported could not be ruled out.

The possible existence of a rare plumage stage of Northern Gannet has raised questions over recent claims.

References:
Birding World 1: 263, 348; 5: 387; *British Birds* 83: 519-526; Macgillivray 1852: 420.

Least Bittern *Ixobrychus exilis*
(North America south to southern Brazil)
1852 North Yorkshire, near York.   [1]

A Little Bittern *Ixobrychus minutus* killed near York, some time around September 1852, was purchased by Joseph Duff of Bishop Aukland and placed in Thomas Nelson's collection. His widow presented his specimens to the Dorman Museum, Middlesborough. Following some doubt regarding the bird's identity, John Mather and Phil Stead confirmed that it was an American Least Bittern in 1984. Despite Mather's claims that the species should be included on the British List it still remains unacceptable.

There does not appear to have been any attempt of fraud as it was not initially claimed as being a Least Bittern and the date would appear to fit established vagrancy patterns.

The skin is still on public display at the Dorman Museum.

References:
Nelson, 1907: 397; Mather, 1985: 93.

Yellow Bittern *Ixobrychus sinensis*
(China and Japan; winters south to Philippines and India)
1962 Dorset, Radipole Lake.   [1]

A bird found dying on 23rd November 1962 by Rex Clive and A G Jackson had collided with the concrete parapet of a bridge near Radipole Lake, Dorset. It was sent to the British Museum where the bird was found to be a first-winter Yellow Bittern but the skin was subsequently lost.

The bird was presumed to be an escape, however none were known to have been held in captivity and it had arrived during a period of extreme weather conditions where freezing temperatures in Siberia spread westwards to Europe.

References:
Morrison 1997: 17-18; Rare Birds in Britain 1993: 30.

Great Blue Heron *Ardea herodias*
(North and Central America)
1968 at sea.   [2]

An immature Great Blue Heron that had boarded the M.V. *Picardy* captained by J G Street, some 550km southwest of Fayal, Azores on 29th October 1968 remained on board until the ship reached Avonmouth, Britain. Following its discovery the bird spent three days at liberty on deck but was found sheltering behind the mast-house following a period of cold weather when water washed the decks. It was kept in the warmth of the crew reception room and fed scraps of food until they approached Lands End. When the bird was thrown overboard it returned to the ship so was eventually taken by the RSPCA to Rhode Tropical Bird Garden, Somerset after docking but later escaped.

An adult was reported spending an afternoon on the M.V. *Sugar Crystal*, bound from Panama to London only two days before the M.V. *Picardy's* bird. It was half way between the Bahamas and the M.V. *Picardy's* position; was it the same bird?

On 9th May 1982 a second immature bird landed on a ship 460 miles southeast of Nova Scotia and remained on board until succumbing 150 miles off the Isles of Scilly on 15th May. It was placed in the Rotterdam Natural History Museum.

As both birds had been sheltered and fed, neither are entitled to a place on the British List.

References:
British Birds 65: 442-3; *Birding World* 8: 424-5; 11: 12.

Ross's Goose *Anser rossii*
(Canadian Arctic, winters south to Mexico)
1970 Lancashire, Plex Moss, Formby. [3]

Ross's Goose is a popular species in captivity and has consequently received little interest from ornithologists. In spite of this, there have been several reports since the 1970s where a wild origin is possible. One of these was seen regularly with Pink-footed Geese *Anser brachyrhynchus* in the Plex Moss and Formby areas of Lancashire during the winters of 1970-74.

A second bird was present at Meikle Loch, Northeast Scotland, on 17th March 1985, with a further report from Slains, on 10th March 1988. A bird that arrived at Lossiemouth, Northeast Scotland, with Icelandic Greylags *Anser anser* on 23rd March 1991 was widely thought to have involved a wild bird.

References:
British Birds 87: 571; *Birding World* 4: 137-140; 6: 367; Evans 1994: 50.

Wood Duck *Aix sponsa*
(North America and Cuba)
1848 Worcestershire, Tenbury.

Col Montagu recorded a "Tree Duck *Dendrossa sponsa*", which was almost certainly the first record of a Wood Duck in Britain. The specimen was shot at Tenbury, near Worcester and reported by Mr Cutler in *Zoologist,* 1848. A bird shot on the River Derwent in Derbyshire in 1853, with another killed on the River Trent near Drakelow, Derbyshire at a similar time, followed this.

Another Wood Duck was shot near Moor Mill, Radlett, in December 1891. All reports are treated as escapes, and breeding regularly takes place.

References:
Birding World 5: 325; *British Birds* 86: 611; 92: 179; Montagu, 1862: 72; Frost. 1978: 159.

Black-shouldered Kite *Elanus caeruleus*
(Africa and South Asia)

IRELAND
1862 Co. Meath, Horsetown Bog [1]

During autumn or winter of 1862, Mr Horan shot a Great *Bittern Botaurus stellaris* and a Black-shouldered Kite on the Bog of Horsetown, an area of impassable marsh with coarse aquatic vegetation (now drained) near Beauparc, south of Slane, Co. Meath. The bird was given to Dr P T Nicolls in fresh condition who skinned and preserved it.

In 1870, Nicolls gave it to John F Dillon of Lismullen stating that it was a "Pied Hawk". On checking Gould's *Birds of Europe* he recognised it as a Black-shouldered Kite and took the bird to Mr A G More at the Dublin Museum who agreed with the identification. He pronounced it to be an immature bird on account of its brown edged breast feathers. Saunders examined this specimen and confirmed the identity. Unfortunately it had lain unrecognised for ten years and there was insufficient evidence to regard it as a genuine vagrant. It was however considered acceptable by some authorities at the time.

References:
Saunders, 1899: 338; *Zool*, 1875: 4455.

American Swallow-tailed Kite *Elanoides forficatus*
(South-eastern North America, Caribbean and northern South America)
1805 North Yorkshire, Shawgill, near Hawes. [7]

The first report of American Swallow-tailed Kite in 1805 was well documented and originally accepted by the BOU, under Newton in 1883, it was later rejected by Saunders in 1899 and not reinstated. He said that there were grounds to suppose that this bird had previously been confined, but did not give details.

On 6th September 1805, Rooks *Corvus frugilegus* were harassing the kite as a thunderstorm approached Shaw-gill, near Hawes, Wenslydale, Yorkshire. To avoid both, it took cover in a thicket. Before it was able to fly out, a stick was thrown at it and the bird was knocked down and caught. The un-named captor kept it for a while before it escaped on 27th when a door was left open as it was being shown to friends. After first flying into a tree and again receiving the unwanted attentions of the Rooks, it then ascended to a great height before heading south and out of sight. Mr W Fothergill of Carr End, near Askrigg, Yorkshire, described this record in a letter to the Linnean Society.

An early report of American Swallow-tailed Kite at Balalchoalist, Argyllshire, was recorded by Dr Walker in his *adversaria* for 1772, but was regarded as being too vague with possible confusion from Red Kites *Milvus milvus*.

References:
Montagu, 1862: 186; Yarrell, 1843: i, 71-72; Saunders, 1899: 338; Nelson, 1907: 347-350; *British Birds* 48: 4-5; Naylor 1996: 182.

Hen Harrier (American Marsh Hawk) *Circus cyaneus hudsonius*
(North America and northern South America)
1957 Norfolk, Cley-next-the-Sea. [7]

A 'ringtail' harrier present in the Cley and Salthouse area of north Norfolk from 26th October 1957 to 13th April 1958 was identified as a first-year Marsh Hawk; the American race of Hen Harrier.

There were at least seven Marsh Hawk reports in Britain up to 1983 with much debate particularly about the individual at Cley. In 1983 Grant laid the subject to rest when he investigated the plumages of immature birds and found that there was a colour morph of Hen Harrier *C. c. cyaneus* that showed the unstreaked rufous underparts present on the Cley bird.

Further reports of this race concerned a bird present on St Mary's, Isles of Scilly, from 22nd October 1982 to 7th June 1983 and another at Sheskinmore Lough, Donegal on 28th September 1997.

References:
British Birds 64: 537-542; 76: 373-376; *Birding World* 11: 454.

Red-tailed Hawk *Buteo jamaicensis*
(North America and West Indies)
1850 Nottinghamshire, between Mansfield and Newstead. [many]

In 1866, at the British Association meeting held in Nottingham, William Felkin, of Lenton, Nottingham stated that he had been given a Common Buzzard *Buteo buteo* in the flesh that had been killed in autumn 1850. It had been shot between Mansfield and Newstead, Nottinghamshire. Failing to identify the bird, Felkin submitted it to John Gould who identified it as a Red-tailed Hawk, the first of several unsuccessful claims for admission to the British List.

Felkin belonged to a family of lace manufacturers and possessed a collection of over 300 specimens that were sold on his death. In 1991, an investigation by county recorder Austin Dobbs revealed that the weather at the time of the bird's discovery involved a deep Atlantic depression, possibly the worst storm of the century. Vessels were driven ashore in the River Thames, severe damage sustained to ships in the Mersey, and two vessels wrecked at Great Yarmouth.

The Red-tailed Hawk specimen cannot be traced and so the BOURC does not accept this record.

Nor does it accept the record of a Red-tailed Hawk said to have been obtained in Kirkwall, Orkney on 16th March 1919, the specimen is held in the Natural History Museum, Tring (BMNH 1939.12.9.3588). While the identification is not questioned the stated origin must be doubtful, given the specimen's provenance from the collection of Sir Vauncey Harpur Crewe.

References:
Whitaker, 1907: 161; BOU, 1915; *Nottinghamshire Birdwatchers Annual Report* 1991: 45-47; *Ibis* 1974: 579; 140: 182-184.

Merlin *Falco columbarius columbarius*
(North America)
1920 Western Isles, South Uist, Outer Hebrides. [1]

An adult male Merlin of the American race *F. c. columbarius* was apparently shot on South Uist, Outer Hebrides, Western Isles on 11th November 1920. This bird was originally thought to have been an aberrant Merlin of the European race *F. c. aesalon* but was eventually accepted as an American race of Merlin. It was a record claimed by Meinertzhagen to have been shot by him but later reportedly collected by a Col Macindoe.

The entry in Meinertzhagen's skin log is placed between two other Merlins; the first obtained on South Uist on 26th October and the second in Argyll on 8th November 1920. The dates do not follow in the correct order and all entries appear to have been written simultaneously.

Col Meinertzhagen skinned his own birds but on investigation all three specimens were skinned in a different manner and stuffed or sewn up with different materials. It is clear therefore that Meinertzhagen's claim is shrouded in doubt.

The record was rejected following an investigation by the BOU in 1993.

References:
British Birds 48: 6; *Ibis* 1993: 324; 495.

Andalusian Hemipode (Little Button Quail) *Turnix sylvatica*
(Africa, east to Taiwan and south to Australia)
1844 Oxfordshire. [2]

A bird, shot on 29th October 1844 by a gamekeeper on Miss Penyston's estate at Cornwall, Oxfordshire, was sent to Mr Goatley of Chipping Norton who wrote down details of bare part coloration and measurements. It was a fat male with husks of barley in its crop. The same gamekeeper later shot a second bird, possibly its mate near the same spot but unfortunately the head was shot off and it was of no use as a specimen.

Mounted together with a Barbary Partridge *Alectoris barbara* it was accepted at first by Yarrell but later ignored and presumed that the birds were released. Adrian Norris rescued the specimen from a council rubbish dump, and it remains at Leeds Museum in the same case as a Barbary Partridge (accession No LEEDM.C.1995.1.2).

A bird caught alive by two Irishmen at Fartown, near Huddersfield on 7th April 1863 (1865 in Montagu and Gould), went into the possession of Sir Vauncey Harpur Crewe of Calke Abbey, Derbyshire and, following his death, was sold at auction on 10th November 1925 for £3 10s.

On the rear of the case was a quotation from Gould's *Birds of Britain*:

> "Andalucean Hemipode, taken alive at Fartown, nr. Huddersfield, April 7, 1865; bought of two Irishmen who thought it was a young partridge, for 6d. by S. D. Mosley of Huddersfield."

This species is now thought to be almost extinct in Europe.

References:
Calke Abbey Auction catalogue 1925: 19; Montagu, 1862: 263-264; Radford, 1966: 82; Leeds Museum 2000.

Purple Gallinule *Porphyrio porphyrio*
(South-east Eurasia, Africa, through south-east Asia to Australia)
1863 Hampshire, Rowner. [Many]

The first record of a Purple Gallinule that had a reasonable chance of arriving in a wild state, and the identity proven, was a bird at Rowner, Hampshire, on 10th August 1863, with one in Northumberland in the same month. The latter bird captured alive at Bolden Flats was healthy, apparently showing no signs of ever being kept in captivity. John Hancock of Newcastle suspected that it might have originally been on an ornamental pond. Many other records followed as the gallinule family became popular in collections.

Of the recent reports worthy of consideration an adult of the Indian race *P. p. poliocephalus* was found dead in Aberdeen, in February 1965, followed by a sub-adult west Mediterranean race bird *P. p. porphyrio* at Field Farm Pool, Sandbach, Cheshire from 13th August to 26th September 1971. Although this individual's origin was not traced, it was believed to have escaped.

In 1978 an adult *P. p. poliocephalus* took up residence at Cley, Norfolk from 20th July to 19th September and an adult possibly of Middle Eastern origin, *P. p. caspius/ seistanicus* remained at Attenborough, Nottinghamshire from 25th August to 14th October 1978.

They were considered by the BBRC or BOURC to have involved escaped birds or there was reasonable doubt about their origins, as was a bird seen by Phil Palmer and Derick Evans at Sandscale Haws, Cumbria on 23rd October 1997.

References:
Hancock: 126; Naylor 1996: 183; Morrison 1997: 65; Riviere 1930; Walpole-Bond, 1938: iii, 336; Evans 1994: 31-132; Taylor 1999: 527; *Birding World* 462-466; *Ibis* 142: 177-179.

Demoiselle Crane *Anthropoides virgo*
(Turkey, eastwards across central Asia to northern China; winters mainly India and Pakistan)
1863 Orkney, Deerness, Mainland. [23]

Two adult 'Numidian' (Demoiselle) Cranes were at Deerness, Mainland Orkney, on 11th May 1863. A male was finally killed on 14th May, the second bird flying off to the neighbouring island of Copinsay. Although it returned two days later after several further attempts to kill it the bird left. The dead bird appeared to have been in good condition weighing five pounds but its stomach was empty except for a few oats. The specimen was preserved for Mr Reid, bookseller, of Kirkwall.

At the time of this record and ever since the Demoiselle Crane has been widely kept in captivity so this, and subsequent records (e.g. 10 others prior to 1958) have been regarded as escapes. Some reports have involved small flocks, the largest being a group of six at Horsey, Norfolk on 23rd April 1967. These birds were never traced to a captive source.

There have been several reports of birds which appeared wild and in perfect condition, but the BOURC consider all records to involve escapes.

References:
Montagu, 1862: 35; Evans 1994: 133; Taylor 1999: 528.

Spur-winged Plover *Hoplopterus spinosus*

(Africa, Greece, East to the Middle East)
1997 Kent, Stodmarsh. [1]

On 30th April 1997, a Spur-winged Plover was seen in flight by Graham Crick and Peter Young at 4.30pm from Marsh Hide at Stodmarsh, Kent. Moving to the Netherlands, the plover returned to Stodmarsh on 3rd June. The presence of a broken primary feather confirmed that the same individual was involved. This may have been the product of wear and moult or on the other hand due to a period of confinement.

The BBRC regarded it as an escape.

The Spur-winged Plover has the potential to reach Britain as a vagrant; it has been recorded in Spain (three birds together), Belgium, Germany and Italy, while all other British reports have been proven escapes. These have included two birds (one with an orange ring) at Crystal Palace and other London sites, including a busy traffic roundabout, from 5th June 1988.

References:
Birding World 1: 187, photo 193; 10: 217-219, photo; *British Birds* 91: 517.

Yellow-billed Sheathbill *Chionis alba*
(Antarctica and South America)

IRELAND
1892 Co. Down, Carlingford Lighthouse. [1]

A bird in the collection of Mr R M Barrington was said to have been shot near Carlingford lighthouse, Co. Down, in December 1892 by the lighthouse keeper, Mr R Hamilton. After missing at 30 yards, the bird flew around and re-landed, allowing him to kill it. Its flight was described as being like an Atlantic Puffin *Fratercula arctica* and it walked boldly and proud. When skinned it was a fat bird found to be containing small eggs. Despite acceptance by Sclater (1893), Howard Saunders (1899) rejected the record claiming that living examples had been sent from the Falkland Islands.

BRITAIN
Following the Falkland Islands dispute the Royal Navy brought a live Yellow-billed Sheathbill to Plymouth in September 1982, courtesy of *RFA Pearleaf*. It had been confined for part of its journey and therefore does not meet the BOURC's criteria for acceptance onto the British List.

References:
Birding World 5: 387; Saunders, 1899: 560; Ussher *et al* 1900: 404.

South Polar Skua *Catharacta maccormicki*
(Southern Oceans)
1869 Norfolk, Great Yarmouth. [1]

The identification of a South Polar Skua specimen in Norwich Castle Museum

(NCM 74.23), claimed to have been obtained at Great Yarmouth, Norfolk in 1869 was accepted by the BOURC but its origin in British waters is unproven. The cabinet skin is in good condition but the head is loose. It was presented to the museum by Gerard H Gurney bearing the label *"Great Skua. Leadenhall. Oct. '69. J. Gatcombe. Yarmouth"* (Dr A G Irwin *in litt*). The bird almost certainly came from a ship serviced at Great Yarmouth as the crew shot birds to sell on to game dealers to supplement their wages. Although most probably obtained in the North Sea the bird cannot be admitted onto the British List but is the first confirmed record in the Northern Hemisphere.

This record was discovered as recently as 1993 when it was examined by Dr W R P Bourne and Dr D S Lee, who re-identified it. As the bird was not claimed to have been anything other than a Great Skua *Catharacta skua* there was no indication of fraud.

The bulk of British South Polar Skua reports have come from Cornwall where the majority of Britain's large Shearwater sightings are recorded. The first was seen at Peterhead, Northeast Scotland on 23rd July 1982 followed by a bird at St Ives, Cornwall on 14th October 1982.

Between 1982 and 1989 there were approximately ten claims for this species to be admitted to the British List.

References:
Birding World 5: 256-270; 6: 476; British Birds 76: 102; 90, painting of a Cornish bird; 90: 520-521; Taylor 1999: 528.

White-cheeked Tern *Sterna repressa*
(Red Sea, Persian Gulf, Gulf of Oman and Indian Ocean)
1989 Kent, Dungeness. [1]

While at Dungeness, Kent on 13th May 1989, David Walker and Anna Hughes spotted an unusual Black Tern *Chlidonias niger* feeding over the nuclear power station's cooling water outflow into the sea. Along with Ray Turley, Steve Gale, Peter Boxall and James Siddle no-one had seen anything like it before and suspected that it may be a White-cheeked Tern. It performed in front of the hide for 30 minutes allowing them to take notes before it flew off east at 10.40am.

The tern was seen briefly at 12.45pm off St Margaret's Bay, Kent by Ian Hodgson and Tony Greenland. This record was not accepted by the BOURC.

References:
Birding World 2: 173-174, painting; 6: 368.

Brown Noddy *Anous stolidus*
(Caribbean and Atlantic south to Gough Island; Red Sea, Indian and Pacific Ocean)

IRELAND
***c.*1830 Co. Dublin,** near Tuskar Lighthouse. [4]

Two specimens of Brown Noddy were recorded by William Thompson, of Belfast, in *Transactions of the Linnean Society* 1835. He had found the birds in the collection of Mr Warren, of Dublin. The birds were said to have been obtained by a sea captain who saw them shot near the Tuskar Lighthouse, Dublin in the summer of 1830. The captain presented the two "odorous" skins to William Massey and the specimens are still available and housed at the Science and Art Museum, Dublin.

BRITAIN
1891 Cheshire, Dee Estuary.

The first claim of Brown Noddy in Britain concerned a bird shot by William Lawton on the Dee Estuary/Marshes, Cheshire, in the winter of 1891. The following letter was published in *Zoologist* (1906):

"Noddy Tern in Cheshire.
The other day, when looking through a collection of stuffed birds, I saw and obtained a specimen which has since been identified as the Noddy Tern, Sterna stolida, Linn.; It is in immature plumage, the grey on the crown being just visible. It was shot on the Dee marshes in winter about six years ago. As I believe this Tern has been only twice recorded in Europe, I think this specimen worth a mention.

F. Congreave. Burton Hall, Neston, Cheshire.

P.S.: *I obtained the Noddy from a small private collection belonging to Mr Lawton, an ex-tenant of my father's. He killed and stuffed it himself. It is at present in our collection at Burton Hall, but it has been identified by the taxidermist of the Liverpool Museum, and by Mr Dobie, of Chester".*

The specimen is now held at Chester Museum.

In 1908, Witherby reported that the Irish taxidermist involved had later produced two Belted Kingfisher *Ceryle alcyon* skins. Messer's Coward and Oldham also cast doubt over the Cheshire record.

The Irish and Cheshire records were deemed acceptable for a considerable period but were later rejected by the BOU in 1915.

References:
Montagu, 1862: 344-345; *Birding World* 5: 389; Saunders 1899: 655; *Zool*, 1897: 510.

Passenger Pigeon *Ectopistes migratorius*
(North America; now Extinct)
1825 Fife, Monymeal. [5+]

The first report of the Passenger Pigeon was recorded in Dr Flemming's *History of British Animals.* The bird was shot on 31st December 1825, while perched on a wall near a pigeon house, at Westhall, near Monymeal, Fife. The specimen was said to have been in good condition with fresh feathers showing no sign of a captive origin. Rev A Esplin, schoolmaster at Monymeal presented it to Dr Fleming.

Prof Newton added the species to the British List but later it was removed by Saunders in 1915, on the grounds that several birds had been liberated from 1830 onwards, indeed one of the records mentioned by Saunders concerned a definite escape.

IRELAND
1848 Co. Kerry, Tralee.

A bird suffering from extreme exhaustion was found at Tralee, Co. Kerry in 1848 having presumably struggled across the Atlantic. However this record has never formally been endorsed.

References:
Saunders, 1899: 487; *British Birds* 48: 6; Yarrell, 1843: ii, 272-276; Eyton 1836: 31-32; *Zool*, 1877:180; Snow & Perrins 1998: 865.

Eagle Owl *Bubo bubo*
(Europe and North Africa east to India, China and Japan)
1830 Orkney, Sanday.   [Many]

Following a BOURC review of all records in 1974, the first dated and acceptable record regarding a wild bird was a bird shot on Sanday, Orkney in 1830.

Following a further review in 1996 the BOU removed the Eagle Owl from the British List.

The first proven breeding of this species involved a pair in Moray and Nairn in 1984 and 1985 which produced a single chick. A pair fledged three young in northern England in 1996 repeating the success in 1997. Both pairs probably stem from captive stock.

There are many old records of the Eagle Owl in Britain including fossil remains, so there is no doubt that the species once occurred here in a wild state.

References:
Thom, 1986; Baxter & Rintoul 1953: 267; Yarrell 1843: I, 107-112; Harrison 1953: 15; *British Birds* 92: 182; 476.

Black Woodpecker *Dryocopus martius*
(Eurasia except south-west China)
1787 Devon.   [110+]

Of over 110 claimed sightings none have been found acceptable. The earliest report concerned a statement by Dr Latham in 1787, who said that the *"species is sometimes met with in the south, and in particular in Devon."*

The first report with any details involved a single bird shot in the nursery, near Blandford Forum, Dorset, some time before 1799; the specimen was in Lord Derby's collection at Knowsley Lancashire. No bird had been seen alive by an ornithologist but in Dr Pulteney's *Catalogue of Dorsetshire Birds* claims were made that it had been killed in the county more than once.

It was rejected by Montagu but Yarrell and various other authorities admitted the species to the British List. J H Gurney then rejected all existing records in his review during the 1870s due to his dislike of sight-only records.

One interesting but unaccepted report concerned a Black Woodpecker that was seen twice by Francis Hall and his wife in the grounds of his house near Mansfield, Nottinghamshire just after Christmas 1907. He was familiar with the three common

British woodpeckers and described it as similar to the northern woodpeckers that he often encountered on his property in Canada. It was described as half as big again as the Green Woodpecker *Picus viridis*, black all over with a scarlet crown. His keeper also reported two sightings of what he took to be a black jay in the same area. James Whitaker, finder of Britain's first Egyptian Nightjar *Caprimulgus aegyptius*, reported this record.

References:
Montagu, 1862: 387-386; *British Birds* 1: 386; Yarrell, 1843: ii, 127-131; *Birding World*: 5, 75-77; D'Urban: 110.

Downy Woodpecker *Picoides pubescens*
(North America)
1836 Dorset, Bloxworth.   [3]

In 1836, two American woodpeckers were recorded in Britain, both reports were mentioned by Montagu but not accepted by the BOU.

The Downy Woodpecker was said to be in the collection of the Rev Octavius Pickard-Cambridge. It was shot by Mr E P Cambridge, from his bedroom window at Bloxworth Rectory, Dorset, in December 1836.

Mr Havell of 77 Oxford Street, London stuffed it and returned the skin with a label stating *"Least Woodpecker, male adult"*. Despite several ornithologists seeing the bird it was Frederick Bond who first noticed that it was different when he visited Mr Pickard-Cambridge in April 1855. Bond took the skin to Yarrell who agreed that it was not a Lesser Spotted Woodpecker *Dendrocopus minor*. The skin is retained in the Dorset County Museum.

A specimen of Downy Woodpecker at the Durham University Museum compared favourably with Pickard-Cambridge's skin and so Mr Gould examined it. As a result a description was printed in *Zoologist* in 1859 and a request made for more observations of the plumage's of small woodpeckers.

Saunders (1899) stated that "American Spotted Woodpeckers were brought to Europe and turned loose more than a century ago" and so the Downy Woodpecker was not accepted onto the British List.

References:
Montagu, 1862: 385; Saunders, 1899: 278; *British Birds* 48: 9; *Zool*, 1859: 6327; 6444-6446.

Northern Flicker *Colaptes auratus*
(North America)

BRITAIN.
1836 Wiltshire, Amesbury Park.   [2]

A "trustworthy man" named Marsh at Amesbury, Wiltshire obtained a "Golden-winged Woodpecker" (Northern Flicker) in the autumn of 1836. Mr Marsh, Member of Parliament for Salisbury, saw the bird just after it was shot and before being skinned. Preserved by Mr Edwards of Amesbury and kept by George, the brother of

Mr Marsh. It was thought to have possibly been liberated locally. This report was mentioned by Montagu but was not accepted by Saunders or the BOURC.

A second report involved a bird that survived a crossing to Liverpool aboard RMS *Sylvania* on about 23rd May 1964. The live bird was later presented to Chester Zoo.

IRELAND
1962 Co. Cork. [1]

A Northern Flicker was seen to fly ashore from the RMS *Mauritania* at Cobh Harbour, Co. Cork, Ireland, at 6pm on 13th October 1962. It had joined the ship with at least ten other flickers on 7th or 8th October. As food was placed on deck by the crew the bird was considered to have been cared for during its passage.

References:
Birding World 10: 145; Montagu, 1862: 385; Saunders, 1899: 278; British Birds 48: 8. Rare Birds 5: 58

Black Lark *Melanocorypha yeltoniensis*
(Central Asia)
1907 East Sussex, Pevensey. [13]

Thirteen Black Lark records from the south-east coast in 1907 and 1915 were later rejected in 1962 as part of the Hastings rarities. In 1907, severe weather on the continent was said to have caused a small influx of the species to Britain, extremely cold and persistent north and north-easterly winds, followed by a day of south-easterly winds on 28th January.

The first record was an adult male shot on Pevensey Level, East Sussex, in the company of two or three others on 29th January 1907; the specimen cannot be traced. A female obtained on 31st January 1907 at Lydd, Kent is occasionally reported as the first record, it had been badly shot and was covered in dirt when shown to Dr N F Ticehurst.

The bird had been in the company of a second female and a single male. During February, additional birds were seen or obtained along the coast, followed by a smaller influx in 1915. Mr W R Butterfield and Ticehurst at the British Ornithologist's Club exhibited three specimens, while several others from the continent were on sale in Leadenhall Market. Some of the specimens involved in the minor invasions are now in the Dyke Road Museum, Brighton.

Although George Bristow, taxidermist, took the other corpses to him as they were killed, Ticehurst was rarely at home so only saw them after being mounted.

References:
Harrison 1953: vol 2. 48: Harrison 1968: 125: 104: 78; Walpole-Bond, 1938: i, 178-1789; British Birds 1:14.

Horned Lark *Eremophila alpestris alpestris*
(North America)

IRELAND
1998 Co. Down, Tyrella Beach. [1]

The 16th Irish Horned Lark record was a bird present at Tyrella Beach, Co. Down from 3rd January until 1st March 1998. It possessed deep rufous lesser coverts, a feature of Nearctic race birds. The clean white underparts contrasted strongly with a very yellow face and photographs show a bird very different to the European birds normally encountered on the East Coast of Britain. At present not enough is known about winter plumages of the various Horned Lark races and so this record has not been formally recognised. Further information may provide the evidence required clinching it as a 'First'.

BRITAIN
1953 Western Isles, South Uist.

There was one accepted record of the American race of Horned Lark in Britain. This was a male obtained at Grogarry, South Uist, Outer Hebrides, Western Isles, by Meinertzhagen on 29th September 1953. It formed part of the British List until an investigation by the BOURC uncovered discrepancies with Meinertzhagen's records and in 1993 was removed from the British List. The specimen was supposed to have been prepared by Meinertzhagen but the style of workmanship differed considerably from his other specimens.

References:
Ibis 1993: 324; *Rare Birds* 4: 160; *Birding World* 12:152-154, photo's.

Purple Martin *Progne subis*
(North and Central America; winters South America)
1842 Greater London, Brent Reservoir. [6]

Two American Purple Martins were said to have been shot by John Calvert of Paddington near the Brent Reservoir, Middlesex, in September 1842. One of the birds, a juvenile male, was added to the collection of Frederick Bond and examined by Yarrell who figured it in his work. The second specimen retained by Calvert but also examined by Yarrell was a glossy adult male.

Bond's case contained five specimens from the area: a Sand Martin *Riparia riparia*, a white Sand Martin, a Common Swift *Apus apus*, a "White-bellied Swift" (Alpine Swift *Apus melba*) from Mr Wheeler's collection and the Purple Martin. It was later purchased by Sir Vauncy Harpur Crewe of Calke Abbey, and following his death, bought at auction for the Booth Museum, Brighton on 10th May 1925 for £7 10s. The specimens were then split and the Purple Martin cased separately remaining at Brighton where the adult is on public display.

The record was accepted by various authorities, including Montagu and Yarrell but Harting suggested that some degree of fraudulent behaviour had taken place. He found that Calvert had bought American skins and relaxed them for mounting in Britain later.

References:
Montagu, 1862: 201; Yarrell. 1843: ii, 232-233; Glegg, 1935: 90; Saunders, 1899: 166; Ruttledge, 1966: 145; Walpole-Bond, 1938: ii, 137; *British Birds* 48: 9.

Daurian Redstart *Phoenicurus auroreus*
(Siberia, China, winters Southeast Asia)
1988 Fife, Isle of May. [1]

On 29th April 1988, Marc Jones found a redstart feeding near the Low Light, Isle of May, Fife, while undertaking a weekly count of Common Eider *Somateria mollissima*. After dictating a hurried description of the bird, which unusually showed a lot of white in the wing, he continued with his survey. Returning to his accommodation on the island, he checked various literatures with his colleagues and decided that it must have been one of the eastern races of Common Redstart *Phoenicurus phoenicurus*.

The following morning, 30th April, Marc relocated the bird close to the original site and together with artist, Keith Brockie, watched it for short period.

It was seen again mid afternoon in the same place but ran down a rabbit burrow before Robert Proctor and Keith Brockie arrived. The bird was taken out of the burrow for examination but died shortly afterwards, entering birding folklore as the aptly named *'Daurian Deadstart'*.

Brockie took the corpse to be compared with skins at the National Museums of Scotland, Edinburgh, where it remains.

The identification as an adult male Daurian Redstart was confirmed and a surprised Marc James was telephoned on the island and informed of the identification as he still thought it was just a race of Common Redstart.

The bird was ascribed to the race *P. a. leucopterous*, which breeds in central China and Tibet. It is a short distance migrant to north Thailand and Vietnam, whereas the more northern race *P. a. auroreus* is a long distance migrant and therefore has the potential to reach Britain.

Daurian Redstart was available for sale in Britain at the time (£50-£80 each); indeed the feathers showed signs of a period in captivity. Together with the fact that it was the least likely race prone to vagrancy, the record was rejected by the BOURC.

References:
British Birds 86: 359-366, photo, Brockie's painting; *Birding World* 1: 162-163, 219

Black Wheatear *Oenanthe leucura*
(Iberia and Northwest Africa)
1943 Cheshire, Altrincham. [4]

Mr W Cullen watched a 'black' wheatear at close range in a cabbage field, half a mile from Altrincham sewage farm, Cheshire, on 1st August 1943, it then flew to a nearby cartshaft where he took note of the tail pattern. His sketches were sent to Mr B W Tucker who agreed with Mr A W Boyd that the bird was a Black Wheatear. This and a further three records were initially accepted until a review by the BOURC in 1993 found the identification was not conclusively proven.

Three records were also rejected as part of the Hastings Rarity scandal.

References:
Scot Nat 1913: 26; Dymond 1991: 95; Walpole-Bond, 1938: ii, 93-94; *British Birds* 37: 135-136.

Golden-crowned Kinglet *Regulus satrapa*
(North America south to Guatemala)
1897 Lancashire, Wharmton Clough, near Oldham. [1]

A Golden-crowned Kinglet was reportedly shot on 19th October 1897 at Wharmton Clough, near Oldham, Lancashire. The mounted specimen was placed in full view under glass for 20 years before being correctly identified in 1922 having originally considered to have been an undiscovered Asiatic race of Firecrest *Regulus ignicapillus*.

It was identified by H F Witherby as a Golden-crowned Kinglet but the bird was thought to have been incapable of crossing the Atlantic, there have however been several reports of individuals being ship assisted to almost halfway across the Atlantic. It was suspected that the specimen was imported.

References:
Saunders 1991; *Birding World*: 5, 198; *British Birds* 48: 11; Snow & Perrins 1998: 1348.

Ruby-crowned Kinglet *Regulus calendula*
(North America; winters south to Central America)
1852 Argyll, Kenmore Wood, Loch Lomond. [2]

Medical student Donald Dewar found a bird that he took for a Firecrest *Regulus ignicapillus* amongst the dozen or so Goldcrests *Regulus regulus* he had shot during a visit to Kenmore Wood, on the west side of Loch Lomond, in the summer of 1852. The bird was skinned by a novice (possibly by Dewar himself) and placed in his collection while he ventured on the Crimean Campaign (1853-57) until it was exhibited at the April 1858 meeting of the Natural History Society of Glasgow. Questioning the identification he showed it to Robert Gray, a leading Scottish ornithologist who named it as a Ruby-crowned Kinglet, an adult male in worn plumage.

The then Dr Dewar gave the bird to John Gould, who exhibited it at the Zoological Society of London on 11th May 1858. Gould's collection was later placed in the British Museum during 1881 and is now at housed at the Natural History Museum, Tring, Hertfordshire. The Ruby-crowned Kinglet took its place on the British List published in the fourth edition of Yarrell's work, by Professor Newton in 1871.

The record was first called into question by Henry Seebohm in the BOU's first list published in 1883, as there had followed a dubious report from Gloucestershire and an incorrectly identified bird in Co. Durham, in 1852 that proved to be a Firecrest.

In 1979 the record was reassessed by the BOURC following suggestions by John Mitchell that it was worthy of inclusion on the British List, however a split decision was reached and the species did not gain acceptance. Nor did it on a second investigation following the arrival of a bird in Iceland during 1987, as Dewar's travels to America were suggested as being the origin of his specimen. The BOURC also regarded the species as a short distance migrant with the record not conforming to an established pattern for Nearctic insectivores in Britain.

The Gloucestershire record unfortunately suffered from the involvement of Sir Vauncey Harpur Crewe of Calke Abbey, Derbyshire with many of his specimens originating from dubious dealers intent on fraud for monetary gain. The bird had been shot by Mr Spring, the head gamekeeper at Higham Court, Gloucestershire, on 21st September 1871. Mr White mounted the bird a "courteous and popular" taxidermist whose shop was in Cheltenham and later purchased from Spring by his grandson, E T Clarke in 1889, also a taxidermist from Cheltenham. In the same year it was purchased by Harpur Crewe and following the sale of his collection in 1925 bought back by Clarke who presented it to the Booth Museum, Brighton, where it remains. Mr Clarke appears to have been a dealer as well as a taxidermist. His list of birds sold to Harpur Crewe included a Hooded Merganser *Lophodytes cucullatus* shot near Cheltenham in 1905, an American race Northern Hawk Owl *Surnia ulula caparoch* shot in Ireland in 1910 and a Northern Hawk Owl shot near Chelmsford, Essex in 1913; non are acceptable records. Without supporting documentation this kinglet record was also rejected by the BOURC.

This species is a candidate for vagrancy to Britain as Iceland has recorded two birds, but the BOURC's decision remained unchanged by 1999.

References:
Birding World: 5, 195-199: 7, 73-78; 11: 417; *British Birds* 48: 11; Frost 1987:142.

Verditer Flycatcher   *Eumyias thalassina*
(Southern Asia, winters in Southeast Asia)
1993 Fife, Crail.   [2]

On 3rd October 1993, an immature bird in pristine plumage was found by Martin Culshaw and his wife feeding in the sycamores of Denburn Wood, Crail, Fife. It had arrived with three other species of flycatcher *Muscicapidae* and lots of other migrants as part of a large fall. Dick Byrne clinched the identification just prior to dark. The bird was only present the following day being seen by c.50 birders. Although the record was rejected as an escape due to the species being a short distance altitudinal migrant, locals thought it had credentials worthy of further investigation. Weather patterns at the time allowed winds to come directly from the Himalayas with dust samples obtained in Fife at the time originating from there. The bird itself was in immaculate plumage with no abraded feathers or signs of confinement (Stuart Rivers *in litt*).

The Rarities Committee thought that the bird had been liberated on the continent rather than escaping in Britain. The following spring, a second bird was found at Landguard, Suffolk, on 12th May 1994

References:
Scot Birds 17: 2, photo; Evans 1995: 278; 1997: 274.

Masked Shrike   *Lanius rubicus*
(Eastern Mediterranean east to Iran; winters sub-Saharan Africa)
1905 Kent, Woodchurch.   [1]

Masked Shrike is one of the few Hastings rarities that have not occurred in Britain since the scandal was uncovered. An adult male in worn plumage was apparently shot at Woodchurch, Kent on 11th July 1905. Examined in the flesh by Michael J Nicoll on

14th July, he reported that the eyes were sunken in and it had begun to smell. Using Dresser's *Manual of European Birds* he identified the bird which was then preserved by George Bristow. The mounted specimen was exhibited at a meeting of the BOU prior to its formal acceptance.

With no further acceptable records of Masked Shrike, the rejection of the Hastings records in 1962 removed the species from the British List.

References:
Harrison 1953: 231; Harrison 1968: 108; *British Birds* 1: 11.

House Crow *Corvus splendens*
(India, east to Thailand; small introduced populations in Middle East and East Africa)

IRELAND
1974 Co. Waterford, Dunmore East. [1]

The House Crow has expanded its breeding range which was restricted to India and Southeast Asia by travelling on ships. A bird was seen frequenting the rigging of a trawler in the harbour at Dunmore East, Co. Waterford, Ireland. Having been present for at least two weeks it was seen by Killian Mullarney, Oran O'Sullivan and John Lovatt on 3rd November 1974, remaining for at least two years (P Milne *in litt*). The bird had arrived during a period when many vessels arrived from the Middle East and the bird regularly visited a local convent for food. This was the first European record but several birds remained near a Dutch port in the 1990s with breeding recorded. As a result the species has begun to colonise and may spread further as it has done in the Middle East.

The IRBC place ship-assisted birds in Category D and so the House Crow forms no part of any list.

References:
Evans 1994: 442: photo *Birding World* 7: 258; Snow & Perrins 1998: 1472-3.

Black-whiskered Vireo *Vireo altioquus*
(Florida south to Brazil)

The mummified corpse of a Black-whiskered Vireo was found on board a tanker arriving at Sullom Voe Oil Terminal, Shetland in June 1991. The skin is currently held at the Natural History Museum, Tring.

Reference:
Naylor 1998: 412.

North African Chaffinch *Fringilla coelebs africana* or *spodiogenys*
(North Africa)
1994 Essex, Fingeringhoe. [3]

A bird showing characteristics of one of the North African races of Chaffinch fed on grain near a farm on South Green Road, at Fingeringhoe, Essex, from 7th to 24th April 1994, returning the following winter.

A second individual was trapped at Great Saltee Co. Wexford, Ireland, during the same spring.

Both birds were regarded as escapes and the true racial identity of the Essex bird questioned.

References:
Evans 1994: 456; *British Birds* 90: 520.

Red-fronted Serin *Serinus pusillus*
(Turkey, east to the Nepal and central Asian mountains)
1992 Suffolk, Landguard. [1]

A group of birders travelling from Devon and Cornwall to see a White-throated Sparrow *Zonotrichia albicollis* at Felixstowe, Suffolk on 6th June 1992, visited nearby Landguard Point afterwards to search for migrants as easterly winds had been prevalent for the previous few days. At 8.15am David Barker from Exeter heard an unusual call as a bird flew overhead then landed on a branch, 30 feet in front of him. It was an unmistakable adult male Red-fronted Serin.

Before flying off south it was seen by Ted Griffiths and Ashleigh Rosier, but was relocated at the point where about 15 birders watched it for about 30 minutes. The bird flew around and fed with Common Linnets *Carduelis cannabina* before heading west over the River Orwell and out of sight.

The identification of Red-fronted Serin was accepted but the bird was regarded as an escape and the record rejected. There were relatively few captive in Britain at the time; a more likely origin was Belgium where they were reportedly more numerous.

Reference:
Birding World: 5, 220-221; *British Birds* 87: 571.

Citril Finch *Serinus citrinella*
(Southern Europe, east to Austria and north to southern Germany)
1904 Norfolk, Great Yarmouth, North Denes.

The North Denes at Great Yarmouth, Norfolk, were an area of sandhills, gorse and marram stretching north to Caister, and a popular haunt of birdcatchers. On 29th January 1904, the wind was force 5, from the southwest, having increased slightly from the previous day when Jack Quinton trapped a female Citril Finch amongst some Common Linnets *Carduelis cannabina* at the Denes. He sold the bird to Edward Charles Saunders a local Taxidermist who claimed to have identified it.

Saunders kept it alive for a few days, he then killed and skinned it before examination by J H Gurney at Norwich, who identified it as an adult female. Howard Saunders on the strength of this record officially added the Citril Finch to the British List.

The skin was then sold to Thomas Gunn of Norwich, probably the best British taxidermist of the era who mounted it before selling it to Sir Vauncy Harpur Crewe of Calke Abbey, Derbyshire.

Harpur Crewe was a well-known collector who paid high prices for rarities or colour mutations and was renown for not authenticating many of his specimens. Indeed a Spotted Nutcracker *Nucifraga caryocatactes* I examined from his collection sold to him as British taken, was of the southern group; the various races of which extend from the Himalayas to China and have never been recorded in Europe! On his death in 1925 the best specimens were auctioned to pay death duties and the Booth Museum at Brighton bought the finch, where still it remains.

The Citril Finch remained firmly on the British List even though it was questioned in 1968 by Paul G R Barbier in *British Birds*.

While researching for his book The Birds of Great Yarmouth (1990), Peter Allard visited the Booth Museum and thought that the specimen looked wrong for Citril Finch. He contacted Lee Evans who in turn spoke to Dr Alan Knox. The museum was visited by Knox on behalf of the BOURC and the bird identified as a male Grey-necked Serin, Cape or Yellow-crowned Canary *Serinus canicollis*.

Cape Canaries were a common cage bird at the time of the 'Citril Finch's' capture, indeed one caught at Brighton Racecourse in 1886, was at first identified as a Citril Finch by Mr Swaysland. Various escaped birds were also found in the Yarmouth area with another African species the Shaft-tailed Whydah *Vidua regia* was trapped on the beach at a similar time. Jack Quinton was the last full time bird catcher at Yarmouth; he was also an excellent field ornithologist. It would be easy however, to confuse the two species, a genuine mistake probably being made.

Citril Finch is not a regular vagrant away from its breeding areas and there are no other British records. There were no descriptions of the bird taken at the time of its capture so without a specimen available the BOURC ruled the record unacceptable in 1994.

Although now firmly rejected the 'Citril Finch' was originally sold at Harpur Crewe's auction in a case with a bird labelled as a female "supposed hybrid Citril Finch and Canary". The specimen in the Booth Museum is on its own having been re-cased since being purchased. Could the specimen on display be the "supposed hybrid" while the real Citril Finch remains yet to be discovered?

There have been further Citril Finch claims in Britain, all rejected.

References:
British Birds 1: 12; 7: 471; Allard, 1990; Riviere 1930: 181; Auction Catalogue of Sir. Vauncy Harpur Crewe, 1925: 17; Saunders 1899: 178; 8 Norfolk Bird & Mammal Report 1994: 366.

American Goldfinch *Carduelis tristis*
(North America)

IRELAND
1894 Co. Mayo, Achill Island. [1]

On 6th September 1894, Mr J R Sheridan saw a bird feeding on a thistle with Common Linnets *Carduelis cannabina* and pipits *Anthus spp.* at Keem Bay, on Achill Island, Co. Mayo, Ireland. He recognised it as an American species from a specimen in his own collection that he had killed there in 1873. He shot the bird and immediately dispatched the corpse to Mr A G More, of Dublin who confirmed it was an American Goldfinch.

This record is presently not accepted as the plumage condition suggested that it had been confined.

References:
British Birds 48: 13; *Zool* 1894: 396; Saunders 1899: 176.

Long-tailed Rosefinch *Uragus sibiricus*
(Eastern Siberia, northern Mongolia, northern and central China, south-east Tibet and Japan)
1993 Borders, St Abbs.   [5+]

There have been at least five records; the first was worthy of consideration being a well watched adult male in pristine condition at St Abbs, Borders.

It was the first record to show any kind of resemblance to a genuine vagrant. It arrived on the east coast on 10th May 1993, along with record numbers of eastern vagrants including a massive influx of at least 46 Common Rosefinches *Carpodacus erythrinus*, some of which remained to breed.

The Long-tailed Rosefinch remained until 16th May with a second (or the same) male seen later that month on 30th and 31st May in Tayside. Whether these birds were genuine vagrants or escapes from the continent caught up in exceptional East Coast fall conditions may never be known.

Three "Siberian Bullfinches" (also called, Long-tailed Rosefinch) were shot at Little Common, Bexhill, East Sussex, on 11th February 1919. One was in poor condition and of no use but W R Butterfield, who considered them genuine vagrants, examined the other two specimens in the flesh. Having been reported by Mr Nicoll, the general opinion of various authorities including Harry F Witherby was that they were escapes. These were the first reports of any Long-tailed Rosefinches in Britain and formed part of the Hastings rarities.

A first-summer male Long-tailed Rosefinch was present at Portland Bird Observatory, Dorset, from 2nd-9th August 1991. It was trapped and ringed by Mick Rogers, chairman of the BBRC but due to the bird's rising popularity as a cage bird, its poor condition and scar tissue above the bill (a feature of many cage birds, caused by putting the bill through the cage bars/wire), it was regarded as an escape.

References:
Walpole-Bond, 1938: i, 101; *Birding World* 4: 321, photo 6: 183; 6: 170-179.

House Finch *Carpodacus mexicanus*
(Western North America)
1966 Shetland, Fair Isle.   [1]

Arriving at a similar time to a Dark-eyed Junco *Junco hyemalis* on nearby Foula, Shetland, a dull-looking finch was present on Fair Isle from 27th to 30th April 1966. Roy Dennis who considered it to be a female House Finch trapped the bird but at the time ship-assistance was a bar to admission to the British List. There is no mention of the event in the Fair Isle log so the identification must remain in doubt, as there can be confusion with Purple Finch *Carpodacus purpureus* and the closely related rosefinches.

Reference:
Rare Birds 5: 59.

Pallas's Rosefinch *Carpodacus roseus*
(Siberia, winters south to China and Japan)
1988 Orkney, North Ronaldsay. [6]

At Holland House on North Ronaldsay, Orkney, on 2nd June 1988, Kevin Woodbridge (warden) and Peter Donnelly (assistant) heard a small bird fly over with a call that resembled a Hedge Accentor *Prunella modularis*, which the bird clearly was not. They carefully approached the clump of New Zealand Flax that the bird had dived into and saw a bright pink rump as the bird moved into the dense Fuschias. They left the bird in the hope that it would enter a mist-net.

The nets were kept open all night and checked regularly but the finch was found feeding at 6.30am in the Kirkyard, where it showed very well and was positively identified as a Pallas's Rosefinch.

It finally entered the net at 1pm on the 5th when it was decided that the bird was probably an immature male. On 19th June the bird was seen to 'flick' a tail feather out and it was presumed to be starting to moult. It was last seen on 14th July and had not completed its moult so was thought to have been eaten by a cat.

The BOURC investigated the report and found that importation of this species was increasing around this time.

In addition the bird had fresh tail feathers that should have been abraded at a time when it would be about to begin moulting. This indicated that the bird had recently lost all of its tail feathers, possibly due to mishandling while in captivity. The timing of this and other recent European records are outside the period of time that vagrants should occur as all vagrancy records of the species prior to 1940 indicate.

The identification of Pallas's Rosefinch was accepted but the record was rejected.

References:
British Birds 87: 247-252, 571; *Birding World* 1: 196-199, photo.

Spotted Towhee *Pipilio maculatus*
(Western North America)
1975 East Yorkshire, Spurn. [1]

A male Spotted Towhee was caught in a mist-net at the Warren, Spurn, East Yorkshire, on 5th September 1975 and despite being trapped on two further occasions remained until 10th January 1976. After the initial capture it was not seen again until 13th.

The bird occasionally fed in the open at the top of the beach behind the Warren Cottage where it was watched by hundreds of birdwatchers before retreating into dense buckthorn. Being shy it would feed in the buckthorn but at times would search for food amongst the tide wrack below the sand-dune.

The bird did not show any signs of captivity but the BOURC regarded the race involved to be an unlikely vagrant to Britain. "Arctic Towhee cocks" had been advertised for sale in Cage and Aviary Birds for £12 each in April 1975, they had been imported from Canada and sold in Leicester. Western races are now treated separately and named Spotted Towhee although there is an overlap zone where hybridisation occurs.

References:
Sharrock 1982: 140; Moore 1969: 278; Mather, 1985: 587-588; YNU 1975: 60.

Field Sparrow *Spizella pusilla*
(Eastern North America, winters south to Mexico)

IRELAND
1962 at sea. [1]

A Field Sparrow was seen on board the RMS Mauritania until the ship reached Irish territorial waters, 200 miles from Ireland at dusk on 12th October 1962. The bird was one of five Field Sparrows and part of a fall of over 130 North American landbirds that joined the ship in the wake of 'Hurricane Daisy' during a six day voyage from New York to Southampton. As food and water was provided by the ships crew the birds were considered to have been 'ship-assisted' and therefore not admitted onto the British and Irish List.

Reference:
Birding World 10: 146, photo; Snow & Perrins 1998: 1635.

(Siberian) Meadow Bunting *Emberiza ciodes*
(Central Asia east to eastern Siberia, eastern China, Korea and Japan)
1886 East Yorkshire, Flamborough. [5]

Mr R W Chase of Birmingham had in his collection a male Siberian Meadow Bunting, which had been caught alive in November 1886. William Gibbon, a fisherman obtained the bird during an easterly gale, at the foot of the cliffs, just south of the Head, at Flamborough, Yorkshire. He sold it to Matthew Bailey, a well-known local naturalist and birdstuffer. Chase saw the bird at Bailey's house and purchased it, as he did not recognise the species. It was dispatched to Canon H B Tristram who identified it and later exhibited it at the Zoological Society on 15th January 1889.

There it was seen by Seebohm, Newton and Saunders who thought it looked more like the Chinese sub-species rather than the migratory Siberian form. Despite this, Saunders accepted the record after interviewing Bailey.

The record is no longer considered satisfactory and the skin is retained in the Chase collection at Birmingham. The bird shows a bar across the forehead, indicative of a period in captivity.

References:
Ibis 1889: 293-294, 296; Saunders, 1899: 215; Nelson, 1907: 206-207, illustration; Mather, 1985:596-597.

Lazuli Bunting *Passerina amoena*
(Western North America)
1990 Cornwall, Murrayton. [8]

Thomas Fry noticed an unusual bird feeding in his cliff-top garden at Murrayton, Cornwall on 15th September 1990 and his wife also noticed it the next day. A week later after hearing about the bird, Steve Madge visited the Fry's armed with some field guides and Fry pointed out a male Lazuli Bunting. Although the bird was not present during his visit Madge saw the bird when he returned in the afternoon confirming the identification as the bird fed 20 feet from the French windows. The bird loosely associated with the local European Greenfinch *Carduelis chloris* flock and remained until 26th September.

The bird arrived at a similar time to a nearby Red-eyed Vireo *Vireo olivaceus* and Britain's first Yellow-throated Vireo *Vireo flavifrons*, however the species is not considered to be a candidate for vagrancy despite a previous Norwegian record. The species is not legally exported from North America and does not breed easily in captivity but still does not find a place on Category A of the British List.

Earlier records were thought to have involved escaped cage birds. while the Cornish bird was thought to have possibly been ship assisted.

References:
Birding World 3: 345-346, photo; 5: 401; 6: 367; *British Birds* 87: 571.

Painted Bunting *Passerina ciris*
(South-eastern USA; winters Mexico south to Panama)
1802 Dorset, Portland. [9]

Listed below are some old records of Painted Buntings that were not accepted by Saunders. The species has received serious consideration from the BOU but the large increase in reports during the 1970s were deemed more likely to stem from the large number imported since the 1960s. Most were adult males in spring.

1802: Taken alive on Portland. Seen by Montagu in the possession of Mrs Steward near Portland, considered to have hopped off of a ship moving past the coast or docked at Weymouth.

1868: A bird was procured by Thomas Edward in Banffshire some time during 1868. At the time, Painted Buntings were known to be on sale in London and Paris so the record never found acceptance.

1869: Oxfordshire no locality or date.

Modern records include four from Shetland, two in Northwest England and one on Skokholm but there is no established pattern and the BOURC place the species in Category E.

References:
Hutcheson, 1986: 117; Montagu, 1862: 136; Saunders 1899: 178; Gray 1871: 133; *Birding World* 5: 401; 6: 367; Snow & Perrins 1998: 1689.

Red-winged Blackbird *Agelaius phoeniceus*
(North America south to Costa Rica and West Indies)
1824 Suffolk, Holton. [17]

In June 1824, a Red-winged Blackbird was killed at Holton, Suffolk. This was the first of at least 17 records from between 1824 and 1885 (including a bird killed at the Nash Lighthouse, in the Bristol Channel at 3am on 27th October 1886) and was the most credible of those reported.

On 20th April 1886, the Duke of Argyll released several birds at Inverarray, probably accounting for a bird found at Rannoch, Perthshire, three weeks later on 10th May.

All records concerned adult males with a concentration of reports in southeast England during the period 1863 to 1866. This would suggest that most or all were escapes as this popular cage bird was regularly imported into Britain at this time.

References:
Saunders 1899: 226; D'Urban: 437; *British Birds* 48: 12-13; Snow & Perrins 1998: 1693.

Yellow headed Blackbird *Xanthocephalus xanthocephalus*
(Western North America and central Canada; winters south to Mexico)
1964 Lancashire, Leighton Moss. [6]

In 1964, an adult Yellow-headed Blackbird was present at Leighton Moss, Lancashire from 4th to 10th August, it was the first British report and at the time it was thought to have escaped.

Between 1964 and 1981 several birds were reported at a time when the species was imported into Britain. Two later reports received more interest as imports had ceased; the first was at Norwick, Shetland on 10th May 1987 moving to Burrafirth, Cullivoe and Mid Yell where it was last seen on 13th. The second was photographed by Kevin Osborn on Fair Isle, Shetland from 26th to 30th April 1990 but, on this bird, one eye showed some damage and some feathers were worn. This wasn't conclusive proof that the bird had been confined although it did not help the bird's cause for general acceptance.

The BOURC still receives reports of this species for consideration, which shows a strong northwesterly bias, but so far all records are considered to have involved escaped cage birds. The species remains a potential vagrant to Britain as several have been seen in the Atlantic including a flock of 30 over 350 miles from New York.

References:
Birding World 3: 160, photos; 5: 401; 6: 367; Evans 1994: 571; Cottridge & Vinicombe 1997: 175; Snow & Perrins 1998: 1693; Naylor 1998: 420.

Eastern Meadowlark *Sturnella magna*
(Eastern North America south to northern South America)
1854 Norfolk, South Walsham. [4]

There are four old Eastern Meadowlark records with little supporting information:

1854: Norfolk, South Walsham, October. Rev H Temple Frere reported that Captain Jary had seen one on three occasions but failed to obtain it.

1860: Suffolk, Thrandeston, shot, March. The bird was considered wild by Mr Sclater and is currently held in storage at the Norwich Museum (Accession no. 88.21), where it is in good condition but lacks glass eyes. (Dr A G Irwin *in litt*).

Pre-1871: Gloucestershire, Cheltenham, no date.

1876: Norfolk, South Walsham, 13th October. At the sale of Sir Vauncey Harpur Crewe's collection in 1926 a specimen was listed as "shot at South Walsham, Norfolk, 13th October 1876". It had been sent to Mr T E Gunn, the Norwich taxidermist as a skin with instructions to mount it, with the labelling details as above.

It seems strange that two Eastern Meadowlarks would be found at the same village in Norfolk and would appear that the second specimen from there was incorrectly labelled or a fraudulent attempt to pass the specimen off as British taken. The Harpur Crewe collection was riddled with inaccuracies and fraudulent specimens, including many of the 'Hastings' birds.

BWP *Concise* states that two of the three dated specimens being found in the prime month for American landbird vagrancy may indicate a natural origin. It should be borne in mind that these are the only Western Palearctic records from a period when the species was being imported into Britain, combined with unreliable data. All records were rejected by the BOURC:

References:
Snow & Perrins 1998: 1692; Naylor 1996: 189; *British Birds* 48: 12; Riviere 1930: 11.

Rusty Blackbird (Rusty Grackle) *Euphragus carolinus*
(North America)
1881 South Glamorgan, Cardiff. [2]

On 4th October 1881, a Rusty Blackbird was shot near Cardiff, South Glamorgan. This bird arrived during a deep Atlantic depression involving a long period of north-westerly winds and was possibly a genuine vagrant. The skin is now at Cardiff Museum.

A second bird was present at St James Park, London in July and August 1938, this was assumed to have been a cage-bird.

Neither report is recognised by the BOU.

Reference:
British Birds 48: 13; Snow & Perrins 1998: 1692.

Additional at sea records

Several Nearctic species were reported boarding ships that crossed the Atlantic between 1961 and 1965. Although arriving naturally on board between 200 and 2000km east of New York the species listed below had departed well to the west of Ireland. Only those that preceded the accepted 'first' record are mentioned while others have not been mentioned at all elsewhere in this work. A more detailed account can be found in British Birds 65: 428-442.

American Kestrel, Mourning Dove, Ruby-throated Hummingbird, Yellow-bellied Sapsucker, Hairy Woodpecker, Purple Martin, Blue Jay, White-breasted Nuthatch, Red-breasted Nuthatch, Brown Creeper, House Wren, Long-billed Marsh Wren, Brown Thrasher, Hermit Thrush, Golden-crowned Kinglet, Ruby-crowned Kinglet, Cedar Waxwing, Yellow Warbler, Magnolia Warbler, Palm Warbler, Mourning Warbler, Common Yellowthroat, Yellow-breasted Chat, Canada Warbler, Eastern Meadowlark, Red-winged Blackbird, Rusty Blackbird, Common Grackle, Indigo Bunting, Purple Finch, Pine Siskin, Savannah Sparrow, Field Sparrow, Lincoln's Sparrow, Swamp Sparrow and Song Sparrow.

AND LAST

Great Auk *Pinguinus impennis*
(Extinct)

Although not a first for Britain and Ireland the last record of the Great Auk is equally worthy of a mention. Ancient remains of this bird have been found proving that it had occurred in the North Atlantic and Northern Britain for a considerable period. Bones belonging to three adult Great Auks were found below Viking level at the Jarlshof settlement, Mainland Shetland. In 1549, Dean Munro mentioned it as being found on the Western Isles and in 1789 it was said to visit St Kilda and breed occasionally. Bones found in old sea-caves at Whitburn and a tame bird taken alive prior to 1769 on the Farne Islands prove that the bird frequented the British coast. By the mid 19th Century it was already on the verge of extinction.

The only place the auk inhabited in Orkney was Papa Westray and while Mr Bullock was on a tour of the Orkneys' in 1813 he wrote:

> *"Only one male had made his appearance for a long time, which had regularly visited Papa Westray for several years. The female (which the natives call the Queen of the Auks) was killed just before Mr Bullock's arrival. The King, or male, Mr Bullock had the pleasure of chasing, for several hours, in a six oared boat, but without being able to kill him, for though he frequently got near him, so expert was the bird in its natural element that it appeared impossible to shoot him"*
>
> (Montagu's British Birds, 1866)

The species was recorded in Ireland and a pair was seen at the entrance to Waterford Harbour in May 1834, one was a young female apparently starving that swam close to a boat. Having accepted a few sprats from a man named Kirby it was hauled aboard. The other bird apparently died or was killed but not preserved.

Kirby kept the female for ten days before selling it to Francis Davis who placed it in the care of Jacob Gough of Horetown, Co. Wexford who eventually persuaded it to eat potatoes mashed in milk.

Four months later the bird died whilst moulting and was promptly despatched to Dr Burkitt for preservation.

Some time later the Dr was tricked into donating the bird to the Dublin University Museum having been assured that it was only worth a few shillings. In a letter to J H Gurney he recounted the event with some bitterness having been deprived of a considerable sum for the last Irish Great Auk.

Malcolm McDonald grabbed a sleeping bird by the neck while it slept on a ledge halfway up Stack-an-Armin, St Kilda in July *c.*1840. He was assisted by four other men including Lauchlán McKinnon and Donald McQueen who confined the 'Garefowl' in a bothy for three days where it occasionally made a loud Gannet-like noise and clacked its bill together loudly. The bird was suspected of being a master of wind and weather, and having caused a storm to blow up the poor creature was violently clubbed to death with two large stones for an hour; executed as a witch! It was the last Great Auk seen alive in Britain.

References:
Baxter & Rintoul 1953: 681-682; Galloway & Meek, 1978: 100; Montagu, 1862: 5; Venables & Venables, 1955: 333; Fuller 1999:56-57; 75; 197-199, photo.

REFERENCES

Allard, P R, 1990. *The Birds of Great Yarmouth*, Norfolk and Norwich Naturalist's Society, Hunstanton.
Atkinson-Willes, G L, 1963. *Wildfowl in Great Britain*, St Albans.

Barber, L, 1980. *The Heyday of Natural History*, Jonathan Cape, London.
Baxter, E V & L J Rintoul, 1953. *The Birds of Scotland*. Oliver & Boyd, Great Britain.
Bell, T, Hedley 1954. *The Birds of Cheshire*, John Sherrat & Son, Altrincham.
Bell, T, Hedley 1967. *A Supplement to The Birds of Cheshire*, John Sherrat & Son, Altrincham.
Booth, C J & Cuthbert, M & Reynolds, P, 1984: *The Birds of Orkney*, The Orkney Press, Stromness.
Bolam, G, 1912. *Birds of Northumberland and the Eastern Borders.*
Bolam, G, 1932: *The Birds of Northumberland,* Trans. Nat. Hist. Soc. Of Northumberland, Durham & Newcastle-upon-Tyne.
Borrer W, 1891: *The Birds of Sussex*, R. H. Porter, London.
BOU 1992: *Checklist of Birds of Britain and Ireland* 6th ED, BOU/ Helm Informaion Ltd, Cambridge.
BOU *The British List*, 1998, Tring.
BOU *The British List*, 1999, Tring.
Bucknill, 1900: *The Birds of Surrey*, R. H. Porter, London.

Calke Abbey Auction Catalogue, 1925. Stevens's Auction Rooms LTD, London.
Clarke, R, 1996. *Montagu's Harrier.* Arlequin, Chelmsford.
Clarke, W E, 1912. *Studies in Bird Migration,* 2 vols., Gurney & Jackson, Edinburgh.
Clement, P, 1995. *The Chiffchaff,* Hamlyn, Hong Kong.
Cole, A, 1993. *In Search of the Cirl Bunting,* Alan Sutton Publishing Ltd, United Kingdom.
Cordeau, J, 1872. *Birds of the Humber District,* John Van Voorst, London.
Cotteridge, D & Vinicombe, K, 1996. *Rare Birds in Britain & Ireland, A Photographic Record*, HarperCollins, London.
Cox, S, 1984. *A New Guide to The Birds of Essex,* Essex Birdwatching & Preservation Society, Ipswich.
Cramp, S, Simmons & Perrins (eds). 1977-1994. *Handbook of the Birds of Europe, the Middle East & North Africa.*Vols 1-9. Oxford University Press, London (vol 1) & Hong Kong (vols 2-9).

Densley, M, 1999. *In Search of Ross's Gull,* Peregrine Books, Otley, West Yorkshire.
Denton, M L, 1995. *Birds in the Yorkshire Museum,* Yorkshire Museum, York.
D'Urban, W S M & Matthew, M A: *The Birds of Devon,* 1895. Porter, London.
Dymond, J N, 1991. *The Birds of Fair Isle,* Ritchie, Edinburgh.

Evans, L G R, 1994. *Rare Birds in Britain 1800-1990*. LGRE Publications Ltd, Buckinghamshire.
Evans, L G R, 1995. *Rare Vagrant, Scarce Migrant and Rare Breeding Birds in Britain 1993*, LGRE Publications LTD, Nottingham.
Evans, L G R, 1997. *Rare Vagrant, Scarce Migrant and Rare Breeding Birds in Britain 1994*, LGRE Productions Inc, Britain.
Eyton, T C, 1836. *A History of the Rarer British Birds*, Longman, Rees, Orme, Brown, Green & Longman, Houlston & Son, London.

Farber, P L, 1982. *Discovering Birds, The Emergence of Ornithology as a Scientific Discipline, 1760-1850*. The John Hopkins University Press, USA.
Fisher, J, 1954. *Birds as Animals I. A History of Birds*. Hutchinson's University Library, Watford.
Frost, C, 1987. A *History of British Taxidermy*, The Lavenham Press, Lavenham, Suffolk.
Frost, R A, 1978. *Birds of Derbyshire*, Moorland Publishing Co. Trowbridge & Esher.
Fuller, E, 1999. *The Great Auk*, Errol Fuller, Southborough, Kent.

Galloway, B, & Meek, E R: *Northumberland's Birds*, 1978. J & P Bealls LTD, Newcastle-upon-Tyne.
Glegg, W, 1935: *A History of the Birds of Middlesex*, Witherby, London.
Gray, R, 1871. *The Birds of West Scotland including the Outer Hebrides*, Murray, Glasgow.
Gurney, J H, 1921 (1972): *Early Annals of Ornithology*, H. F. & G Witherby, London. (Minet, Trowbridge).

Hagemeijer, W J M & Blair, M J (eds), 1997: *The EBCC Atlas of European Breeding Birds*, T & A D Poyser, Norfolk.
Hancock, J, 1874: *Natural History Transactions of Northumberland and Durham*, Williams & Norgate, Newcastle-upon-Tyne.
Harrison, J, 1953: *A History of the Birds of Kent*, Witherby, England.
Harrison, J, 1968: *Bristow and the Hastings Rarities Affair*, A.H. Butler Ltd, St Leonards-on-Sea.
Harthan, A J, 1945: *The Birds of Worcestershire*, Littlebury & Co. LTD, Worcester.
Holloway, S, 1996: *The Historical Atlas of Breeding Birds in Britain & Ireland 1875-1900*. Poyser, Frome.
Hunt, D, 1986: *Confessions of a Scilly Birdman*, Croom Helm, Great Britain.
Hunt, J, 1815: *British Ornithology*.
Hutcheson, M, 1986: *Cumbrian Birds*, Frank Peters, Kendal.
Hutchinson, C D, 1989: *Birds in Ireland*, Poyser, London.
Hutchinson, Clive, 1998: A list supplied to *Concise Edition of The Birds of the Western Palearctic*, UK400 website.

Kear, J, 1990: *Man & Wildfowl*, Poyser, Bath.
Kear, J & Berger, A J, 1980: *The Hawaiian Goose*, Poyser, Bath.
Kelsall, Rev. J E & Munn, P W, 1905: *The Birds of Hampshire and the Isle of Wight*, Witherby, London.
Kennedy, P G, Ruttledge, R F & Scroope, C F, 1954: *Birds of Ireland*, Oliver & Boyd, Edinburgh.
Knifton, J, 1992: *Rare Birds in Nottinghamshire 1759-1992*, privately published, Nottingham.

Lack, D, 1934: *The Birds of Cambridgeshire,* Cambridge Bird Club. Cambridge.
Lack, D, 1986: *The Atlas of Wintering Birds in Britain & Ireland,* T & A D Poyser, Bath.
Latham: *General Synopsis of British Birds 1787.* Leigh & Sotherby, London.
Latham: *General Synopsis of Birds, 1st Supplementary Volume.* Leigh & Sotherby, London.
Leeds Museum, 2000: *archive letters/documents accompanying specimens.*
Lewington I, Alstrom P & Colston P, 1991: *A Field Guide to the Rare Birds of Britain and Europe.* HarperCollins, Great Britain.
Lorand, S & Atkin, K, 1989: *The Birds of Lincolnshire & South Humberside,* Leading Edge Press & Publishing, Hawes, N. Yorks.
Lovegrove, R, Williams, G, & Williams, I, 1994: *Birds in Wales,* Poyser, Bath.

Marchant, J H, Hudson, R, Carter, S P & Whittington, P, 1990: *Population Trends In British Breeding Birds,*BTO, Tring.
Mather, J R, 1985: *The Birds of Yorkshire,* Croom Helm, London.
Macgillivray, W, 1837-1852: *History of British Birds,* 5 vols. Scott, Webster & Geary, Edinburgh.
Mays, R, 1978: *Henry Doubleday. The Epping Naturalist,* Precision Press, Marlow.
Mearns, R & B, 1998: *Biographies for Birdwatchers,* Academic Press, England.
Mitchell, D & Young S, 1997: *Rare Birds of Britain & Europe,* New Holland, Singapore.
Montagu Col. 1862: *Dictionary of British Birds, Newman's ed.,* Van Voorst, London.
Moore, R, 1969: *The Birds of Devon,* David & Charles, Newton Abbot.
Morris, the Rev. F O, 1868: *History of British Birds,* 1868 Groombridge,.
Morrison, S, 1997: *Rare Birds in Dorset,* Privately Published.
Moss, S, 1995: *Birds & Weather,* Hamlyn LTD, Hong Kong.

Naylor, K, 1996 & 1998:. *A Reference to the Rare Birds of Britain,* Vol 1 & 2. Privately published, Nottingham.
Nelson, T H, 1907: *The Birds of Yorkshire,* 2 vols. A. Brown & Sons Ltd, London.

Paget Bros, 1829: *Sketch of the Natural History of Yarmouth,* Yarmouth.
Palmer, E M & Balance, D K, 1968: *The Birds of Somerset,* Longmans.
Pashley, H N, 1992: *Notes on the Birds of Cley,* 2nd ed. Christopher Frost, privately published.
Paterson, A H, 1929: *Wild-fowlers & Poachers,* Methuen, London.
Paterson, A H, 1905: *Nature in Eastern Norfolk,* Methuen, London.
Payn, W H, 1962, 2nd Ed. 1978: *The Birds of Suffolk,* Barry & Rockliff, London.
Penhallurick, R D, 1969: *Birds of the Cornish Coast,* Headland Publications, Cornwall.
Pennant, T, 1761-1776: *British Zoology,* Benjamin White, London.
Prendergast, Col. E D V & Boys, J V, 1983: *The Birds of Dorset,* David & Charles, Newton Abbot.

Radford, M C, 1966: *The Birds of Berkshire and Oxfordshire,* Longmans, London.
Rhodes, R J, 1988: *Birds in the Doncaster District,* Doncaster & District Ornithological Society, Doncaster.
Rising, J D, 1996:. *A Guide to the Identification & Natural History of the Sparrows of N. America & Canada,* Academic Press, Bath.
Riviere, B B, 1930:. *A History of the Birds of Norfolk,* Witherby, Great Britain.
Rodd, E H, 1880: *The Birds of Cornwall & the Scilly Islands,* Trubner & Co, London.
Ruttledge, R F, 1966: *Irelands Birds,* Witherby, London.

Sage, B L, 1959:. *A History of the Birds of Hertfordshire,* Barrie & Rockliff, Hertfordshire.
Saunders, H, 1899: *Manual of British Birds,* 2nd ed., Gurney & Jackson, London.
Sharrock, J T R and Grant P J, 1982: *Birds new to Britain & Ireland.* Poyser, Calton.
Shrubb, M: *The Birds of Sussex,* 1979: Phillimore & Co, Chichister.
Smith, A C: *Birds of Wiltshire,* 1887: R. H. Porter, London.
Smith, A E & Cornwallis, R K, 1955: *The Birds of Lincolnshire,* Lincolnshire Naturalists' Union, Lincoln.
Smith, C, 1869: *Birds of Somersetshire,* Van Voorst, London.
Snow, D W & Perrins C M, 1998: *The Birds of the Western palearctic, Concise Edition,* Oxford University Press, China.
Somerset Ornithological Society, 1988: *Birds of Somerset,* Longman, London.
Sterland & Whitaker 1879: *Descriptive List of The Birds of Nottinghamshire,* William Gouk, Mansfield.
Stevenson, 1890: *Birds of Norfolk,* Van Voorst, London.
Stearn, W T, 1981: *The Natural History Museum at South Kensington,* Heinemann, Fakenham.
Swaine, C M, 1982: *Birds of Gloucestershire,* Alan Sutton, Norwich.

Taylor, M, Seago, M, Allard, P, & Dorling, D, 1999: *The Birds of Norfolk,* Pica Press, Sussex.
Thom, V, 1986: *Birds in Scotland,* T & A D Poyser, Bath.
Temperley, G W, 1951: *A History of the Birds of Durham,* The Natural History Society of Northumberland, Durham & Newcastle Upon Tyne, Newcastle Upon Tyne.
Ticehurst, C B, 1932: *The Birds of Suffolk,* Gurney & Jackson, Edinburgh.

Ussher, R J & Warren, R, 1900: *Birds of Ireland,* Gurney & Jackson, London.

Venables, L S V & Venables, U M, 1955: *Birds and Mammals of Shetland,* Oliver & Boyd, Edinburgh.

Walpole-Bond, J, 1938: *A History of Sussex Birds,* Witherby, London.
Whitaker, J, 1907: *Notes on The Birds of Nottinghamshire,* Walter Black & Co Ltd, Nottingham.
Willughby, F, 1676 (1972): *The Ornithology of Francis Willughby,* Paul P. B. Minet, Menston, Yorkshire.
Wingfield Gibbons, D, Reid, J, B, Chapman, R A, 1993: *The New Atlas of Breeding Birds in Britain & Ireland 1988-1991.* T & A D Poyser, Somerset.
Wood, N (Ed): *The Naturalist.* Vol 2-5, 1837-1839. London.

Yapp, B, 1981: *Birds in Medieval Manuscripts,* The British Library, Hong Kong.
Yarrell, W, 1843: *A History of British Birds,* 3 vols. John Van Voorst, London.

Bird Reports & Journals
Annals of Scottish Natural History

Birds in Cornwall
British Birds
Birdwatch
BirdWatching
BOU Reports 23rd-26th published in Ibis
Cambridgeshire Bird report
Cape Clear Bird Observatory Report
Cheshire & Wirral Bird Report, 1995
Dutch Birding
Essex Bird Report
Fair Isle Bird Observatory Trust Bulletin, February 1957
Fair Isle Bird Observatory Report, 1981
Kent Bird Report
Ibis
Isles of Scilly Bird Reports
Natural World
Norfolk Bird Club Bulletin
Norfolk Naturalists Trust: *Norfolk Bird & Mammal Report*
Nottinghamshire Birdwatchers Annual Report: *The Birds of Nottinghamshire*
Rare Birds: Magazine of the UK400 club
Scottish Birds
Skokholm Bird Observatory Report 1967
Spurn Bird Observatory Report
Suffolk Birds
Sussex Bird Report
The Field
The Naturalist
Twitching 1987
Yorkshire Naturalist's Union Bird Reports
Zoologist

INDEX
(English Names)

A
Accentor – Alpine 182
   Hedge 182
Albatross – Black-browed 43
   Wandering 16, 287
Auk – Great 317
   Little 37, 280

B
Barrow's Goldeneye 79
Bee-eater – Blue-cheeked 161
   European 33, 162
Bittern – American 54
   Least 292
   Little 55
   Yellow 292
Blackbird – Red-winged 315
   Rusty 316
   Yellow-headed 315
Bluetail – Red-flanked 186
Bluethroat – Red-spotted 31, 185
   White-spotted 30, 185
Bobolink 266
Bufflehead 78
Bullfinch – Common (Northern) 241
Bunting – Black-faced 258
   Black-headed 17, 263
   Chestnut 264
   Cirl 259
   Cretzschmar's 260
   Indigo 265
   Lazuli 314
   Little 17, 262
   Meadow (Siberian) 313
   Ortolan 260
   Painted 314
   Pallas's 263
   Pine 258
   Red-headed 284
   Rock 30, 33, 259
   Rustic 17, 261
   Yellow-breasted 262
   Yellow-browed 261
Bustard – Houbara 35, 98
   Great 11, 99
   Little 98
Buzzard – Common (Steppe) 85

C
Capercaillie – Western 91
Canvasback 71
Catbird – Grey 181
Chaffinch (North African) 308
Chiffchaff – Common (Siberian) 224
   Iberian 224
Cisticola – Zitting 201
Coot – American 95
Cormorant – Great 10, 53
   Double-crested 53
Courser – Cream-coloured 99
Cowbird – Brown-headed 266
Crake – Little 93
   Baillon's 93
Crane – Common 9, 10, 96
   Demoiselle 297
   Sandhill 97
Crossbill – Parrot 239
   Two-barred 238
Crow-House 308
Curlew – Little 119
   Eskimo 32, 120
   Slender-billed 30, 31, 32, 39, 272
Cuckoo – Black-billed 150
   Great Spotted 149
   Yellow-billed 22, 151

D
Diver – Yellow-billed 41
Dove – Eurasian Collared 147
   Mourning 148
   Oriental Turtle 147
Dowitcher – Long-billed 118
   Short-billed 117
Duck – American Black 70
   Falcated 278
   Ferruginous 74
   Harlequin 76
   Long-tailed 76
   Mandarin 69
   Marbled 279
   Ring-necked 73
   Ruddy 80
   Wood 293

E

Eagle – Bald 35, 81
  Booted 39, 270
  Short-toed 39, 269
  Greater Spotted 86
Egret – Cattle 57
  Great 59
  Little 58
Eider – King 75
  Steller's 75

F

Falcon – Eleonora's 89
  Gyr 90
  Peregrine (American) 90
  Red-footed 88
  Saker 280
Finch – Citril 309
  House 311
  Trumpeter 239
Firecrest 225
Flamingo – Greater 277
Flicker – Northern 302
Flycatcher – Asian Brown 30, 280
  Collared 33, 226
  Mugimaki 282
  Red-breasted 225
  Verditer 307
Frigatebird – Magnificent 54

G

Gallinule – Allen's 94
  Purple 94
  (American) Purple 297
Gannet – Cape 291
Godwit – Hudsonian 119
Goldfinch – American 310
Goose – Brent 66
  Brent (Black Brant) 66
  Canada 65
  Egyptian 67
  Lesser White-fronted 63
  Pink-footed 63
  Red-breasted 67
  Ross's 293
  Snow 64
Goshawk – Northern 85
Grebe – Black-necked Grebe 42
  Pied-billed 41
  Red-necked 287
  Slavonian 15, 42
Grosbeak – Blue 285
  Evening 240
  Pine 33, 240
  Rose-breasted 264
Gull – (American) Herring 133
  Audouin's 273
  Bonaparte's 130
  Franklin's 129

Gull – *(cont.)*
  Iceland 134
  Ivory 136
  Kumlien's 134
  Laughing 128
  Lesser Black-backed 15, 132
  Little 129
  Mediterranean 127
  Mew 131
  Pallas's 127
  Ring-billed 131
  Ross's 35, 36, 135
  Sabine's 129
  Slender-billed 130
  Thayer's 273
  Yellow-legged 132
Guillemot – Brünnich's 35, 144

H

Harrier – Hen (American Marsh Hawk) 295
  Montagu's 84
  Pallid 83
Hawk – Red-tailed 295
Hemipode – andalusian 296
Heron – Black-crowned Night 56
  Great Blue 292
  Green 56
  Purple 59
  Squacco 57
Hoopoe 11, 13, 32, 163

I

Ibis – Glossy 61

J

Jackdaw – Eurasian 233
Junco – Dark-eyed 256

K

Kestrel – Lesser 87
  American 87
Killdeer 103
Kingfisher – Belted 30, 33, 160
Kinglet – Golden-crowned 306
  Ruby-crowned 306
Kite – Black 81
  Black-shouldered 294
  American Swallow-tailed 294
Knot – Great 108

L

Lapwing – Sociable 31, 107
  White-tailed 107
Lark – Bimaculated 165
  Black 30, 31, 33, 303
  Calandra 165
  Crested 168
  Greater Short-toed 166

Lark – *(cont).*
  Horned 37, 169, 303
  Lesser Short-toed 167
  White-winged 33, 166
Longspur – Lapland 257

M
Martin – Eurasian Crag 170
  Purple 304
Meadowlark – Eastern 315
Merganser – Hooded 79
Merlin 37, 296
Mockingbird – Northern 180
Murrelet – Ancient 145

N
Needletail – White-throated 157
Nighthawk – Common 156
Nightingale – Common (eastern) 184
  Thrush 183
Nightjar – Red-necked 154
  Egyptian 155
Noddy – Brown 30, 33, 299
Nutcracker – Spotted 233
Nuthatch – Red-breasted 228

O
Oriole – Baltimore 267
  Eurasian Golden 14, 230
Ovenbird 249
Owl – Barn 151
  Eagle 301
  Eurasian Scops 152
  Little 153
  Northern Hawk 153
  Snowy 152
  Tengmalm's 154

P
Parakeet – Rose-ringed 149
Partridge – Red-legged 91
Parula – Northern 243
Pelican – Great White 276
Petrel – Bulwer's 32, 46
  Capped 45
  Collared 289
  Kermadec 289
  Soft-plumaged 44
  Southern Giant 288
Phalarope – Grey 15, 125
  Red-necked 125
  Wilson's 125
Pheasant – Golden 92
  Lady Amherst's 92
Phoebe – Eastern 164
Pigeon – Cape 32, 288
  Passenger 300
Pintado 32, 288

Pipit – Blyth's 17, 172
  Buff-bellied 175
  Olive-backed 173
  Pechora 174
  Red-throated 174
  Richard's 171
  Tawny 173
  Water 174
Plover – American Golden 105
  Caspian 31, 32, 104
  Lesser Sand 103
  Little Ringed 101
  Greater Sand 104
  Kentish 103
  Pacific Golden 106
  Ringed 102
  Semipalmated 102
  Spur-winged 298
Pratincole – Black-winged 30, 101
  Collared 100
  Oriental 100

R
Razorbill 145
Redhead 72
Redpoll – Arctic 238
Redstart – American 248
  Black 187
  Daurian 305
  Moussier's 187
Robin – American 200
  Rufous-tailed Scrub 183
  Siberian Blue 186
  White-throated 187
Roller – European 162
Rosefinch – Common 17, 240
  Long-tailed 30, 33, 311
  Pallas's 312
Rubythroat – Siberian 184

S
Sandgrouse – Pallas's 146
Sandpiper – Baird's 30, 31, 111
  Broad-billed 113
  Buff-breasted 33, 114
  Curlew 113
  Least 111
  Marsh 30, 121
  Pectoral 31, 112
  Semipalmated 30, 108
  Sharp-tailed 112
  Solitary 31, 122
  Spotted 35, 123
  Stilt 114
  Terek 30, 123
  Upland 121
  Western 109
  White-rumped 111
Sapsucker – Yellow-bellied 163

Scaup – Lesser 74
Scoter – Black 77
   Surf 77
Serin – European 238
   Red-fronted 309
Shearwater – Audubon's 290
   Cory's 30, 46
   Great 47
   Little 49
   Mediterranean 48
   Sooty 47
Sheathbill – Yellow-billed 298
Shelduck – Ruddy 68
Shrike – Brown 230
   Isabelline 231
   Lesser Grey 232
   Masked 30, 307
   Southern Grey (Steppe) 232
   Woodchat 31, 232
Skua – Pomarine 126
   South Polar 298
Snipe – Common (Wilson's) 37, 115
   Great 116
Snowfinch – White-winged 30, 283
Sora 93
Sparrow – Field 313
   Fox 254
   Lark 253
   Rock 235
   Savannah 253
   Song 255
   Spanish 234
   White-crowned 255
   White-throated 22, 256
Spoonbill – Eurasian 61
Starling – Daurian 282
   Rosy 14, 234
Stilt – Black-winged 99
Stint – Little 110
   Long-toed 110
   Red-necked 109
Stonechat – Siberian 30, 188
Stork – Black 60
   White 11, 60
Storm-petrel – Leach's 13, 51
   Madeiran 30, 52
   Markham's 290
   Matsudaira's 290
   Swinhoe's 52
   White-faced 50
   Wilson's 50
Swallow – Cliff 171
   Red-rumped 170
   Tree 169
Swan – Tundra (Bewick's) 62
   Tundra (Whistling) 62
Swift – Alpine 159
   Chimney 156
   Little 160

Swift – *(cont.)*
   Pacific 158
   Pallid 157

T
Tanager – Scarlet 252
   Summer 251
Tattler – Grey-tailed 30, 124
Teal – Baikal 278
   Blue-winged 71
   Green-winged 69
Tern – Aleutian 141
   (American) Black 274
   (American) Sandwich 140
   Bridled 142
   Caspian 138
   Elegant 140
   Forster's 141
   Gull-billed 137
   Lesser Crested 139
   Little (Least) 274
   Roseate 140
   Royal 30, 33, 138
   Sandwich 139
   Sooty 142
   Whiskered 143
   White-cheeked 299
   White-winged 143
Thrasher – Brown 180
Tit – Eurasian Penduline 229
   Willow 227
   Willow (Boreal) 228
Thrush – Blue Rock 191
   Grey-cheeked 196
   Dark – (Black) throated 199
   Dark – (Red) throated 199
   Dusky 33, 198
   Eyebrowed 197
   Hermit 195
   Naumann's 197
   Rufous-tailed Rock 191
   Siberian 193
   Swainson's 195
   Varied 194
   White's 192
   Wood 194
Towhee – Eastern 252
   Spotted 312
Treecreeper – Short-toed 229
Tropicbird – Red-billed 291

V
Veery 196
Vireo – Black-whiskered 308
   Philadelphia 308
   Red-eyed 237
   Yellow-throated 236
Vulture – Eurasian Griffon 83
   Egyptian 82
   Monk 279

W

Wagtail – Ashy-headed 176
  Blue-headed 175
  Black-headed 30, 176
  Citrine 177
  Grey-headed 176
  Pied 178
  White 178
Wallcreeper 229
Warbler – Arctic 30, 219
  Aquatic 205
  Barred 31, 216
  Bay-breasted 248
  Black-and-white 22, 242
  Blackburnian 245
  Blackpoll 247
  Blyth's Reed 31, 206
  Booted 209
  Cape May 246
  Cetti's 30, 200
  Chestnut-sided 244
  Dartford 15, 212
  Desert 214
  Dusky 221
  Eastern Bonelli's 222
  Eurasian Reed 207
  Garden 217
  Great Reed 208
  Green 217
  Greenish 30, 219
  Golden-winged 242
  Hooded 250
  Hume's Leaf 220
  Icterine 210
  Lanceolated 202
  Magnolia 246
  Marmora's 211
  Marsh 206
  Melodious 30, 211
  Moustached 30, 204
  Olivaceous 33, 308
  Orphean 33, 215

Warbler – *(cont.)*
  Paddyfield 206
  Pallas's Grasshopper 202
  Pallas's Leaf 30, 220
  Palm 284
  Radde's 221
  River 203
  Rüppell's 30, 33, 214
  Sardinian 213
  Savi's 203
  Spectacled 212
  Subalpine 213
  Syke's 210
  Tennessee 243
  Thick-billed 208
  Two-barred Greenish 218
  Western Bonelli's 222
  Wilson's 251
  Wood 131, 223
  Yellow 244
  Yellow-browed 220
  Yellow-rumped 247
Waterthrush – Northern 249
Waxwing – Bohemian 178
  Cedar 178
Wheatear – Black 30, 205
  Black-eared 190
  Desert 190
  Isabelline 189
  Pied 22, 189
  White-tailed 191
Whitethroat – Blyth's Lesser 217
  Lesser 216
Whimbrel (Hudsonian) 121
Wigeon – American 69
Woodpecker – Black 301
  Downy 302
  Great Spotted 164

Y

Yellowlegs – Greater 122
  Lesser 122
Yellowthroat – Common 250